Wisdom With Understanding is Better Than Rubies

Lurine Karon Greenberg
Fine Arts Collection

THE STORY OF

NAXOS

THE EXTRAORDINARY STORY OF
THE INDEPENDENT RECORD
LABEL THAT CHANGED CLASSICAL
RECORDING FOR EVER

NICOLAS SOAMES

piatkus

PIATKUS

First published in Great Britain in 2012 by Piatkus

Copyright © 2012 Naxos AudioBooks UK Ltd.

The moral right of the author has been asserted.

All rights reserved.
No part of this publication may be reproduced, stored in a
retrieval system, or transmitted in any form or by any means, without
the prior permission in writing of the publisher, nor be otherwise circulated
in any form of binding or cover other than that in which it is published
and without a similar condition including this condition being
imposed on the subsequent purchaser.

A CIP catalogue record for this book
is available from the British Library.

ISBN 978-0-7499-5689-9

Typeset in Janson by M Rules
Printed and bound in Great Britain by
Clays Ltd, St Ives plc

Papers used by Piatkus are from well-managed forests
and other responsible sources.

MIX
Paper from
responsible sources
FSC
www.fsc.org   FSC® C104740

Piatkus
An imprint of
Little, Brown Book Group
100 Victoria Embankment
London EC4Y 0DY

An Hachette UK Company
www.hachette.co.uk

www.piatkus.co.uk

Contents

Foreword by Klaus Heymann   vii

Preface by Nicolas Soames   xi

One   **Dramatic Change in Classical Recording,**   1
1977–1990

Two   **Klaus Heymann: A Profile**   19

Three   **The Early Years: From Frankfurt**   29
to Hong Kong 1936–1967

Four   **A New Home in the Far East: Building**   36
a Business Career 1967–1982

Five   **Marco Polo: An International Label**   50
1982–1987

Six   **Naxos: A Classical Revolution 1987–1994**   67

Seven   **Naxos: A World Force 1994–2000**   87

Eight   **Naxos: The Digital Age 1996–2011**   107

Nine   **The Artists: Soloists and Chamber**   123
Musicians

Takako Nishizaki – Violin   127
Jenő Jandó – Piano   137
Idil Biret – Piano   142
Maria Kliegel – Cello   146
Kodály Quartet   149
Ilya Kaler – Violin   154

Maggini Quartet 155
Patrick Gallois – Flute and Conductor 161
Norbert Kraft – Guitar and the 'Guitar Collection' 164
Ulrich Eisenlohr – Piano 168
The New Generation 170
Tianwa Yang – Violin 170
Ashley Wass – Piano 171
Eldar Nebolsin – Piano 174
Christopher Hinterhuber – Piano 176

Ten   **The Artists: Conductors**   **178**

Marin Alsop 181
Antoni Wit 187
Dmitry Yablonsky 191
Michael Halász 196
Jeremy Summerly 201
Helmut Müller-Brühl 206
Takuo Yuasa 208
Leonard Slatkin 212
Robert Craft 216
James Judd 219

Eleven   **Composers of Our Time**   **223**

United States 225
Poland 234
United Kingdom 236
Other Contemporary Voices 241

Twelve   **Naxos and Its Labels**   **247**

The Naxos Catalogue 248
The Central Classics 250
Opera Classics 261
American Classics 262
Spanish Classics 264
Italian Classics 266
Guitar Collection 267
Organ Encyclopedia 268
Amadis, Donau, Lydian and Linz 269
Naxos Jazz 270
Naxos World 271
Naxos Historical 272
Naxos DVD 278
Deletions 280

Thirteen   **Marco Polo**   **281**

The Marco Polo Catalogue 283
Chinese Classics 283

	Marco Polo Classics	284
	Marco Polo Film Music	290
	Yellow River and Middle Kingdom	291
	Postlude	292
Fourteen	**Publishing**	**293**
	Naxos AudioBooks	293
	Naxos Hörbücher	299
	Naxos Educational	300
	Naxos Books	302
	Artaria Editions	304
Fifteen	**Behind the Scenes**	**307**
	A&R, New Recordings and the Release Schedule	307
	Recording, Producing and Editing	311
	Contracts and the Organisation of Recordings	323
	Booklets and Designs	325
Sixteen	**Naxos on the Web**	**335**
	Developing the Digital Services	335
	The Platforms	342
	Naxos Website	342
	Naxos Music Library	344
	ClassicsOnline	346
	Naxos Video Library	346
	Naxos Spoken Word Library	347
	Naxos Web Radio	348
Seventeen	**Distribution: The Growth of an Empire**	**349**
	Naxos Global Logistics	351
	Naxos Distribution Around the World	354
	United Kingdom: Select Music and Video Distribution	354
	United States: Naxos of America	369
	Germany: Naxos Deutschland	382
	The Nordic Countries: Naxos Sweden	388
	Naxos Japan	396
	Australia: Select Audio and Video Distribution	399
	Naxos Far East	401
	Naxos Korea	403
	France: Abeille Musique	405
Eighteen	**Naxos: The Future**	**410**
	Appendix: Awards	425
	Acknowledgements	435
	Index	437

Foreword by Klaus Heymann

When I look back over the past quarter of a century of the Naxos label – and even further, to the start of Marco Polo in 1982 – I am surprised at how much it all seemed to grow of its own accord. Although I certainly made plans, Naxos developed in unexpected ways, without rigidly following a grand business plan.

The label, with its primary purpose of providing good, new, digital recordings at a price everyone could afford, certainly emerged at the right time. But I know how much of its success was made possible by a few key individuals who believed in what I wanted to do, who were as convinced as I was that the classical recording industry needed to change. They were not establishment die-hards (or they would never have joined a classical music label created by a businessman based in Hong Kong!). And they were not all classical music enthusiasts: some actually knew very little about classical music at the start, though they learned quickly. They just had faith in what I was trying to achieve.

Naxos changed the culture and industry of classical music recording; there is no doubt about that. This book tells how it happened. It is clear, even from the Contents, that this story features a very varied group of men and women who put their talents and energy into a young company that was finding new ways of doing things. There were the fine musicians who would never have been given an international platform by the classical establishment yet proved time and again that out-standing performances can come from unexpected quarters. There were the capable producers and engineers working within the new digital fields; the knowledgeable writers and designers prepared to work to tight deadlines without compromising musicological standards.

Just as important were the distributors, who not only developed efficient networks but also devised fresh and sometimes extremely bold marketing campaigns to make Naxos the most highly visible classical label in the world. The different characters of these individuals were reflected in the way Naxos evolved in countries as far apart as the US, Germany, Japan, France, Korea and the UK. The label's underlying purpose was international, but there were often discernible national characteristics in what was released and how titles were promoted.

From the start I wanted Naxos, despite its budget price, to be at the forefront of technology, and I am particularly pleased that we remain there twenty-five years on, offering specialist classical web services that are simply unmatched by any other company.

The Story of Naxos recounts how the label became the single most identifiable classical music brand in the world: we were moving so quickly that only in retrospect has it become clear how we did it. It also confirms that with our breadth of artists and repertoire, and our sheer number of releases both popular and specialist, we are now the leading provider of classical recorded music: we have travelled far beyond being a 'budget' label. It is a continuing journey. The environment of classical music and the recording world – commercially and technologically – is changing even more rapidly than in 1987, when the first Naxos CDs emerged. Nevertheless I am still as excited when I open a box of new Naxos releases in Hong Kong as I was when I began collecting classical records as a teenager in Frankfurt.

As a non-musician, I have been extremely fortunate to live my life inside music: to see my wife, Takako Nishizaki, recording the great violin concertos of the world and helping them to become worldwide bestsellers; to create a comprehensive classical catalogue with an extremely wide repertoire; and to build a company that has brought classical music to millions who otherwise may not have encountered it.

Klaus Heymann, 2012

Preface by Nicolas Soames

I first encountered Klaus Heymann's record labels when I was classical editor of *Music Week*, the UK's leading trade magazine for the record industry, covering the main issues of the time and the new releases. I wrote about Marco Polo and then, when it arrived, Naxos, and I met Klaus himself. I also wrote for *Gramophone* and many national newspapers, and as a journalist I always enjoyed a good story, so I was intrigued by the controversy that soon surrounded these ventures of 'the German businessman from Hong Kong' – especially as he was being praised and heavily criticised in equal measure.

In fact, I can remember the first time we met: we were having a drink in a hotel bar in London. I had been warned by my friends in the majors that he was of dubious provenance, and I was rather pleasantly surprised to find not Mephistopheles – which really was how he had been painted – but a straightforward, no-nonsense businessman, who clearly knew his music and musicians extremely well. He was also acutely aware of the issues of the day. I think it must have been around 1990, when Naxos ended its Woolworths exclusivity.

We met fairly regularly after that, either at MIDEM (the music trade fair in Cannes, which I covered annually for various newspapers and journals) or in London. Klaus was always the source of interesting news, or had an angle I could pursue: despite living in Hong Kong he was very well informed.

In 1992 my sister, the clarinettist Victoria Soames, and I

started Clarinet Classics; it was an independent label with a clear purpose. I knew various distributors, but I first approached Graham Haysom who had recently set up Select Music as a joint venture with Klaus to distribute Naxos in the UK, because I felt the company was going places. Shortly afterwards, at one of our meetings, Klaus suggested that Naxos could distribute Clarinet Classics worldwide, and with some exceptions we were happy to take him up on it.

On the evening of 23 January 1994, after the Naxos conference day at MIDEM Classique, Klaus hosted a supper at a Cannes hotel for all the Naxos distributors. I had attended the conference during the day, partly as a journalist and partly as a record-label owner. I sat next to Klaus at the meal, which he announced at the start would conclude at 11 p.m. German efficiency, I thought. At 10.50 p.m. I started to talk to him about my next venture: an audiobook label that would offer abridged versions of the great classics accompanied by classical music, making the likes of Homer and Dante easier to approach. Klaus listened attentively; at 10.56 p.m. he proposed a joint venture, specifying the number of releases in its first two years, the financial details, even the basic office set-up; we discussed it for four minutes and at 11 p.m. on the dot we agreed and shook hands. Klaus stood up, thanked everyone for coming, and left the room. I sat there, stunned, trying to take on board that my life had changed direction.

It is eighteen years since that day. The intervening time has seen Naxos AudioBooks win awards on both sides of the Atlantic and grow to become the leading spoken-word label for literary classics. This enterprise has been my primary focus, but I have always kept a close eye on the growth of Naxos itself – after all, for two decades I had written about classical recording and then I found myself inside one of the most exciting classical record stories in the history of the industry. I saw expansion at a remarkable rate and I travelled to most of the Naxos offices. It wasn't all plain sailing: I saw Klaus right the ship time and time again when his enthusiasm and investment in new recordings had overtaken sensible cash flow. Month after month the new CD releases would come through to the Naxos AudioBooks office and each time I opened the boxes I was astounded by the diversity of music and musicians; here were not only the popular classics but composers I had never heard of – and this was supposed to be a budget label.

These years inside Naxos have been hugely exciting. There have been times of confusion, times of delay, missed sales targets, projects that have gone awry, series with good recordings that have failed for marketing reasons; but the successes have far outweighed the failures, and every month there are those new-release boxes with a remarkable variety of music – and audiobooks – that no other company in the world could begin to match.

I have been privileged, as a former journalist, to see Naxos develop from its original position as an outsider (challenging for a place in classical recording and shrugging off the disdain poured on it by the establishment) to its current position of prominence. It is without question the world leader in the breadth of classical repertoire regularly produced; it is the strongest and most comprehensive worldwide distributor of classical music; and it is the front runner in digital delivery (in various forms) of the classics. Although it can be difficult to mark changes from within, it is clear that the classical music industry has altered forever, and that this is partly due to Naxos.

After a few years of exclusive work on Naxos AudioBooks as well as some occasional work for Naxos, such as producing the much-loved Johnny Morris narrating *The Carnival of the Animals*, I became involved in other sections of Naxos's classical music activity. I produced audiobook composer biographies, then general music biographies and histories. After fifteen years I knew that someone, at some point, had to write *The Story of Naxos*. It wasn't going to be easy to draw a portrait of such a multi-faceted company, even if that company had a single man at the head of it all. In the end, I simply couldn't keep away from the task – it was such a good tale.

I didn't want to write a company history: I wanted to tell the story for the average Naxos buyers – the people who go into the record shops and head straight for the Naxos section. They are such a diverse range of people: students who can afford only Naxos; newcomers to classical music who see a work they recognise clearly titled on the cover; more occasional, discerning CD buyers interested in some of the unusual repertoire; serious collectors, who, like children in a sweet shop, really go to town at Naxos prices. That is the extraordinary thing about the following that Naxos has built up over the years – people come from all walks of life, united by the fact that they know a Naxos CD when they see one.

So this book is written with them in mind. I have set out to chart how it happened, when it happened and in what way it happened. Frankly there is no real 'why', other than that Naxos's founder, Klaus Heymann, saw an opportunity, which he thought would be short-term but which he turned into twenty-five years of unforeseen growth and which was fuelled more than anything else by the love of the thing – and that thing was music.

Nicolas Soames, 2012

One
Dramatic Change in Classical Recording 1977–1990

In 1977, a decade before the first Naxos budget CDs hit the streets in Europe and Asia, sales of the previous format – vinyl LPs – were approaching their zenith. The classical record industry, in profile and character, was very different from the one to which we have become accustomed in the twenty-first century. It was, back then, a very paternalistic affair. It was ruled by a handful of self-proclaimed glorious (at least that was the way they saw themselves) companies – called informally by the industry 'the majors' – with a select roster of star artists who were largely exclusive, fêted (even pampered) and promoted as the master musical artists of the world. The leading conductors, soloists and singers of these 'majors' were regarded by the companies, the retailers and the classical buyers themselves as an aristocratic breed that would deliver definitive interpretations of the great composers – definitive, that is, until the next generation came along to be marketed and promoted in their place.

There were four European companies: Deutsche Grammophon (DG), Philips, Decca and EMI. Deutsche Grammophon (popularly called the 'Yellow Label' because of its distinctive yellow cartouche) was based in Hamburg and probably carried the greatest cachet: its full name was Deutsche Grammophon Gesellschaft, shortened to 'DGG' but later abridged even further to 'DG'. Philips was originally a Dutch company allied to the electronics giant. For many years Decca was a UK company with a curiously divided business activity of classical recording and military electronics. EMI was also based in the UK and carried its long heritage with pride: its roots lay in the earliest days of the classical recording industry and its recordings carried the famous dog-and-trumpet logo of His Master's Voice, until some clever marketing initiative wiped it from the sleeves.

There were also two American labels, RCA and CBS. RCA was created out of the merger in the late 1920s of the mighty Victor Company and the Radio Corporation of America, and was led for decades by a titan of American capitalism, David Sarnoff. One of the key RCA artists was Arturo Toscanini. CBS (originally Columbia) was led by another mid-twentieth-century media giant, William Paley, who created strong competition for RCA's record division with the purchase of the American Record Corporation in 1938. Both RCA and CBS used their radio and television arms to promote their key artists, who included Sir Thomas Beecham.

The content of these six catalogues stretched back to the start of the recording era in the first decade of the twentieth century. There were remarkable archives from those early years when the race was on to capture forever the finest performers and performances of the day. And these had to be good: editing did not become commonplace until after the Second World War (when tape was used as a recording medium).

By 1977 the six international majors commanded the lion's share of both classical music record sales and the publicity and reviews in classical magazines all over the world. They had well-developed machines to promote their stars; and they could exploit the back catalogue with mid-price releases, popular compilations, and specially priced boxed sets for the Christmas market.

Living alongside these magnificent whales were the 'independents' – classical labels that had often been created by enthusiasts hoping to fill a variety of specialist niches. The 'indies' were ever enterprising and they truly filled the needs of the collectors. They offered rare repertoire, which more often than not was chamber music but did include orchestral works and even opera in certain circumstances. These independents lived on their wits, surviving frequently through the energies and imagination of the founder; they reflected the nation of their headquarters, promoting, at least initially, the music or musicians of that country; and generally they declined as age and exhaustion crept up on the owner.

It was a busy scene. In the mid-1970s there were CRD, Unicorn-Kanchana, Nimbus, Meridian and Lyrita, among others, in the UK; the two sizeable labels Harmonia Mundi and Erato led the indies in France, as did Acanta and Deutsche Harmonia Mundi in Germany. There was BIS in Scandinavia; and Elektra Nonesuch, Varèse Sarabande and Telarc featured strongly in the US. In the Eastern European Communist Bloc countries, the classical record scene was dominated by the national labels: Supraphon and Opus in Czechoslovakia, Hungaroton in Hungary, Polskie Nagrania in Poland, VEB Deutsche Schallplatten in East Germany, and the mighty Melodiya in the Soviet Union. These had a double-sided status: majors in their own countries, independents in the rest of the world.

The perception was that the six majors were firmly at the top of the pile, with their *maestri*. Unassailable king of all was Herbert von Karajan. He was the prize of two companies – DG and EMI – simply because his gargantuan appetite for record-ing and the costs involved were both too great for one, even a major. There were other star conductors, of course: Georg Solti with Decca, Leonard Bernstein with CBS, the late Otto Klemperer with EMI, the young James Levine with RCA, and Bernard Haitink with Philips. They all had their symphonic cycles, though none matched the prolific Karajan, who recorded no fewer than five Beethoven symphony cycles during the course of his recording career. Comparing the merits of Bernstein's Mahler versus Haitink's, for example, was a central discussion of the day, and to be classed as an average collector one had to have at least three or four versions of the complete cycle.

Then there were the soloists. Take the pianists: Ashkenazy on Decca, Pollini on DG, Perahia on CBS; or the violinists: Menuhin on EMI, Stern on CBS; or the singers: Pavarotti and Sutherland on Decca, Sherrill Milnes and Placido Domingo on RCA. This was just the surface. Most of the majors had a rich roster of contracted artists covering the principal instruments and offered different performances of the same works. Of course they covered the central repertoire (which, during the 1980s, became known by the phrase 'core repertoire') but the promotional effort focused on the artists. The majors both created stars and built on the success of established concert performers. It was the purpose of the press and marketing departments to relay the message to the collectors that for serious interpretations of core repertoire it was necessary to invest in full-price recordings by these top artists with the world's top ten orchestras. To invest in anything else would be to support a bold attempt, perhaps, but it would not bring the finest quality.

This sense of grandeur was backed by a financial base that did not merely allow excess but encouraged it. Artists were given royalty deals and other rewards which matched the pampering of pop stars. They had the right to veto recordings if they disliked the end result – no matter how many days had been spent in the studio. Carlos Kleiber refused to record again for DG after the label insisted on releasing his recording of *Tristan und Isolde*. He spent days recording it, DG spent months editing it, but he did not think the final edit was good enough to release and refused to pass it. In the end, DG, in an unusual show of determination, managed to persuade him; it was released (and received well) but Kleiber never did record for the company again.

Many signed artists also had approval rights on photographs. It was almost commonplace for a release to be delayed for months, even years, because an artist disliked the cover picture and had no time to go into a photographic studio for more sessions. Flying a photographer halfway round the world to take a picture of a singer in full operatic regalia for the front cover was a relatively small outlay.

This was all matched by lavish promotional budgets, which took classical music writers worldwide to interview, listen and comment on concerts, festivals and recordings. These budgets allowed equally generous funds for advertising in classical music magazines and classical music sections in newspapers, thereby ensuring that the majors had the lion's share of editorial column inches, with the indies jockeying below for what was left.

That was just how it was, and few complained. In its way it was a golden time, and the danger of producing inflated reputations was just part of the party. It was all possible because, from the 1950s and the growth of pop music, and the expansion of record-buying as a popular commercial habit, classical music had carved for itself a special, elevated place in the record industry. It was Art, with a capital A, and the musicians were Artists, with an even larger A. It was not expected that this area of cultural life should make a profit, or contribute to the bottom line of a company, any more than the Royal Opera House, Covent Garden did; or, at least, there was a lot of leeway. The classical departments of these majors lived in a magical world.

There is no doubt that this aura was only partially earned and deserved, burnished as it was by the powerful marketing machines of the international companies; yet out of this period came extraordinary recordings that will always be regarded as among the unique achievements of Western culture. Few who saw Karajan conduct or who met him could deny that here was an extraordinary man in any terms – similarly Bernstein or Kleiber, Klemperer or Giulini. It wasn't just about the big stars, either. There was a substratum of highly knowledgeable and dedicated engineers, producers and A&R (artists and repertoire) experts who made this world live. They inhabited an arena that combined aspects of the protective realm of academia, the star quality of showbiz, the rarefied air of an R&D department, and the profligacy of Hollywood.

There was genuine integrity, too. Often there was a quality of the crusader in some of the projects: Decca, for example, took up the mantle of promoting period performance – a trend that had been started by the independents – and, with its Mozart symphony cycle by Christopher Hogwood and the Academy of Ancient Music, brought the genre into the mainstream. This was initiated not by the artists but by the head of marketing at Decca: it was an event that actually helped to broaden the period-music movement.

Another example, again from Decca, was the release of Bach's complete organ music. For this the company chose an English organist, Peter Hurford, who was a respected figure though not well known outside organ circles; and it took the imaginative decision to record around the world on only new organs. So Hurford and the Decca recording team travelled throughout Europe, America and Australia to realise the project. It wasn't cheap. It is unlikely they recouped the investment. But it was certainly a statement.

For two or three decades, classical recording lived in the supercharged, protected world of the majors, with enough crumbs and space left over for individuals of enterprise to start small labels of their own. The classical share of the record industry varied from 5 per cent in the US, rising to 11 per cent in Germany, with around 7 per cent in the UK; but it remained fairly stable, only shifting now and again following an unexpected crossover blockbuster.

In the 1970s the classical picture was changing. The pop label Warner dipped its toe in the classical waters by absorbing the independent label Elektra Nonesuch. EMI was investing in local recording centres around the world, giving it a unique character of its own among the majors. In 1979 Deutsche Grammophon and Philips, which comprised the classical labels of the huge record company PolyGram, were joined by Decca. Edward Lewis, the Decca founder and a dedicated classical music lover, had run into financial trouble and needed to sell. He died two weeks later. Although ostensibly the three labels maintained their separate identities, PolyGram Classics, the group's new title, was now the single most powerful worldwide classical force. Pop companies with their commercial attitudes were beginning to take note of the classical backwaters (though without any real understanding – which may have been why, when Decca was absorbed into PolyGram, all its precious 78 rpm metal masters were destroyed).

In 1979 LP record sales began to plateau. There were a number of reasons for this. LPs had been around for nearly forty years, and perhaps people were beginning to question whether, when they already had perfectly adequate recordings of Beethoven's symphonies on LP, it was really necessary to add to them or replace them with a set by the latest conductor. They may have been slightly scratched, but they were much more durable than 78s. The main cause, however, was the advent of home taping. It was in the late 1970s that 'music centres' – which combined a radio, an LP record player and a cassette deck – began to make their way over from Japan, and home taping became common practice. Blank cassettes were relatively expensive but it was still cheaper to copy than to buy a new LP. The recording industry launched its first anti-piracy campaign, with a skull-and-crossbones as the logo, but nothing could stem the tide. So the industry began to look for a medium that could not be copied.

It was also in 1979 that the first commercial digital recordings were made. This system used PCM (pulse code modulation) recorders, which could produce a sound without any analogue 'hiss'. Classical LPs began to appear with 'DIG-ITAL' as a selling point, offering, it was claimed, absolutely silent background; and it was true, except that there was an analogue 'moment' at the microphone end, and when the needle hit the vinyl an analogue process was involved. Nevertheless it did make a discernible difference, and the classical world jumped on this as a major step forward in the engineering of recordings.

The Philips videodisc introduced digital technology to the home in 1978, and after the engineers of Philips and Sony came together the compact disc was born. Manufacturing CDs was complex and involved a huge investment. Nevertheless, following their initial release in Japan in 1982 and the rest of the world in 1983, CDs transformed the record world. All the record companies hoped that this remarkable fidelity would set such a standard that no one would want to copy onto cassette. In any case, until CD and cassette players were combined in one machine it was quite complex to do; and it was some years before the advent of home computers made copying from CD to CD relatively easy. So, for some time, the industry was convinced that CD would be the answer to home piracy. Ironically digital recording and the CD were to create the greatest home-piracy headache of all for the record companies; but in 1983 they were the perfect solution. They also ushered in a gravy train the like of which classical recording had never seen.

Initially there were some questions over the nature of the CD sound. Collectors, accustomed to the perceived 'warm' sound quality of the LP, did have some criticisms of the first-generation discs and players. However, the technology improved over the years – computers transformed techniques of recording and production as the playback equipment itself evolved – and there was no doubt that the convenience of the medium and the excitement of the new 'modern' technology meant that it carried all before it. The playing length was determined, curiously, by Herbert von Karajan. Sony asked him what the length should be and he replied that it should be enough to contain Beethoven's Symphony No. 9. This was quite illogical: it would have made more sense to set it at around sixty minutes (two sides of an LP) or ninety minutes (two sides of a cassette tape).

The format provided a bona fide reason for the hardcore classical collector to go out and buy again all his favourite recordings on CD: the back catalogues of Karajan, Klemperer, Solti, Giulini; of Michelangeli, Stern; of opera and even historical performances going back into the early years of recording. It was a little while before the record companies really began to exploit the back catalogue – but when they did, it proved very profitable. The new medium also opened the door for a much wider public to sample classical music. While people were buying their Pink Floyd and The Beatles on CD they would throw a classical CD into their basket. It looked good on the shelves, and a full orchestra did sound impressive on CD.

The only issue for the first four or five years was that the CDs were very expensive (their silver appearance was designed to endorse this). There was restricted manufacturing capacity at the few CD plants around the world. Record companies could demand high prices from the consumer for the privilege of owning this technology and sold CDs for three times the price of LPs. There was a clear indication that classical music was in the vanguard of the CD movement, even though the discs were not cheap. This was primarily because the longer playing times more obviously benefitted classical music than pop; but it had also clearly been deemed that the higher spending power of the classical collectors, and their interest in hi-fi – they did not play their LPs on a multi-changer Dansette – would make them early adopters. The assumption proved correct.

The commercial success of the CD's early years meant that classical record companies began to show their heads above the record-industry parapet. This could be seen by the growth of the classical presence at MIDEM (the annual record-industry trade fair held in Cannes each January), which led to the establishment of MIDEM Classique. It gave an energy to the industry in general and classical music in particular. New technology was helping to make classical music a bit fashionable.

At the same time, the general public's perception of classical musicians was on the rise. Karajan may have been in the last years of his life, but his profile was high. For some time his concerts in Japan with the Berlin Philharmonic were not only packing out concert halls but were being relayed on NHK radio and television, reaching audiences of fifteen million. He realised the importance of connecting with the wider public and began to have all his concerts filmed: it was a massive investment in terms of cost but it would provide him, he hoped, with a kind of immortality. All this attention had a remarkable effect on record sales, and by the time of Karajan's death in 1989 he represented 25 per cent of all DG's sales.

There was a fresh energy in classical recording. This was created partly by the advent of the CD, but also by the flowering of a new generation of independent labels. In the UK, Hyperion, Chandos, Nimbus, ASV and others began to make a significant artistic and sales impact. In Germany, ECM, under its highly individualistic founder Manfred Eicher, was developing a cult following, while Capriccio emerged as the CD was launched. BIS, founded by Robert von Bahr in 1973, had already established itself as the leading independent in Sweden and grasped the opportunity of the CD with both hands.

From Hong Kong, in 1982, came another initiative: Marco Polo Records, founded by the German-born businessman Klaus Heymann to record and release world-premiere recordings of music from the Romantic and late Romantic periods. It was a clear marketing strategy which sat well beside the other independent labels so far established. It was not normal for such an initiative to originate in Hong Kong, but the world was becoming smaller. The first recordings came out on LP; and even though the CD was introduced soon after the formation of the company, the lack of manufacturing capacity meant that it was some time before Heymann could get Marco Polo accepted for pressing by a CD plant.

Together these small but bold labels began to be a force of their own, changing the face of classical recording and playing their part in raising its profile. On the whole, the driving force was the music rather than the artists; and the growth of the CD helped enormously as, month by month, increased production meant a wider and more varied representation of music and labels on the shelves.

During the mid-1980s CD manufacturing plants began to proliferate. The CD as a medium was clearly here to stay, and the general financial investment sector had decided to put money in. To begin with, the manufacturing prices were high as the piper called the tune. By 1985 they were starting to drop as competition among plants and greater capacity steadied the market. By 1987 there was even some spare capacity – enough for one Japanese manufacturer to agree to press CDs for $3 each (compared with $1 for an LP).

It was at this point that a new era in classical recording was about to begin, in the unlikely surroundings of French hypermarkets. A Hong Kong buying office, Fargo, had placed an extremely large order with a Hong Kong company for digital recordings of popular classics to be sold at budget price. The first Naxos CDs rolled off the Denon presses in Yokohama.

It was not only the advent of the CD that laid the ground for a new enterprise such as Naxos: there were other considerable changes to the classical record industry in the late 1980s. Some of the majors had new owners who began to question the traditional, comfortable ways of operating. Large multinational companies became interested in the potential profits of classical music as consumers replaced their LPs with CDs. In 1986 Bertelsmann, the German publishing and magazine group, bought RCA so that it could have music alongside print. In 1987 Sony bought CBS Records and created Sony Classics as part of its drive to acquire content: it didn't want purely to make the CDs. In 1988 the Time Warner group decided to get deeper into classics and bought the German company Teldec; four years later the group was joined by former EMI president Peter Andry, who brought Erato into the fold and founded a separate label, Warner Classics. Thus there was created a new 'major' with three arrows in its quiver, plus Elektra Nonesuch as a kind of 'independent' within. All these classical companies, though they didn't know it, were soon to be subject to tougher business-accounting policies: a target return on investment of less than two years rather than the hitherto relaxed return that had predominated.

Along with these changes on the label side of the business, equally important changes were happening in the retail world. For years, classical record sales had been driven by the classical departments of chain record stores and a network of independent classical music shops run by highly knowledgeable enthusiasts. Both these channels had gained a reputation for being, at times, somewhat forbidding. Those who were less than confident in their classical knowledge could find the experience of buying a recording a daunting one.

These stores had previously concentrated their efforts on full-price product and mid-price reissues. The advent of the CD changed that. By 1987 there were already mid-price and even budget CD lines on the market. In October 1987, in the UK, EMI introduced the CD equivalent of its popular 'Music for Pleasure' line of LPs, retailing at £6.99. British multi-chain stores with record sections, such as WH Smith and Boots, began sourcing cheap CDs to retail at £4.99 and even £3.99. Enterprising independent distributors were scouring the world to meet this demand. Recordings were acquired from Yugoslavia and Slovakia, though rumours rapidly began to spread about their dubious provenance and sometimes questionable quality.

It was at this moment that Naxos appeared, started almost by accident by Klaus Heymann, the Hong Kong-based entrepreneur who loved classical music as much as he loved grasping a business opportunity. If his Marco Polo was a result of the former, Naxos was a product – at the start – of the latter. It entered the record retail channels in a variety of ways, starting with supermarkets and general-store chains, and only gradually found its way into the classical mainstream. For example, in the UK Naxos became the exclusive classical label for Woolworths in 1988, at the time one of the leading record retailers in the country with 10 per cent of the market and a need for a budget classical line. It was the first key step to breaking into the UK market on a national basis. It wasn't particularly auspicious because it restricted a label that had aspirations for a serious international classical presence, and Naxos was initially in danger of being lumped with the other fly-by-night labels that featured Eastern European orchestras. The fact that it presented new digital recordings ('DIGITAL/DDD' was prominently displayed on all the covers) of reliable performances was not often noted by rivals, journalists or even retailers in those early days. It could have sunk into obscurity and the nondescript bargain bins with the others. That fact that it didn't remains one of the remarkable stories of classical recording.

The reason for its survival was due partly to its being in the right place at the right time and partly to the immense energy and true dedication to classical music that went into its development and expansion. It was certainly the right moment for a budget CD label to come through. *Music Week*, the UK trade magazine, noted in the summer of 1988: 'Established classical consumers will be looking to change their home library over the next five years to a new hi-tech medium, providing steady income for retailers with a basic stock of classical repertoire.' And so they did. Sales of CD recordings were growing by 20 per cent per year. By 1988 CD sales were equalling LP sales. It was boom time – clearly helped by cheaper CDs.

Even the majors recognised this. Late in 1988 PolyGram announced budget lines of CDs using back-catalogue analogue recordings, retailing at £5.99. There were known names in these lists – at least known to classical aficionados – but that was not of interest to the new buyers of classical CDs in Woolworths. They wanted to see the words 'DIGITAL/DDD' stamped on the CD covers. The majors thought that 'star' names on CDs, albeit in remastered analogue recordings (AAD), would brush aside these upstart versions from Eastern Europe. They were wrong.

In fact, it would have been extraordinarily prescient for anyone in PolyGram HQ to think that this little label from Hong Kong would pose a threat to the established order of things. DG had much more important things to think about. In 1989 Herbert von Karajan died. It was truly the end of an era, and DG executives despaired at the thought of finding a replacement. They hoped it would be Claudio Abbado, who succeeded Karajan at the Berlin Philharmonic and was on their books; but in their hearts they knew that he would never match the old master for sheer presence.

They must have felt doubly threatened because, over at EMI, a scruffy but brilliant violinist by the name of Nigel Kennedy was racking up two million sales with a patchy recording of *The Four Seasons* (which had been recorded at different times and edited together) through force of personality and pop-style marketing. It was still a celebrity event, but with a totally different character and a new popular reach. Karajan never attempted to be popular – though he became so, in a way – just grand.

In 1990 the Kennedy campaign was put into the shadows by the success of The Three Tenors and their *tour de force* at the World Cup in Rome, in the ruins of the Baths of Caracalla. Luciano Pavarotti (Decca), Placido Domingo (DG) and José

Carreras (Philips) each represented one leg of the PolyGram stool; superbly marketed, they sold millions, creating a wave that all three were able to ride for years. They were given a superb start by the clever idea to use Pavarotti's recording of 'Nessun dorma' as the theme music for all the UK television broadcasts of World Cup matches. Decca had a hit on its hands before The Three Tenors CD was even pressed.

However, it also put the spotlight of investment finance on the majors. Suddenly classical music was not only prestigious but a commercial commodity. The spectre of financial expectations slid into the classical boardrooms: the money men wanted a part of the cake. The majors, within multinational companies, now found themselves in a darker environment, where financial targets needed to be met and awareness of the bottom line was about profit, not a good bass section. Many expectations were simply unrealistic for regular classical sales. Meanwhile, Naxos's fast-growing catalogue, efficiently marketed and distributed, and sold at a price anyone could afford, began eating into the core classical sales as well as appealing to a wider, non-specialist classical audience. Its slimline operation was fashioned for the times.

Unable to produce a 'Three Tenors' success year after year to meet the financial targets expected of them, the classical managers at the majors were forced to change their ways. Through the 1990s it became clear that the old, gentlemanly methods of running a major classical record company could no longer apply. A large roster of star artists on generous contracts could not be maintained; horror on horror, many who had been with the labels for a considerable number of years had to be 'let go'. Cuts undreamed of a decade earlier had to be made. The demands of the new accountants were unrealistic and unsustainable in the classical music world, but the damage was done. No longer could core repertoire be repeated for the benefit of new artists wanting to give the world *their* Beethoven, *their* Brahms. No longer could these majors nurture young artists.

Instead, stars with popular appeal had to be found, propelled into the public eye, and ditched if they didn't make an instant mark. Promotional budgets, for advertising and for journalistic trips, were cut. Recording budgets were cut. No longer were the majors able to carry the torch for new interpretations: only successful crossover projects could meet the requirements of the bottom line.

These new pressures had a knock-on effect throughout the classical music industry and resulted in a further development: artist labels. When Colin Davis's association with Philips was ended, he, the London Symphony Orchestra and the LSO's manager Clive Gillinson decided to form their own label, LSO Live. Other orchestras followed suit, including the London Philharmonic Orchestra. Independents, which had traditionally kept away from core repertoire, began moving into the central classical road. Artists who found themselves adrift without a record company began looking for other possibilities.

Meanwhile there was the continuing pressure exerted by the small, seemingly insignificant label based in Hong Kong, which was selling its CDs for less than the value of the smallest banknote in each country. The main nineteenth-century symphonies played by Eastern European orchestras under the baton of unknown conductors could not really be of any significance, could they? Surely the main violin concertos played by an unknown Japanese violinist and the piano concertos by a quiet Hungarian could not compete in the main classical marketplace?

They could. From being an exclusive line at Woolworths in 1988, the company moved to the mainstream UK record shops, and within a short time the famous 'Naxos White Wall' began appearing all over the country. It was a pattern that was repeated all over the world – at different speeds, in different ways, yet always describing an upward graph. The white cover with its simple, basic graphics had created a standard look that made the label instantly identifiable. It stood out from all others. In a remarkably short time Naxos became perceived as a brand, the only brand of its kind in mainstream classical music. People started to home in on it; and because the repertoire was expanding rapidly, Naxos became a brand that they wanted to revisit. It began to change the face of the classical record departments. As the concept of 'own branding' took hold, it also began to appear in other, non-traditional outlets, such as bookshops. By the early 1990s it had established a ubiquitous presence in many markets.

There was continued development in the last two decades of the twentieth century and an exciting volatility in classical recording. There were opportunities everywhere, and those who emerged and still survive demonstrated not only a deep classical commitment but also the ability to move with the changes and even see them coming. The majors had a swan-song with the celebrity culture; the new independents showed themselves to be truly inventive in terms of repertoire, bringing lost or forgotten music to consumers of recorded music. Both majors and independents recognised the rise of period performance.

Equally significant was the provision of classical music to a vast popular audience at a desirable price. This was achieved more by Naxos than by any other company, and through curiously plain, traditional values: providing reliable performances of central repertoire in new digital recordings on CD, even with basic but dependable liner notes. Classical recording would never be the same again.

By the middle of the 1990s it was clear, to those who could see the signs, that a new order was emerging. The dominant hold maintained for so long by the majors over the classical record industry was being undermined from both inside and out. The digital international world was a different one. A new customer base was going into record shops willing to walk out with bundles of white-liveried budget CDs, knowing that reliability was assured and a real gem might be discovered. These recordings were not coming from grand offices in the capital cities with long classical traditions (which was, ironically, one reason for the company's success – for many years, the majors simply didn't take it seriously as a threat): Naxos had its headquarters in Hong Kong. In the UK, for the first key years of its growth, there was an office in Sheffield and then in Redhill, Surrey. In the US it was based in Cherry Hill, New Jersey and then in Nashville, Tennessee. In Sweden it was in the country town of Örebro; in Germany it was in Münster.

Increasingly, as the 1990s progressed, these Naxos offices became distribution points for other classical labels, in some cases becoming the main classical distributor in the country. It was not a plot that the grand men who ran PolyGram or EMI or Sony could have imagined would happen. By the first decade of the twenty-first century, however, it was very clear where their main opposition was coming from.

Two
Klaus Heymann: A Profile

Klaus Heymann is tall: 1.93m (6′3″). Now in his mid-seventies, he is white-haired, slim and walks with a slight stoop, perhaps the result of spending so many years in the Far East where he towers over most, or maybe an inevitable consequence of all those years hunched over a keyboard – typewriter or computer. His principal home has been in Hong Kong for more than forty years, and although he now spends a few months each year in his second home in Auckland, New Zealand there is little suggestion that he will leave China in the near future.

He has always found it particularly satisfying that the revolution caused by Naxos in the classical record industry came not from Europe, the established centre of classical music, or from the United States, but from Hong Kong. He often says that had he been based in Europe he would not have been able to do what he did. It was precisely because Hong Kong was not a classical music centre that Naxos was able to grow in size and strength, and expand worldwide. None of the major classical companies was looking to see what was coming out of the East. By the time they did, it was too late.

He has never been tempted to move. The headquarters of Naxos remain there – in the hi-tech quarter of Cyberport. His wife, the Japanese violinist Takako Nishizaki, has a growing violin-teaching practice (Suzuki Method); and his son Rick, now in his mid-thirties, runs Naxos Far East from Hong Kong.

Heymann's roots in Hong Kong go deep. The entrepreneurial, risky, high-octane atmosphere, flavoured by the Chinese ability for commerce, has always suited Heymann. He scored his first commercial successes there, and built a comfortable fortune well before Naxos. He has made the most of his position as a businessman comfortable within Chinese circles in particular and Far Eastern circles in general, though he started his business life in Europe. German by birth but European by education (Portugal, Paris and London as well as Frankfurt; fluent in four languages and conversational in more), he is international in outlook.

This even applies to his name. He generally introduces himself as Klaus 'Hay-man' rather than rigidly insisting on the correct German pronunciation of 'Hei-mann'. When he goes into his offices in Cyberport most of the staff address him as 'Mr Hayman'. He studied linguistics and his English is impeccable; but he speaks, curiously for a European, with a noticeable American colour. This was probably a legacy of his early years in Hong Kong and Southeast Asia, the time of the Vietnam War, when he was dealing mostly with Americans. He absorbed the tones, and in any case it was more appropriate for business.

For Klaus Heymann is, at heart, a businessman. He has an arts and humanities background. Mention Seneca or *Don Quixote* and it transpires that he read them in the original language. Literature, history, politics and political theory were the stuff of his student years and he has not lost them. Yet he is the first to admit that now he does not read books. He gets on the plane (first class) and reads business or classical music magazines, or *The Economist* or the *Financial Times*, or business analyses. He absorbs the current concepts of 'the long tail' or 'the global market' or 'the tipping point' or 'the black swan'; he keeps up with world politics, mainly insofar as it touches his business, and technological developments.

For a septuagenarian, he is exceptionally well informed concerning digital directions and developments. When fax technology came in he was one of the first to leap at it, and he insisted that all his business colleagues kept up. It is similar with email: he receives hundreds of messages a day, but any of his vast number of regular correspondents around the world will say that he almost always responds within a day – more often than not within hours, even minutes. It seems effortless. He was a very early adopter of Skype: Naxos offices around the world were required to get on to it. He drew the line at Skype video, however – because he says it uses too much bandwidth. In his late sixties he began to suffer from repetitive strain injury due to the hours he spent using his mouse. He switched to a pen mouse, and then adopted the early versions of speech recognition software. If you watch him at his computer now, you see him mainly speaking to it. He has top-of-the-range speech recognition software that allows him to answer all emails with barely any need to touch the keyboard. Nothing must stand in the way of fielding the torrent of communication that comes in from all time zones.

Mostly he works from the office in his home in Hong Kong, an ante room beside the main drawing room. The desk is impeccably tidy. The laptop computer sits in pride of place. In the background can be heard his wife practising or teaching. He may have the Naxos Music Library playing. If a document comes through that requires careful reading, he prints it out and reads it on paper rather than on the screen. Otherwise, donning his headphones with a microphone, looking for all the world like a call-centre person, he speaks to his machine, and to the world, and runs the Naxos empire.

And that is exactly what he does. All Naxos roads lead to this little office. Sometimes, the email or Skype line may lead to his more impressive steel-and-glass office – with a larger desk –

in Cyberport, though he now goes there only a couple of times a week. Those lines could lead anywhere in the world of course – to Shanghai, Nashville, London, Munich – wherever he happens to be.

From his early days in post-war Germany he found he had a natural aptitude for business, for commercial opportunity. This was partly due to his facility for mental arithmetic. He is extremely quick at weighing up costs and profit margins, and he has an instinct for what the market will take. At first it was just trade. He preferred it to be something technological – cameras, the latest hi-fi equipment, cutting-edge studio equipment – because he read about them anyway. He loved a challenge, particularly when circumstances forced him to think sideways to resolve a situation. Not for him were the formal avenues to trade. If it could be done faster, more profitably – be it in a somewhat unorthodox manner – it was all the better. He picked up the nuts and bolts of advertising and marketing while working for Braun; and he learned how to start a business from scratch when he went to Hong Kong to open the office of an American newspaper.

Underpinning all this were the two central passions of his life: sport and music (principally classical). A useful tennis player, helped by his height and ball skill, he played competitively and coached. Most people who take up sport to a good level of skill and competition retain the lessons learned in that activity. Klaus Heymann was competitive as a teenager and remained so in business. To him, a skilful return of serve followed a few parries later by a neat passing shot was particularly satisfying. His tennis was not based on overt aggression, the unstoppable volley.

So it has been in business. His business style is not to crush rivals but to play his game to his strengths, and neatly make a move in a time of his own choosing. On the other hand, Heymann is the first to acknowledge that on many occasions he has been lucky with the way the ball has bounced or with a net cord just when he needed it. Winning is the name of the game, without a doubt, and there has been little room for sentimentality. Despite his wife being a violinist he holds no sentimental attitude towards musicians. Of course, being married to a musician, he is acutely aware of what it means to be a performing artist; but as the owner of a record company he can rarely allow his feelings or preferences for an artist to take priority over the needs of the company to make a profit. His view is pragmatic: 'no profit, no record company, no recordings'.

He knows he holds the aces. He does not have long-term contracts with his musicians but has, from the start, expected his artists to be loyal to him and to Naxos. If a musician was disloyal, by recording for someone else, for example, he would censure them without regret or ensure that they never recorded for him again. This was particularly the case in the early years, when he was building the company and felt that he couldn't afford to send out the wrong messages. The attitude extended to his business dealings, too: he was capable of sidestepping a business partner who was not performing his or her side of the deal, especially if an opportunity arose. Nevertheless he is sharp rather than ruthless. He has also been known to apologise at a later stage for actions he took but subsequently regretted.

On the other hand, he can be long-suffering and surprisingly generous. This side of his personality can astound those who don't know him well. One former employee who left under a cloud threatened to sue him and frequently insulted him personally; but Heymann continued to pay for his children's education as he had promised to do.

He pours resources into music-education projects because he wants to promote classical music, even sing its praises. Some make money; most do not. But he doesn't seem to mind because the cause is right. Rarely does he take credit for it: despite leading Naxos from the front, he has never been into the personality cult. He is frequently interviewed for classical music or business columns but he is also content to be anonymous. In China, where Nishizaki is a very well-known soloist, he can be referred to as 'Mr Nishizaki' and it amuses him; perhaps he is even proud of it. In 2010, at the Hong Kong Business Awards, he was on the stage with some of the richest men in the city (that means mega-rich) after winning the Owner-Operator Award. If the truth be told, he nearly declined it because the event interrupted plans for a break in New Zealand where he would play golf every day. He chose to stay because the exposure was good for Naxos's profile in its home town.

As with many highly successful men, there are contradictory traits in his character; or maybe it is more accurate to say that there are different traits which manage to co-exist. He makes cool business decisions, quite unemotionally; yet his response to music is clearly emotional. Few business partners of long standing have heard him talk about his passion for music in any intimate way, and would be surprised to hear him describe his response to Richard Strauss's *Der Rosenkavalier*, for instance:

> Rosenkavalier *is one of the few things that makes me cry. I do not cry at deaths of heroines, or when someone dies on stage ... but dramatic resolutions, such as when the Marschallin gives away Octavian to Sophie because she knows that this is the right thing to do – this moves me. In the same way, I was deeply moved when I first saw Pfitzner's* Palestrina, *and it still affects me today. Nobody gets killed. But Palestrina's reconciliation with his persecutor Cardinal Borromeo, and the sense of spiritual release, is extremely powerful. And I prefer Bruckner to Mahler. Bruckner doesn't have downs: he is an uplifting composer, even in his slow movements, except perhaps the slow movement of the Ninth Symphony. For me, his symphonies are all about the good*

things of the world: his architecture is grand, his world is whole. Mahler, by comparison, is for me more uneven emotionally, wilder, less sure.

Heymann is direct and refreshingly unpretentious when he talks about music. He did not learn to read it or to play an instrument because there was no such tradition in his family. In any event, there was no money after the war for buying an instrument and funding lessons. From a very young age he had to work because he did not receive pocket money from his parents. He declares that not having learned, at the very least, to play the piano or read music is one of his great regrets in life, though he has famously turned it to his advantage with the creation of Naxos. After a lifetime in music, and years of marriage to a violinist, he still talks of a musician playing 'high' or 'low' rather than 'sharp' or 'flat'. He has been offered honorary doctorates by a number of universities but has always declined them; he feels that because he doesn't read music it would be pretentious to accept. Yet he is still confident to stand up at the annual sales conference and sing the praises of Schumann's *Scenes from Goethe's Faust* or Mozart's Divertimento in E flat, sublime works with which only the knowledgeable are generally familiar. Furthermore, he knows that in the current climate the recent recording of *Scenes from Goethe's Faust* (a large-scale work with full orchestra, soloists and chorus) will probably never recoup its investment. For projects which are particularly dear to him, he doesn't mind.

Like many entrepreneurs, he is a risk-taker. He says that he never takes a big risk that could sink the company, but he is very prepared to make many small bets, or sink resources into new areas, in the hope that one or two of them will bear fruit. He has probably had more failures than successes in his business life, but all the failures have been small while he made the right decisions in some really crucial areas.

It is not often realised that Naxos is actually the product of a husband-and-wife team. The relationship between Klaus Heymann and Takako Nishizaki is unusually close, both in personal and business terms. Heymann always acknowledges the contribution that his wife has made, though it is not often recognised because he is the label's most prominent figure. Nishizaki's recordings helped to start the label, but it is also she who has recommended which musicians should record for Naxos, and even their area of repertoire, after hearing them in concert or on demonstration recordings. She has had a considerable influence on the musical character of Naxos. It should be said that the equality of women has never been an issue with Heymann.

But Naxos the company has been made by one man, which has been its strength and its weakness. For all its twenty-five years Heymann has run the company, even down to a detailed level. Most of the new ideas and directions come from him. He listens to his employees at every level and he supports them, but ultimately nothing happens without his approval. This is both a help and a hindrance. It means that instant decisions are possible. It also means that, despite some capable and dedicated people around him, it has been difficult for the company to move on to a more corporate footing, even when it was evidently too large for one pair of hands. Heymann has been acutely aware of this, and of the track record of companies that have outgrown the entrepreneur–founder: only too often they have closed, or been subsumed into a larger company. Over the years, he has tried to find someone to take over from him, or at least to become CEO and take over the day-to-day running of the company. He has put people in place but few have lasted beyond two or three years. Very simply, Heymann has never found anyone who can match him in the key areas of classical music, business, vision *and* swift opportunism, as well as an untiring commitment to work. Unsurprisingly he has little patience for people he deems to have fallen short – a trait that applies at all levels. If people do not come up to his expectations they generally last a short time. To those who do, he gives the kind of loyalty he expects from them.

He has for many years maintained a board, consisting principally of the managing directors of Select Music UK, Naxos of America and Naxos Sweden, plus other occasional, co-opted members. Matters are discussed, and on the whole Heymann does not force issues through, especially on matters that directly affect the distribution companies. He does not interfere in the running of the national companies unless there are problems. The national CEOs run their companies as if they were their own. Most are 'lifers' with ten years or more experience with Naxos. He is, however, prone to start new projects, even major initiatives, without discussion or agreement at board level. All his senior executives now expect to find, from time to time, a new venture already committed to, a new person appointed, a new label taken on for worldwide distribution, a new composer cycle underway. Heymann is shrewd but spontaneous; he has an instinctive feel for an overview of a subject, particularly a deal. But in rapidly coming to a conclusion, he sometimes makes mistakes. Paradoxically, he can pay great attention to detail, whether it be in a lawyer's brief – he has frequently pointed out issues that his own lawyers have missed and thereby won a case – or in the proof-reading of a cover or booklet notes. The underlying explanation is that if he is deeply interested in a topic the scrutiny is minute; if he has marginal interest, or has other, more pressing business, the scrutiny will be cursory.

Heymann is consumed by work. It is not so much that he is driven by it, but more that he is fascinated by it, be it business or the arts. It may have been the oscillation between both, or involvement in them in parallel, that has kept him so fresh and curious. Nevertheless he does have his recreational interests. For some years, wine and golf have held probably equal status. He prefers New World wines to European vintages, and he knows them well: wine was one of the great attractions for him of Australia and New Zealand. Even when he is in Europe he drinks New World wines. He is not a collector because his preferred wines don't last very long. He is an accomplished golfer, and still walks from hole to hole, declining transport. It is his exercise, his break from the computer and the email (he rarely uses a mobile phone). It is also his opportunity to experience again the spark of competition. He always plays better when he plays against someone – and without doubt he carries that into his business life.

Heymann muses from time to time about retiring, even if it is only partial retirement. He is not really serious, though. In Asia there are many businessmen, both Chinese and Western, who run international companies into their eighties, and in his heart he sees no reason why he should not be one of them. There are few signs that his sharpness or his eagerness for new business have diminished in any way. He remains the most far-sighted figure among his colleagues, and is probably still the greatest risk-taker. There is no doubt that Naxos remains his own, and he does with it what he wants while being mindful of the fact that he now has more than 300 employees, many of whom, especially the executives, have devoted their lives to the company. After all, in the end, he sees that he is risking his own money, and that is that.

Three

The Early Years: From Frankfurt to Hong Kong 1936–1967

Klaus Heymann was born in a suburb of Frankfurt on 22 October 1936. His father, Ferdinand, was an administrator working for the city government and his mother, Paula, was a traditional housewife, a role which she resented though she had only had a primary school education. She was bright and capable, and when his father was drafted into the army in 1939, as war clouds gathered, she took his job in City Hall. Ferdinand was an anti-aircraft officer and was mainly based around German towns. When Heymann was four years old he was evacuated, in common with other children, to the countryside, to be joined by his mother only later. First of all he was housed in villages in Hesse, then towns in Alsace, and finally, at the end of the war, in Bavaria. When the family returned to Frankfurt in 1945 they found that their apartment had been turned over to displaced persons, and they (Ferdinand, Paula, Klaus and his younger sister Brigitte) moved into the attic of Heymann's grandmother. A second sister, Barbara, was born three years later. Eventually, in 1948, they moved back to their flat and normal life began. Heymann was twelve. He remembers his childhood home as a 'cultured' household:

We were a book-reading family. I remember that as a kid, myself, my two sisters and my mother would be sitting in four different corners of the room, everyone with a different book. The culture was a reading culture. Music came a little later for me, though my parents always liked classical music and went to concerts. Just after the end of the war, in late 1945 when I was nine, I went to my first concert in a spa on the other side of the lake – the Munich Philharmonic Orchestra playing Beethoven's Leonore 3, *the Fourth Piano Concerto and Schubert's 'Unfinished' Symphony. I remember the pianist was Rosl Schmid and the conductor Hans Rosbaud (I heard many concerts with him later on after he had become music director of the Hesse Radio Orchestra). I found it fascinating. The music made a great impression on me and, back in Frankfurt, I started to go to all the 'youth concerts' at the Hessischer Rundfunk. I went to a lot of concerts.*

My grandmother on my mother's side had a house in one of the other suburbs and had friends who lived in the countryside, so she had food. We went there on weekends on a bicycle – a 20-kilometre bicycle ride to eat. And she had a piano in the hallway but she would never let me touch it. I remember her saying: 'You're going to destroy it. Don't touch the piano!' Perhaps, if she had let me play on it, or just touch it, things might have worked out differently and I might have learned an instrument. But that didn't happen and I never did. Neither of my parents played, so that was the way of the family. And I never learned to read music either.

I became more involved with music around 1955 when my father bought his first record player, which played LPs. I remember I was in high school because I was still making money as a caddy; I was nineteen. We had one of those old radios, of course, but it had a pretty good sound. The first disc my father bought was Mendelssohn's Hebrides *overture on 45 rpm. And then to aggravate my father, whose musical preferences stopped around 1900, I bought Stravinsky's* Petrushka, *Richard Strauss's* Till Eulenspiegel *and* Don Juan, *as well as the* Symphonie fantastique *by Berlioz. Those were my first three LPs. I think they were all Philips and conducted by Willem van Otterloo [the Dutch conductor of the Residentie Orkest in The Hague], who was particularly known for his recordings of twentieth-century music.*

Although I didn't play an instrument, which is something I regret very much to this day, I did read books. When I was in high school I read lots of adventures by a German author called Karl May. He set his stories around the world – the American Old West and the Middle East – countries which he had never visited. He himself wrote about forty or fifty, and after he died other people concocted others. I had a classmate whose father was an industrialist and he had the money to buy all of them, so I borrowed them from him. My ambition was to read every one of his novels, and I did.

I also read other things. I read everything! I think I was probably the best customer of our local city library. I read under the blanket at night; I read all the time. But not about music. I read the programme notes to the concerts but reading about classical music came later when I began record-collecting seriously, after university.

Heymann learned to earn money from a very young age. At ten he had started buying reading sheets from a kiosk in the early morning and reselling them at school for a small profit. Sport was also a keen interest and he got himself a job at a big tennis club as a ball-boy, and then as a caddy at Frankfurt's only golf club. In his student years he did many other jobs, ranging from cleaning and removing labels from bottles for re-use to loading mail on the night trains and being a witness at weddings. He was an able tennis player – he became the playing coach of the Frankfurt University tennis team – and made money by giving tennis lessons at the Frankfurt Press Club and, during the summer holidays, at a big industrial plant near Wiesbaden. He went to Frankfurt University in 1956, just before he turned twenty, to read English and Romance languages and literature. He was always attracted by travel; he became fascinated by Brazil and decided to learn Portuguese. The winter term of 1958 was spent studying Portuguese language and literature at Lisbon University and living with a Portuguese family. He established a pattern of playing and teaching tennis during the summer, and earning sufficient money to fund a winter term at a university abroad. It became an important preparation for his later life.

> *I learned a lot about the different way people lived. I was some sort of a doer. While studying in Lisbon I also played tennis for the university and met a lot of people. I had two very good professors: one, a Brazilian, had written the most important history of the Portuguese language, and the other one was teaching both linguistics and literature. The Portuguese have many dialects: there were many little valleys that were separated from the rest of the country at the time. This professor would write out the phonetic transcription of a sentence and we would have to guess from which part of the country it came. He spoke very movingly about the extreme poverty there – how some villages had only one suit: when one of the villagers had to go to the city for an official visit he put on the one village suit.*
>
> *Because I had studied abroad I got a part-time job running a seminar for my fellow students at Frankfurt University, and this, together with coaching tennis, meant that I was actually starting to become quite well off. And my languages were expanding. I spoke German, English and Portuguese, and I was reading in French, Spanish and Italian – and I took some courses in Romanian, which was half Romance language, half Slav.*

In 1959 Heymann spent the winter term at King's College London; he was ostensibly studying in the Portuguese department but he also went to lectures on French and English. He regards his time there as crucial because he learned 'a critical approach to literature', which was very different from the more deferential German attitude. In 1960 it was back to Frankfurt for the summer, earning well, and then to Paris and the Sorbonne for the winter, where he had the good fortune to study with the distinguished professor and author Antoine Adam. Heymann had brought with him his tape recorder and recorded the lectures while all his fellow students took notes. These winter study periods also introduced him to a lot of opera, theatre and concerts: the San Carlos Opera in Lisbon, the Royal Opera House, Covent Garden in London (it was the early years of Georg Solti), and the Opéra and Comédie-Française in Paris. But it was a life that couldn't continue: he decided that five years as a student had been enough. He was told that in order to finish his Frankfurt degree he would need to stay for another two years, so he dropped out.

It was 1961 and he was accustomed to earning a living in a variety of ways. Tennis was not an option as a profession: 'I was a good state-level player but no more – and there was no professional circuit as there is now.' He didn't want the life of a club tennis coach, either. But it was through his tennis coaching at the Frankfurt Press Club that he got a job as an advertising sales supervisor for a newspaper called *The Overseas Weekly* (which was nicknamed 'The Over-Sexed Weekly' because of the cheesecake pictures that featured in all issues). It was an English-language tabloid for the 300,000 troops in the American armed forces stationed in Germany.

My boss was a hi-fi nut and also a classical music lover. We hit on the idea of publishing a hi-fi supplement, which is where I got to learn about hi-fi. Then people came to me and said they needed translations of hi-fi manuals from German into English. So I started a very lucrative business of doing translations of operating instructions and advertisements which would be polished up by my boss. Even today, if you buy a Braun shaver, you will find a lot of terminology in the instructions that came from me many years ago. Then I started freelance copywriting on the side. I was working all the time, doing my day job, and then having translations or copywriting delivered to me at 7 p.m. which had to be completed overnight. It was proper on-the-job training. I got to know the ad agencies not only as a translator or writer but also as a model for brochures. I modelled as a Lufthansa captain once, with a gorgeous blonde model sitting next to me in a fancy car; it was winter, but I was dressed in the captain's summer uniform because the advertisement was scheduled to run in summer. It was freezing. The advertising-agency people put a fur coat on the model between shoots but I was standing there, shivering, in my summer uniform. On another occasion I did a cigarette commercial and had to hold a cigarette; but I had never smoked, and my eyes began watering and I started to cough. I learned that you never look into a camera but have to focus on a spot, like the shoulder of the cameraman; otherwise you look vague. So now, whenever we do a shoot with a musician or if a press photographer takes pictures of me, I know what to do.

It became clear that there was not a real future in *The Overseas Weekly* and when, at the start of 1966, Braun offered Heymann a job as the export advertising manager, he changed paths. It was an important step because he learned key sales and marketing methods that he was later to use in his classical music business. Braun was famous for its classic, clean design, but Heymann realised that the export markets were not carrying this through in their advertising. He therefore wrote a Braun style guide for advertising – and many of these principles were carried through to Naxos.

Braun did lots of tests on which typography and layouts are easiest to read and used the results in their designs. No indentation because it delays the reading speed; dark blue on white is easier to read than black on white; sans serif type is easier to read than serif. Braun used templates for layouts into which the text and pictures had to fit, and, as a result, all their advertisements and printed material had a very clean look. I learned a lot.

After Heymann had spent a year with Braun, *The Overseas Weekly* invited him to open an office in Hong Kong. It was the time of the Vietnam War, and he arrived in Hong Kong on 6 January 1967 with a suitcase and a two-year contract. Although he has travelled the world, Hong Kong has remained his base ever since.

Four

A New Home in the Far East: Building a Business Career 1967–1982

The move to Hong Kong set Heymann on a steep learning curve, setting up an office, and solving problems with printers, distributors, and not least the military authorities. They were not supporters of the paper because it had been critical of the military, and they refused to allow it on the military newsstands. Yet without distribution there could be no advertising. Heymann travelled around Asia – Thailand, the Philippines, Korea, Taiwan, Japan and, of course, Vietnam – finding outlets in front of the bases. He made a go of it, but realised that there were better ways to get wider distribution. He managed to get hold of military phone books, base by base, which carried details of key personnel, and these became the core of an unrivalled network. He devised a way of shipping out the newspaper in bulk to an international mail exchange centre in Japan, which then shipped it free of charge to the key personnel – even to soldiers and airmen in the front line! What's more, he made no charge to the readers for the newspaper itself – a very early example of a free newspaper funded by advertising, which included most of the main Japanese camera and hi-fi makers. After two years he left and went out on his own. The next step was a direct-advertising business, Davidson and Partners; and then a mail-order company for the US armed forces in Asia, Pacific Mail Order System. It was 1969.

I knew how to convert military phonebooks into mailing lists and so I hit on the idea of starting a mail-order business, because as I travelled around the military bases I kept being asked: 'Where can I buy a camera?' So I began a mail-order business and sold cameras. I made a camera catalogue. I didn't know much about cameras and it had rather a lot of mistakes! But I mailed it out and three weeks later I looked in my letter-box and hundreds of envelopes containing cheques fell out. I was a dollar millionaire within the year. I was thirty-three. It sounds easy, but there were many problems to be overcome, especially the posting difficulties – getting the cameras to the buyers on the military bases. I found out that the nearest US territory to Hong Kong was a place called Guam. I set up a warehouse there, and shipped the parcels in bulk by air freight from Hong Kong to Guam. Our people in Guam posted the parcels at the local post office and the goods were then sent all over Asia to the armed forces by the US Government, at US domestic postage rates.

It was an exciting time. Heymann flew in military helicopters over the Vietnamese terrain and saw, at first hand, the testing circumstances, with guns jamming and communications wild and difficult. He was in Saigon during the Tet Offensive: he learned not to sit near windows in cafés because the Vietcong might throw explosive devices through them. He became involved in travel tourism for soldiers on R&R, working with a big American airline.

Then came the Paris Peace Accords of 1973 and the writing

was on the wall for this form of mail-order activity. However, he wasn't quite finished: he adapted the business, offering hi-fi equipment to members of the military who were preparing to return to the US; they would buy it while still in the Far East, and have it shipped home for their arrival. Although it was clear that his life in Hong Kong and the Far East would be very different, Heymann had no thought of returning to Europe. 'I couldn't imagine living anywhere else.'

During this time he continued to listen to music, but mainly on LP: there was very little live music-making of any reasonable standard in Hong Kong. He also maintained an interest in hi-fi equipment. He had been selling Revox tape recorders and Bose speakers to the GIs, and it was this that led to the next major step in his career: he had a meeting with the innovative designer of speakers, Dr Amar G. Bose. Dr Bose had come to Hong Kong to visit the distributor of his unusual speakers but was disappointed in the distributor's performance. He offered the distribution of Bose in Hong Kong and China to Heymann. It was the beginning of a fruitful relationship that was to last more than twenty-five years and later make a crucial contribution to Naxos itself. Revox also gave him the distributorship of its tape recorders for Hong Kong and China. It was a natural step for Heymann because, even during those heady and busy days since his arrival in the Far East, music had remained a central part of his life, an emotional lifeline to his Western heritage.

From the start of my life in Hong Kong I collected records. I used to read all the catalogues and buy LPs from all over the world – including the Eastern European recordings from Hungaroton, Supraphon and Opus. I got these from a little distributor in Hong Kong called Essex Trading. The company's salesman David Levy knew a lot of unusual music – all the Polish and Czech and Hungarian composers – as well as the central repertoire. I had hundreds of LPs lined up on

*my shelves at home. I tried cataloguing them but didn't have
the time to keep it up, and eventually I shelved them according to the order in which I bought them.*

*I knew mainly about orchestral music and opera. I liked
the big piano and violin concertos, and the symphonic repertoire – Bruckner and Mahler: particularly music that was fast
and loud. It was only later, after I met my wife, Takako
Nishizaki, that I really learned about chamber music, and
how to listen to music intelligently and sensitively. As the
Revox and Bose distributor, I decided it was a good idea to
promote the equipment by organising concerts. But also I
was missing the European environment. I had been accustomed to going to concerts and opera in Europe, and while
I loved being in the Far East, and could listen to records, I
felt the lack of live music. So I started to correct that myself.*

The first concert Heymann organised was a recital by the
American pianist Michael Ponti, arranged through family contacts. Ponti had recorded extensively for the American
independent company Vox-Turnabout, making some eighty
titles – including largely forgotten Romantic piano concertos
by Moscheles, Bronsart, Thalberg and others on its rarities
label Candide. Heymann knew the recordings, and learned
from Michael how a label like Vox could reduce recording
costs in order to make such discs economically viable – such a
contrast to the grand ways of the majors, such as Deutsche
Grammophon or EMI. This initial contact was fortuitous
because Vox, with its subsidiary label Turnabout, was one of
the first low-price record labels, pioneering the 'cheap LPs'
approach in the 1950s. It launched the recording careers of a
number of great artists, including the pianist Alfred Brendel
and the conductors Jascha Horenstein and Otto Klemperer. It
was just as innovative in its choice of repertoire, which
included both specialist and core works. It released the first
complete recordings of Bach's *St Matthew Passion* and Orff's

Carmina Burana as well as Baroque music that subsequently became standard fare: composers such as Vivaldi, Corelli and Tartini were brought to a wider audience, almost for the first time. For a collector like Heymann it was a label of particular interest: he was intrigued as to how its founder, George Mendelssohn-Bartholdy (a descendant of Felix Mendelssohn), could issue acceptable, and sometimes very good, recordings of both standard and rare repertoire at a low price. Until the moment Ponti arrived in Hong Kong, the interest was at arm's length: Heymann was running his mail-order business and had no thought of going into classical records. The idea was prompted inadvertently by Michael Ponti's expressing disappointment that his discs were not available in the record shops in Hong Kong. Could Heymann, who was involved in the import–export business, remedy this?

At the start, importing LPs was a hobby. The main business was importing and selling studio equipment, principally Revox and Studer. In 1969 he had formed Revox (HK) Ltd which, in 1976, he was to change to Studer-Revox (HK) Ltd because by then the company had started to market professional recording equipment.

> *The company that manufactured the Revox tape recorders also made the famous Studer professional recording machines. They asked me to take on the distribution of these machines for Hong Kong and China, and I decided that it was difficult to sell only tape machines so I started looking for other equipment (mixing consoles, reverb units, equalisers, microphones) that would enable us to offer people turnkey studio projects.*

In the early 1970s he spotted a gap in the international camera market and began to buy cameras – Minolta, Canon, Nikon – in Japan through semi-official routes and parallel-export them to Germany. He sidestepped the main processes which kept

Japanese export prices high. Using barter arrangements with airlines, maintained from his days in the direct-mail business, he would fly first-class from Japan to Hong Kong with 2,000 cameras in thirty to forty boxes that were classed as excess baggage. Payment to his Japanese suppliers was often in cash and he found himself travelling with millions of Yen in a brief-case. It was totally legal, so he could turn up to customs in Japan, declare it, and stand in front of customs officers as they opened up his briefcase stuffed with bank notes. 'It kept me fed between the close of the mail-order business and the start of the studio business.'

By 1973 Heymann was a well-known figure in Hong Kong recording and studio circles, and his love for classical music brought him into contact with other expatriates who had similar interests. His work in putting on concerts such as Ponti's recital was noticed by the conductor of the semi-professional Hong Kong Philharmonic Orchestra and he was invited to join the board. He accepted on the basis that the orchestra would turn fully professional, and he set out to make this happen. Heymann was appointed chairman of the fund-raising committee and honorary general manager. One of the members of the fund-raising committee was a senior executive in the chemical branch of Esso and he introduced Heymann to all the 'big shots' in Hong Kong. Heymann sold them his concept: that Hong Kong would benefit from a professional orchestra and that it gave them an opportunity to entertain their visiting guests as well as advertise and promote their companies. Would they help fund it?

I came up with a good little scheme without really knowing anything about it, but they had never seen anybody like me and had never thought of the concept themselves. I got the necessary funding and in January 1974 we launched the fully professional Hong Kong Philharmonic. We had a mixed bag of musicians: we brought in some Koreans and a few

Japanese and others who lived in Hong Kong; we also advertised and hired people based on taped auditions. There were a lot of problems later on, but that's how we started. When we wanted to do bigger pieces, we would hire Filipino musicians from the night clubs to make up the numbers. I got to learn the repertoire – I studied all the publishers' catalogues – and even today I can tell you the instrumentation for most of the standard symphonic works.

I didn't know a lot about soloists, so I made some rules. Among them was to hire only artists who either had a contract with a major record company or had won an important competition in the last three years. One soloist who was offered to me was Takako Nishizaki, but she didn't fulfil any of these criteria. She was a gifted Japanese violinist who had been Shinichi Suzuki's first pupil (though her main teacher was her father, a colleague of Suzuki). She had studied at Juilliard with Joseph Fuchs and had been awarded the Fritz Kreisler Scholarship, given to the top violin student every year. She had come second in the Leventritt Competition in 1964 (behind Itzhak Perlman) but that was ten years earlier, and then after touring a lot she had returned to Japan. So I rejected her. But in early 1974 I got a phone-call from her Japanese manager, saying that she was coming to Hong Kong to play with the Philharmonic and to give a recital with a Korean pianist, and would I meet her and hear her. As it happened, the orchestra had a cancellation by a Romanian violinist who was to play Wieniawski's Violin Concerto No. 2, so the management agreed that Takako should replace her. By that time I was no longer involved with the orchestra but I met her at the airport on 13 August 1974, and that is how the whole thing started.

In fact, when we first met, she was distraught. Somebody had stepped on her violin on the plane and she was very concerned. As it happened he was very light, the case had taken the impact, and the violin was fine. She walked past me, saying, 'My violin, my violin!' and got into the car the orchestra had sent, which dropped her off at the Mandarin Hotel. I hadn't heard her play yet but I thought she was cute. I invited her out for dinner but she said she had had dinner. How about a drink? She said she didn't drink. How about a cup of tea? She couldn't say no to that, so we went out for a cup of tea at 8.30 and stayed talking until 1.30 a.m. We were the last ones to leave. She told me later that she had expected me to be an elderly gentleman with three children, and she was amazed how much I knew about classical music.

When I heard her play the Wieniawski I was very impressed: it was really good. She was a fabulous player. Then I went to the recital. She was a wonderful musician and performer with a terrific stage presence. After the concert and the recital she stayed in Hong Kong for a few more days; I managed to get invited to some dinners and met her again, and we clicked. Shortly afterwards I had to do a two-week business trip to Japan and I visited her at her family home in Nagoya. Her father was a highly respected music teacher who had co-founded the famous Suzuki Method with Shinichi Suzuki. I didn't speak Japanese and they didn't speak English, so Takako translated. Not long after, I asked her father for permission to marry her. He was quite shocked. He had just built an annex to the house as a music studio and Takako was supposed to take over his students. But he was happy that I liked classical music because when Takako's sister married, her husband, a university professor, forbade her to give any more concerts although she was a very good pianist. Her father also said that he had been the person who kept Takako practising, but now I would be responsible for that!

They were married in January 1975. On 29 December 1976 their son was born. They named him Henryk after the composer Henryk Wieniawski, whose concerto had brought them together. Now known as Rick, he works in Naxos, responsible for Hong Kong and the rest of Southeast Asia.

While the studio and hi-fi activities were his central business, Heymann became increasingly involved in importing music and records. His distribution network in Hong Kong and the Far East was beginning to work well with the Eastern European labels and he became more ambitious. At one point he even started his own classical record shop in Hong Kong called Hong Kong Records, but it failed to make any money and after three years he closed it down.

> *It was more of a hobby and I had an idiosyncratic manager who wanted to stock what he liked, not what sold. The trouble was that I understood that! Also I got into trouble because we imported some boxed sets by the majors which I had found cheaper elsewhere without realising that I was breaking the parallel import laws. PolyGram took me to court and I had to eat humble pie.*

He preferred to concentrate on distribution, a business which grew steadily throughout the 1970s since the first discussions with Michael Ponti regarding his Vox recordings. Heymann, both consciously and unconsciously, gained useful information for the future from this first-hand contact with a low-price label.

> *I approached George Mendelssohn [owner of Vox-Turnabout and Candide] and he said he didn't have distribution in Hong Kong, so I started importing and distributing Vox-Turnabout and Candide. They were very interesting labels for collectors, but I had heard a lot about George and his business methods from Michael so I didn't have many illusions. Michael told me that when he recorded his famous set of Scriabin sonatas (which on release became widely regarded as the finest on the market) it was on an*

upright piano; and that he wasn't given any money for a hotel, so he slept on the floor of the studio! George also skimped on production values, using poor orchestras for too long and cheap pressings. It gave the labels a poor reputation. But you would never have guessed this from meeting the man himself. I met George when I went to New York on Bose business. He had an office on the Upper East Side, quite a nice neighbourhood, and he proved to be the perfect gentleman. He always assumed a rather aristocratic posture – he used to call himself George de Mendelssohn-Bartholdy! I learned from him certain things to observe when I started my labels: not to try to save money on production or pressings; and to treat artists with respect. That wasn't so difficult – after all, I was married to one!

He wrote to Eurodisc, the classical wing of Bertelsmann (BMG), which had the pop label Ariola. He was offered distribution of not only Eurodisc but also Ariola itself and Hansa, which produced disco music. Heymann wasn't sure – he didn't know anything about this kind of music – but he spoke to his two Hong Kong salesmen and they were very pleased because they knew that pop music would be easier to get into the shops. Then came other classical labels, including Telefunken. At the same time, he spotted a gap in the Asian market for cheap classical cassettes and he formed his own label, Budget Classics, with fifty titles licensed from Hungaroton and Supraphon; it launched in 1977. It had the original logos of the two labels and the words 'Budget Classics', with a very basic design involving colour coding – green for Baroque music, pink for Classical and blue for Romantic. There were no pictures.

It was actually quite successful. I sold them for HK$10 each when at the time an LP cost around HK$40. Full-price cassettes sold for about the same price, so this was a novel approach. It became quite a big range, and, in many ways, *was a precursor to Naxos. They were just for the Hong Kong market. We sold 2,000 to 3,000 of most titles and I kept them going until the arrival of Naxos.*

In 1978 Heymann made his first trip to MIDEM, the annual music trade fair held every January in Cannes. It was a pivotal moment. Hong Kong and the Far East had a reputation for music piracy, but Heymann, with his company Studer-Revox (HK) Ltd, was clearly a legitimate operator. He became the licensee for Virgin Records and, having shown that he could get good results while providing clear and regular sales reports, began to pick up other important pop labels. He was joined by a young Englishman in Hong Kong, Steve Beaver, who was a pop specialist, and they soon signed up Chrysalis, Jive, Mute and others.

I remember being at MIDEM in 1980, and Steve was signing up labels one after another. He would come to me and say, 'Klaus, I need a $10,000 advance to sign up Jive Records,' or whatever it was, so I would write a cheque on the spot – that was the way it worked.

When BMG, whose Ariola and Eurodisc labels he had been distributing, bought RCA, Heymann found himself with not only the RCA classical label but also the RCA, Arista and Motown pop and rock catalogues. By 1984, he owned the biggest record distribution company in Asia outside Japan, all thanks to these pop and rock labels. He even distributed the first recording of Whitney Houston. Yet classical remained his first musical commitment, and, of course, he was married to a top-class violinist so was keen to keep her busy and help her career. As early as 1978 he had begun to make recordings with her.

Takako had won the Fritz Kreisler Scholarship at Juilliard, and her father had always played Kreisler, so she grew up with his music and clearly had an affinity for it. There were no modern recordings of his music, so it was an obvious choice for Takako. She made ten LPs in all, some of which were released on Telefunken and some on Camerata, both labels which I distributed. They are all available digitally now. And then came the recording of The Butterfly Lovers, which had a huge impact on her playing career and made her one of the most well-known violinists in Asia.

Behind that recording was a story of conflict within the classical music circles of Hong Kong. Heymann did not run the Hong Kong Philharmonic Orchestra for very long. He found that although he was doing all the work, he was supposed to take orders from a committee when it came to the choice of repertoire and artists. This is not his way of doing things, and they parted company. Not afraid to be combative, he became the orchestra's main critic and also started his own music magazine: *Hong Kong Hi-Fi and Music Review*. In 1978 the orchestra decided that its standard was good enough to start recording and chose to begin principally with *The Butterfly Lovers*, the most popular work of 'Western' Chinese classical music, by the composers Chen Gang and He Zhanhao. Takako Nishizaki was not asked to play the solo part. Heymann took that as a challenge and immediately decided that he would record it with her himself. He persuaded her to learn it, and she grew to like it. He decided to record it in Nagoya with the Nagoya Philharmonic Orchestra under the baton of the former music director of the Hong Kong Philharmonic Lim Kek-tjiang. They went to Nagoya but the first attempt at recording was beset with problems over union and management issues, and it was abandoned. They returned four months later to complete it, also recording Shande Ding's *Long March Symphony*; in the end they recorded nearly four LPs of Chinese music. Initially the response of the Chinese commentators was that Nishizaki was Japanese and could not play Chinese music with the appropriate Chinese expression. But it was the first modern recording of the piece with a good orchestra and a good sound, and it was a popular success, selling 60,000 copies in a short time in Hong Kong alone – a number unheard of for a classical music LP. It put the Hong Kong Philharmonic's recording, which had come out first and been made with the German resident conductor, totally in the shade. It showed Heymann that not only could he take on the competition and win, but there was also a business here.

Takako played it as if it was the Tchaikovsky. She threw herself into it and treated the composition as if it was great music, which it can be. Even today the composer He Zhanhao says she plays it best of all. It came out in 1979 on the HK label that I started – so it was HK 1. It sold all over Asia where there were Chinese communities. We were not allowed to sell it in Taiwan because as mainland music it was forbidden: we sold it under its English name (the Chinese name being Liang Shan Bo *and* Zhu Ying Tai, *after the names of the two protagonists in the Chinese Opera on which the story is based) and it got through for a while, but when the authorities realised what it was they banned it. Then it was sold underground and pirated. We couldn't sell our recordings in mainland China because the normal channels were not open. But we succeeded in licensing the recordings to Victor in Japan. We licensed the four discs we had made – that was our first big international success. Victor made a beautiful red box with a wonderful booklet and launched it with a big reception.*

A few years later, Chen Gang came to Hong Kong and he said publicly that Takako didn't understand the piece. He came to our house and she went through the piece with him bar by bar.

So Nishizaki made another recording, again in Japan but with a different Chinese conductor and a different Japanese orchestra (she has now recorded the work some seven times). When it was released the Hong Kong critics complained that it was not Chinese enough. However, the first two and the subsequent *Butterfly Lovers* recordings established her in China – and in her home town of Hong Kong – as the leading performer of Chinese violin music; she began playing to huge audiences at the Hong Kong Coliseum and toured for the next three decades. Heymann also commissioned violin concertos (one from Chen Gang and one from Du Mingxin, another of China's well-known composers), which Nishizaki recorded. Both Nishizaki and Heymann feel that these recordings contributed considerably to Chinese and Japanese friendship in the closing decades of the twentieth century.

Heymann has always said that having a world-class violinist as his wife was a spur to creating and establishing his record labels. He admired her as a musician and a performer from the first time he saw her play.

Takako has always had real charisma on the concert platform. She walks out on stage like a queen and people start clapping – it is a natural stage presence. And she really makes a good show when she plays.

Five

Marco Polo: An International Label 1982–1987

While Heymann continued to make recordings of classical Chinese music for his HK label (around fifty in total) he saw the opportunity to make recordings for the worldwide market. Relations with the Hong Kong Philharmonic Orchestra had healed following the arrival of a new manager, and the orchestra wanted to record. Heymann felt that it was inappropriate for it to record such mainstream composers as Mahler or Bruckner, but here was a chance for him to realise a long-held ambition to record rarities – music from the later years of the nineteenth and early twentieth centuries that had never been recorded. He wanted to establish a label that would release only world-premiere recordings, introducing new works to classical collectors. He named the label 'HK Marco Polo', which brought together both the label's Chinese base and a sense of exploration. It was launched in 1982, selling at full price, and shortly afterwards the 'HK' prefix was dropped.

We began with a disc of overtures and marches by Wagner which, extraordinarily, had never been recorded before: it included Rule Britannia, Polonia *and the* Imperial March *with the Hong Kong Philharmonic. Another early recording was Respighi's* Concerto gregoriano *and* Poema autunnale *played by the Singapore Symphony Orchestra. I had begun to study the history of music, looking for unknown works by famous composers or the best-known works by unknown composers which had never been recorded before. Takako was also part of that and she had to learn lots of new music, starting with the* Concerto gregoriano *and then Spohr concertos and a lot more. Many of the Marco Polo recordings are still the only available versions of these works.*

I started reading The Grove Dictionary of Music and Musicians, Die Musik in Geschichte und Gegenwart *(MGG) and publishers' catalogues. Actually the publishers were quite supportive and we didn't have to pay a lot for rental material. I rang up the publishers myself – there was nobody in Hong Kong who could do this for me. That is one of the problems of being in Hong Kong, especially in those days – there was very little scholastic backup. We were very isolated. But the advantage was that I could do things my way. I didn't have any bad precedents. I could do things economically. I would read the catalogues, select the music, arrange the timings into LP length. I even commissioned oil paintings from China to go on the covers. On a visit to Shanghai I met a painter called Chai Benshan at the Shanghai Conservatory. He looked at black-and-white drawings or paintings of these composers and reproduced his own versions. He continues to this day. He did Spohr, Wagner, Joachim, Respighi – and all the rare composers we recorded. People were quite surprised ... they had never seen an oil painting of Joseph Joachim. And actually I think some of the paintings were really first class! We did this for the first recordings, but they all turned out to be men with beards. After Volume 50 we felt this couldn't go on and we had to change.*

It was a very exciting time. During the day I was running my various businesses – pop distribution, hi-fi sales and organising new studios – and in the evening I would go home and read publishers' catalogues. I hadn't heard any of this music because it had never been recorded, but there was just enough information in the catalogues to give me an idea of what to expect. We ordered scores and Takako would look at them and indicate which pieces she thought were good, or not worth doing.

My appreciation of music had changed since Takako came into my life. I had started to look at it more professionally when I began building programmes for the Hong Kong Philharmonic in the early 1970s, but then I began appreciating music from a musician's perspective. Takako taught me how to listen, especially to chamber music. She taught me about intonation, ensemble, expression, and how to appreciate good music rather than what was loud and fast. That was a really very important time for me. And then I started to go to auditions of musicians for the orchestra, and attend rehearsals. I suppose I could say that after getting involved in concerts professionally I didn't enjoy them so much because I now had a more critical ear, listening for what was wrong instead of just enjoying the music. But without Takako teaching me it would have been difficult to develop my musical awareness, which enabled me to guide these record labels. To this day she's the main arbiter of who gets to record for us and who doesn't. We often do blind tests – listen to this, listen to that – without her knowing who are the musicians.

The start of Marco Polo prompted, very early on, a major change: moving the recording activities to Europe. Distributing and licensing recordings from Hungaroton, Supraphon and Opus meant developing close connections with Hungary and Czechoslovakia. Shortly after the first Marco Polo discs came out, executives from Hungaroton and Slovart suggested that Heymann make recordings for the label in Hungary and Slovakia. Why not record in Bratislava and Budapest?

I said, 'Fine!' and we started in 1984. These orchestras cost no more than we paid in Hong Kong and Singapore, and worldwide they were much easier to sell. Many record buyers felt that recordings by the Hong Kong Philharmonic or the Singapore Symphony were probably pretty suspect. They had never heard of these orchestras. No recordings by Japanese orchestras were available outside Japan, and I figured that the Slovak Philharmonic Orchestra or the Budapest Radio Symphony Orchestra sounded much better on paper – and that's how it turned out. But also it must be said that they were better recordings. The Slovak Philharmonic was and remains a very good orchestra, at the time actually much better than the Hong Kong Philharmonic or Singapore Symphony Orchestra who were themselves relying on imported players (many of them Czechs and Poles in the case of Singapore).

Heymann acknowledges that at the start there was no long-term planning for Marco Polo. He made up lists of works that he wanted to record and arranged them in programmes of around fifty minutes, which was an appropriate length for LPs. When an orchestra became free, and the parts were available, a recording took place. Between ten and fifteen LPs a year were released, so that by 1985, when the recordings were largely being made in Eastern Europe, it was a label approaching fifty titles. It was apparent that however worthwhile it was as an artistic enterprise – and there was no doubt that these discoveries were making an important contribution to classical recording – the recording process was not glamorous at all – it was more like hard graft. Nishizaki needed stamina, determination and concentration to deal with the challenges she faced. Heymann has never forgotten the punishing schedules of those early days.

We were still making recordings in the Far East when the right opportunities arose. We went to Singapore to record

Respighi's Concerto gregoriano. *It is a wonderful piece, but suddenly it turns into really difficult Paganini! We were recording with the Singapore Symphony Orchestra at the Victoria Concert Hall and it began to rain ... and the hall was not soundproof. You could hear the rain. So we had to stop. Then when it stopped you could hear the traffic, so we had to start recording at night. It is a work full of the most beautiful Gregorian melodies (I can still sing them today) but Respighi goes crazy at the end. It is super, super difficult for the soloist. We were running very short of time and the orchestra had problems with the music; we were all tired and I was quite nervous. It was really very tense. But we finished it in the end. We were four days in Singapore getting that recording done. It was occasions like that which turned Takako into a very experienced recording artist, ready for the best and the worst.*

Hong Kong had a good concert hall for recordings. The Slovak Philharmonic Orchestra in Bratislava had some very fine musicians but, as in Singapore, the concert hall was not soundproof. There was also a tram stop right in front of it. Everyone had to learn to work with traffic noise, not stopping just because the tram trundled by but continuing to play and then patching afterwards. Fortunately, during the communist era, it was generally quite quiet in the evenings so it was decided to start recording at 7 p.m. and go through to five minutes before midnight, which allowed just enough time for the musicians to pack up and catch the last tram home. That was the pattern for many years. It was an economy package from the start: flying economy class (not comfortable if you are Heymann's 1.93m in height) to communist countries where the hotels and general facilities were basic. Heymann would be up early on the phone, dealing with a flood of telexes (the forerunner of faxes) and ensuring that his businesses back in Hong Kong were going smoothly; Nishizaki would be practising in the hotel during the day; then they would record at night in difficult circumstances. But it was a package that suited everyone, and the fee – suggested by the orchestra, not by Heymann – was reasonable.

> *We paid a flat fee per minute of recorded time per musician: DM2 per minute per musician. Therefore, a sixty-minute work which required eighty musicians cost DM9,600. They were paid in foreign currency which they loved because there was a thriving black market for changing German marks into local currency. It was a good deal for both sides. They were not such fast sight-readers as English orchestral musicians but there were some good players in the orchestra and we got some good recordings. I also agreed a flat fee per recording for the conductors and the producers. To be honest, I didn't do break-even budgets for the recordings. I just did the recordings in the most economical way I could, and I knew what it would cost, plus or minus 10 per cent. I also made a guess of the number I could sell.*

The contract was clear and relatively simple, and has, in essence, carried on through the decades. No artist was brought under contract to the label: the artist was contracted for a particular project or series; there might be further recordings or not, depending on both parties. A clear, non-royalty fee structure was also developed for soloists. It was based on a buy-out fee of $1,000 for a solo recording, with a duo getting $1,500, a trio $1,800 and a quartet $2,000.

> *Anything below would have been an insult and anything above would have been unaffordable. I also felt it was important that everyone got the same – I didn't want to make any exceptions because I know artists talk to each other. A lot of independent labels work on this basis and pay upfront in order to own the recordings. It is a risk for the*

*company, but only the independent labels that can't afford
the initial investment pay royalties.*

In the closing years of the LP era, when royalties were
expected, some soloists baulked at the buy-out, but many
acknowledged that actually it was a better deal: they were paid
in advance rather than getting money in dribs and drabs years
later (or never, if the records failed to sell sufficiently – for they
were only due payment once the labels had recouped their
recording costs). Remembering Michael Ponti's experience,
Heymann also ensured that the Marco Polo (and, later, Naxos)
contracts included travel, hotel expenses and per diems.

*In these early days we were not recording with artists whose
names would sell many more copies, so there was no reason
to pay royalties. We wanted to give a fair deal, but that is all.
I have always felt it is an open market. If an artist wanted to
be paid more, and could get the increased fee from someone
else, he or she was free to go elsewhere. Of course, I understood!*

Parallel to this contractual system was a clear process for the
cover design of those first LPs – a concept which is still continued on both Marco Polo and Naxos nearly three decades
later.

*I established a simple but direct design format which could be
carried over easily from one disc to another. It was clear to
me that the composer should be at the top, then the work and
then the artist. It doesn't mean that the artist is unimportant,
but these were not 'name' artists, so why stress them?*

Of course, recording was only the beginning. Just as important
to the success of a classical label is distribution. Heymann knew
how to distribute in the Far East but he had no experience of

distributing in the West; and he knew that Marco Polo, by its very nature, was primarily a label for the West, not Asia.

We were not recording for the Hong Kong classical market: it was too small and Marco Polo was too specialist. I had to aim for the world market. I actually wanted to make money from it, or at least not to lose money. I needed distributors in the major classical markets in Europe and the US, and I found that because it was interesting repertoire played by respectable orchestras, distributors did take it. It was very busy at MIDEM in those first years – running up and down the aisles looking for distributors in various territories. When back in Hong Kong, I sent samples to distributors all over the world. When I travelled to countries on other business, I would take samples of LPs – which were a lot bigger than CDs! – and visit classical shops and distributors.

One of the first places that he visited was the main classical record shop in Vienna, Gramola, owned and run by Richard Winter. Winter still remembers today a tall stranger turning up at his counter one day in 1983 and pulling out of a big case the first five discs of a new label, Marco Polo. Heymann knows first hand what it is like to be a record sales rep – an experience which has enabled him to speak, cajole, persuade reps all over the world to go out and sell his classical recordings. And Marco Polo worked.

I never lost money on Marco Polo. It was funded by the profits from the Bose audio business but I think I can say that we always recouped our investment. Everything sold, probably because we concentrated on rarities – for a long time, at any rate, if it wasn't a world premiere we didn't do it. We did occasionally do some works as fillers because we wanted to offer good recording times, but for many years every LP or CD had 'world premiere' on the cover.

This was noticed early on by the critics because people like that enjoy having new things to write about. I remember that Takako's first review in Gramophone *(for Concerto gregoriano) was bad because the critic said that he couldn't hear the soloist ... but our producer thought the soloist should be embedded in the orchestra rather than playing up front. I remember how disappointed I was. I did think that the reviewer was right in this case, and I learned an important lesson from it. Generally, at a recording, classical producers listen at a very high level, on fancy monitor speakers. But this is not the way most people listen at home. I knew from my experience in recording studios that the pop producers always have a pair of little speakers to which they can switch and hear the music in a way that most people will hear it. In the best studio conditions you may hear the violin clearly, while at low, normal listening volume the balance is different and the violin can become submerged into the orchestra. A producer has to ensure that the balance is right at all levels.*

Marco Polo quickly developed into a dream label for collectors of Romantic and late Romantic music. The music itself was sometimes inconsistent in its achievements, but nearly every work released had something to offer – a good melody, a grand moment, even a genuine milestone in recording history. This was certainly the case with Havergal Brian's Symphony No. 1 'The Gothic', which Heymann decided to record in 1989.

Sometime in 1988, the conductor Kenneth Jean told me about Brian's 'Gothic' Symphony and said that this was one work which would never be recorded. The forces required were just so humungous: two orchestras, a male chorus, a children's chorus – hundreds of people and it lasts for one hour forty minutes. I took that as a challenge and planned it. I decided to do it in 1989 in the concert hall of the Slovak Radio, Bratislava with the Slovak Philharmonic Orchestra *and the Slovak Radio Symphony Orchestra conducted by Ondrej Lenárd. It was, at the time, by far the biggest project we had ever undertaken, and the most expensive. It cost $75,000 and I was pretty sure the money was never coming back. The recording seemed to go well, but when it was being edited we found that five bars were missing! Fortunately, it was only the a cappella chorus so we got the small choir back together again, recorded the missing bars, and edited them in.*

We were all amazed at how well it did. First of all, it put Marco Polo on the map. Everyone in classical music knew about it because 'The Gothic' Symphony is such a legendary work. But even better, it became by far the bestseller on the label, selling some 30,000 copies at full price within a few years and surprisingly recouping the investment. Even now that it is on Naxos it continues to sell regularly – as it should do, because it is a bargain at the Naxos price. Not surprisingly, no one else has ever even thought of doing it!

'The Gothic' Symphony was an atypical Marco Polo work in its size but typical in its adventure. The label brought so many forgotten or half-forgotten composers to the attention of classical music lovers. There was big orchestral music by Glazunov, Szymanowski, Rubinstein, Raff, Lachner, Kalinnikov and Myaskovsky, as well as chamber music by French composers such as Félicien David and Jacques Ibert, and piano music by Alkan, Erkel and Čiurlionis. At its height there were forty-five releases a year; some 900 titles have been made over two decades and more.

It was within Marco Polo that Heymann began to develop his taste for complete cycles (often the financial ruin of the true collector). It was one thing to do the complete symphonies of Raff or orchestral music of Glazunov, but the complete waltzes, polkas and marches by Johann Strauss Junior and Senior, and Josef Strauss? That way madness lies, surely.

*This was a completely crazy idea, I admit. But it was not
something that I just started and couldn't stop. I started
planning it in 1985, at first with the conductor Alfred Walter
and then in association with the late Professor Franz Mailer,
who was the world authority on the Strauss family. The first
problem was finding the music because it wasn't all in one
place, so we started with what was available. Piece by piece,
we gathered the rest. Professor Mailer got access to all the
manuscripts and wrote out many of the scores and parts by
hand. We recorded almost all with Slovak orchestras because
they had the right feeling for the music: Bratislava is almost
a suburb of Vienna. And we always used Viennese conductors. Johann Strauss the Younger took about ten years to do.
It was fifty-two CDs. Then we started with Josef, which took
about another five years and ran to twenty-six volumes; and
then we turned to Johann I, which will amount to around
twenty-four.*

Marco Polo remains, for Heymann, one of his most satisfying
achievements. 'I created a label but I did it in a way that made
it become a brand.' He says that it was largely unplanned at the
start, with the right decisions made at key moments. The
simple but effective design – you could always recognise a
Marco Polo record with its deep blue (inherited from his Braun
experience) and the Marco Polo name centred – in some ways
presaged the Naxos look; and though at the start the choice of
works may have been haphazard, method was quickly introduced. Certainly by the late 1980s he had compiled
exhaustive lists of works that he planned to do. In 1988 Peter
Bromley, who later became production manager of Naxos but
was at the time working for the English label Gimell, wrote to
Heymann, suggesting a series of neglected late Romantic
Italian orchestral works. He was astounded to find, by return
post from Hong Kong, a neat list of the principal Italian
Novecento works scheduled for Marco Polo in the near future.

At the time of writing, some have been re-released on Naxos but many are still waiting to be recorded: works by Casella, Pizzetti, Montemezzi, Martucci, Mascagni, Sinigaglia and many others. What was interesting was that the list was carefully typed out, with notes of publisher, length, date of composition, and likely place to find the score. This was an overview of just one corner of classical music, and it is an indication of the careful research that went into the creation of Marco Polo.

> *There are many excellent pieces on Marco Polo. But when you look at these composers, I think the most common fault was that few of them seemed to know how to write a good ending. They would get lost in empty repetitions, or run dry of melodic invention. Often, the works are like a late Romantic movie show.*

Marco Polo continues to operate to this day, though in a reduced form. Recordings of light music continue and so do the operas of Siegfried Wagner, but the main target label for all new recordings is Naxos. Many important Marco Polo recordings have been deleted and reissued on Naxos itself, giving rare repertoire new life at budget price. Marco Polo CDs also dropped to mid-price, a shift requested by distribution companies though Heymann was not totally in favour of it.

> *There is a lot more competition in the area of rarities now. Everyone is looking for unusual or forgotten works to record because they know they can't make money out of standard repertoire. So we thought we could compete more ably by releasing new Marco Polo recordings at mid-price, though it hasn't been a great success.*

Although Marco Polo and then Naxos represented the worldwide public persona of Heymann's music enterprises, the financial engine room comprised the studio and hi-fi businesses. Without these successful ventures it would have been impossible to maintain the continued investment necessary to fund thousands of ambitious recordings. Heymann made money by standard commercial activity, and ploughed it back – sometimes even recklessly – into a raft of businesses: recordings, videos, books, music publishing, concert promotion, educational products and many more. He used his natural entrepreneurial instincts, supported by a strong competitive streak, to the full. He had found Hong Kong the perfect environment for his abilities. Essentially, it was his involvement in studios and hi-fi, which had begun after he left the newspaper business and turned to mail-order in 1970, that formed the basis of his fortune. It continued for more than thirty years to 2003, when his Bose distributorship in Hong Kong and China was finally terminated; but it wasn't a clear path.

> *A lot of my success has to do with Asia and the flavour of Hong Kong. It's a wheeling, dealing place. My favourite saying is: 'For the Chinese, if there is no way there is a way around.' If there is an obstacle, there will always be a way around it, and even today that's my thing: finding solutions to problems and connecting the dots. That is what I am good at: recognising the opportunity and going with it, and, when it is not smooth sailing, finding solutions.*

Throughout the 1970s and '80s, Heymann ran a number of businesses: when an opportunity came his way he simply couldn't ignore it. Studios and hi-fi were the result of his search for a more sustainable business. He had sold Revox tape recorders to US military personnel during the Vietnam War, and had subsequently become the Revox distributor in Hong Kong. The company that manufactured the Revox machines also made the Studer range of professional tape recorders and had eventually appointed Heymann its distributor for Hong

Kong and China. When those distributorships were revoked by the companies in circumstances he felt were unjust, he was determined to show that he could not be crushed. By good fortune, on the day he received the termination letter from the Studer-Revox people he also received a call from a representative of MCI (a major competitor to Studer in the studio business), who happened to be in Hong Kong. They met and Heymann was offered the distributorship of MCI for Southeast Asia and China.

I wanted to show those people at Studer. I am not a quitter. I could have gotten out of the business but I didn't. I had no idea how to supply complete recording studios, but I found a Japanese studio designer who designed everything and we started building studios. We turned the whole Chinese market from Studer to MCI equipment. In the very first month we sold five recording studios to Radio Television Brunei. And I took risks. In the winter of 1985, on pure speculation, I took a whole TV audio recording system to Tianjin for an exhibition at the TV station. I didn't know what I was going to do with it if I couldn't sell it. But I did – to China Central Television in Beijing. They played hardball for two weeks, and I just sat in my hotel room in Beijing working on price quotations; but they finally bought it. I knew they wanted it because it was the first modern TV audio recording studio in China. In that time I learned the basics of the business: not only how to install the equipment, but what each piece of equipment – the tape recorders, mixing consoles, reverb units, equalisers, microphones – would do in a professional recording studio. I had to know what I represented. I will never forget those weeks.

We built that studio successfully and it established our reputation in China for quality work and good after-sales service. Over the following years we sold and built the first modern audio recording studios for China Central Broadcasting and China Records.

At the same time as I was demonstrating and selling the equipment in Tianjin, I had an Englishman and an American engineer installing the studios in Brunei. The American came from Idaho and all he would eat was meat and potatoes, but you couldn't get potatoes in Brunei and not much meat – it was seafood and rice – and he was very unhappy. In the middle of the second day of the exhibition in Tianjin I got a call from Brunei saying they had run out of shrink-wrap, the special plastic sheeting for cables that was applied with a torch. So here I am in China around Christmas time (they don't celebrate Christmas in China, but they do where you buy shrink-wrap). It was the first time I had palpitations. I was so stressed out – and I had all the heavy drinking with the Chinese officials. Then it was straight back to the hotel and on the telephone: where can I find shrink-wrap? But I got them the shrink-wrap the day after Christmas. Those were the days! Before email, before fax: just telephone and telex.

Although seemingly always ready to turn his hand to any promising business, by 1980 Heymann had largely narrowed down his enterprises to consumer and professional audio equipment, recording studio and sound reinforcement design and installation, and music. Having lost the Studer and Revox agency and, shortly after, gained the MCI agency, he restructured his business. He changed the name of Studer-Revox (HK) Ltd to Pacific Music Co. Ltd in order to reflect his increasing focus on music. At the same time, he established two new companies: Audio Consultants Ltd, to handle the recording studio design and installation side of the business; and Pacific Audio Supplies Ltd, to look after the Bose consumer and professional audio business and the design and installation of sound reinforcement systems. This was the state of play by the mid-1980s. In 1992 he sold Audio Consultants

Ltd to his partner John Ho in order to focus on the Bose and the music businesses.

> *It was a crazy time. In the 1970s and 1980s all the Asian markets were pirate markets, even Singapore. But gradually they became more legitimate, first of all Hong Kong, then Singapore, and others followed gradually. I was in the right place at the right time. Piracy lasted longer in Korea, Thailand, the Philippines and Indonesia, but things changed as the big shops, first of all, went clean. It was very important because of the distribution businesses.*

It was in the mid-1980s that change hit the whole recording industry worldwide. In 1983 the compact disc arrived, bringing digital technology and a huge commercial boost to records. Digital recording had already started to overtake analogue recording, so the move towards the complete digital path had begun. Heymann was in the perfect position. His studio and hi-fi businesses had put him right at the cutting edge of recording technology; his placement in Asia, a technology hot-house with a massive population keen to be early adopters, meant that he had early warning of the speed with which the new system would take over from the LP; and furthermore, his activities as a pop distributor gave him a far more encompassing overview of the record industry than that of other classical label owners. His personal commitment, however, was to classical music: Marco Polo had just started, and his reaction was to bring the new technology to classical recordings rather than to expand his recording activities to pop, where he had little experience. He began recording music for Marco Polo in the new digital format in 1983, producing the first CDs in 1984 and dropping LP production in 1985 (probably the first classical label to do so).

> *We started releasing Marco Polo recordings on CDs as soon as we could get capacity from the Japanese manufacturers, in*

particular JVC and Denon. The manufacturers throughout the world were quite ruthless and looked after their bigger customers first. I had no doubt that this was the future. There was talk in the hi-fi magazines and especially the classical industry that the sound of the 16-bit technology was inferior to the LP; but there was no doubt in my mind that this was the direction everything was going. My distributors were surprised – no, shocked – when I stopped pressing LPs! I could hear that the sound wasn't as good as on vinyl but that was because we were getting used to working with the whole digital technology. We first started recording digitally on those huge old U-matic tape machines, and we had to adapt to it. But we were early adopters on Marco Polo because we were in Asia. Our Japanese producer had his own digital recording equipment and soon we bought a set of our own, so we did not have to rent the machine for every project. The pressing was expensive, too: we paid $3 for pressing a CD against $1 for an LP – a substantial difference. And mastering was also very costly. This was at a time when we were only charging $5 for an LP; we had to charge more for the CD but the market took it, for there was no doubt in anyone's mind that, despite the greater production costs, the CD was the carrier of the future.

Six

Naxos: A Classical Revolution 1987–1994

By 1987 Marco Polo had a catalogue of around 150 titles. It was a comfortable business. The stream of new recordings had settled to around thirty a year, it was establishing itself with classical distributors around the world, and the change to CD had raised its profile. CD had now settled as the primary medium and the record industry was reaping the benefits of this shift in technology: people were buying CDs of their favourite music to replace their old – and in many cases scratched – LPs. CD factories were springing up all over the world and the pressure on capacity was beginning to ease. There was talk of the initial high launch price dropping in both manufacture and retail; and, in Korea in 1987, a butterfly flapped its wings for Klaus Heymann. His life and his work was about to change. Naxos was on the horizon.

> *Well, to be honest, it was purely accidental. I wish I could say I had the foresight to realise that classical budget CDs were going to be big and so on, but the true story is this. For many years I had a very good business in Korea, licensing classical content to companies selling cassette or LP packages door to*

*door. They were big packages – forty or fifty cassettes in a
box. I licensed Supraphon, Melodiya, all those things we had
the rights for. It was a bit of a strange business. A record company would put together the package but it would be sold
through special companies with specialised salesmen. It was
high-pressure selling. Some packages were sold to salarymen
who were drunk in a bar at night; but most were door-to-
door sales. Sales happened everywhere except in the normal
music shops, and record companies left it to these special
organisations to operate the market. One day, I think in late
1986, I got a call from Mr Lee at SRB Records (I had sold
them material for many packages in recent years). He said,
'Mr Heymann, we would like to be the first company to sell
classical music in thirty CD packages door to door.' He
insisted on original digital recordings, not analogue transfers
to digital. I said, 'Mr Lee, I don't have any digital recordings
but I'll see what I can find.' I called Ivan Marton, my contact
in Bratislava, and said, 'Do you know of anybody?' He
explained that yes, there was a company that had digital masters of popular classical works. They had recorded them
digitally, but then they couldn't release them on CD because
they couldn't get capacity at the plants. As a result, they got
into financial difficulties. Ivan said that a Slovak gentleman in
Paris could get me the rights. I contacted the man and said we
would like the licences of the masters for a package in Korea,
but could I buy the rights for the Far East. I bought them for
the price of $500 per master – buyout. No termination date.
I paid for them and received the masters in Hong Kong.*

*Then I rang Mr Lee and said, 'I have the masters, can I
send them to you?' He replied, 'Oh, I'm so sorry, we made
our calculation, the mastering and the pressing costs: we
cannot go through with the project.' We hung up and I
thought, 'What the hell am I going to do?' These were recordings by the Slovak Philharmonic, Capella Istropolitana –
good musicians but unknown artists and conductors. So I*

talked to my guys and said, 'You know I'm stuck with these thirty masters – what are we going to do? We can sell them, but because they are unknown musicians we cannot sell them at full price.' Now, at the time, the price of a CD was about $25 and LPs were selling at about $5–6 each. I said, 'Guys, let's sell them for the price of an LP.' And that was the crucial decision.

So we released the first five titles in Hong Kong on the 'Naxos' label at HK$50 each, which was about US$6.25. Almost the day after, the telephones started ringing: people had heard about the first budget CD label. The telephone continued ringing and I realised I had a business on my hands. I called my contact in Paris and said, 'I want to have a licence for the rest of the world.' So I got a licence for the rest of the world, and we started.

That licence was royalty-based and more complicated; but Heymann now had thirty masters which he could use world-wide. He manufactured them in Japan, with Denon, and the first big customer was the Hong Kong buying agent for French hypermarkets, Fargo. They placed the first orders of 50,000 and 100,000 pieces (3,000 to 5,000 per title) – numbers very rare in the classical industry. But as worldwide manufacturing capacity grew, and the manufacturing price dropped, the original licensor sold the same recordings to other labels and it became a bit of a mess. By early 1988 the European market was being flooded with these budget CDs on many different labels and they started being shipped into the Asian market from Europe. The bubble had lasted eight months but now it had burst and become a dogfight.

Then I was faced with the decision of whether to continue or to throw in the towel. I thought to myself, 'I've had one good year so should I say, "That's it", or should I invest in this business?' So because I was already producing recordings in

Hungary and Slovakia for Marco Polo, and I knew how to do it, I said, 'Ok, we will use those production facilities to record our own masters of standard repertoire.' Actually, I had already started recording a few titles for Naxos in 1987. When I saw how well those thirty digital titles were selling, I wanted to expand the repertoire because there were a lot of things I didn't have. So by 1988 I already had some new recordings of my own coming through, though not at a great pace because I had those thirty in the catalogue. Having taken the decision that I was going to invest in recordings for the budget market, I immediately started re-recording those original thirty titles in order to build a proper catalogue from scratch.

He also decided to continue with the name 'Naxos'. It had started to gain a profile of its own, and he felt he could develop it. In truth, this name had come through happenstance.

I wanted to buy a condominium. In Hong Kong some people purchase a condominium through a shelf company for tax advantages. I called my lawyer and said, 'Look, I want to buy a shelf company, what can you offer?' And I guess they have people who come up with ideas for these companies, and register them, and some guy had gone through all the Greek islands. So my lawyer offered me Crete Ltd, Rhodes Ltd, Lesbos Ltd and I said, 'No, thank you.' But I liked Naxos Ltd, partly because of Ariadne auf Naxos, Richard Strauss's *opera. So I bought Naxos Ltd and Naxos Ltd bought the apartment. That was in 1985. Then in 1987, there I was, stuck with those masters and looking for a label name, and I said, 'Well, I own Naxos Ltd, let's call it Naxos.'*

It turned out to be one of the best and worst decisions. It's a great label name but in many countries you cannot register a place name as a trademark. If a Manchester cloth-merchant, when Manchester cloth was a sign of quality, had been able to register that place as a trademark, all the other Manchester cloth-merchants would have gone out of business. Like Sheffield steel. But anyway, stupidly I didn't think, so I used 'Naxos' as a logo. On the other hand, it's a great name, easy to pronounce in almost every language. There's the classical reference and the classical music connotation Ariadne auf Naxos, so not only the Greek myth but also opera. I designed the logo myself – the columns with the name in the middle – and I then gave it to the artist to do it professionally. 'This is what I want, the columns, Naxos in there,' and so on. I don't like serif typefaces but I had to accept that a sans serif typeface with those pillars and the capitals would not have looked good.

For the covers, we followed the house style devised for Marco Polo. I decided on the fine-art approach, then famous paintings out of copyright. On our slim margins I had to watch the costs. We didn't put the artists on the cover for the same reasons: the artists weren't famous, and good portrait photo shoots cost money. You don't want artist pictures looking like mug shots from the police albums.

The serif typography was very simple to start with. I decided that white would become the trademark – blue on white or black on white, as I learned at Braun. It was also my idea to have blurbs on the back, to explain to people what the music was like, and I introduced those later. Most Naxos recordings still have this, and I am surprised it has not been adopted by many other labels. We could probably get away without blurbs today, but I still think it is helpful for specialist repertoire.

I decided not to skimp on the liner notes. I wanted proper notes, and I was very fortunate to come across Keith Anderson, who from the beginning wrote them all. He was a music lecturer in Hong Kong, and in a way he became one of the fathers of Naxos. He had been writing notes for Marco Polo and started to write all the Naxos notes. He was very knowledgeable and very meticulous and I am proud of the fact that, in the history of the label, we have never been caught out with wrong facts. We did the notes in English mainly, though we decided that if the artists or the composers came from a specific country and were likely to sell in that country, we would add another language (other than German composers – there were so many, and Germans can read English!).

Over the years I have had so many distributors come up to me and say what a wonderful label Naxos is, but that so much more could be done to make the design attractive and interesting. They have all missed the point. Part of the success can be put down to the fact that it is very straightforward and instantly recognisable. You get what you see on the cover.

Heymann recalls that the repertoire on the first thirty recordings was, on the whole, solid, but key things were missing. After they had been released and had started to appear on other labels, Heymann sat down with record catalogues to plan his recording schedule. He marked all the works that had been recorded more than ten times, and that is how the first master plan came about.

Vivaldi's Four Seasons *was not there: that was the first new recording that we made in Bratislava for Naxos. Takako had it in her repertoire, of course; and in Bratislava was the excellent chamber orchestra Capella Istropolitana, formed from some of the best players in Slovakia. At that time, in the communist era, Bratislava was amazing – a city of 300,000 with five orchestras: the Slovak Philharmonic, the Radio Symphony Orchestra, the National Opera Orchestra, the Slovak Chamber Orchestra and the Capella Istropolitana. And there was a big band as well.*

Takako recorded The Four Seasons *conducted by the*

American conductor Stephen Gunzenhauser, chief conductor of the Delaware Symphony Orchestra. He was very good – he had done a recording for Marco Polo previously – and he became, for Naxos, one of the first conductors of the first hour, so to speak. We made the recording in the autumn of 1987 in two days, but the sessions were not without problems. We had to exchange the harpsichordist halfway through because she wasn't up to it. We got another harpsichordist at short notice, and so the last concerto was not actually rehearsed. We had to do it in rehearse–record, rehearse–record method. And we were on a serious time limit because the musicians had to catch the last tram home at midnight. I remember, we finished the final bar and immediately they jumped up and rushed to get that tram. Then they recorded the Concerto alla rustica, *the filler, a few days later.*

Other key works followed with the Capella Istropolitana, including Handel's *Water Music* and *The Fireworks*, and Bach's *Brandenburg Concertos*. More and more musicians and ensembles were coming on board. The Hungarian pianist Jenő Jandó, who was to prove a remarkable stalwart for the label, recording so much of the central piano repertoire, was one of the first. He was recommended by Hungaroton, who actually made the first recordings for Naxos. Jandó started with the popular Beethoven sonatas and when Nishizaki heard them she said, 'That is a really wonderful pianist.' He did other things, including Mussorgsky's *Pictures at an Exhibition* and chamber music with Nishizaki, and soon Heymann entrusted him with the complete Beethoven piano sonatas.

One of the things I am most pleased with about Naxos is that it enabled people who were not well known, but still wonderful musicians, to shine. Jenő Jandó won the Hungarian Radio Competition one year and András Schiff

*another. I think Jenő (we call him 'JJ') is one of the finest
pianists in the world today. People always ask how he could
possibly have made so many recordings in a relatively short
time. His answer is that once he had figured out the style and
musical language of the composer, the rest was just technique – of which he had plenty. Perhaps he lacks a few social
graces, which is maybe why he didn't make a career before
and doesn't have the career, even today, that he deserves. But
he is a wonderful musician. I know when he and Takako
recorded the Beethoven sonatas they hardly talked before the
sessions: there was complete agreement on musical things –
perfect harmony.*

Jandó was delighted to find himself recording almost full time
for Naxos, often at the Italian Institute in Budapest. The only
complaint that he had in the early days was that Naxos did not
spell his name correctly, with two accents on the 'o' in 'Jenő'
and one on the 'o' in 'Jandó'. The Naxos CDs were designed
with a simple computer programme which had diacritics but
not the double accent which his name required: the strokes are
long, unlike the two dots of an umlaut. These were later corrected!

In those early Naxos days Heymann was maintaining many
businesses simultaneously – the Asian pop and classical distribution network, the hi-fi distribution business, Marco Polo and
others – so it was not until two years after Jandó's first
Beethoven piano recording that they met, in Budapest.
Heymann went to Bratislava as often as he could, but it was
mainly when Nishizaki was recording there: dealing with his
network was still not easy from a hotel room in communist
Slovakia or Hungary and the phones were extremely expensive. In the first years of Naxos, therefore, it was inevitable that
there were many Hong Kong connections to the recordings and
that Heymann relied on recommendations by the Slovaks.
Kenneth Schermerhorn, music director of the Hong Kong

Philharmonic Orchestra and a recipient of the Sibelius Medal from the Finnish government, went to Bratislava and conducted the Slovak Radio Symphony Orchestra in *Finlandia* and other tone poems. Among the Slovak recommendations were the conductors Anthony Bramall (who made early orchestral recordings) and Peter Breiner (who later arranged a lot of music as well, including the world's national anthems); and Hungaroton recommended the pianists István Székely and Péter Nagy, both of whom made many of the early Naxos recordings. The conductor Barry Wordsworth came on board, as did Wolf Harden, whom Heymann had known before Naxos. So the musicians of those early days arose from a variety of contacts. There was simply no time to consider very carefully, meet and audition musicians, not least because of the Hong Kong base. There was too much to do. In the first year of Naxos, Heymann recorded thirty new titles before re-recording the repertoire of the first thirty he had licensed, and they had to be brought out to the market extremely quickly. Of course, this was in addition to the Marco Polo programme. It was frenetic.

In those days I listened to everything. For years, DATs [Digital Audio Tapes] of the final edits would be sent to me for approval in Hong Kong and, after supper, Takako and I would listen. Then in 1988, with the business going well, we increased the recording schedule to around sixty. It was in 1988 that Takako started to record all the standard repertoire: the Mozart concertos, Bach concertos, Beethoven, Mendelssohn, Brahms, Bruch. Then, more gradually, came Mozart sonatas, Beethoven sonatas ... Looking back, I think there were some very good recordings that have stood the test of time. This is true of The Four Seasons, *which has sold more than 1.5 million copies – Takako is a musician who had some interesting things to say about the music, and you can hear that the Capella Istropolitana was a first-class string orchestra. The Mozart concertos, the Tchaikovsky,*

Mendelssohn and Bruch were very good. The Brahms was not one of her favourite works but she learned it and came to like it more. She had always played the Bach concertos and Mozart's 3, 4 and 5; but she had to learn Mozart 1 and 2, and the 'Haffner' Serenade, which has a mini concerto in the middle. This kind of pressure brought out the best in her. She was always superbly prepared and had tremendous stamina. And these recordings are all still selling!

Heymann was so committed to classical music that the distinctions between 'popular', 'core' and even 'specialist' repertoire were slightly blurred in his mind. He says today that Naxos started to become a 'specialist' label in the 1990s, yet it was just one year after the label began that the first volume of Haydn quartets was recorded. This included popular quartets such as the 'Emperor' and the 'Sunrise', and it surprised everyone by selling extremely well. It was helped by the chosen musicians, the Kodály Quartet, an outstanding ensemble initially recommended by Hungaroton. This also reaped benefits later on: when Naxos decided to do the Haydn quartet cycle Heymann naturally chose the Kodály Quartet, and it was one of these recordings that brought Naxos an early rave review from a prominent British critic in 1990.

At the beginning I always thought that this was not going to last. Surely the majors were going to come out with great stuff from their back catalogues. But it was not until the early 1990s that PolyGram produced their first budget CD label, Eloquence – and they got that wrong because the recordings were not digital recordings nor did they feature top names. That meant that ours could compete. They did not put Karajan out at budget price, or other big-name conductors, because they were still trying to make a lot of money from releasing their old recordings at full price, as people re-established their music collections on the CD platform. And

*I suppose the artists themselves didn't want to be seen on a
budget label. Things have changed now!*

*To be honest, I would probably have done the same,
except that I would have watched Naxos and seen that it
was becoming a danger. But we were far away in Hong
Kong. A friend of mine participated in a board meeting of
PolyGram where Naxos was discussed; the consensus was
that it was a phantom that would disappear in a few years at
worst, and possibly in the very near future. The price was a
threat, but they couldn't believe that there would be a public
interested in buying the standard repertoire played by musicians they hadn't heard of. Hong Kong was also a long way
away and they couldn't conceive of a serious classical music
label being run from there. Perhaps if I had started Naxos in
Germany or England under their noses it would have been
different. An executive of a major classical label was quoted
referring to me as 'that crazy German in Hong Kong with his
budget label'.*

In 1989 Heymann decided to restructure his businesses again.
Bertelsmann (BMG) wanted a foothold in Asia and offered him
a good price for Pacific Music and its subsidiaries in the region,
and he accepted. Pacific Music was a powerful force, with distribution companies not only in Hong Kong but also in
Singapore, Thailand and Malaysia ('We had all the top pop
artists in Malaysia at one point').

*Fortunately BMG didn't want Naxos. They didn't think it
had a future. Probably if they had taken it I would have sold
it. But they would have destroyed it. They bought the
Chinese catalogue, though, which was a pity because it
meant I lost Takako's first recording of The Butterfly Lovers
and a lot of other Chinese classical music. I would like to get
them back, actually – not for CD release but to put them
online. Sony owns BMG and I hope that I can make a deal*

with Sony. But what happened with BMG is so typical of the majors. Why do they buy things which they don't use? They wanted the Chinese classical music, including the Violin Concerto by Du Mingxin, but most of the recordings disappeared not long after BMG bought Pacific. We did license some titles back from BMG once but the licence expired a long time ago.

But they didn't buy Naxos because they didn't recognise its potential, which was very lucky. They didn't understand the basic concept (nor did PolyGram at the time) that we had built a substantial catalogue of new digital recordings to be sold at a budget price. The key thing none of the major record labels understood was that it was not an 'exploitation' label but something completely new. The only way they could respond was to start a similar label of their own, with different people. BMG eventually did try it with Arte Nova: that was the first serious attempt. But it failed to dislodge Naxos and did not become an important factor in the classical CD market.

From 1987 to the early 1990s I was looking over my shoulder to see where the majors were; when I could not see them, I started to make plans for a comprehensive catalogue of all important classical music, including many complete cycles. Already, in 1989, I decided to do the complete Beethoven symphonies. It was the first 'complete' project we did on Naxos. We had some hitches. We recorded seven symphonies with the Zagreb Philharmonic conducted by Richard Edlinger, but we had problems and had to use earlier recordings of Nos. 3 and 6 from Bratislava to complete the set. It was a risk when we started, but we ended up by selling 200,000 sets within three years. We were offering good quality at a good price, and we were also speaking to a different buyer – not only the standard classical buyers. We were attractive to those who had an LP collection and wanted to switch to CD but didn't care so much who the performers were. We sold to young people, to students who didn't have much money, and to the LP-to-CD converts. That was the original market – not like today where the connoisseur buys Naxos for the repertoire.

Throughout the 1980s and the first few years of the 1990s, Naxos and Heymann's efforts were either ignored by the classical music establishment – the main magazines and the main critics – or vilified. There were quite a few cowboys peddling cheap classical CD product – opportunists who saw the commercial success of Naxos and tried to jump on the bandwagon. To some extent Naxos itself was viewed in this way by the classical stalwarts; but mainly it was just ignored. So Heymann ploughed on. Of course, the success didn't land in his lap.

The sales didn't just happen! I couldn't produce all those recordings and somehow magically issue them to the world where a willing public simply rushed out and bought them. I had to build a distribution network that could make the CDs available in the major markets and then tell the public about them and persuade them that though they were cheap they were very good! This was the toughest part of the whole business.

A major part of the Naxos success comes down to Heymann's establishing worldwide distribution. It does not appear as glamorous as recording Mozart and Beethoven but it was, very simply, crucial. What's more, Heymann enjoyed the cut and thrust of the commercial business as much as dealing with artists and recordings. He derived satisfaction from the competitive chase, the overcoming of continuous problems – even the occasional failures, because they meant the challenge of restructure and re-evaluation. Distribution has proved the graveyard of many a commercial activity, in classical music as in soap products, and sentimentality or preciousness has no place there. In the beginning, distribution was not a problem because budget CDs were a novelty; but consolidating the distribution network to allow a proper classical, albeit budget, label to flower proved even tougher than getting worldwide distribution for Marco Polo. Mistakes were made. Routes were taken up the wrong alleyways. Companies in every country came and went; some grew and some went bust. Now, however, Naxos has an unrivalled worldwide classical distribution network.

The established classical distributors understood Marco Polo when we started and were generally ready to take it on. And they knew what to do with it. But Naxos was another thing. It was so different, they didn't know how to handle it. Many Marco Polo distributors wouldn't touch it because they were afraid for their reputation. I couldn't find a distributor in Japan – a huge classical market – until my brother-in-law stepped in. Richard Winter at Gramola in Vienna was an exception: he took it and sold it with all his other classical labels. We went with another distributor in Germany who sold our Naxos CDs at full price because they were pressed by Denon, the Japanese manufacturer which had a very good reputation. He was a parallel importer of high-end audio equipment and thought he could sell the CDs at high-end prices. He did well initially, but this was not the idea of Naxos – it was clearly a budget label – so we had to get rid of him. In England we had a small operator in the very early years who did very little with the label, and then closed down. I was left with a one-man representative. One day I read that Boots, the big pharmacist chain, had taken one of the cheap labels and I asked my representative to contact Woolworths. Woolworths took Naxos. They insisted on exclusivity and I agreed, but eventually they didn't do such a good job and they agreed to non-exclusivity. So we went to Harmonia Mundi, at the time an important independent classical distributor in the UK, and we were with them for a short time. Sales of Naxos began to affect the sales of the Harmonia Mundi label, and the Harmonia Mundi team of Graham Haysom and Fergus Lawlor were told by head office to drop Naxos. But they saw its potential and suggested we start a distribution company together on a 50/50 basis. I agreed, and, in 1991, this became my first classical distribution company in the West: Select Music, based in Redhill, Surrey.

If the classical distributors struggled to make sense of Naxos, so did the retailers – both the independents and the classical sections of chain record stores. Where should the CDs be displayed?

The retailers thought they wouldn't put these junk CDs in with all the other 'important' classical CDs, so they put us in racks in the corners. They didn't want to mix Naxos with their good recordings, but they couldn't ignore us because people wanted to buy Naxos. It was out of that prejudice that the famous 'Naxos White Wall' grew. There we were in racks in the corner, on our own – clearly distinguishable. Customers would go into the shops and head directly for those Naxos bins, flick through them, choose two or three, and go to the till. Eventually, the retailers realised that sales could be improved by making it simple for the buyer and actually devoting a whole display unit to Naxos, which became easier as the label grew so quickly. This played a key role in turning Naxos into a brand – the leading classical brand. Even now, it is the only label in the world that is racked as a label. And it happened by accident!

For the next decade and more, a sizeable portion of Heymann's time and energy went into developing the Naxos distribution network, solving problems, changing personnel, and investing in people and infrastructure. He bailed out companies going bankrupt, bought some of them out, closed others, and struggled in some key territories. There were boom times in Scandinavia, then bumpy years. Every January he could be found in Cannes at MIDEM, making new deals, consolidating others, holding distribution conferences to announce the coming year's new releases, and reviewing campaigns of the past year and proposals for the next twelve months. He gradually gathered around him a multi-faceted international team – or, more precisely, a group of strong individuals in the various territories, with different abilities and temperaments. Extraordinarily he would maintain regular, almost daily, contact with them.

In the core Hong Kong team were Keith Anderson, an expatriate music lecturer who became the scholar of Naxos and wrote an unbelievable number of liner notes, blurbs and essays, both short and extensive, for Marco Polo as well as Naxos; and Keith's son Anthony Anderson who, having graduated in Classics at Durham University, arrived in Hong Kong and started at the bottom, learning every aspect of the business to become, in some ways, Heymann's right-hand man. There were also many key people around the world. David Denton, a music writer in Sheffield, England took over the public relations work and also established contacts with UK artists and orchestras; he helped Select Music to become a major classical force in Britain. In Sweden, the largest Scandinavian territory, Heymann began with a Christian music distributor; when it went bust he joined forces with Håkan Lagerqvist, a shrewd record marketing executive, and his business partner Mats Byrén. Lagerqvist did not know much about classical music but ran some extraordinary campaigns in Scandinavia, including *Swedish Classical Favourites*, a TV-promoted boxed set that eventually, it was reported, got into 80 per cent of middle-class homes in Sweden. Naxos Sweden is now the leading classical music distributor in the country, with some 75 per cent of classical sales going through its portals. After some difficult times, Heymann effectively bought out other third-party distributors in Scandinavia and now owns the distribution networks in Finland, Denmark and Norway. The US proved one of the most challenging markets. Various expensive false starts (including one with a heavy-metal distributor) led to Heymann solving the problem by creating his own company with Jim Sturgeon and Jim Selby, a couple of smart Canadians with experience in the pop business. They settled Naxos of America in Nashville, the home of country music, and put the label on a successful path. There were good times and difficult times in Australia; they settled when Heymann established his own distribution company. It was a similar case in Germany, where he eventually set up with Chris Voll, a music salesman who had worked for a previous Naxos distributor. France went through uneven patches depending on the individual on the ground, and it is still the only major record market in which Naxos does not have a subsidiary.

Heymann maintained personal contact with all these individuals, first by phone and fax, then by phone and email (adopting the new technology immediately), and more latterly by Skype. He simply worked all the time, advising, cajoling, persuading, suggesting. Accessible to all, he seemed never to lose the thread of a campaign proposal or a promotion, or the terms of a deal, whether it was a discount proposal, a licensing offer or the rental of offices. Even into the millennium he still listened to everything, read all the CD notes and checked the covers.

Behind this was his more directly remunerative consumer and professional audio business, as well as a thriving dance-music label: after the sale of Pacific Music to BMG in 1989 he immediately formed a new company with Steve Beaver to market EuroBeat in Asia.

BMG didn't want Steve, which was another mistake. He really is a genius in recognising trends in the music industry and I couldn't miss the opportunity. So we started Beaver Records and it became the biggest dance-music label in Asia. At one point we had 50 per cent of the Japanese dance-music charts. EuroBeat had been the king of European electronic disco music in the late 1980s and early 1990s but there was also a lot of interest in Asia. Many recordings became so popular that the Japanese licensees wanted them to tour. This was electronic music created by studio musicians. We had had to ring up Italy and say, 'Hey, can you find a few musicians to do that stuff again and tour Japan?'

Before I had sold Pacific Music to BMG I had already made a lot of money with disco music. Steve had signed all the most important new labels and we came out with a series of enormously successful compilations because we could draw on all the hits from these specialised labels. We sold more than 50,000 copies of some of these disco compilations in Hong Kong, and then we started selling them in Korea. We had already established sub-licensees there for all the labels we represented. It was a fascinating business. The Koreans were not allowed to pay advances and the only way we could get the money was for me to carry the cash out – otherwise there would have been no business. We had the same problem in the Philippines and Taiwan as well: $10,000, $15,000, $20,000 in cash in bags on the plane, coming through customs. There were some tense moments.

Eventually I was getting tired of the EuroBeat business. We were making a lot of money from it, but somehow it was embarrassing because most of the music was electronic garbage and when Steve Beaver offered me a fair price for my share of Beaver Records in 1992 I accepted it. Now I could concentrate on the Bose business, Marco Polo and Naxos. Whatever money I made in Bose I put into Naxos. I ploughed all my money into that. I didn't make a real profit from the recordings for years, but making a success of Naxos became an important goal. I could have sold it and lived a comfortable life, but as the years went on I found I was surviving in an industry I loved to be in, and I managed to make money in other ways to fund the growth of the label.

Those funds were sorely needed because the number of CDs that Naxos and Marco Polo were now recording annually was beginning to run into three figures, and some of them were very expensive. In 1990 Heymann took another big step with Naxos, recording his first complete opera. When he had started the label, and for some years afterwards, he had never even thought of recording opera, a ruinously expensive business ('the most expensive noise known to man', according to Molière). But by the turn of the decade he felt the time was right for selling digitally recorded standard opera at budget price. The first one was *Così fan tutte* recorded early in 1990 in Bratislava with singers from the Vienna State Opera, the Slovak Philharmonic Chorus and Capella Istropolitana, conducted by Johannes Wildner. Its moderate size made it a good initial step into opera recording. But even before its release, Heymann was sufficiently encouraged to move ahead with a much bolder project – *Carmen*, one of the ten most frequently performed and recorded operas of all time.

At the time, I didn't know good singers in Europe who could be entrusted with such a key project. I turned to Alexander Rahbari, the Persian-born conductor who was the principal conductor of the Belgian Radio and Television Philharmonic Orchestra. In 1989 the BRT Philharmonic had become our house orchestra for some of the more demanding reper- toire – Debussy, Brahms symphonies and many other things. Rahbari wanted to do opera and he lived in Vienna and found singers. So we recorded Carmen *in Bratislava in July 1990. It cost $50,000, which for a two-CD set being sold at budget price was a great risk. But it sold like hot cakes: 300,000 copies in a short time. So we went ahead with* La

Bohème, Rigoletto *and others. They all made money because there was no budget opera on the market and certainly no new recordings at that price. Even now I think the musical performances are pretty good, and we had singers that were later to go on and be big names: Giorgio Lamberti in* Carmen *and* Tosca, *with Nelly Miricioiu as Tosca, and Luba Orgonášová as Mimì in* La Bohème. *Once again, there was a lot of good talent around in provincial opera houses – singers who had no chance of being recorded by major record labels and were glad to record for us.*

In 1990 a leading English critic, Edward Greenfield of the *Guardian*, wrote a major article in that newspaper, acknowledging the work and achievements of Naxos. It was a key turning point. The first recommendations for Naxos recordings appeared in *The Penguin Guide to Classical Music*, and by the mid-1990s there were well over 100. Even *Gramophone*, the prestigious UK classical record magazine, started to take notice, with its first unqualified praise going to a recording of Haydn's quartets played by the Kodály Quartet. There was confidence in the label, confidence in the company.

Seven

Naxos: A World Force 1994–2000

The opera recordings and the stream of orchestral and chamber music that now far surpassed the confines of 'popular' repertoire had made an impact, and serious collectors and the classical establishment had begun to accept that here was a significant label.

In 1994 we were an important label, selling seven to eight million CDs a year. We made more profit in the early years because most of the repertoire we recorded was in the public domain, so there was not much copyright to pay. In the late 1980s CD manufacturing prices were quite high, but as more factories opened there was increased capacity and in the early 1990s prices dropped; but our selling price didn't drop and Naxos became a better business. Even after they stopped falling, we were making about $1.50 per disc profit. The export price was about $2.00 and manufacturing was 50c, so we made $1.50. That was when the CD was retailing at $5.99 in the US. I had consciously tried to fix the price of a Naxos CD to the consumer at the lowest bank note of the country. It was £4.99 in the UK, DM9.99 in Germany, KR49 in Sweden. That was what we were aiming for.

Unfortunately, it didn't work in the US. But the idea was there, and it was only very reluctantly that we changed, as the financial situation dictated. The price gradually crept up in all markets, though in retrospect the increases were relatively small. And even with a profit of $1.50 it was quite a challenge to recoup all the recording and design costs. Some CDs sold in large numbers but many did not, and when we started doing music in copyright – Stravinsky, Shostakovich, Sibelius and many others – margins shrank. For many years I tried to persuade our distributors to adopt a two-tier price structure – one for public-domain music and one for music with copyright – which made commercial sense but did not make sense to the consumer, who is not aware of factors such as mechanical copyright.

Heymann's expansionist, entrepreneurial temperament made him an habitual investor in new ideas and new products. This and his readiness to take risks in a spontaneous manner have been at the core of his success. It was in 1994 that he expanded the range of Naxos beyond the classical music sphere, moving into spoken-word recordings with Naxos AudioBooks.

I was at the Naxos distribution supper at MIDEM, sitting next to the music journalist Nicolas Soames. He had interviewed me for various newspapers and magazines, and we also distributed a small label he had, Clarinet Classics. Right at the end of the evening he mentioned he was going to start a new spoken-word line of abridged classic literature on cassette, which was the dominant spoken-word medium at the time. The idea was to make 'difficult' writers such as Homer, Milton, Dante and Joyce more accessible and bring them to a wider audience, with the productions enhanced by classical music. I was interested in the idea but thought that for the project to become successful it needed unique selling points. Music was one, and releasing all titles on CD as well as cassette – at a time when the audiobook departments in bookstores were still called 'books on tape' – was another. I called along my UK, US and Australian distributors who were on the next table and explained the idea. I also said that I thought we could use the audiobooks as door-openers to bookstores. They said they weren't particularly interested in the spoken word but they agreed that it could enable them to go into bookshops with these recordings and pull Naxos classical CDs out of their back pockets, so to speak. They envisioned Naxos spinners in main bookshops. Ideal! So I turned back to Nicolas and suggested we do it together. I proposed terms, and that he should record twenty-five releases to be out on the market from September to December, with a further fifty releases in 1995. We shook hands on the deal. It was 11 p.m., the time for the formal end of the supper, and I left for my hotel room to prepare for the morning.

It was a rather typical piece of fast Klaus Heymann decision-making but the ensuing Naxos AudioBooks story was not quite so simple. Within eighteen months it won awards for James Joyce, Dickens and poetry, and developed a reputation for top-class productions with outstanding actors. It carried the Naxos brand into a new area. However, it took a decade of faith and investment to turn it into a commercial success. The problem was the knotty one of distribution: although these were recordings, the principal area for selling audiobooks was bookshops, and bookshops were not where the Naxos strengths lay. So it took some years to establish a reasonable network in the English-speaking countries. Creating the audio-book wing nevertheless gave Naxos an expertise in making and publishing books, which was to bear fruit later.

This enterprise demonstrated once again the importance of distribution. The strength of Naxos's classical distribution in key countries enabled each of the subsidiaries to start a local recording programme, so that the Naxos name was not only a global brand but had a local connotation too. It was started in the UK in the mid-1990s by David Denton, responsible for UK Naxos promotion and marketing. He introduced Jeremy Summerly and the Oxford Camerata to the label, which by now really needed a strand of early choral music. Denton also initiated the programmes of English music, beginning with the orchestral music of Bax. Over the next decade and more, Naxos built a reputation for recordings of English music which could rival that of the full-price labels such as Hyperion and Chandos. This was continued by Anthony Anderson when he left Hong Kong and returned to England to run Select Music, after Heymann had bought out Haysom and Lawlor in 1997. Select Music was the first distribution company in the West owned fully by Heymann and it formed the template for others – part of which was the commitment to local recordings. These were not vanity projects: they had to be commercially viable, and it was challenging because often, by their very nature, they were not an easy worldwide sale. With margins quite slim for budget labels, exacerbated by copyright payments, it was touch and go. But Anderson showed that it could work and, in that sense, paved the way for similar projects elsewhere, particularly in America.

We tried to do only local repertoire that we could sell elsewhere, one of the exceptions being the 'Japanese Classics' series which came much later. English music sells in all the former colonies, Australia, New Zealand and North America as well as the UK: it is a very multinational repertoire. And 'American Classics', which became one of our strongest sublabels, was a conscious effort finally to establish Naxos on the American market. And it worked. The label had never really been very successful there until then. We sold 'American Classics' in reasonable quantities but its real importance was that it put the label on the map in the world's biggest music market. And America had never really had a label that recorded its own music and distributed it worldwide. Columbia issued quite a lot of American music – they did Bernstein and others – but there wasn't a comprehensive project to record American music for both the home and the export market. With 'American Classics' there was, for the first time, an international record company making recordings of substantial chunks of American music that were instantly available around the globe. The range included symphonies by Roy Harris and William Schuman, as well as Bernstein. We recorded the complete orchestral works of Samuel Barber and the complete John Philip Sousa, which, astoundingly, had never been done. I must admit that I had never heard of William Schuman or Roy Harris before we started. As before, I started reading histories and catalogues. And I had American repertoire advisors, in the beginning Victor and Marina Ledin and later a formal editorial board that included the writer Joseph Horowitz and the musicologists Wiley Hitchcock and Wayne Shirley. They gave the 'American Classics' series the gravitas it deserved.

The series was launched in 2002, Naxos's fifteenth anniversary year, and brought the label exceptional press recognition. Heymann was pleasantly surprised by the sales, too, some of the Barber achieving nearly 30,000 copies worldwide. Even for composers like Harris and Schuman who were not so well known abroad, one third of the sales came from outside the US. Heymann began the Barber series with the Royal Scottish National Orchestra because its principal guest conductor was the fiery and talented Marin Alsop, a Bernstein protégée; and also because the strictly unionised American orchestras were simply too expensive even to contemplate. That was soon to change, but initially American music was recorded in Scotland. At the same time, there came French music from France, Spanish music from Spain, Polish music from Poland, and so on. With the Bose business generating funds, Heymann could afford to be eclectic and take risks. (However, it must be said that Bose was not an infallible cash cow. There were many times when cash flow was tight and he had to consider cutting his ambitious recording and development plans; but he always managed somehow to get finance from around the world and continue with the expansion of the label.)

The local recording projects often had another effect: they gave Naxos such a strong reputation in the local territories that other labels wanted to join in. It was counter-intuitive – after all, they were supposed to be rivals – but results soon showed that there were many advantages in competing classical labels being distributed and sold together. They strengthened the position of the Naxos distribution. The concept started in the UK.

It was not easy at the start to persuade key independent labels to join our distribution network. In some ways, we seemed to be everything they didn't like and our success was threatening. Were we undermining their business? Understandably they were also concerned that they would be regarded as second to Naxos when our salesmen visited shops. But we showed that this was not the case. The first major label to come to us was Hyperion in the UK, and that surprised everyone because Ted Perry's label was one of the most respected in the UK and the world. It helped that our UK company was called 'Select' not 'Naxos' – Graham Haysom's idea – though in the end it worked just as well in Sweden and the USA where we kept the name Naxos, and where labels came to us without worrying about what we were called. Select Music became a model for others and, to tell the truth, we needed the labels as much as they needed us: it gave us the market power and the higher turnover to engage more salesmen and grow.

America was a tough nut to crack because there were other established classical distributors which had many of the main European labels. CPO came to us early on and gradually others joined us. For years I had to inject cash into the US to keep it going. This was the case elsewhere, too – from time to time I have had to prop up our distribution subsidiaries. It took fifteen years to establish a strong and stable distribution network. But ultimately it was the strength of the worldwide distribution network that turned Naxos into a real force in the world of classical music.

In 1995 there was another critical development that would affect Naxos considerably: the start of the in-house recording, editing and mastering facilities of K&A (Klaus and Andrew) Productions. For over a decade, since the start of Marco Polo in 1982, Heymann had relied on a bank of freelance producers and engineers to make the recordings. All of them were funnelled through a German editing and recording operation run by the Dutchman Teije van Geest. It had worked reasonably well, but it could not be said that Naxos or Marco Polo had state-of-the-art recordings. It was the purpose of an in-house production and editing department to match the audio standards to the growing international reputation. Consistency was the first target. David Denton found Andrew Walton, a violinist with the English Chamber Orchestra who was already making a name for himself as a recording engineer and editor. K&A Productions, based in Potters Bar just north of London, rapidly became the hub of the production wheel.

In 1994 we were making around 120 recordings, but it was beginning to get out of hand. One year we recorded as many as 300, and we had masters stacking up! Some years we had a backlog of 600 masters waiting for release, which was a huge investment just sitting there and not recouping. It became even more crucial to have a process of quality control, and this K&A provided. It began checking, editing and mastering the backlog. Then it took on a considerable amount of the recording, not just in the UK but in Europe and the US as well. As its reputation grew, other labels started to come to it for high-standard recording as well, so K&A became a leading classical production company in its own right.

The quantity of work in all its aspects now going through the Naxos portals was staggering.

The trouble was that in some ways we were becoming too successful. The original idea was that we would make one recording of everything that had ten recordings in the record catalogues. That was my definition of popular! At the start, it never crossed my mind we would do so many Haydn quartets, and certainly not C.P.E. Bach. Now we are even considering the complete C.P.E. Bach with a modern C.P.E. edition! But once we had survived the first five years, the plan changed. I wanted Naxos to become a virtual encyclopedia of classical music on CD, and throughout the 1990s we diversified into many different areas of the repertoire. We needed to have a strong new-release programme, and our customers were clamouring for more. Naxos may have started by producing popular classics for supermarket customers, but now the central classical music buyers were scouring the lists to see what we were bringing out next. So I wanted to have everything and invested constantly, and that approach is paying off today.

But I didn't rush into everything, even core repertoire. Shostakovich symphonies were offered to me by the Slovak Radio Symphony Orchestra in a very good deal. The symphonies were conducted by the veteran Ladislav Slovák, who had been present at the first performances of several of the symphonies in Russia. The interpretations were terrific but the orchestra, of course, had its limitations. My own musical parameters and criteria were changing. It was not enough to get recordings out onto the market which would be acceptable at budget price: they had to be first class and compete directly with the full-price labels. From the mid-1990s onwards I was beginning to get sick and tired of Naxos being regarded just as 'a budget label' with recordings suiting the price. The critics weren't listening. They were judging us on past perceptions of Naxos.

I really took my time over the Bruckner symphonies. For me, Bruckner was the ultimate composer and I loved the symphonies from when I was a young man. I knew Horenstein's recording of Symphony No. 9 on Vox which is still one of the finest. So I decided to wait until I felt we were ready to do something special. One day in October 1994 I got a phonecall from Anthony Camden, the English oboist [former principal of the London Symphony Orchestra] who was the dean of music at the Hong Kong Academy for Performing Arts. He said, 'Georg Tintner is in town.' I had never heard of him. 'He is the greatest living Bruckner conductor and maybe you would like to talk to him.'

So Georg and his wife Tanya (with whom I am still in contact) came to the house and I sort of interviewed him. I asked him what he thought of Bruckner and how he would interpret the symphonies, and he impressed me so much. He struck me as being a man of the utmost sincerity when he talked about Bruckner. He had a saintly demeanour. I think he was anything but saintly in some areas, but he was a vegan and he was wearing nothing made from animal skin – in some ways he was quite radical! But he really impressed me as a human being and I felt that a man like that could do Bruckner justice. Of course, I also did a little bit of checking and it all matched, so I agreed to give the symphony cycle a try.

It didn't get off to a particularly good start. Tintner had been in New Zealand for a while after the war and had a reputation there, so the cycle started with the New Zealand Symphony Orchestra. It was not a good time for them. They were in turmoil, and when the Ninth Symphony was planned the first chairs refused to participate. A recording was made but not released. The Sixth had been finished before the trouble started; and although some players complained about Tintner's conducting style, his head buried in the score, that recording (released in 1998) was unquestionably fine and received very good reviews. But Heymann decided to shift the project elsewhere, recording with the Royal Scottish National Orchestra and the National Symphony Orchestra of Ireland (introduced to Naxos by David Denton) and was happy with the results. 'I think it is one of the best Bruckner cycles in the world today.'

The decision to record with orchestras that were particularly suitable for certain repertoire was made possible by the easing of commercial constraints. British musicians were – and remain – the finest sight-readers in the world, so although they may have been slightly more expensive, the economies of time were often a greater factor. Higher expectations of quality also dictated a more careful choice of orchestra. David Denton opened the way for further Naxos associations with various groups, including the Bournemouth Symphony Orchestra. Other regional UK orchestras followed, especially those who had musicians on full-time contracts and needed engagements when the concert life was quiet. Concurrently the early-music programme was gaining pace.

When David introduced the Oxford Camerata to me I asked Jeremy Summerly to make a recording plan for early choral music. He produced fifteen programmes, and we did them. I do listen to people, though I also check. Similarly with Hervé Niquet and Le Concert Spirituel who did Charpentier, Lully and other French Baroque composers for us: I said to him, 'Make a plan!'

But not all these new ventures went well. Quite a few were started, ate up a considerable amount of investment which they never recouped, and were then stopped or slowed down. Heymann is adept at putting a positive spin on things and says that now, with the digital world and its long tail, almost all the recordings are serving some purpose or other. However, a lot of money from the Bose business (and, when Bose finished, Heymann's personal fortune) went down various classical and non-classical drains, to be seen only much later!

Audiobooks took a long time to turn around; his world music and jazz labels never did.

Artistically the jazz label was extremely successful. But I did not know the business or the jazz environment and relied on the well-known Australian jazz pianist Mike Nock, who had all the contacts. It seemed to be just one branch of music but it was totally different. Composers were our headlines on our classical recordings, but it is the artists who headline a jazz record. That was a major difference I didn't appreciate at the start. We also paid too much to produce the recordings.

The biggest surprise was that the largest jazz markets in the world – US, France and also Japan – do not buy much non-American jazz. It is as simple as that. We had gold-record awards in Finland and Sweden but couldn't sell fifty copies in the US.

I wanted to have frontline jazz – the best available in Scandinavia, Germany, Australia, New Zealand, wherever we could find it (we had American jazz as well). But the simple fact was that our distributors knew how to sell classical music, not jazz; and it didn't sell well in the bigger markets, only in the smaller ones. We also made the mistake of putting contemporary art on the cover and not pictures of the artists; and we sold at budget price, which was unnecessary. The reviews were fantastic; nevertheless it was a failure.

*I sometimes think I would like to get back into jazz, espe-
cially as our distributors have now learned how to sell it, but
I would have to find a much more economical way of doing
it.*

Much the same thing was happening, simultaneously, with
world music. Some very good recordings were made. One, a
recording of sacred Tibetan chant by the monks of Sherab Ling
Monastery, won a GRAMMY Award and still sells. A lot of
money was spent on trying to make Naxos World, but the
genre proved to be too different a culture for the label.

The story was repeated with ambient/new-age music and the
label White Cloud. It was run by Jon Mark of Mark-Almond
fame – one of the big rock bands of the 1970s.

*Jon was a very creative guy and I think some of the music he
produced on White Cloud was very beautiful. But it didn't fit
into the company and was also a failure, even if it is still
online and we use it for compilations.*

Historical recordings were a different story altogether. The
company debated, in the early 1990s, whether to move into
historical records. The received wisdom at the time was that
there was a limited market for old recordings. Heymann felt
that if Naxos were to go into this area it should be able to offer
something unique, not simply produce the same things that
others were trotting out. He started with a collection of original masters of live recordings that had been offered to him and
had never been released. He called them 'Immortal
Performances'. That was in 1995. Then one of the recognised
historical restorers, Mark Obert-Thorn, contacted Heymann
and suggested a much wider range of great commercial recordings from the past to which he would apply the most
up-to-date restoration technology, starting with Rachmaninov
playing his own piano concertos. It was an immediate hit,

selling tens of thousands of copies; the CDs still sell about 2,000 copies a year.

At the time, most of the existing historical reissue labels put out old recordings at full price. We were committed to the best restorations possible so that we could offer a really high-quality historical label, at budget price. Sales rocketed and I wanted more, beyond the number Mark could do. So he brought Ward Marston, also widely known as a superb restorer, onto the team. We now had two of the best people in the business, which helped us with critics who were still opposed to Naxos. They could not but grudgingly respect the work that we were doing in the historical area. We were bringing out some of the greatest and most iconic recordings at budget price; and, they admitted, many of them sounded better than the versions released by the original labels.

Why did the major companies, including EMI, not release more historical recordings from their archives? Well, we found out why, because in the end it did not turn out to be such a good commercial business after all. The majors did not release all that music in their archives with good reason: they released only the big names because the others didn't sell enough. It was as simple as that.

I found out from experience that with the exception of some people like Rachmaninov, only artists who had a career that reached into the second half of the twentieth century had sales appeal: Jascha Heifetz, Arthur Rubinstein, Maria Callas, Pablo Casals – and even with him, only the Bach solo suites. Walter Gieseking's historical recordings sold in Germany because he was still playing there in the second half of the twentieth century. But Fritz Kreisler does not sell so well. The complete Benno Moiseiwitsch is a labour of love. Jussi Björling is a labour of love though he sells well in Sweden. So the majors knew what they were doing!

However, the historical label has done tremendously for

*our reputation as a label and is seen as providing an
invaluable service to serious collectors. In that sense it has
been a good investment, though not a profitable one. And
the historical recordings have really come into their own on
the digital platform.*

The simplest way of creating revenue was to use existing
recordings by licensing them to others in a way that would
not affect CD sales. Heymann's single ownership of all the
recordings, and streamlined way of doing business, meant that
instant decisions could be given to myriad other media organisations that needed classical music: advertisers, film makers,
publishers and corporate bodies. Growing this revenue stream
became a focus for Heymann and the Naxos distributors. In
1997 he formed an association with Isabel Gortázar, a
Spanish publisher, businesswoman and writer, to expand
licensing in Europe and elsewhere. Heymann granted her
company (TEC, SL) exclusive rights in several European and
all Spanish-speaking countries to license Naxos and Marco
Polo recordings: for special editions, such as premium packages for promotions; and, particularly, for book publishers to
sell in partworks, school material and other products distributed through non-retail channels. This involved the sales of
millions of CDs through kiosks and other networks. It proved
a lucrative venture.

The mid-1990s was generally a time of expansion, with
Heymann keen to move into new areas. He formed Artaria
Editions, a specialist publishing house that concentrated on
contemporaries of Haydn and Mozart.

*For nine years I ran a chamber music festival as a hobby in
New Zealand, where I have my second home. The festival
was an opportunity to meet my artists! While in Wellington
in 1994 I met Allan Badley, who by profession is an academic – a musicologist specialising in the contemporaries of*

Haydn and Mozart, and especially Leopold Hofmann – but who also happened to run the New Zealand Chamber Orchestra.

We discussed recording Stamitz's orchestral trios and then he started talking about many other composers from the period whom I had never heard of – François-Joseph Gossec, Franz Ignaz Beck and, of course, Leopold Hofmann. I said we could record some of these and he explained that there were no scores and parts available, but that the music was good. The performance material would have to be prepared from the original manuscripts.

It was the beginning of a new company. In 1995 we started a publishing business called Artaria Editions, named after Haydn's Viennese publisher. It was a business I knew nothing about but over the years we published a lot of previously unavailable works and now we have over 500 titles. They are highly respected and universities all over the world subscribe to new publications. Artaria could do a lot better, but we have never had a business person actually running it as a business: Allan is a musicologist who goes into libraries, gets microfilms and edits them himself.

Nevertheless Artaria has given us a lot of unique repertoire: the Saint-Georges violin concertos, which Takako recorded; the concertos and symphonies by Vanhal and Pleyel; and the piano concertos by Ferdinand Ries, which have been quite a success commercially. Altogether we have done more than sixty CDs. Artaria has given us a unique repertoire so to a large extent we have succeeded, and, of course, we have gained experience in music publishing.

In 2004 Heymann gave the go-ahead for the Naxos AudioBooks team to develop a range of products for the book market. The audiobooks had a certain presence in the bookshops and it seemed that music books would be just a small sidestep within that. So Naxos Books produced biographies of composers:

books with two CDs and a website. It also published the first general history of American classical music; and an important book of memoirs by the conductor Robert Craft, whose close association with Stravinsky had placed him in the centre of the post-war cultural milieu. Once again, distribution caused these artistic plans to falter: paper books and audiobooks went into different departments! Nevertheless there was some commercial success with two children's books by the editorial manager of Naxos Books, Genevieve Helsby: *Meet the Instruments of the Orchestra!* and *My First Classical Music Book.* All these titles underscored Heymann's keenness to develop educational projects.

> *There were some excellent books, translated into various languages, and though we didn't see an immediate profit some did quite well in the end. We also learned how to publish and sell books, e-texts and apps, expanding the expertise within the company.*

The Naxos label began with new technology – the CD – and innovation has been a constant theme of the company, and a constant challenge. It has not always been easy to spot the next big technological development.

> *No one really likes having to maintain an inventory in different formats and I tried to keep it to a minimum. Naxos was designed as a CD label but there was some demand still for cassettes, so we introduced a limited range of Naxos cassettes. Then came minidisk and we released a few of those; and the various 'improved' CD formats, DVD-Audio and SACD. At one point we were the only company releasing suitable titles in three different formats: CD, DVD-Audio and SACD. I made the wrong call with DVD-Audio, and SACD won, though that is declining too. Now we are also releasing some Blu-ray audio discs.*

And then there was the temptation of video – on VHS and Laserdisc, and finally DVD. I was approached by someone who said that there would be TV stations all over the world who would buy simple travel programmes with music to take the place of what were then called 'test cards' – when the station was not broadcasting programmes. We bought the equipment and made programmes of many of the major world cities (from Helsinki to Venice, from Vienna to London), taking some nice footage to illustrate the music. The shoots were planned in a way which allowed the footage to be edited in synch with the music. It was, and is still, pleasant watching though it was not commercially successful on video tape. I was doing too many things and I didn't go systematically to TV companies to sell the stuff. In any case, it wasn't really something we could have done ourselves: to sell to television stations one has to go through specialist marketing companies who sell a wide range of productions. And we didn't have the right carrier. If we had had DVD then, it might have been different; they are all out on DVD now and doing quite well, and there is the online revenue stream. We get a small annual income of around €40,000 a year. But I invested around $4 million in our musical journeys which I doubt I will ever recoup fully.

Typically Heymann turned that 'failure' experience into a 'learning' experience and then into a commercial success. He began to understand the video business and it sharpened his eye on this aspect of the classical music business. He was ready to act when DVD became the standard format.

There had been scepticism about the demand for classical concerts as well as opera on video but it was clear that we were turning increasingly into a visual culture. One only had to look at the success of MTV. The digital medium played an important part, but there were other factors. It was clear that if people bought an opera on DVD often for less money than a two-CD or three-CD music set, and could also play it just as a sound recording if they wanted, DVD must have a strong future. And if so, there were strategic reasons why we needed to be there.

It began for us in Germany. One day in early 2000 I got a call from Chris Voll, the CEO of Naxos Germany. He told me about a new classical DVD label called Arthaus and that he had been offered the distribution of the label for Germany. I told him on the spot to try to get the worldwide distribution of the label for us. And Arthaus did go with us for the world and has been with us ever since. Next came Opus Arte, with whom Anthony Anderson had established contact: they had seen what we had done for Arthaus and wanted to join our distribution network. We reached the classical collectors whom they had identified as their core customer. They felt their product needed to be in specialist classical outlets rather than being in racks beside the latest blockbuster films. Our subsidiaries and third-party distributors had to step out of their comfort zone. But we proved we could do this, and now we are the leading distributors of classical DVDs in the world.

By the turn of the century the classical record industry was undergoing serious changes. The majors were doing less and less, and more was coming to Naxos – in terms of both repertoire and musicians. The major companies were shedding their contracted artists who realised that the only way they were going to get their recordings out on the market was through independents: through Naxos. Even Heymann was surprised by some of the musicians with strong international reputations who were now beginning to appear on his label. The greatest change was the drop in CD sales: from being a boom industry, music on CD (especially pop) was going into decline. This was prompted by the growth of music on the web, and the culture of illegally downloading pop music. Classical music was scarcely affected at first, but the lifeblood of the whole chain of recorded music began to suffer some serious body blows and classical could not escape.

The 1990s had seen Naxos change gradually from a budget label with a toe in the specialist water to a classical label offering exceptional value (with its low price and improving quality) and an unprecedented range of releases. When the major companies were cutting back on classical releases Naxos was expanding, re-recording core works where it was evident that improvements could be made. It was aiming increasingly at offering complete cycles of composers as well as a range of specialist repertoire almost unmatched in classical recording history. In the first decade of the new millennium, the monthly release schedule would often top twenty or thirty recordings, with scarcely a reissue.

The early years of the twenty-first century also saw Naxos finally appreciated for what it was: a major player in classical recording and not just a budget label.

Critics in the UK and the US increasingly praised Naxos recordings regardless of their budget price. A new CD was welcomed unconditionally. Yet there were still Beckmessers all over the world, and it wasn't until 2001 that a Naxos disc won a Gramophone *Award: Vaughan Williams quartets played by the Maggini Quartet. The tide had turned, and in 2005 we were even* Gramophone *Label of the Year. In the US we started to get GRAMMY nominations and have now won sixteen of these coveted awards. We still occasionally get reviews from old critics who say, damning with faint praise, that a particular recording is good considering its modest price. That annoys me if I see it now, but it doesn't happen often anymore.*

Klaus Heymann himself was no longer regarded as some kind of classical pariah but more of a pioneer.

Recognition for what Naxos has done was a long time in coming. I had been accused for years of having destroyed the classical music industry by offering classical music cheaply. That was nonsense of course. I couldn't do that with only 10 per cent of the market. I simply didn't have the market power. The majors destroyed themselves by the way they ran their businesses, spending inordinate amounts on the star system. They ran their companies like the film industry whereas the independents ran theirs like well-controlled small businesses.

I know exactly what I have spent on each recording, and where there is an overrun I know how many copies of a recording I have to sell to break even. I make sure that my artists have prepared for the recording sessions: they don't appear and start to rehearse and find out they can't play the music. These were all things that the majors got wrong: they let the recording costs go out of control; they let artists' fees escalate; they gave approval rights to artists for covers, which resulted in some serious abuses by 'star' performers; and when they had The Three Tenors everyone tried to emulate that success with ruinous consequences.

The majors fared no better in spotting and harnessing the next great change that faced the record industry.

Eight

Naxos: The Digital Age
1996–2011

Then there was the Internet. Heymann was perhaps the only significant player in classical recording who not only saw it coming but actually prepared his company accordingly. It was remarkable prescience, and enabled Naxos to become the strongest single classical force in the early years of the twenty-first century.

In the mid-1990s I was not aware of the Internet at all. But one of the great advantages of being in a modern city like Hong Kong is that we are very close to the cutting edge of technology. One day in 1995 Mr S.K. Wong, my Hong Kong warehouse manager, came into my office. He was into computing as a hobby and spent time on the Internet for his own amusement. He said, 'Let us do a website for our company.' I asked him, 'What is a website?' He told me. I said, 'Ok, let's do a website.' So he created one. There was no music on it, or maybe just a little, but I didn't really pay any attention. He suggested registering both 'naxos.com' and 'marcopolo.com'. I didn't understand the importance of having your brand names registered and told him to register

*'hnh.com' [the name of the Naxos parent company] instead.
I didn't understand why one had to have two websites if you
could have one. It was a really stupid decision! It took us a
lot of effort and money to get naxos.com later on, and it
proved too late for marcopolo.com.*

One day I read in The Wall Street Journal *that in years to
come music would be distributed digitally – that it would be
the future of the business. I thought, 'Wait a minute, let me
look at our website.' I saw it was a very unsuitable design: it
took three minutes to load and the database was in a mess.
I said, 'Close it down, let's start from scratch. Clean up the
data. Come up with a homepage that loads in thirty seconds
and not three minutes.'*

*Then I realised that this was a great platform on which to
let people listen before they buy. So I decided to put the
whole catalogue on the Internet so that people could listen,
track by track, at low fidelity. It had to be low fidelity
because of the cost of the bandwidth. But it was completely
free. Most of the world was still working with dial-up
Internet access so it wasn't fast. But that changed more rapidly in Hong Kong and some other Asian countries, before
the US and Europe, so I was always able to be ahead of the
game. I could see possibilities before the rest of the main
classical world. hnh.com had started in 1996 and by 1997
our whole catalogue, both Naxos and Marco Polo recordings, was available for streaming on the site.*

*For a long time I regarded it as a promotional tool. We
had about 2,500 titles at the time and all of that had to go
up on the Internet, along with covers and notes! We had a
room full of young computer-savvy Hong Kong boys doing
all the input. It involved tremendous expenditure because
bandwidth was so expensive in those days.*

Things were moving fast: the concept of what was then dubbed
'the information super highway' was becoming a popular

media topic. By 1998 other classical websites were beginning to appear and some people spent a huge amount of money on projects which were only to come and go. Heymann's websites hnh.com and later naxos.com survived partly because Naxos could afford to subsidise the service from the physical business, but also because the company didn't burn cash to promote the sites and it did all the development work in-house.

I didn't see it as a business to start with because of the cost of the bandwidth. In any case, the Internet market wasn't big enough. It was just a promotional tool for us. I wasn't too ambitious. But when the bandwidth costs started to drop I began to think how we could use the best features of the Internet in a way that would really serve the classical music consumer.

Downloads were a bit of a conundrum for the classical consumer because of the importance of sound quality. For many listeners high fidelity was essential, and where dial-up predominated and speed of delivery was slow, low-quality sound was inevitable. It was less of a problem for a three-minute pop song, but a real obstacle for a Beethoven symphony. This was compounded by the average classical consumer's reluctance to accept the concept of keeping a classical music collection on the computer, which was connected to only low-quality speakers. So Heymann came up with a totally different concept: streaming classical music to subscribers.

I started with the Naxos Music Library, the NML, in 2002. The concept was that we would sell access to this collection on a subscription basis. I thought there would be a wide range of users. There was the academic market – universities, schools, libraries of all kinds. They needed to listen for study purposes. This sometimes means listening to a whole work, but often it means listening to a particular movement or section. I knew that all the booklet notes we had spent so much time and money on – which at the beginning of Naxos were considered unnecessary for a budget label! – would be very welcome. So we not only digitised the recordings, but the notes and the covers as well. I wanted to ensure that anyone who accessed our recordings online would get the same as those who bought the CDs. I wanted to make the subscription worthwhile.

So the academic world was our first target: they would save considerable sums in not having to buy CDs that went missing or were broken. Then there would be individual subscribers; and professional subscribers, such as people in the classical music business who needed quick and accurate access to classical information of this kind. I also wondered about upmarket hotels and other public places, for them either to stream music centrally or offer a wide choice of music to guests in their own rooms.

Turning this conception into reality was a huge task and involved huge amounts of investment. Most of the senior executives within Naxos thought that Heymann had been bitten by a digital bug – and they were right! The distributors could all see that their business was based on CD sales, and either they couldn't envisage how to make money from this digital pathway or they couldn't be bothered. Scepticism predominated. Heymann used all his persuasive powers to explain that this was the future, and that if they wanted to be alive and kicking after the first decade of the twenty-first century they had to change and invest in new areas. He was proved absolutely right, but it was an uphill battle for him. At every MIDEM meeting from 2002 he would organise seminars for his distributors on selling digital music. It was slightly easier with his own Naxos-owned distribution companies (although even there he struggled to engender change); but most others were either reluctant to shift or did not even understand the concept.

What was curious to note was that most of them were far younger than Heymann, who was, at that time, approaching seventy.

I explained that it was necessary to set up new departments to sell the Naxos Music Library and the concept of digital delivery to these new markets. They had to think outside the box if they wanted to be around in the future. And of course, I needed them to succeed because otherwise the NML would fail. There was progress in the US, then in the UK, and, slowly, the awareness grew.

It was a particularly tough call for the independent distributors in the smaller markets – often classical enthusiasts who were very traditional in their approach to selling classical music. Their companies did not have the infrastructure to allow them easily to expand.

At the same time, Heymann was trying to persuade other labels to come on board. Naxos was, by 2002, a large collection but it was by no means comprehensive, and to attract subscribers he needed many more labels.

I wanted to bring in all the classical labels so that subscribers would have not only one performance of a work but many, and could compare. I wanted to provide all the information about each work – its playing length, the orchestration, the background history, the performers, everything – so that the service would become an incredibly useful asset for everyone interested in classical music. And ultimately my ambition was to have in the library at least one recording of every work ever recorded.

Bringing other labels on board was not easy. Few could understand the concept: why was it necessary? Heymann would forget that he was in the vanguard – that his vision of instant access to all classical music was a puzzling or threatening concept for many. There was also a residual suspicion of Naxos. This new idea meant that a label would have to give its entire catalogue – its family jewels – to Naxos for uploading to a network that could be accessed by everyone in the world! Would people just copy and pirate the recordings? Internet piracy was already a hot topic. Would Heymann exploit the material? Did he have horns? Meanwhile, Heymann himself had no idea whether the library would be a commercial success or how much money the labels would make from the service.

The first label to join the Naxos Music Library was the Swedish classical label BIS, run by Robert von Bahr. He had been one of the first to give distribution to Naxos in various territories, including the UK and Scandinavia, and he paved the way for others on the NML. His experience with Naxos had allowed him to trust the company.

While Heymann was getting other labels to join he was also adding new features to the service; his IT department was now led by former warehouse manager Mr S.K. Wong.

We had been constantly upgrading from the start of our Internet platform, but that is the nature of a venture like this. At the beginning of naxos.com, when it was actually hnh.com, we delivered music at 20 kbps (the sound was acceptable then, but it's not now!) using RealPlayer, which was the standard at the time. That was 1996. Then Windows Media became the standard. When the NML came along we offered our recordings at 20, 64 and 128 kbps, allowing users to access the service according to the bandwidth available to them: many places were still limited to dial-up speed. All this required a considerable amount of back-room activity and an even greater investment in hardware: offering all the content in three different formats meant storing it in these formats as well. But this had an unexpected bonus. A year after the launch of the NML, iTunes started [in 2003], and we could immediately offer them our whole catalogue – digitised with all the metadata in place. We were the first classical label to have its whole catalogue on iTunes, and even today I think they still have a soft spot for us.

Turning Naxos into a digital service provider was not as easy as it sounds. There were innumerable problems with servers, files and data, and the Internet was not as stable as it is today.

At times it was a major headache. There are many good reasons for not being ahead of the game, especially when it comes to technology. You make all the mistakes that those following can learn from. And the consumers were on a big learning curve themselves. Customer service was very busy. But it did put us in the forefront of the classical digital medium. Of course, there were competitors – things were moving very quickly. There was something called classical.com, which was UK-based and had actually started before naxos.com. Initially it was a battle for the US market, but they were not very strong outside the US and did not have the same focus as we had. We could also keep investing in our service because we had a strong physical business, and until 2003 the profit from Bose was subsidising Naxos. These days we don't really have a serious competitor for our subscription services.

More labels began to join, especially when it became clear that fears of the NML affecting CD sales were not being realised. There was a market trend towards digital sales, which was inevitable; but the death of the CD would take a lot longer than pundits were predicting. In the meantime the NML was an additional source of revenue for labels. Even Chandos, the independent UK label that had developed its own competent digital web presence, was happy to sign up.

The ambition was, and remains, to create a place where you can find every work ever recorded; and we are getting pretty close, with over 50,000 CDs and 750,000 tracks. I found it interesting that as late as 2010 not one 'major' label had signed up to the NML. They were on iTunes, eMusic and other digital platforms, but these classical majors would not come to the NML. Yet speak to any music student in any country and it is very likely that they have personal experience of it.

By 2005 Naxos had became a huge operation, beyond the scope of its headquarters in Kowloon, and it moved into new offices in Cyberport. This was, as its name suggests, a new development in Hong Kong that aimed to attract IT companies. All the buildings were wired for the twenty-first century and had a first-class technical infrastructure. Naxos, however, remained primarily a classical record company and a specialist Internet team was required to cope with the increasing number of technical changes being prompted by users' demands. In 2007 the company was joined by Riyaz Moorani, a Canadian who had sold his Internet hotel sales company and was looking for a new challenge. He was an expert in the use of the Internet as a selling tool, and he set up a new IT operation in Manila, where he was based; it eventually grew to sixty people, including musicologists, systems analysts, developers and web designers. It was an example of Heymann's international frame of reference that he could see the advantages in moving to Manila, where economy of pay transects with English as an official language. It could have been India, but the Philippines was closer to Hong Kong. The NML database was completely reconstructed, the interface was redesigned to make it more consumer-friendly, and many, many more elements were added.

Then in 2007 came classicsonline.com, a site with the specific purpose of selling downloads (rather than a subscription for streaming). It was given a generic name so that the general classical consumer would not think it offered only Naxos recordings: all the fifty or so independent labels that had so far joined the NML were included. These files were also free of DRM (digital rights management) as they were in the MP3 format without any kind of copyright protection. In this issue – which was highly controversial at the time – Heymann was once again a classical pioneer.

Around the turn of the millennium, as the download era began to grow rapidly, a philosophical and commercial divide opened between those labels who insisted on copy protection and those who felt it was no longer practical. The issue was initially brought into the main arena by various e-tailers such as iTunes and eMusic. Heymann was quite clear where Naxos, and recorded music as a whole, had to go.

The recording industry was trying to shut the stable door after the horse had bolted. When the CD first came on the market, the cost of building manufacturing plants was so enormous that everyone, including myself, thought that finally we will get rid of piracy. As a result nobody thought, or made a priority, of adding copy protection to the CD. Then CD factories became much cheaper and smaller, so that today you can get an automated production line into a relatively small room. Stick a disc in the front and a CD comes out the other side! The CD pirates found it was incredibly easy to make a perfect copy of perfect masters, and the legitimate industry realised that copy protection should have been included. When downloads came, the industry thought that now was the time to add it. But the consumer had become accustomed to doing with his CDs what he wanted, and he didn't accept that. Sites to share music across the Internet made piracy relatively easy.

My view from the very beginning was this: if people wanted to copy CDs they could copy CDs very easily, so what was the point of adding copy protection to downloads? We had to approach sales from a different point of view. Of course, I had certain advantages which enabled me to be quite bullish about this. First of all, I had the benefit of not being hampered by a corporate legal apparatus, by big star artists demanding copy protection because they had suffered from no copy protection on the CDs. Also, as Naxos was sold at budget price there was probably less incentive for people to download a file that was not of the same quality as the CD and then copy it indiscriminately. The CDs were so cheap that Naxos didn't attract the attention of pirates. It was certainly more challenging for pop music, with shorter playing length and therefore smaller files. By the time the industry introduced the DVD it had learned the lesson: DVDs came with copy protection from the very beginning, so people were used to it.

The first Naxos company to issue non-protected MP3 downloads was Naxos AudioBooks, through its dedicated website naxosaudiobooks.com in 2004. There was little evidence of piracy. By the time ClassicsOnline was underway, the battle over copy protection had largely been settled. The attention was now on pushing for growth in the digital arena.

ClassicsOnline was slow to take off, but now it is in the top five of sites selling classical music. It can only grow. And the NML is also on a satisfactory growth curve. It was tough in the beginning because universities and school libraries still had their CD libraries and couldn't always see the point. There was also the issue of librarians worried that they would lose their jobs. But now more and more libraries are switching to digital formats, so their patrons can access content from wherever they are. The province of Ontario bought the NML for every school library. Some provinces in Spain are buying it for all their schools. After all, which other library has a collection of over 50,000 CDs with 1,000 new ones added every month?

Heymann's ideal view of the worldwide market is one of international sales unhampered by trade barriers of any kind. The reality is not like that. Protectionism exists, even in the digital sphere. It was in the digital age that Heymann's ambitious investment in historical recordings paid off. Moiseiwitsch may not have sold well on CD but collectors and students across the world could now access his recordings online. In that sense, the historical series made a handsome contribution to the range of digital content on the NML. But even there, uniquely (and ironically) in the case of historical recordings, it is necessary to observe territorial rights. It was the arcane world of these recordings that embroiled Naxos in expensive and time-consuming court cases.

We had the first run-in concerning our historicals with The Metropolitan Opera, which sued us after we launched the 'Immortal Performances' series. When we announced our plans on our website we immediately got a letter from The Met, saying, 'Don't release it in the US.' It was quite clear that Jonathan Wearn, who created the series for us, had licensed it for the States – and had the specific licence. We decided not to release them in the US because I didn't want to get into a law suit there. I just wanted to go about my business. But people imported them anyway and then The Met sued us. In the end, that case was thrown out because we were sued in New York State and there weren't any sales there. And The Met never came back.

Before we launched Naxos Historical in the United States I went to the law firm that had represented us in the Met case for a legal opinion, to make sure there were no copyright issues. Our lawyers gave us the all-clear and we started releasing the series in the United States. But EMI, worried about what they saw as inroads into their heritage (pop as well as classical), sued, and we had a long, drawn-out court case. I came to know my lawyer's telephone number in New York off by heart, which is a bad sign. We won the first round; EMI appealed and the Court of Appeals sent the case back to the District Court. We eventually settled and the case was never decided.

EMI withdrew its case but I had to withdraw the product. I sued the lawyers, who had given me the bad opinion, for malpractice. I got some money back from them – not all of it, but a substantial proportion. Now we can sell our historical restorations in the rest of the world but not in the US. Because of free trade agreements with the US, Singapore and Australia extended copyright protection for sound recordings from fifty to seventy years. So there is now a gap: in Australia and Singapore anything after 1955 cannot be sold for another twenty years – some free trade!

Of course, as a holder of many copyright recordings myself, my own archive benefits handsomely from this ruling! But as a collector, which I am still at heart, it pains me to know that the majors have perhaps 200,000 titles in their archives and only about 10 per cent of these are available in physical or digital form. It pains me that the majors buy catalogues which then disappear. But I also have to be realistic and understand that if they made available everything that they have recorded it would completely destroy the market for new recordings.

I always say there are about one million classical collectors in the world who buy ten CDs a year. That is how I define a serious collector. There are about 100,000 titles available, physically or digitally, so it means that every title sells on average 100 times: 100 copies per title per year. So what happens if 200,000 titles become available: will the collectors buy twenty CDs? No, they will still buy ten. This means that average sales will drop to fifty – and that doesn't work commercially.

That is the conundrum for the whole industry. An enormous number of recordings are sitting in archives and could be accessed now (and, increasingly, they are). The BBC, the Norddeutsche Rundfunk, the Süddeutsche Rundfunk, Swedish Radio and all the other national broadcasters in Europe – they all have huge archives and keep producing hundreds of new recordings every year. Then there are the major record companies with their archives of more than 200,000 album-length masters. If all that stuff ever becomes available, who will buy it?

So deletion is a process that the industry has to undergo. What does distress me is that so often the choices made of what to release and what to delete are indiscriminate. They are decided by people who really don't know what is important. Key recordings are allowed to go out of the catalogue. In the end, crazy as it sounds, it is part of nature. People have to die and a new generation comes up – and the people who collect these recordings are dying out.

For the classical recording world, the second decade of the twenty-first century is very different from the start of the CD era. Naxos itself has changed dramatically, maturing into the world's leading collector's label, issuing more recordings per month than any other. When he began, Heymann was quoted as saying he would only have one recording of each main work on the label, that he would not endlessly re-record the masterpieces. Standards rose, however, and he saw that better recordings needed to be made. Vasily Petrenko's cycle of Shostakovich symphonies with the Royal Liverpool Philharmonic Orchestra and Marin Alsop's Brahms symphonies with the London Philharmonic Orchestra are examples of this. They stand scrutiny with the very best. Similarly, Naxos is issuing more specialist works for the collector that are either premiere recordings or important new recordings of forgotten works. On both counts it would be justifiable to turn Naxos into a full-price label; but it will not happen.

I went down the budget route because I could not sell the artists I had at full price. Now, we are reluctant to abandon the budget price even though 90 per cent of the things we do would qualify for full-price treatment. But we have our place at a certain price-point and I don't think the Naxos buyer would accept such a change. I feel it with some reluctance because it gets tougher to keep the price down; and I feel increasing annoyance when I look at the full-price labels and see that we are doing things which are certainly equal and in many cases better. After all, quite a few artists who now regularly record for us have come from major labels. But we do not have a choice.

If Naxos has been consistent in maintaining a budget price to its consumers, it has also been consistent in its relationship with its artists, even the 'big-name' artists. The equal-fee basis remains the same, as does the contractual basis. No artists can record for another label within one year of the final recording session, nor can they start a recording for Naxos within one year of finishing a session for another label. Heymann also makes it clear that if a Naxos artist does record for someone else, without asking for clearance, he or she will not be welcomed back to the label. This does not apply to chamber music, and there are exceptions (a conductor asked by a soloist to conduct a concerto, for example).

We can really say that we do promote our artists well with our websites and our distribution. Now, being a Naxos artist is very prestigious. Ten years ago it was not. People are now identified with Naxos and Naxos is identified with them. Artists do ask to be allowed to record for other labels, and this is considered on a case-by-case basis. For example, I am not so concerned about a conductor recording a concerto disc for another label – especially if it is a label which we distribute. But on the whole, I don't want Naxos artists appearing on other competing labels. If they choose to go, that is fine; it is their decision. But they can't come back.

In the early years, Naxos's unconventional approach became a target for criticism from the establishment; now, it still finds itself occasionally a target, but perhaps because it has been so successful.

In 2007 the English publisher Penguin launched a new book by the controversial English classical music journalist Norman Lebrecht called *Maestros, Masterpieces and Madness: The Secret Life and Shameful Death of the Classical Record Industry.* Although the Naxos section was not long – just five pages – it was littered with factual errors, showing the company and Klaus Heymann in a poor light and accusing Heymann of serious business malpractices. Heymann sued Lebrecht and Penguin in London's High Court of Justice, pointing out fifteen statements that he claimed were inaccurate. The case concluded with Penguin publicly apologising, paying an undisclosed sum towards legal costs as well as damages, and agreeing to pull all unsold books off the shelves of bookshops in the UK. Penguin later reissued the book in the UK in 2008 without the offending passages.

Heymann's own view of Naxos is changing. It started as a budget label offering the core classics and then became a repertoire label. The company also expanded into a worldwide distribution network offering classical music in all its forms, at all price levels. As the second decade of the twenty-first century progresses, Heymann is moving towards a different vision: Naxos as a service provider for classical recording. Naxos now has a wider purpose, which is to enable recordings to happen, whether through the Naxos label or an artist's own label. Heymann feels that the Naxos distributors worldwide can advise on the whole gamut of the industry: contracts, production, distribution, press and marketing, even label management. The company, he declares, has the experience in all these fields.

Things are moving so fast that this book itself, perforce, offers an historical perspective on the company. The fact that it all stems from classical music may suggest that Naxos is really about music of the past; but from Klaus Heymann's point of view, nothing could be further from the truth.

Nine

The Artists: Soloists and Chamber Musicians

Traditionally the soloists, along with the conductors, play a crucial role – arguably the most crucial role of all – in any standard classical CD catalogue. They are the stars who reinterpret music that has been played for generations. It is their talent or their personalities, or both, which persuade the buyer to invest in that recording and affirm the label owner's choice in selecting them to play that repertoire. The received wisdom is that the best soloists have something new to say about a Chopin piano concerto, or breathe fresh spirit into Beethoven or Rachmaninov, or effortlessly make Tchaikovsky's Violin Concerto more thrilling than ever before. This, however, was not the *raison d'être* of Naxos, at least not in the early days. Klaus Heymann famously said, on many occasions, that he would record the great works of classical music only once, that he would not have multiple versions of Mozart or Beethoven in the Naxos catalogue. When he started the label his basic purpose was to provide good performances of the classics. Naxos was a repertoire label. On the CD covers, the composers – not the performers – were headline news. Photographs of the performers were not on the covers; they were not even on the back.

His first challenge was to find outstanding musicians who could produce quality recordings. He knew that there were many soloists giving concerts whose performances matched those of artists taken up by the majors, but who, for one reason or another, were without a record company. Heymann was convinced that they would jump at the chance to perform the greatest works of classical music in the studio, just as they did, week after week, in concerts. They would be paid for the recording but receive no royalties; there would be a short biography and photo inside but not outside; they would record when he stipulated and with whom. This was so contrary to the accepted practice of the time, when soloists were fêted, that the musicians themselves had to make a leap of faith.

The remarkable thing is that all this came together very quickly. Heymann discovered that there were many musicians out there who were indeed outstanding players, who matched the highly promoted stars of the major labels in technique and musicianship, yet did not have starry egos or expectations that were artificially raised. How he found these excellent musicians, one after another, was a combination of circumstance, shrewd choice and a bit of luck.

Marco Polo had given him the experience of working with production teams as well as links with orchestras in Eastern Europe. It was 'The Label of Discovery', and as such was not expected, either by critics or collectors, to feature star artists on the recordings. Heymann had also been involved in concert promotion in Hong Kong, where good soloists came to perform – one of them being his future wife. So when the opportunity of Naxos arose he already knew musicians and he also knew people to ask for recommendations. Yet even now he smiles to himself when he thinks of his luck in finding certain musicians who laid the foundations of Naxos. He had asked Hungaroton early on to recommend a pianist for the popular Beethoven sonatas, and he was sitting at home in Hong Kong with his wife, Takako Nishizaki, when the listening DAT arrived. He put it on the machine and they were both astounded by the playing. Here was a real performance, full of character and purpose. It was Jenő Jandó.

Heymann came to rely on Jandó for a vast amount of central repertoire, from Mozart to Bartók. Few label owners would have assigned so much music to one pianist but Heymann has never regretted it. It was less surprising that all the main violin concertos and a lot of chamber music featured Nishizaki; but, as he had felt with Jandó, Heymann knew that here was a fine musician with a sound technique who came fully prepared to every recording – and could really perform when the red light came on. The cellist Maria Kliegel proved much the same kind of musician; she joined the Naxos family, fulfilling the role of solo cellist. The roster of Naxos house artists grew, but on a basis of mutual loyalty. It was a two-way contract. Unexpectedly perhaps, the resulting consistency became a positive factor for sales and marketing. Consumers, both classical collectors and new Naxos devotees, found that they could trust these names and did not seem to want variety for variety's sake.

After the first few years, during which Heymann had relied on just a few house artists to record most of the basic standard repertoire, the policy changed. More and more artists and orchestras were interested in recording for the label. Heymann decided the repertoire and then selected the artists most suitable for it, an approach most unlike that of the established companies, which signed artists first and then chose repertoire for the artists to record. As Naxos started to record more international repertoire he also decided that, where possible, recordings should have a national component. English repertoire was recorded with English artists and orchestras, or at least with an English conductor; French repertoire was similarly treated; and when it came to lieder and chansons, Heymann insisted on native German or Austrian singers for lieder and French singers for chansons.

There came a time (surprisingly early) when Heymann found he could no longer maintain his stance of having only one recording of each work. There were a variety of reasons for this. Sometimes it was clear that the earlier recordings could be bettered for musical or technical reasons; sometimes there was a good marketing reason – perhaps an opportunity for a different coupling; and sometimes along came a young musician who was just so stunning that it would have been self-defeating to reject the opportunity. As Naxos matured, new recordings of works already in the catalogue became more frequent. Heymann was pressured by his distribution companies around the world to repeat popular pieces. A collector himself, he always wanted to bring new repertoire to Naxos rather than new performances; but his sales teams told him that they couldn't sell a CD of an obscure composer, even if it was a world-premiere recording, the way they could sell Mendelssohn's Violin Concerto. He knows that no new recording of *The Four Seasons* will ever sell as many as did Nishizaki's recording, but even Naxos has to ring the changes. There is now a new generation of performers on Naxos who are undeniably exciting, who do offer something fresh. What is heartening is that they themselves often want to do more than the core repertoire: playing Ferdinand Ries is a discovery for a youthful talent like Christopher Hinterhuber; Tianwa Yang actually asked to record the complete chamber music for violin and piano by Wolfgang Rihm.

This shift in perspective coincided with a change in the commercial background to recording. Before the turn of the century, both classical and pop musicians looked to recording as an extra source of revenue. But as the Internet spread, with its creation of both opportunities and problems, recordings began to be seen as marketing tools rather than income streams. Of course for the megastars recordings remain lucrative. For the vast majority of performers, however, a recording is more a calling card, a personal connection with the audience or fan base. On this basis a growing number of musicians, even with fairly established names, have been prepared to record for very little to ensure that their work is available outside the concert hall. As digital delivery has grown, this continues to be true – in a way even more so. Now, with streaming and downloads, especially on the mature platforms offered by Naxos, musicians can really market themselves across the world.

Concomitantly Naxos has developed its criteria for the selection of artists. It is no longer sufficient only to play well when the red light comes on. Naxos looks for talent, personality and an active concert career so that recordings are just one thread of the performing life.

What has it been like for these soloists to be Naxos artists? How did they come to join Naxos? How do they view the recording studio? There are hundreds of performers on Naxos, and the list grows. Here they are represented by a few, of differing age and background – musicians from different parts of Europe and the Far East who now live and play all over the world. It is a truly international selection, which reflects Naxos itself.

Takako Nishizaki – Violin

If any musician embodies the truly international provenance of Naxos and Marco Polo it is the Japanese-born Takako Nishizaki. The first pupil of Shinichi Suzuki, founder of the Suzuki Method, she went on to study at the leading American music school, Juilliard, principally with Joseph Fuchs. In 1964 she was one of four finalists in the Leventritt Competition (Itzhak Perlman won first prize that year) and in 1969 she won first prize in the Juilliard Concerto Competition, performing Mozart's *Sinfonia concertante* with Nobuko Imai. After exhausting coast-to-coast tours of the USA she decided to return to Japan: it was a decision that led to a concert in Hong

Kong in 1974, meeting and marrying Klaus Heymannn, and an unmatched recording career spanning more than thirty years. This remarkable union produced well over 100 recordings, a number rarely, if ever, matched by a classical violinist; certainly the breadth of music remains unchallenged.

Nishizaki may be best known in the West for having recorded much of the mainstream repertoire: all the principal concertos and sonatas for Naxos, many selling in their hundreds of thousands (her recording of *The Four Seasons* is the eighth bestselling classical CD of all time). She has also recorded numerous forgotten works for Marco Polo, ranging from concertos by Rubinstein to the complete Fritz Kreisler Edition in ten volumes (while at Juilliard she was awarded the Fritz Kreisler scholarship). But uniquely she is equally well known in China, where her recordings of the Chinese modern classic violin concerto *The Butterfly Lovers* have outsold all Chinese versions (more than three million copies have been bought in the Far East alone). She has performed the work countless times in most of the major Chinese cities in front of audiences numbering many thousands. It has been suggested that her performances and profile in China have contributed to the improved relations between Japan and China in the last quarter of the twentieth century, after decades of tension.

Nishizaki's recording achievement is exceptional in any terms. Had she known beforehand the number and variety of works that she would go on to record between the late 1970s and the first decade of the twenty-first century, possibly even she would have paled before the task. Yet her recordings reveal total commitment, whether she is playing Tchaikovsky's Concerto and Mozart's sonatas, bringing fresh attention to the concertos of Saint-Georges, or performing arrangements of traditional Chinese and Thai music.

Her success was made possible only by the confluence of a number of key factors: a supportive and musical family; a sound and virtuosic technique underpinned by a natural gift;

a commitment to diligent preparation at all times; and, it must be said, a courageous and marathon-like ability to put up with the constant pressure of concerts, recordings, new works, travel and daily practice. It was surely stimulating to be married to a man of continuous energy and ambition who was always producing ideas for new recordings; but as a performer living on an artistic tightrope she must have felt under pressure to meet these demands.

It helped being Japanese, a nationality that respects discipline and hard work. Born in Nagoya, Takako Nishizaki was taught, from the age of three and a half, by her father Shinji, who worked with Shinichi Suzuki in developing the Suzuki Method; and she acknowledges as a key support her pianist mother Masako, who worked with her three times a day when she was a child and who sometimes fanned her when she had to practise on hot days. Nishizaki's natural facility and relaxed posture was allowed to develop as she was taught initially by ear, only learning to read music when she was relatively advanced (aged six). She later studied with Broadus Erle (leader of the Japan Philharmonic Orchestra at the time; he subsequently became a violin professor at Yale) and, after he left Japan, with Hideo Saito at the Toho School of Music.

Her success at Juilliard, as well as an appearance on the American television programme *The Bell Telephone Hour*, ensured that she was inundated with concert offers, which at one point topped 100 concerts in a season. However, this unremitting schedule of concerts and travel was not the life she wanted and she returned to Japan to build a concert life there. This was just getting underway when she met Klaus Heymann. 'At that time, I had no intention of having a boyfriend or getting married because I was going to have my own TV programme in Nagoya. The concept was for me to travel the world, visit all the important music cities, introduce musicians and orchestras in the cities, recommend restaurants and museums, and so on. I had also just started my own chamber orchestra in Nagoya and my father had built a new music room for me on our property. And I wanted to help my father teach his many students.'

She had already made recordings by this time (Grieg's violin sonatas and Kreisler pieces for RCA, and Schubert and Franck for Balkanton) and had not been particularly drawn to the recording process. 'In the beginning I didn't like recordings because I was used to playing concerts. In a way, it was too easy to fix mistakes and the performances were not really all that natural. But eventually I got to enjoy recording and became very good at it. I understood that recording music had special requirements, different from the total spontaneity of a concert. For example, if it was necessary to do a retake, I had to do it in exactly the same tempo as before so that it could be edited in – though of course we always strive for long takes, and even whole movements!'

In 1979 her career took a new turn with the recording of Chen and He's *The Butterfly Lovers* for solo violin and orchestra, one of the most popular modern Chinese works. It was a move that brought together various strands in her husband's business enterprises and their Hong Kong life, and it launched her popularity in China. To house the recording Klaus Heymann created a new label, called simply 'HK', and in so doing he started a highly successful Chinese music series. Some thirty-five years later she was still playing this work in the public eye of the largest nation on earth: she performed *The Butterfly Lovers* at a televised concert in the Great Hall of the People, Beijing in 2009 that was broadcast to millions. These kinds of concert demands from the Far East generally and China in particular have certainly affected the number of concerts she has given in the West during the course of her career. She had returned to Japan from the USA because she was reluctant to spend her life alone in airports, and, even when her name became well known in Europe and the USA from the Naxos recordings, she chose to restrict her travelling for the sake of her family and Asian commitments.

Her first recording for Marco Polo, in 1984, was Respighi's *Concerto gregoriano* and *Poema autunnale* with the Singapore Symphony Orchestra. 'I had to learn the concerto specially for the recording but later I played it in concert quite often.' It was the start of a series of forgotten violin concertos for this new label of Heymann's, which was designed to present premiere recordings of Romantic and late Romantic repertoire. By definition these were obscure works, all of which she had to learn from scratch for the sessions.

'I liked the Rubinstein Concerto a lot and played it in concert quite a few times after the first recording. The same goes for Spohr's Concerto No. 7, which I later played at the Musikverein in Vienna. And the Respighi is a great piece, except for the ending where the composer tried to out-Paganini Paganini. It still amazes me why pieces like the Respighi, Joachim's Third Concerto and the Rubinstein are not performed more often. Both the Joachim and the Rubinstein have gorgeous slow movements, but my recordings are still the only ones available today.' Nishizaki has continued to champion forgotten works for Naxos, recording concertos by Saint-Georges, Vanhal and Kraus.

Respighi's Concerto was recorded in Singapore, but increasingly during the 1980s Nishizaki found herself in Europe – often in Bratislava, recording Tchaikovsky, Mendelssohn, Brahms or Bruch with the Slovak Philharmonic Orchestra. This enabled her, on occasion, to use the time in Europe to give concerts. Of course she knew most of the major works and had played them in the US or the Far East. Now she had the enjoyable experience of playing them with a good European orchestra (although the Slovak Philharmonic Orchestra was not particularly well known, its qualities were acknowledged by conductors such as Michael Halász). She remembers the sessions in Bratislava with affection ... most of the time. 'Generally they went very well. I was well prepared and there was normally enough time to work on details. Sometimes I had to push the producers to get the balance between the violin and the orchestra right but there were no major disagreements with the conductors about style and we always worked out any differences beforehand.' Using a piano, Nishizaki and the conductor would go through the work before the recording session to settle their approach and tempi.

More troublesome was what happened outside the hall! 'Occasionally, some of the external circumstances were challenging. The concert hall of the Slovak Philharmonic where I recorded most of the standard concertos was not soundproof and the sessions were frequently interrupted by the tram that passed in front of the hall and sometimes by bands playing on the riverboats on the nearby Danube. Very frustrating!'

There was also the issue of travel during the communist era, which Nishizaki remembers only too clearly. 'Conditions were tough. Klaus and I travelled on the very cheapest airlines, and hotels at the time in Bratislava were very basic. Sometimes we had to wait at the border between Austria and Slovakia for two hours or more. Often I had to start recording the following day.'

In addition to this, she was a mother. Her son, Rick, was six when Marco Polo started and approaching twelve when Naxos first made its impact. So Nishizaki had to balance the roles of musician and mother, which was particularly difficult when so much travel was involved.

These were far from ideal conditions, but even now she is happy with these early recordings, if not with every detail. She acknowledges that she is less comfortable in the Baroque period, which is why, despite the *Four Seasons* recording being her single bestseller of Western repertoire, it is the central Classical and Romantic concertos (Mozart, Beethoven, Mendelssohn, Tchaikovsky *et al.*) that are her touchstones. 'I was quite lucky to have had Kenneth Jean and Stephen Gunzenhauser conducting for the most important concertos. Those sessions always went smoothly. Of course, I would have liked to record some of the concertos again, not because there was anything wrong with the original recordings but because I would have liked to do some of the concertos differently and over the years I had learned more about the recording process and how to get the best possible results.'

Chamber music has always been a part of her performing career, especially when she was at Juilliard, and the opportunity to record many of the works that were central to her musical life was one she particularly appreciated. She chose her chamber music partners carefully and developed a particular rapport with the pianist Jenő Jandó. 'He's a wonderful musician and we had an easy understanding. When we prepared for the sessions there were very few discussions. We easily agreed on the style of the pieces and only had to work on a few details and on ensemble.'

The Beethoven and Mozart violin sonata cycles were all recorded in Budapest. 'I knew the Mozart concertos (except Nos. 1 and 2 which very few artists get to play in concert) but I had to learn a few of the Mozart and Beethoven sonatas specially for the recordings.' The persuasive requests by her husband for complete cycles did ensure that she always had music new to her on her stand at home. Her partners for much of the ten-volume Kreisler Edition (originally recorded in the late 1970s for Telefunken and Camerata and released on LP before being collected together and reissued on Marco Polo) were Wolf Harden and Michael Ponti.

Behind her rapidly expanding recording career were a few changes of instruments. During her student life and early concert career she played on an early eighteenth-century Italian instrument by Lorenzo Ventapane, bought for her by her father. By the time she started recording the major concertos for Naxos she had chosen a Guarneri. It was sold to her by a wealthy Japanese doctor who had bought it from a Japanese violin dealer. It had an exceptional sound but turned out to be a fake (noticed by a visiting German violin expert). Fortunately the violin dealer replaced it with a genuine Stradivari which she subsequently sold, buying an early Guarneri del Gesù. This she later traded for the 1732 Guarneri she has now: appropriately it was an instrument owned by Fritz Kreisler (and, before him, by Tivadar Nachéz). However, she explains that most of the time she plays on a copy of this instrument made for her by Joseph Curtin, one of the finest American instrument makers. This is particularly the case if she is playing in a televised concert where the sound will be amplified anyway and the lights are hot.

Recording violin music may have been Nishizaki's public contribution to the growth of Naxos and Marco Polo, but she played an equally influential role behind the scenes. Living with a husband totally absorbed in business and music meant that work rarely stopped. Not being a trained musician, Heymann has always relied on his wife for musical advice and comment. On most evenings, after supper at home in Hong Kong or New Zealand, they would settle down to listen to the latest batch of first edits or masters (originally on DATs; later on CDs) sent from recording centres around the world for approval. 'For the first ten years I listened to all the most important recordings. By and large, there were no serious problems but I sometimes insisted on ensemble and intonation being corrected. Only in very rare cases did I have to tell Klaus that we should not release a recording because it was not of an acceptable standard.'

Even in those early days, the number of works and the variety was extraordinary. An evening's listen could involve a symphony by Ludwig Spohr, Schubert piano trios, Palestrina, Szymanowski, a piano sonata by Mozart, or Suppé overtures. With hundreds of recordings being produced by the efficient Naxos and Marco Polo machines, there was simply no end to the listening tasks; and Heymann relied on his wife's acute ears and critical musical taste.

This was nothing new to Nishizaki because she had always

listened to the first edits of her own recordings and approved the final edit. It was a crucial part of raising the musical standards for Naxos and Marco Polo and was another indication of the extent to which both Heymann and Nishizaki were 'hands-on'. They cared about the recordings going out, regardless of whether they were full-price Marco Polo or budget-price Naxos. They had to accept compromises, but the lessons learned in their drawing room, in front of their hi-fi (and with Heymann's background in professional sound equipment, this was top of the range), had a direct effect on the quality and the process of future recordings – and on which musicians made them. He often says that his wife provided the ears for Naxos. At his request she has also listened to recordings of musicians who hope to make CDs for Naxos. 'Klaus gets me to listen to every new artist and orchestra and I probably have the final say in who gets recorded. Klaus trusts my judgement. I am impressed by what I hear these days. Technically the standards are very high, so I always listen for musicality, a beautiful tone, a wide range of dynamics and expressive playing.'

Nishizaki's life has taken a different route in the last few years. She still makes recordings, though rarely: concertos by Saint-Georges, Vanhal and Kraus are among her most recent. She has also enjoyed recording Peter Breiner's arrangements, including operatic potpourris and popular collections such as *Russian Romance*, *Chinese Pop Evergreens* and *Tchaikovsky: None but the Lonely Heart*.

She now gives only about ten concerts per year, 'though I could probably play *The Butterfly Lovers* somewhere in China every week!' When she performs *The Butterfly Lovers* in a bright concert dress to an audience of thousands in a major Chinese city, Takako Nishizaki is every inch the international virtuoso. In Hong Kong she is very much the leading musical celebrity, a recognised figure among not only classical audiences but also a wider public. Her popularity has given her a place in Hong Kong society, and when the couple attend functions Klaus

Heymann is sometimes introduced as the husband of Takako Nishizaki. In the rest of the world she performs with grace the role of Mrs Heymann, violinist wife of a leading classical music entrepreneur.

She still practises daily, even though she gives few concerts. 'I don't feel good if I don't practise every day.' But she has turned her principal attention to teaching, having formed the Takako Nishizaki Violin Studio in 2005. If you phone the Heymann household in Hong Kong you can often hear in the background the sound of a violin lesson, and sometimes it is clearly a beginner. Nishizaki has adjudicated at leading international violin competitions, such as the Kreisler Competition in Vienna, and could take her pick of advanced students, but she prefers to work with children taking their first steps. 'A white sheet,' she calls it. Not surprisingly she works with the children and their mothers together: the Suzuki background is there, although she doesn't follow the Method slavishly. 'I use the best elements of the Suzuki Method and combine them with traditional teaching. I insist on a parent being involved from the beginning and I use the ten books of the Suzuki Violin School: it is still the most complete collection of well-graded study pieces, even though there's too much Baroque music and nothing after Mozart. But my students have to learn to read music virtually from day one and they also have to do exercises.'

Prompted by her interest in teaching, Nishizaki has recently recorded all the Suzuki pieces in seven volumes of *Suzuki Evergreens*. 'I really wanted to pass on to young people what I had learned from my father and from Mr Suzuki, and also what I have learned from teaching all these pieces myself for many years. I was also keen on adding the original versions of many arrangements so children realise that all of this is music and not just a collection of exercises which they have to complete.' The project brought together, once again, the mutual interests of this husband-and-wife team that is perhaps unique in music. It must have been a salutary experience for Takako

Nishizaki, after a life spent recording some of the greatest and most challenging music written for the violin, to pick up her Guarneri, watch for the red light, and play *Twinkle, Twinkle, Little Star*.

Jenő Jandó – Piano

For a man who is one of the most recorded classical musicians in history Jenő Jandó presents a surprisingly modest figure. Sitting in the green room of Budapest's Franz Liszt Academy of Music – where Bartók, Kodály, Dohnányi and many other great performers (including Jandó himself!) have warmed up before giving recitals in the Art Nouveau hall – it is difficult to match the man and his music-making. White hair, white beard, slight – a man perhaps more comfortable on a piano stool than a sofa.

It is difficult to prove, but there are probably more CDs available of Jandó than of any other single pianist. He may also hold the classical pianist's record for the sheer number of CD sales: many of his early recordings have sold in excess of 500,000 units. Naxos CDs on which Jandó features number a stupendous 400. About half of those are special compilations – *Chill with Mozart, Bach for Meditation, Night Music, Music to Die For* – but they should not be discounted (and he doesn't mind them). After all, they probably take him into more homes around the world than do the original recordings! They also demonstrate the extent to which Jandó's pianism is one of the central pillars of the core Naxos catalogue.

The most concise way of putting it is that Jandó has recorded for Naxos the major piano works of the Classical and Romantic periods – and much more. This does exaggerate a bit, since there are plenty of works which were not undertaken by him (Chopin's piano works or all Liszt, for example); but he did record all of Haydn's piano sonatas, most of Mozart's piano music (all the piano concertos and sonatas), all of

Beethoven's sonatas and all the piano music of Schubert. The big concertos entrusted to him by Klaus Heymann include those of Brahms, Grieg, Dvořák and Rachmaninov, not to mention all three of Bartók's (as well as all of Bartók's solo piano music and even Mussorgsky's *Pictures at an Exhibition*).

There is also all the chamber music of the same period. This includes Mozart's and Beethoven's violin sonatas with Takako Nishizaki (a Naxos partnership highly valued by both musicians) and other works recorded with the Hungarian colleagues and friends whom he gathered together (Schubert's 'Trout' Quintet, Beethoven's cello sonatas with Csaba Onczay, as well as Brahms's clarinet sonatas, his Trio and Quintet). Then, quite late in a career which is as long as Naxos is old, came Bach's Forty-Eight Preludes and Fugues. 'It was a marvellous task,' he declares. 'Incredible. You can find everything in *The Well-Tempered Clavier*. It is a jewellery box and all that is inside is beautiful.'

Jandó's discography is a remarkable testament to an exceptional talent. It would not appear such an achievement were Jandó more of a known personality in the classical world – an Alfred Brendel or an Evgeny Kissin. He isn't. His own story is more unusual in that a leading record company continued to give a pianist, relatively unknown in the major international concert halls, so many central piano works. In two and a half decades of recording, as he charged through the repertoire with often ten discs or more per year and maintained a busy concert career, he just did what came naturally.

He would set off in the morning to the Italian Institute in central Budapest, where many of the early recordings took place, to record some more sonatas by Haydn, or maybe a Mozart piano concerto. He would have a morning cup of coffee and a cigarette (one of many that day) and chat a little with Ibolya Tóth – producer, friend, and key Naxos figure in Hungary for many years. In the hall would be his own piano, a Steinway Model C, chosen because Jandó prefers what he calls 'its clearer bass' for recording. Then, between 10 a.m. and 2 p.m., or sometimes 4 p.m., he would record.

Even now, Jandó continues to follow a simple recording pattern. 'I always play the whole movement, and then do a few retakes. Sometimes I have to repeat because my throat is very loud when I am playing – it is an ugly sound, but less than Glen Gould!' On occasions, he has been persuaded to put an unlit cigarette in his mouth to prevent him from humming along too vigorously with the music. He does take scores to the recording but his considerable memory means that most of the time the music is laid to one side.

When he and his producer know they have covered all the details, he will often play it once more 'as if in concert'. It may be a day for delicacy of touch in a charming, effortlessly captivating Haydn sonata; or for bravura in Liszt's B minor Sonata – clarity partnered by fireworks; or for dexterity and composure in a four-part fugue by Bach. After decades Jandó is totally at ease in front of the microphone, and somehow he always manages to produce a sense of concert excitement.

His first recording for Naxos was the collection of three popular Beethoven sonatas: 'Pathétique', 'Moonlight' and 'Appassionata'. It was made at the Italian Institute in Budapest, 21–23 April 1987; it was the first year of Naxos, though the disc was actually released in March 1988. Heymann, having previously worked with the Hungarian national record label Hungaroton for other recordings, had asked for a recommendation of a good pianist who could potentially record all of Beethoven's sonatas. They suggested Jandó. So this first recording, though he was unaware of it, was effectively a trial disc.

When the DAT copy reached Hong Kong it sounded excellent, but it still took a leap of faith for Heymann to entrust all of Beethoven's piano sonatas to a man he had never met. It was not Jandó's first CD (he had recorded some of Liszt's transcriptions for Hungaroton) and he had won competitions; but he was already in his early thirties with a steady, not spectacular, playing career. He came from a generation of fine Hungarian pianists – András Schiff and Zoltán Kocsis had been at the Liszt Academy with him – but his concert life was mainly within Hungary and Eastern Europe. This one Beethoven disc changed his life. Heymann called him from Hong Kong and asked if he would like to do the cycle. The terms were clear if unusually straightforward for the time: payment by disc. He would like Jandó to record them as soon as possible but certainly within three years. Jandó had no doubts. About half of them were in his repertoire but he knew he was a quick learner. He completed them six months early.

Even now he remembers certain sessions: 'Especially Opus 110. I think it was my best. And I am also very proud of the D minor Sonata, the 'Tempest', because it is there, on disc, without any edits! I had learned this piece very carefully under the supervision of the composer Pál Kadosa at the Academy, and when I came to record it, I just played it. One take.'

A year into the Beethoven cycle, Jandó received another call. 'We were in the middle of this great and difficult project and Mr Heymann asked me to record all the Mozart concertos.' Jandó knew and played about ten of them so had to learn the rest. The main challenge for him was in making decisions about some of the cadenzas. 'Mozart didn't write cadenzas for all the concertos, especially not for the early ones. If they were available I used the Hummel cadenzas, but on occasions I decided to shorten them. Mozart had a shorter keyboard than Hummel, so I adjusted Hummel's range to make it suit the smaller piano that Mozart would have written for. I didn't want to play out of Mozart's style.'

He recorded the cycle with the chamber orchestra Concentus Hungaricus, which was full of his Hungarian musical friends, many of whom had been with him at the Liszt Academy. It was also this Mozart cycle that gave rise to his association with the producer Ibolya Tóth, who was also a fellow student at the Liszt Academy. The project took three years, but Tóth was with him as support and advisor throughout. In fact she has produced the vast majority of the discs that he has since recorded for Naxos, including the journeys through Haydn, Schubert and Bartók. Such an enduring link between musician and producer has unquestionably contributed to the substance of the Jandó discography. From 1995 Tóth's recording sessions were located in her purpose-built recording studio (Phoenix Studio) in Diósd on the outskirts of Budapest.

Although Jandó has recorded individual works from other eras, the truth is that he always felt particularly at home in the Viennese milieu, with cycles of music by a single composer. 'You change your view of a composer when you do so many of his pieces.' Mozart was followed by Schubert, and then it was back to Haydn. 'They are all connected to each other and it is interesting to experience the Classical world like that. Schubert is a different challenge. He is more difficult than Beethoven because his music is harder to grasp. Beethoven can take many different approaches but Schubert is more fragile. I think you can put more personal views into Beethoven, but with Schubert you have to be just Schubert. I only hope that my character is close to Schubert's character because I am Aquarius and Mozart and Schubert were both Aquarius.' He smiles with a hint of self-deprecation.

To chamber music he takes an intuitive approach. His rehearsals for the recordings of the Mozart and Beethoven violin sonatas with Nishizaki, he remembers, involved very little discussion. 'First you have to read the notes correctly and study the whole piece. If you are good musicians you don't need to talk. You have to be very sensitive and feel the approach of the other person, and you can hear if you feel it in the same way. That is the basis of chamber music. If you cannot find the vibration of the other, or the view is very different, you cannot play together.'

Recording for Naxos became a regular theme to his musical

life but he was also busy giving concerts. His recordings opened the door to more appearances outside Europe – in Japan, the US, Canada and Hong Kong. The effect was particularly felt in Japan, where concerts were always followed by CD signings. His stamina is legendary. He is known for being able to record in the morning and give a concert in the evening. On a few occasions he has stepped in to save a concert, playing the work from memory despite having recorded something completely different only hours earlier.

The years passed quickly, but there seemed to be no end to the requests from Naxos. It was Jandó's own wish to do the Haydn sonatas, but generally the impetus came from Heymann. Even now, Jandó is surprised at the way in which Naxos developed and the works that came in his direction: Liszt's B minor Sonata, Bach's *Goldberg Variations*, even Dohnányi (who may be viewed primarily as a Classicist, but his range is much wider). It was a risk for the label to rely so heavily on one pianist but it seems to have worked. Naxos's twenty-fifth anniversary falls in Jandó's sixtieth year. There are a few works he would still like to record, including those which would complete the Bartók cycle; but with an almost unrivalled discography he is certainly content with what he has done.

Idil Biret – Piano

In 1989 Klaus Heymann met the Turkish-born pianist Idil Biret in Brussels. It was two years into Naxos and he was looking for a musician to undertake a landmark in recording history: the first time that one pianist would put on disc the complete piano works by Chopin, both the solo works and the concertos. Biret's reputation as a remarkable performer – child prodigy, student of Wilhelm Kempff and Alfred Cortot – was already established, and reinforced by her existing recordings of Liszt's piano transcriptions of Beethoven's nine symphonies.

Curiously, despite having played a wide range of music, memorising most of Brahms's works before she was a teenager and recording a lot of contemporary repertoire (including Boulez's Sonata No. 2), she had played relatively little Chopin. 'I had listened to very bad and sentimental Chopin performances during my childhood. In some circles Chopin had become the synonym of teary, sentimental music. It was sad that a musician who composed, in Classical perfection, the least self-complacent works had become so misunderstood.' Studies with Kempff gave her a very different view of the composer, and this was underlined, strangely, by her love for the music of Scriabin. 'In my search for the origins of *his* inspiration, I found Chopin.' For Biret the Nocturnes and Mazurkas were no longer sentimental, slightly gloomy and moonstruck – a view which was then properly banished by further studies with Alfred Cortot.

Chopin began to feature in her recital programmes more frequently, and Heymann's appearance and offer happened at just the right time. Nevertheless it still came as a surprise, largely because it was accompanied by the request that the project be completed as soon as possible, ideally within two years. Biret's stamina and natural talent were legendary but she faced quite a task. Living in both Brussels and Istanbul, she immersed herself in Chopin, studying scores, listening to historic recordings and reading essays on Chopin interpretation. Between March 1990 and February 1992, in the Clara Wieck Auditorium, Heidelberg (then West Germany) and the House of Arts, Košice (Slovakia), she recorded the complete works. She started and finished with the studies, completing the cycle with *Trois Nouvelles Études*. The Naxos release schedule tried to keep pace, putting out individual CDs; eventually the complete cycle comprised fifteen CDs containing seventeen hours of Chopin, with notes for every work. The set won the Grand Prix du Disque Frédéric Chopin in 1995; and twelve years later the President of Poland, Lech Kaczyński, presented Idil Biret with

the Order of Merit of the Republic of Poland at the Polish
Embassy in Ankara during a state visit on 23 January 2007,
'for her outstanding efforts in spreading the music of Chopin
throughout the world with her recordings and performances of
the composer's works'.

In the middle of those two busy years of Chopin, Biret also
started recording complete cycles of Brahms and Rachmaninov
for Naxos. In fact the first Biret disc released on Naxos contained Piano Concertos Nos. 2 and 4 by Saint-Saëns with the
Philharmonia Orchestra conducted by James Loughran (a
recording she had originally intended for Vox). Then came
Chopin, Brahms and Rachmaninov.

Contemporary music had always been a strong part of
Biret's performance and recording life before Naxos; she had
recorded many works for Atlantic/Finnadar, including Boulez's
Piano Sonata No. 2. So when Yves Riesel, the Naxos label
manager in France, suggested that she record all three of
Boulez's piano sonatas for Naxos she was delighted. 'Klaus and
I had developed a good relationship, and I said this would be
very good for the label. But I knew it wasn't Klaus's kind of
music and he was very sceptical that it would sell, and at first
he was very reluctant to agree to it.' In the end, he did agree,
and in typical fashion he wanted it quickly. 'I knew the Second
Sonata but not the other two. This was now December 1994
and Klaus wanted me to record them in January and February
1995, at a studio in Radio France. It was a great challenge for
me. I had to work very intensively for a month, but when I
came to record them they seemed to go very well, with few
problems.' The sales figures surprised everyone and continue to
astonish Heymann: over 40,000 CDs have been sold worldwide to date.

Biret admires the works themselves. 'They are great works.
For me the Boulez piano sonatas are classics of the twentieth
century. They hold together, they are very logical, and they have
meaning. I think they are among the few works of that period

which will remain in the repertoire in the future. Actually, we were all very surprised how well they sold. It proves that people have curiosity. And when, six years later, I suggested to Klaus that I record Ligeti's Études (another work which, like Boulez's sonatas, stands on very solid ground), he agreed. I had played them in concert a lot.' Since their release in 2003, these have sold well over 20,000 CDs.

Biret throws a wide purview over music for the piano. She has also recorded Bach transcriptions – not by Busoni but by her teacher Wilhelm Kempff. 'They are wonderful. I prefer them to Busoni's. They are simpler and more in the spirit of this religious music.' The most recent recording that Idil Biret made for Naxos was Stravinsky's own (1910) piano transcription of *The Firebird*. 'I heard a piano roll of Stravinsky himself playing it. It was beautiful and I wanted to do it.' To date, her recordings on Naxos – the Chopin, Brahms and Rachmaninov cycles alone cover thirty-seven CDs – have sold in excess of two million discs.

Her enterprise has now taken her in a new direction. She has always wanted to record the Beethoven sonata cycle, as well as many other works, including more Liszt transcriptions (*Harold in Italy* for viola and piano, as well as *Symphonie fantastique* for piano). To this end, with her husband Şefik Yüksel, she has founded the Idil Biret Archive. She is bringing as many of her earlier, pre-Naxos recordings as possible into this collection (including Liszt's transcriptions of Beethoven's symphonies) and adding new titles by the dozen. Naxos could not accommodate all the music that she still wants to record but Heymann did offer her the umbrella of the Naxos worldwide network; so the IBA, distributed by Naxos, now appears as an independent label with Naxos catalogue numbers. It is an ideal compromise for both.

Biret divides her time between her homes in Brussels, Paris and Istanbul. She has an 1889 Pleyel grand piano in Brussels and a 1960 Steinway and 1916 Schröder in Istanbul, but she also prepares for her recordings and concerts at night on electronic and even silent keyboards. She is now in her seventh decade and her energy in performance appears undimmed. During Chopin's 200th anniversary year, 2010, she gave many Chopin recitals; and when a leading Polish newspaper published a fifteen-volume partwork on the composer's life and work, it was Idil Biret's Chopin recordings that were chosen to accompany it: a rather particular endorsement.

Maria Kliegel – Cello

It was quite a recording coup that put the German-born cellist Maria Kliegel in touch with Klaus Heymann: the world-premiere recording of Alfred Schnittke's Cello Concerto. The work had been written for and premiered by Natalia Gutman, and she was given a two-year window to make the first recording. But plans went awry, the time expired, and by that point Maria Kliegel had already learned it and begun to play it in concert. Heymann had heard about this and asked her to record it for Marco Polo. Something of a race developed between the two planned recordings, and each one had its problems. The composer himself had been to the Gutman recording sessions but a second work to go on the disc had yet to be finished. Meanwhile, shortly before the start of the Marco Polo sessions with Kliegel and the Saarbrucken Radio Symphony Orchestra, the conductor suddenly dropped out. Kliegel persuaded the orchestra to accept Gerhard Markson, who had conducted her first concert performance of the work, and the Marco Polo CD came out in 1991 as a world premiere. It was highly praised by the composer (he called it the 'definitive' performance).

This was a pivotal moment for Maria Kliegel, the first step in a long association with Marco Polo and then Naxos. Her recording career has played a central role in her performing life. She was born in Hesse and studied with János Starker and Mstislav

Klaus Heymann coaching on the centre court, Frankfurt Stadium, 1958

Klaus Heymann wearing a pilot's summer uniform in a cigarette commercial, 1960s

Klaus Heymann in his Bose office in Hong Kong in the late 1970s

In 1999, Klaus Heymann was awarded the Das Österreichische Ehrenkreuz für Wissenschaft und Kunst, in recognition of the Johann Strauss II project.

The Heymann family: Klaus, Takako and Rick

Takako Nishizaki and Klaus Heymann in the late 1990s

Klaus Heymann in the computer room at Naxos HQ in Hong Kong

Klaus Heymann in a rare relaxed moment at Naxos HQ in Hong Kong

Klaus Heymann in the Naxos archive in Hong Kong

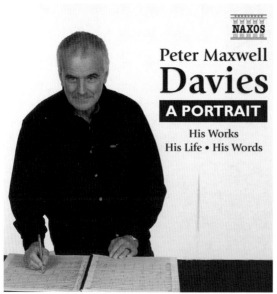

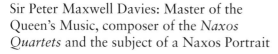

Sir Peter Maxwell Davies: Master of the Queen's Music, composer of the *Naxos Quartets* and the subject of a Naxos Portrait

Idil Biret, the Turkish pianist whose Naxos recordings include cycles of Chopin and Brahms, as well as the Boulez sonatas

The recording of William Bolcom's three-hour work *Songs of Innocence and of Experience* won Naxos's first two classical GRAMMYs.

(Photo credit: Katryn Conlin)

Austrian-born pianist Christopher Hinterhuber brought the forgotten piano concertos of Ferdinand Ries to worldwide attention.

(Photo credit: Nancy Horowitz)

The pianist Ashley Wass, whose Naxos recordings vary from English music to Liszt

Though based in the US, Ilya Kaler comes from the Russian school, his musicality allied to a virtuoso technique.

Flamboyant cello playing from Maria Kliegel

The Maggini Quartet
with producer
Andrew Walton
(centre)

The Kodály Quartet,
which has recorded much
of the central Classical
repertoire for Naxos

Among the younger
generation of soloists on
Naxos is the Uzbek pianist
Eldar Nebolsin, who
plays Chopin, Liszt and
Schubert.

(Photo credit: Kirill Bashkirov)

Takako Nishizaki playing *The Butterfly Lovers* in the Great Hall of the People in Beijing in 2009, a televised production marking the 50th anniversary of the work

Takako Nishizaki at home in Kowloon

Enterprising and vigorous, Marin Alsop has stamped her musical personality on Naxos.

(Photo credit: Grant Leighton)

Though he holds a baton here, Patrick Gallois is represented as both flautist and conductor on Naxos.

(Photo credit: Matti Salmi)

Arranger extraordinaire and conductor Peter Breiner (Photo credit: Roderick Kucavik)

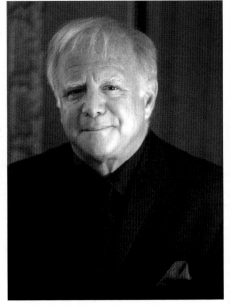

Leonard Slatkin, GRAMMY Award-winning conductor (Photo credit: Donald Dietz)

Rostropovich (winning the Grand Prix of the Paris Concours Rostropovich in 1981), and she was particularly pleased that she began her recording career with Schnittke's Concerto. 'I was so happy that I could begin with a piece that was not Dvořák or Saint-Saëns or Tchaikovsky – but Schnittke. He was a very important composer, and also I was in love with that piece.'

Schnittke's Concerto is fiendishly difficult and it demonstrated clearly the talents that both Starker and Rostropovich had recognised. Aware that he needed a cellist to record the standard cello repertoire on Naxos, and having been impressed with the Schnittke recording, Heymann turned to Kliegel. With some financial support from the foundation that had provided her with her Stradivarius cello, the next recording, of concertos by Dvořák and Elgar, was made in the relatively lavish circumstances (by early Naxos standards) of the Henry Wood Hall in London, with the Royal Philharmonic Orchestra conducted by Michael Halász. 'It was fantastic,' says Kliegel. 'I was a little afraid because I didn't know what the English musicians would say about an unknown German cellist playing the Elgar Concerto. But they were very attentive and very nice – it felt like being in a big, comfortable, warm bed with them, and I loved it.' The CD was released in 1992, and, having never been out of the catalogue, has sold in excess of 160,000 copies. For Kliegel it set a pattern of regular recording that was to last nearly fifteen years.

'In the beginning years all the suggestions came from Klaus. He said he preferred one-composer CDs which were easier to sell but I knew this is more difficult for the cello because cello repertoire written by individual composers is not so large.' Nevertheless, for the first couple of years it worked out well. 'I wanted to record things I had played in concert but also pieces I actually wanted to play – not just recording for recording's sake – and combine this with Klaus's wishes.'

Kliegel recorded concertos by Saint-Saëns and Shostakovich, Tchaikovsky's *Rococo Variations* and Bruch's *Kol Nidrei*.

Working with various pianists, she also recorded the central sonata repertoire (Beethoven, Mendelssohn, Chopin, Brahms) and attractive programmes of encore pieces, including a collection of works by the cellist–composer David Popper. Her recording of Tavener's *The Protecting Veil* sold more than 40,000 discs.

It was inevitable that at some point she would record Bach's cello suites. 'Klaus was very patient – it took me many years to prepare for it. I do love the Baroque and Classical pieces, but Romantic music touches me more.' She compared the four existing manuscripts of the suites and eventually recorded them in Budapest with Ibolya Tóth producing; the recording was released in 2005.

Undoubtedly the most unique CD in Kliegel's recording career for Naxos and Marco Polo is *Hommage à Nelson Mandela*. Inspired by the autobiography of Mandela which she read while on holiday in Hawaii, Kliegel, a musician of passion and enterprise, was determined to meet him and to mark her admiration for him in a special way. She commissioned a work for cello and percussion from the composer Wilhelm Kaiser-Lindemann and gave the first performance in Düsseldorf in 1996. In the following year she was in Capetown playing the Concerto by Saint-Saëns, and she included some extracts of *Hommage à Nelson Mandela* in the concert: within three months she was back in South Africa and playing sections of the work early one morning to Nelson Mandela himself. 'I had a personal meeting with him for a whole hour,' she recalls. 'I played one of the movements for him – it was based on a lullaby from Xhosa ... I decided I would take the song, sing it as a lullaby, and accompany myself on open strings and knock the rhythm on the back of my cello. It was complicated, but he was very touched. It was a wonderful experience. It had taken four years from first reading the book to have my wish fulfilled.' It was released on Marco Polo with a photograph of Mandela and Kliegel together, and received worldwide publicity.

Kliegel has now made some thirty-five recordings for Naxos. She declares that curiously she has not developed a concert career to match her discography and her international sales. She puts it down to personal reasons, and possibly management issues. Instead she developed a career as a teacher, in recent years releasing books and DVDs addressing the many challenges facing cellists in the main repertoire. She looks back with affection on her association with Naxos.

'I feel I have had a special relationship with the label because from the start all my correspondence was with Klaus Heymann personally. He has been in my house many times. We have had some disagreements, which is normal, but we have developed a certain trust. In the beginning I was very grateful because he trusted me enough to offer me the main cello repertoire and I knew he would have only one recording of these main works for ten years. At the start I was very sceptical about doing these for Naxos because it was a budget label and people said, "Why don't you go to Deutsche Grammophon." I said, "It is not easy!" In those first years, the presentation of Naxos and Marco Polo in the shops was very bad and the prices *were* cheap. But then I thought that I had a good orchestra with a good recording, so the result was very good, and I hoped that the distribution would get better in the coming years. And it did. And then I heard from other musicians that if their recordings don't sell so well they are deleted, and I thought, "Well, this hasn't happened with *my* recordings on Naxos and Marco Polo!"'

Kodály Quartet

Attila Falvay, 1st violin · Erika Tóth, 2nd violin · János Fejérvári, viola · György Éder, cello

Haydn is the bedrock of the string quartet. Most groups maintain a few Haydn quartets in their repertoire and almost all players express a continuing delight in them. Relatively few experience the privilege of playing them all, and even fewer have recorded the complete cycle. Attila Falvay, first violinist of the Kodály Quartet, is very clear that in nearly a quarter of a century spent recording for Naxos this was the highlight for him – a continuing highlight, for the cycle was recorded organically over a decade. Between 17 and 19 June 1988 in the Italian Institute, Budapest the Kodály Quartet (at the time, Attila Falvay, 1st violin; Tamás Szabó, 2nd violin; Gábor Fias, viola; János Devich, cello) played Op. 76 No. 3 in C ('Emperor'), Op. 76 No. 2 in D minor ('Fifths') and Op. 76 No. 4 in B flat ('Sunrise'). These were all in the group's repertoire, so it was simply a pleasure. None of them – certainly not Falvay, who had joined the Quartet in 1980 (it was founded in 1966) – had any idea that it was the start of a cycle. As far as they knew, it was just a one-off disc for an obscure budget label, though that did not lessen the enjoyment of the sessions. It turned out to be an important disc for Naxos because it brought the first very positive review in the UK, in November 1990 on BBC Radio 3's influential programme *Record Review*, and this helped to establish the label as a reliable source for classical music despite its low price.

The Kodály Quartet had as many as half of Haydn's quartets in its concert repertoire, so it was relatively easy for the musicians to move into the studio and put them on disc. Each time was pure pleasure, as Attila Falvay explains. 'If I had the fortune to record them again, I would start with the early ones and step by step go with the quartets as they were composed. But in those early days, we didn't have the best scores: it was the communist era, and the urtext scores were not available. We only had the Peters Edition and there were lots of questions about those. Sometimes we just had to go on our instincts. But it is a fantastic thing to do for a string quartet, especially for the first violin, and I was very happy. It is a dream to do all the Haydn quartets, to know and play this wonderful literature.'

The commissions for the recordings came from Heymann, who initially asked for the 'named' quartets because they were more popular. Fairly soon, however, the Quartet recorded programmes in order of opus number, which Falvay feels was right. 'What we found so very interesting was the Haydn "laboratory" of string quartets. Musical ideas that he tried in No. 1 of an opus would appear in No. 2 and No. 3 of that same opus. It was a family of thematic ideas, growing and being worked out further by Haydn. And tempo is so important. And asking what kind of music is it: a kind of peasant dance or, like the 'Emperor', more aristocratic, more noble?'

By 1994 it was clear that the group was on course to do the whole cycle, and the composer was a regular feature in its annual recording programme. Sometimes it was two Haydn discs a year, sometimes more. The last disc in the cycle was recorded in 2000: it contained the arrangements, now known to be spurious, of two cassations as Op. 2 Nos. 3 and 5, as well as the two Op. 3 quartets now normally attributed to Hoffstetter; but it was decided to do these for completeness' sake. The whole set (twenty-five CDs) came out in 2008 and was well received critically. Falvay comments: 'Inevitably, over the twelve years, we changed our approach and our style. The personnel changed [the current membership dates from 2005] and so the way we played the quartets changed slightly. But this is natural – all musicians change individually over that spread of time.'

Interpretation was particularly crucial when it came to Haydn because awareness of period performance was burgeoning during the 1990s. Falvay took note of the differing views and the gut-string performances, and, although all four musicians play on modern instruments, the style of the Quartet's Haydn evolved. 'My way of playing is very close to singing, a natural singing voice, without too much mannerism. I like the pure musicality, when the character comes out by itself.' A Hungarian quartet is a natural choice to play Haydn because he wrote so many of the works at the Esterházy court.

Certainly Falvay thinks that the Kodály Quartet may have a distinctive Hungarian flavour, and it follows a strong tradition of Hungarian quartet playing. 'Perhaps it is more Classical, less academic and scientific, than an American or a French quartet.'

The success of the Haydn cycle set the Kodály Quartet on the road to the central Classical repertoire, resulting in complete cycles of Beethoven and Schubert. Falvay suggested the Beethoven cycle to Heymann. The group had already performed all the works in concert, though this did not mean the recordings were simple to do. 'The Beethoven quartets are very complicated – it is a very different project. In the Haydn quartets, most of the melody is played by the first violin. In Beethoven's quartets, everyone is playing important things. Take the *Grosse Fugue*. If everybody plays the dynamic written it is a terrible work because the listener cannot hear any melodic line – everyone is just playing fragments. We had to bring out the continuity; we had to rewrite the dynamics many times, even from *fortissimo* to *piano*, because other parts may be much more important. It was a very difficult work to do. It really helped to record this, because when we listened to the playback we could hear what we were all doing and how our theories functioned. I was pleased that we got good reviews for this because we worked very hard on it!'

The recording process was different for Beethoven. Haydn sessions would involve one quartet a day; for middle-period Beethoven, the Quartet would be happy with one or two movements a day. But most sessions followed a pattern: 9 a.m., warm up; 10 a.m., record for two or three hours without a break; then lunch and record again until 5 or 6 p.m. 'I don't like the breaks because you lose the tension and it is difficult to find the character. I am completely exhausted after each session because it takes a great amount of concentration and energy not to become boring when you repeat. We have to keep the playing fresh, which is much more difficult to do without an audience. It is such a different feeling in a recording session! When you are giving a concert it is much easier to be alive and full of vigour, though in a concert you only have one shot. Sometimes, when you listen to the playback in a recording session, you are surprised by what you hear – you didn't expect a phrase you have just played to sound like that!'

Most of the recordings took place with the producer Ibolya Tóth (as did so many recordings in Hungary) first at the Italian Institute and then at the Phoenix Studio in Diósd. However, the difference with many of the later Kodály Quartet recordings is that they were edited by Falvay's wife, Mária. Falvay would listen to the first edit then trust his wife and Tóth to finish it. 'They listen in a different way from me.' Over twenty years the Kodály Quartet made more than fifty recordings for Naxos, with their three main cycles of Haydn, Beethoven and Schubert happening simultaneously. The group also recorded other things, including the octets by Mendelssohn, Schubert and Bruch ('that was a discovery for us'); the quartets by Ravel and Debussy; and Schubert's 'Trout' Quintet and Bartók's Quintet (both with Jenő Jandó). They regret not having been able to record for Naxos other works that they play a lot in concert – quartets by Bartók, for example (recorded for Naxos by the Vermeer Quartet), or Dohnányi or even Kodály himself. But Falvay does not complain. 'We were very grateful for the opportunity to do all this central Classical quartet repertoire for Naxos. At first, we didn't think about the company we were doing it for – whether it was a budget label, or what nationality it was. We were just happy to have the chance to do this. We did meet with some prejudice at the beginning from some people who did not care for Naxos because it was sold at a budget price. People thought that maybe it was a budget performance – cheap in some way. But fortunately this perception changed completely. And it certainly helped our concert career. It was very good to take our recordings with the good reviews to concert agents.'

Ilya Kaler – Violin

After the Russian-born virtuoso Ilya Kaler had won three of the leading international violin competitions in the mid-1980s (Tchaikovsky, Sibelius and Paganini), it was not so obvious that he was going to migrate to Naxos in the early 1990s. The appearance of his first recordings, however (Paganini's Concertos Nos. 1 and 2 and the same composer's Twenty-Four Caprices), brought worldwide recognition and demonstrated the emerging appeal that Naxos was having for outstanding players. It was clear that Naxos could provide them with an international platform equal to that of any established label.

Stephen Gunzenhauser, already a Naxos artist, conducted two concerts with Kaler in the US and recommended him to Klaus Heymann, who responded immediately with the Paganini offers. Other recordings, including concertos by Glazunov and Dvořák, followed swiftly. 'He was clearly one of the great violinists in the Russian tradition of today but didn't have the career he deserved,' says Heymann. 'He is very musical, excellent technically, and a very intelligent player.' Over the following years Kaler extended the Naxos violin repertoire so far established by Takako Nishizaki, adding his own performances of core repertoire but also recording lesser-known works (a path he continues to tread). Sonatas by Brahms came in 2002, and then major concertos by Tchaikovsky, Brahms and Schumann as well as both of the concertos by Shostakovich.

Kaler is unequivocal in his commitment to Naxos. 'It was a wonderful opportunity for me to record these great pieces, and they helped me enormously in my career.' From his home in Illinois he pursues an international playing career with major orchestras and encounters the Naxos distribution in all corners of the world. 'The other day I was playing in Santa Domingo in the Dominican Republic, and out of the blue these young people came up after the concert and asked me to sign the

Naxos recordings they had bought – Paganini's Caprices. It was very sweet to see that.'

He now records once or twice a year. 'Most of my work takes place in a concert hall, so it can feel a little bit strange to stand again in front of the microphone, though it doesn't take me long to get used to it. I look at it always as a learning experience for me because when you stand before a microphone your ears somehow work differently. You start listening intently to what you are doing, and why you are doing it, and then you hear the playback and you discover new things in your playing – which sometimes you like and sometimes you do not! It is very stimulating for me as an instrumentalist. But generally I think my recordings honestly reflect my way of playing, the way I sound in life.'

Inevitably his reputation as a recording artist stands by the more popular repertoire. He has also recorded Bach's unaccompanied sonatas and partitas, where violin playing is put under the clearest of spotlights, and Ysaÿe's solo sonatas. Yet looking back at his two decades of recording for Naxos, he is equally engaged by the lesser-known works that he has put on disc. These have included Taneyev's *Suite de concert*; Szymanowski's two concertos with the Warsaw Philharmonic Orchestra under Antoni Wit (a recording which led to a series of concert performances, as promoters picked up on the works); and the Violin Concerto by Mieczysław Karłowicz, again with the Warsaw Philharmonic and Wit. Kaler knew about Karłowicz's Concerto because it was played in Russia when he was young, but he never thought he would have the chance to record it. 'That is why working with Naxos has been such an interesting experience,' he says.

Maggini Quartet

The Maggini Quartet has made a unique contribution to Naxos in general and English chamber music in particular.

From its first appearance on the label in 1996 there was a steady stream of recordings that championed the heart of English chamber music in the twentieth century, especially from 1900 to 1950.

The offer to record this music for an international budget label was a considerable surprise to the Quartet. Surely English chamber music was the domain of the full-price English independent labels? But this special collaboration (part of the English music series established by David Denton) helped to give Naxos an English character in England – a 'localising' feature that was to be replicated elsewhere in the world by other Naxos companies. It started with the music of Frank Bridge and E.J. Moeran and finished fifteen years and some thirty CDs later with the music of Ronald Corp; in the middle was the momentous undertaking of Peter Maxwell Davies's *Naxos Quartets*.

The relationship between Naxos and the Quartet began with a simple proposition. In 1994 its members – Laurence Jackson and David Angel, violins; Martin Outram, viola; Michal Kaznowski, cello – decided to record privately two CDs of English music and offer them to record companies. In a North London church they recorded short, attractive works for string quartet by Bridge and the string quartets and String Trio by Moeran. The engineer–producer was a friend of theirs, Andrew Walton: though a violinist with the English Chamber Orchestra, he was very interested in the recording process.

The master tapes went off to three labels. The Quartet received a highly positive response from David Denton, representing Naxos, who not only agreed to take the recordings but offered a contract for further discs of English music. He was also happy for them to be produced by Andrew Walton. It was a life-changing moment for the Quartet (and for Walton), as David Angel remembers. 'I was on the train when I got the call from Andrew and neither of us could believe it. It was the most fabulous offer to both him as a producer and us as a quartet.'

It was the turning point for the Quartet musically, for suddenly English music became the central part of their concert life. 'When we started the Maggini in 1988, we didn't see ourselves as a vehicle for British composers. It all came by chance. We chose Moeran for the recording because we had happened to be asked to perform some of the music at a festival near Tunbridge Wells and we thought it was wonderful. We knew one of Britten's quartets and our viola player, Martin, was very keen on it; but we played the central European quartet repertoire – we had already recorded some Haydn, Schubert and Szymanowski for other independent labels. We had no plans to play so much English music until Naxos asked us to record it!'

The next CD was of Elgar's Piano Quintet, with Peter Donohoe, which went on to win a Diapason d'Or in France. It was particularly satisfying recognition, and ironic that it should come from outside England. When Anthony Anderson arrived at Select Music in 1997 he took over responsibility for the Maggini recordings, and over the following decade developed a close relationship with the group. The first volume of Britten's string quartets (Nos. 1 and 2) followed in 1998, and a pattern was established of two recordings per year. The Quartet continued to play a broader range of repertoire in concert, but more often than not the middle work in the programme would be an English one – because of the Naxos commissions. The group planned carefully and quite far ahead, choosing the work to be recorded and scheduling it for concert performance before taking it into the studio.

British music became the hallmark of the Maggini Quartet although Angel points out that it only represented a third of their concert repertoire. The regular reviews received for their two releases a year – generally high praise indeed – helped to raise the Quartet's profile and certainly increased the number of concerts it gave. After Britten came Walton; after Walton came Vaughan Williams. The collection of Vaughan Williams's two string quartets and Phantasy Quintet with Garfield

Jackson brought Naxos's first *Gramophone* Award. 'It began as a typical project for us,' remembers Angel. 'We didn't know the music very well before we started working on it, and I wasn't particularly keen on Vaughan Williams. But I fell in love with the quartets and in 2000 I ate, drank and slept Vaughan Williams. I read everything about him and his music that I could lay my hands on, and we played him all over the place. As with the Britten, we immersed ourselves in it.'

It turned out to be a special recording, and the sessions themselves demonstrated what a close team the Maggini Quartet and Andrew Walton had become. Angel recalls: 'There was a moment when we were doing the slow movement of No. 2, the central movement, which begins *pianissimo* but with no vibrato. It is a very haunting and touching moment. We did a first take. Andrew in the control room said, "I think we can go one of two ways with this. We can either go down the slightly stony Shostakovich-like way, or we can go for something extraordinarily misty that perhaps we couldn't achieve in the concert hall very easily" – and that was the one he wanted to push us down. The five of us worked at it and when I listened to the first take, I had to get nearer to my speakers to hear it. But I had to admit there was something extraordinary about it and he had driven us to it, actually. Somehow it did sum up how special we thought the music was.'

So they were particularly pleased that it was this disc that won them the *Gramophone*'s Chamber Award in 2001. They played a movement at the London awards ceremony, and during that evening a well-known conductor came up to them and criticised them for recording for Naxos. The prejudice against the company was still there, fourteen years later. 'He said he understood that we had to get recordings where we could but accused us of "sleeping with the enemy!"' The Vaughan Williams CD became the Quartet's bestseller: 20,000 CDs were sold within a year of winning the award and some 45,000 CDs have been sold to date, which is an exceptional figure for relatively specialised repertoire.

The next year saw the beginning of the project with which the Maggini Quartet will be forever linked: the *Naxos Quartets*, the ten works written especially for the group by Sir Peter Maxwell Davies, Master of the Queen's Music. This remarkable commitment by composer, performers and record label to a startling musical venture was unprecedented in classical music. Angel says: 'Max had been wanting to write a series of ten quartets – he felt it was the time – but he wanted to find something on which to hook it. He had had a long relationship with the Belcea Quartet and initially spoke to them, but they turned it down, probably realising the immense commitment it was going to require.

'Then Klaus Heymann became involved and Naxos approached us. We were the Quartet that recorded English music; we were the natural people to do it. We knew at the beginning what a daunting project it was and we thought long and hard about it, but in the end we couldn't turn it down. It was *too* exciting and unprecedented – to have an actual contractual agreement with an outstanding composer like Maxwell Davies for ten quartets over five years. It meant working with him intensively for five years, and when I look back on it I think it was one of the most important things musically I have ever done. It turned out to be absolutely extraordinary. All I can say is, "Thank God we got on!" I remember Max saying at the start that he didn't know us, we didn't know him, and we had no idea what was going to happen. What put our minds at rest was that the very first time we played to him, a week before the premiere of the First Quartet, we discovered that he was essentially musical! It wasn't maths. Even though he is a maths wizard he uses that purely as a tool to help him compose. He can dance every rhythm he writes; he can feel it bodily.

'He rehearsed us much as if it were a Haydn quartet (Haydn was the starting point for him anyway) so we got off on just the right foot for the first work. Then it was a road the five of us travelled together, really, him finding out more and more about how to write quartets and us finding out more and more about how to play them! They were playable but sometimes they were fiendish. It wasn't that they got more difficult as the series progressed but we felt his writing got clearer and clearer. There were always remarkable sounds right from Quartet No. 1, but I don't think he ever went back to the dense writing in No. 2, gigantic and impressive though that Quartet is. If anything, he got more and more transparent. On the other hand, I am not sure whether he would agree with me. When we got to the Fourth Quartet, and mentioned this, he said: "But it is merely that you are becoming used to my sense of tonality, and if you went back to the other three now you would play them differently." (I reminded him of that when we were preparing the Seventh Quartet and he said: "Did I really say that? What a cheek!")' As always, the Quartet toured the works before recording them. The poet laureate Andrew Motion even wrote a set of sonnets for himself to read in concert in between the movements of Quartet No. 7.

While these ten quartets were making their mark on English musical history they still had to take their place in the Maggini's overall Naxos recording programme. During each of the five years that the players spent recording the *Naxos Quartets* they always made at least one other CD, and often more. There was music by Alwyn, Arnold, Bax, Bliss, Ireland, Rawsthorne and Lennox Berkeley. In a way, however, the end of the *Naxos Quartets* project presaged the end of an era for the Maggini Quartet. Laurence Jackson, the first violinist, had left and they were joined by different leaders for short periods before settling with Susanne Stanzeleit. Music by Edmund Rubbra was followed by the quartets of Ronald Corp, both discs released in 2011. It was then that the Maggini Quartet and Naxos decided to part company. The Quartet wanted to record works outside the English repertoire, to reflect the broad interests of the musicians themselves, and Naxos had other groups to do this. It was an amicable separation because both recognised that something exceptional had been achieved by the partnership over fifteen busy years.

Patrick Gallois – Flute and Conductor

Patrick Gallois is almost unique among Naxos artists in featuring equally as a solo instrumentalist and a conductor. His recordings of the main flute repertoire bear the distinctive quality of his special instrument: a wooden flute made to his own specifications, with square holes and square keys. His recordings of orchestral works, from Haydn to Gershwin, bear a particular hallmark of vivacity, for above all Gallois enjoys the process of making music. He is not a conductor who operates like an efficient managing director in the recording studio: he insists on working with his orchestra for as long as it takes. The fact that he has managed to achieve that in the context of Naxos, where budgetary concerns are a major consideration, is a tribute both to his own commitment and ingenuity, and to Klaus Heymann's ability to accommodate different kinds of talents. Selecting a Finnish chamber orchestra conducted by a French flautist to record music as disparate as early Haydn symphonies, Mendelssohn's Violin Concerto, and music for clarinet and strings by George Gershwin is not an obvious strategy; but the musical results have justified the decision.

Gallois began his recording career at the traditional top, with Deutsche Grammophon. The prestige reflected his exceptional qualities as a flautist but he was unhappy in the environment. 'I went to London and recorded the Rodrigo Concerto in one session and the Khachaturian in another. I can do it but I asked myself, where is the music?' So after making around ten recordings with the Yellow Label, he stopped. 'They wanted me to record Mozart with the Vienna Philharmonic Orchestra. They are good musicians, but that is not my style.'

The recording was never released, and Gallois switched to Naxos. 'The DG way of making recordings is fantastic if you want to make a career but I wanted to be a musician. I tried to find a company who would do the things I wanted to do, not Mendelssohn's Violin Concerto or Franck's Sonata on the flute, which is terrible. The flute does have a lot of music but people don't know it.' He also wanted to do more conducting, especially of orchestras with whom he had a close association. For almost a decade his relationship with the Sinfonia Finlandia Jyväskylä has formed a central part of his work: he lives in Finland for much of the year.

His first disc for Naxos was Mozart's concertos for flute, including the Flute and Harp Concerto, with the Swedish Chamber Orchestra and the harpist Fabrice Pierre, released in 2003. Typically Gallois wrote his own cadenzas, stamping his personality even more distinctly on the recording. Other flute recordings appeared over the following decade, including the Flute Concerto by Friedrich Witt (in a programme with two Witt symphonies); the Concerto for two flutes written specially for Gallois by the contemporary Bulgarian composer Emil Tabakov (and recorded with Philippe Bernold); Reinecke's Flute Concerto; the complete flute concertos by C.P.E. Bach; and music for two flutes and orchestra by Franz and Karl Doppler (recorded with Kazunori Seo).

All the recordings he made for DG were on a gold flute. Underlining the change that took place, on all the recordings made for Naxos Gallois used the wooden flute of his own devising, even for twentieth-century works. 'I didn't want to play on a period flute with a period orchestra. I did that many years ago. But you have to know what is your specific voice, and my voice is very specific. My instrument, the wooden flute with square keys and square holes, is unique. You must be like a singer with your own voice; you must be able to do everything. I was frustrated with the *traverso* because in the end I was making the same sound. That is not the sound of me but the sound of the instrument.' He points out that Reinecke's music was written for a player who used a wooden instrument, though an unusual one with twenty keys. 'I played it and it is interesting but it is very hard.' While Gallois acknowledges that authenticity in the choice of instruments does have a place, he believes it can be overstated. 'The Romantic instrument has eleven keys and there are three or four different fingerings for every note ... some Baroque flutes have one key, others five keys. You cannot be a specialist in all these flutes. It is better to be a specialist in the music.' So he uses his special flute for composers ranging from Einojuhani Rautavaara to François Devienne to Saverio Mercadante, whose chamber arrangements feature on one of his most recent recordings.

'Making music' is a constant statement and a constant theme for Gallois. His special relationship with the Sinfonia Finlandia Jyväskylä, a salaried orchestra, enables him to schedule a week's rehearsal for one Naxos disc – a highly unusual circumstance. 'It is a luxury! I can make mistakes with my orchestra. We can try things out, we can even record, and, when I sleep on it and feel it didn't really work, we can record again!'

It started simply. 'I went to Klaus and asked him if I could record as a conductor. He trusted me and he said yes. It was very easy. The main problem with conductors is that they conduct. It is quite easy to get an orchestra to play together and play in tune. The main difficulty is having a musical direction, to know where you are going. A conductor should be an artistic director, a guy who says we go in this style or that style, to the left or to the right, but we go somewhere!'

This was particularly the case with the early Haydn symphonies that Gallois recorded in the Suolahti Hall. 'These symphonies are another world. They are not Baroque music; they come from C.P.E. Bach and Wilhelm Friedemann Bach, and you cannot simply perform them the way they are written. It would be boring. You have to look for the music. I took a position, using so much harpsichord in improvisation, moving around the harmony, making the joke. I am 200 per cent sure that this is what would have happened. Generally, musicians never really work on early Haydn, in much the same way as Vivaldi. They just play it. But you have to use *more* imagination with this kind of music; you have to have *more* rehearsal to really make music out of it. With Mozart there is less space for creativity, there is less room for interpretation: it is just perfect. There is more room with Haydn. It is the same with Ravel next to Debussy: Ravel and Mozart, Debussy and Haydn.

'With my recordings for Naxos I feel I am free as a musician. I have been with the Sinfonia Finlandia for nine years and the style and the sound is really quite specific. The orchestra gets better and better. You cannot work this way in London – the musicians are just too busy.'

Since they are based in Finland, it is natural that Gallois and the Sinfonia Finlandia Jyväskylä have made many recordings also for the Finnish label Ondine, which is now owned by Naxos. They continue to record for Ondine but Gallois is equally busy with Naxos itself. His recent flute recordings include music by Ignaz Pleyel; recent orchestral recordings include American Classical music 'that not even the Americans know', as well as overtures and ballet music by Joseph Martin Kraus; and at the time of speaking he was scheduling overtures by Cimarosa with the Sinfonia Finlandia. 'I will cook spaghetti for the orchestra that week ...'

Norbert Kraft – Guitar and the 'Guitar Collection'

'The guitar is a bit of an odd duck in the classical world,' declares Norbert Kraft, the Canadian guitarist. Nevertheless Klaus Heymann was keen to accommodate it, and started the 'Guitar Collection' with Kraft in 1994; it now has the largest catalogue of classical guitar recordings of any single label in the world. Furthermore, Heymann recounts that virtually every CD in the series has moved into profit, or at least broken even, which is a testament to its reach within the international guitar community.

Norbert Kraft, the Toronto-based virtuoso and teacher, had been making recordings for an English company but the relationship had become increasingly fractious. It was SRI, the Naxos distributor in Canada at the time, who suggested Kraft look at this emerging label. 'At the start I was sceptical because a "budget" label meant cheap product to me at the time,' recalls Kraft. 'But the distributor told me that Naxos would be the only company standing in a few years' time so I thought I should investigate!' Heymann heard Kraft's existing CDs, approved, and asked him what he would like to record. Kraft put together a list of thirty CDs, expecting a small selection to be made, and was taken aback when he was told that he could do the lot – but in a year!

Kraft's life had suddenly changed. He had a busy concert career but he needed to create some space, so he started by reducing his teaching. He recorded the popular guitar concertos by Rodrigo, Castelnuovo-Tedesco and Villa-Lobos in Manchester with the Northern Chamber Orchestra under Nicholas Ward; the recording was released in May 1994 and went on to sell more than 250,000 copies. It was followed later that year by *19th Century Guitar Favourites*, which carried the series title 'Guitar Collection' and set the pattern for the future.

Then there was a gear shift. Unlike most performing musicians Kraft had always been interested in the recording process; following a discussion with Heymann, it was decided that he try out recording in Canada under his own auspices, with his wife, Bonnie (a pianist and harpsichordist), as producer and editor. After an extensive search the Krafts found St John Chrysostom, a church in Newmarket, just outside Toronto: they felt it had the perfect acoustic for guitar recordings. The first trial recording was passed by the Naxos team and the life of the Krafts set off in another new direction. With many recordings on the books, they even moved home to be closer to the studio environment.

It became apparent to Norbert Kraft that one guitarist could not satisfactorily do all the recording that Naxos wanted in so short a time. In any case, he wanted to build a representative guitar catalogue and this meant drawing on the talents of other players. He first of all had to persuade Heymann to change some established Naxos patterns. 'Klaus saw Naxos as a repertoire label not an artist-dominated label, without the artist's photograph on the cover. He also wanted one-composer discs. But this approach is not always appropriate for a guitar catalogue. There are composers who can fill discs – we do have Sor, whose music extends to sixteen CDs, and others – but composers such as Britten or Ginastera, with just one major work, are more common. We also wanted to do themed discs, such as *Guitar Music of Argentina*.' In addition, there was quite an abundant repertoire for the guitar as a chamber music instrument. Heymann accepted the differences and the 'Guitar Collection' went from strength to strength.

Kraft felt that he himself could comfortably record two or three recital discs per year. In the end, his interest in recording and producing took over, and to date he has made just a dozen recital discs. Norbert and Bonnie Kraft rapidly became the Naxos recording team for Canada and began to attract musicians from North America and much further afield. Initially the focus was on the guitar, though this was not without its tensions. Some of Norbert's contemporaries were not entirely comfortable with a colleague on the other side of the glass giving them notes about performance or making suggestions. 'There were times when we felt it was better that I set up the microphones, leave, and let Bonnie take over the production,' smiles Kraft. But as a new generation of guitarists emerged, the younger players were happy to draw on his expertise. 'During a recording we act like musical coaches. Of course people bring their own interpretations, but we can help. If we hear that an intended crescendo is not working, that it just isn't coming to the microphone, I can suggest certain things. So we work very closely with the artist. Of course, we are traffic cops for bad notes or intonation, but we are also intimately involved in helping the players to create their best possible performance.'

Although the Krafts' production work for Naxos has expanded to take in chamber, orchestral and even choral music, so that they have become the main Naxos recording team in North America, they remain dedicated to building the 'Guitar Collection'. Over the years, they developed close links with the major international guitar competitions, starting with the Guitar Foundation of America. 'The guitar is an instrument that lives slightly outside the limelight of the classical world. It has created its own integral, thriving world with its own organisations and societies.' The combination of the Krafts' specialist guitar knowledge and the world distribution of Naxos was able to produce discs to accompany competition winners as they toured the international concert circuit. These young guitarists launched the Naxos 'Laureate Series', which later extended to other instruments. It meant that everyone in the chain of Naxos production had to work at top speed. 'Often the winners wouldn't get to our studio until four to six months after the competition, and we had to record, edit and get the disc manufactured and distributed in time for the forthcoming concert tours.' The Krafts and Naxos now maintain links with three other major international guitar competitions (two in Spain and one in Italy) in addition to the GFA. Each competition offers a Naxos recording as part of the top prize.

In 2003 Norbert Kraft made his final appearance on a Naxos disc, playing in the collection of chamber music by Takemitsu. Although he still gives concerts and teaches, he is principally committed to the recording process. 'There is still a lot of guitar repertoire to be recorded – we haven't completed the music of

Napoléon Coste or Rodrigo, and we haven't even touched Leo Brouwer's concertos.' The Krafts now record around eight CDs of plucked strings per year: four 'Laureate' recordings and four others that also include lute. Nigel North's CDs have proved among the most popular, and his short video extracts posted on YouTube by the Krafts are accessed by thousands. The breadth of guitar repertoire encompassed is unrivalled, from the quintets of Boccherini to the music of Henze, via Barrios Mangoré and Piazzolla. The 'Guitar Collection' is a guitarist's dream.

Ulrich Eisenlohr – Piano

The *Deutsche Schubert-Lied-Edition*, encompassing some 650 songs, is one of the greatest musical collections. One masterpiece follows another using only the simplest of means: voice and piano. It was a project very close to Klaus Heymann's heart, not least because the vast majority were settings of poems written in his mother tongue. He had always found it difficult to listen to these works sung by even the finest singers if they were not native German speakers. After all, he felt, these songs were Schubert's passionate response to the very sound of German poetry as well as its meaning, and he determined that Naxos's complete set would represent the language faithfully.

The distinguished accompanist Ulrich Eisenlohr joined the baritone Roman Trekel for Volume 1 of the *Schubert-Lied-Edition* with *Winterreise*, Schubert's most remarkable song cycle. It was recorded in Berlin in 1998 and released in 1999. Just over a decade later, in March 2010, Volume 35 – the final volume, entitled 'Rarities, Fragments and Alternative Versions' – was released.

It was quite a journey for Eisenlohr. An academic as well as a pianist, he had taught at conservatories in Europe and Japan; he knew most of the songs and had played many in concert. But spending a decade so intensely involved in the wellspring of Schubert's fertile imagination proved both invigorating and exhausting. The pianist Stefan Laux was there at the beginning of the series, but soon the *Edition* came under Eisenlohr's sole guidance. Not only did he choose the singers and accompany them; he also wrote many of the detailed notes, researching the background and content of songs and fragments. This scholarly work underpinned the series and enabled Eisenlohr to produce the most comprehensive set ever recorded.

'We have 672 tracks. This includes many different settings [new compositions based on the same poem] as well as some different versions [modifications of the same composition] and also some fragments and part songs.' As Eisenlohr explains, his decision to organise the collection by the poets was to follow Schubert's own approach. 'Sorting the songs by poets and poet groups brings numerous advantages,' he says. 'First of all, Schubert himself followed this concept in significant parts of his lieder composing career. Secondly, it becomes evident that Schubert was a master in assimilating the styles and characters of poets and their lyrics. You will find specific approaches in sound, musical speech and construction for every important poet or poet group. Finally, grouping by poets shows evidently that poem and music, as well as poet and composer, come to an indissoluble symbiosis in the genre of classical art song.'

Perhaps the most challenging part of the project was the choice of the singers. The decision to match tenor or baritone to a set of songs could only be a personal response to the works themselves, but central to that selection was Eisenlohr's performing experience over the years. 'Knowing, hearing, working with the singers was the most important part. It was a question of choosing musicians who were not only good singers, but good lieder singers. And native German speaking. This may not be a "must" for Schubert lieder singing, but we have found it to be very beneficial.'

Eisenlohr used the authoritative Bärenreiter *Neue Schubert-Ausgabe*. Although no formal academic research was necessary, he worked closely with the singers on the text before going into the studio. 'We had to look with fresh eyes at many aspects of performance. Take "Poets of Sensibility", Vol. 6 with Jan Kobow: we wanted to really work out musical variations for different strophes. Maybe this comes quite close to the way Schubert and his singers performed these songs.'

The *Deutsche Schubert-Lied-Edition* was a project that Eisenlohr will never forget: it has enriched his own concert life and he hopes that it will lead listeners to discoveries. 'We found that there are lots of songs of the highest quality and beauty which are almost unknown and rarely appear in lied recital programmes.'

The New Generation

Tianwa Yang – Violin

The young Chinese violinist Tianwa Yang made her mark on Naxos with fresh and lively recordings of the violin music by Sarasate, starting in 2004; there are six volumes to date. Virtuosity is a hallmark. A child prodigy, she recorded Paganini's Twenty-Four Caprices at the age of thirteen; but she has since matured into a violinist with an international solo career taking her throughout the US and Europe. She also made a recording of Vivaldi's *The Four Seasons* (an important promotional landmark for a young musician) but lifted the character of the disc by coupling it with *The Four Seasons* of Piazzolla. Current projects for Naxos include the complete music for violin and piano by the German composer Wolfgang Rihm and Ysaÿe's solo sonatas.

Yang studied in China until the age of sixteen before spending three years in Germany. Among her stated influences are Jörg-Wolfgang Jahn of the Bartholdy Quartet and the Baroque cellist Anner Bylsma; yet, as seen in her Sarasate recordings, grace, lightness of touch and freedom in performance are very much part of her own style.

It was Heymann who suggested that she begin her Naxos recording career with Sarasate. 'That's how it all began. He asked me to programme the most popular works but also other favourites, perhaps of my own, and he left me to choose that. I didn't at that time know the rest of Sarasate very well at all. I just knew a couple of pieces. Even for the first record I chose one thing that I didn't know beforehand. Sarasate's best is very good. I like all of his opera fantasies, which certainly deserve to be better known – especially the *Carmen*, *Magic Flute* and *Don Giovanni* fantasies, and *Romeo and Juliet*. So many of these are never played in public, which I think is a shame. And of course the violin writing is wonderful. His work shows – how can I put it? – the lightest and most elegant aspects of the violin: it's so often so delicate, so very fine and detailed and sensitive. And of course, being a great violinist, he had a wonderful knowledge of how to make the instrument sound best.'

Ashley Wass – Piano

Competitions are derided by most musicians yet they often provide launch pads for soloists. This was certainly true for the English pianist Ashley Wass. Part of his reward for winning the UK-based World Piano Competition in 1997 was a recording for Naxos, which set him, albeit slightly circuitously, on the road to a fruitful recording career – fruitful both for himself and for English music.

After the competition Naxos sent him a long list of works that were needed for the catalogue, from which he was invited to choose repertoire to record. He went for a selection of works by César Franck, a characteristically idiosyncratic choice for a first recording. It is principally with English music of the early twentieth century that he has made his mark on the label, though he is the first to admit that recording the repertoire has been a journey of discovery as much for him as for many collectors – especially the music of Arnold Bax.

'I didn't know anything about Bax at the start. There seemed to be a revival of interest in his music at the beginning of this century, led by recordings of the symphonies on Naxos conducted mainly by David Lloyd-Jones. I got to know the music a little bit through those CDs and it began to appeal to me. I did the first disc [Piano Sonatas Nos. 1 and 2] and it was well received and we went on from there.' There was a gap of some seven years from winning the competition to the release of the first volume of Bax in 2004, but then things moved more quickly. Wass recorded a further eight volumes, encompassing all of Bax's solo, orchestral and chamber music with piano; he was the first to do it. 'I think the Symphonic Variations is a masterpiece – wonderful – and it was fabulous fun to record. The First Sonata has regularly found its way into my concert programmes over the past three or four years, and has always been well received. And the big forty-five-minute *Winter Legends*, a proper monster of a work, is also very remarkable. It's a fine piece – quite dark at times, typically Baxian in its rather wandering structure and its elusive melodies; one thing Bax could really do was write music which is immensely beautiful.'

The Bax cycle and the other recordings of English music meant that Wass had to learn many works extremely quickly, but this is one of his particular skills. Not all the music is of top quality, he concedes, but it meant that he got to know some outstanding works which will always remain in his repertoire. Of the English composers he has recorded for Naxos he reserves his highest praise for Frank Bridge, whose music 'I just fell in love with … Of all the projects I've undertaken, the Bridge recordings have been by far the most rewarding for me. At his best he's a truly extraordinary composer. The Sonata, for instance, is an absolutely wonderful piece though unfortunately it remains much less well known than many lesser works by more famous composers.'

He was concerned that by recording so much English music he would become typecast as an 'English specialist' but he acknowledges that he has benefitted from this Naxos profile. He was the obvious choice to play Vaughan Williams's Piano Concerto in the BBC Proms in 2008, and he went on to record it for Naxos with the Royal Liverpool Philharmonic Orchestra conducted by James Judd. He is frequently asked to include an English piece when giving recitals abroad. Yet he was especially pleased to record two volumes of Liszt as part of the 'Liszt Complete Piano Music' project. In 2005 he played at a celebratory concert for Naxos's eighteenth birthday, a private event in London. It was a memorable occasion, for not only was this performance given in the middle of the party – not a formal concert event at all – but it was also being filmed, and the cameraman took advantage of the informality to get in extremely close. Standing only a few feet away on his other side was Klaus Heymann himself, interested to see this English pianist in performance, having only heard him on disc. Despite the pressure, Wass gave a superb virtuosic performance of some challenging Liszt pieces and was invited shortly afterwards to record for the Liszt edition. The first CD was, at his suggestion, the transcription for two pianos of Beethoven's Symphony No. 9 (recorded with Leon McCawley); the second was the *Album d'un voyageur*, the first incarnation of Book I of the famous *Années de pèlerinage*, which Wass had played many times in concert.

He also has a particular commitment to chamber music – he runs his own festival in Lincolnshire – and Naxos has given him the opportunity to record Bridge's piano trios and, with the Tippett Quartet (another Naxos ensemble), piano quintets by Bax.

Wass is dedicated not to making a career but to making music, and a couple of years ago, though just thirty-three, he took a four-month sabbatical from the piano and recording. 'The danger is that you get burnt out and tired, and it all starts to feel like a job rather than a passion. You need to remind yourself every now and then why you have chosen to do this; and when you are running around stressed and tired and worried, and feeling that you can't really manage it, I think you need to take a step back.' When he does step back, his discography alone – which also includes music by Elgar and Alwyn – can keep him in the public eye.

Eldar Nebolsin – Piano

The Uzbek-born pianist Eldar Nebolsin has undertaken particularly challenging assignments for Naxos, recording anew some of the music written by pianists for pianists, such as the concertos by Liszt and Chopin, and Rachmaninov's preludes, as well as Schubert's *Wanderer-Fantasie*. Equally active as a chamber musician in the concert hall, his first chamber recording for Naxos features Brahms's piano quartets. Most recently he was in the studio with the two piano concertos by the twentieth-century Portuguese composer Fernando Lopes-Graça, which indicates his breadth of interest.

A relaxed and personable man, he takes an easy view of his career path, studded inevitably as it is by competitions. 'I only took part in four competitions and I think it was far too much. In all of them I was lucky to get first prizes, and I always wondered why it happened ...' These included the Santander and Moscow competitions, where in both he won not only the top prize but also the Mozart Piano Concerto prize (which says more about his sensibilities than his luck).

The concertos by Chopin and Liszt are core ingredients in the catalogue of any record label, and with these Nebolsin follows in the Naxos footsteps of Idil Biret and Jenő Jandó, who set the benchmark in the early years. 'One of the most popular composers, Chopin will always remain, in my opinion, one of the most demanding. He is like a touchstone or like litmus paper: even a few bars of his music immediately reveal what material you are made of as a performer. Something similar happens in Mozart's music. It's impossible to lie when playing Chopin. His music makes you tell the truth, so to speak. In every sentence of Chopin's music there could be a different soul gesture. It is very important to understand how the harmonies are interrelated and what they mean in each case. By contrast, Liszt demands a kind of "orchestral" imagination, so the pianist's goal is to learn to hear an extra-pianistic dimension in order to convince listeners that Liszt's fast and difficult passages go far beyond simple typewriting-machine noise, which sadly happens too often. His virtuosity is primarily a means to an end, not merely an end in itself. That's what I think is meant by the "transcendental" character of his writing for piano: it opens the way to a sublime realm of music.'

Nebolsin recorded Liszt's piano concertos with Vasily Petrenko, another Naxos artist from the younger generation. 'Vasily is one of the most talented musicians I have ever known. He has an incredibly sharp ear, perfect technical skills, deep musical knowledge and an infinite richness of gestures to express the most subtle musical nuance or colour. I also admire his spontaneity, his sense of humour and his human qualities both on and off stage. It was an unforgettable experience to work with him both on stage and in the recording studio and I hope I will have more opportunities to record something else with him, maybe Russian or German repertoire.'

Having begun his recording career with Decca, Nebolsin is now content to be with Naxos. 'I feel very grateful to Naxos and would like to thank Klaus Heymann for opportunities to record and work with people like Vasily Petrenko, JoAnn Falletta and Antoni Wit. I think Naxos is doing a fantastic job in the educational field and especially in promoting new and unknown music. It has a tremendous importance in our practical and cynical society because music makes us better and helps us to develop a higher spiritual level and understanding of the world we are living in.'

Christopher Hinterhuber – Piano

Ferdinand Ries, contemporary of Beethoven, was a bit of a
revelation for the Austrian pianist Christopher Hinterhuber.
When Naxos asked him if he would like to record Ries's eight
piano concertos, he had to admit that he didn't know them. He
had heard some violin pieces and symphonies on the radio but
he was unaware that the piano concertos even existed. He was
not alone; the recording proposal was only possible because
Heymann's publishing house, Artaria Editions (jointly owned
with New Zealand-based Allan Badley), had resurrected them
from library archives and was preparing performing editions.
Hinterhuber thought he had better look at the music before
agreeing and went to the library of the Musikverein in his
home city of Vienna to consult the scores kept there. He was
forbidden to take them out so he sat at the desk and read
through them. He was pleasantly surprised: the piano parts
were lively and interesting (Ries himself was a known virtuoso
pianist of his time) even if the orchestral parts were little more
than accompaniments. 'There are a lot of notes for me but not
many notes for the orchestra,' Hinterhuber admits, almost
apologetically.

He felt the concertos were definitely worth learning afresh
and performing. The series was thoughtfully designed – one or
two concertos per disc coupled with other works for piano and
orchestra – and covers five volumes. The couplings suggested
the orchestras so that Hinterhuber found himself travelling the
world to record the series, which was conducted by Uwe
Grodd: Volumes 1 and 5 were recorded with the New Zealand
Symphony Orchestra so that Badley could see the start and
finish of the cycle; Volume 2 was recorded with the Gävle
Symphony Orchestra in Sweden because the CD also contained
Variations on Swedish National Airs; and Volume 3 was
recorded with the Royal Liverpool Philharmonic Orchestra
because the accompanying works included *Grand Variations*

on *'Rule Britannia'*. It has meant, of course, that Hinterhuber has been asked to play them in concert in Europe. 'They are such attractive pieces pianistically but they are not superficial showpieces – like Kalkbrenner, for example.'

He has been recording for Naxos for a decade. His first Naxos CD was Volume 4 of the 'Piano Works for Four Hands' by Schubert, recorded with Rico Gulda in 2002. Three years later a recording of his own suggestion – sonatas and rondos by C.P.E. Bach – was released and was shortly followed by works for piano and orchestra by Hummel, including *Oberons Zauberhorn*. In danger of being typecast by period, he was rather pleased to record chamber music by Zemlinsky: the Clarinet Trio and the substantial Cello Sonata – which he describes as 'an extra Brahms Sonata' – with the clarinettist Ernst Ottensamer and the cellist Othmar Müller.

Hinterhuber's discography for Naxos has largely settled on late Classical and early Romantic works more by chance than as a reflection of his concert repertoire. He can be found just as often playing Liszt's piano concertos or twentieth-century music such as Frederic Rzewski's *The People United Will Never Be Defeated!*, which is to be expected of a searching musician from his generation; and he is equally happy to discover music of earlier centuries. In addition to his Naxos recording work Christopher Hinterhuber played the piano (Schubert, Rachmaninov and Schoenberg) for Michael Haneke's film *The Piano Teacher* – and it is his own hands that are shown on the screen!

Ten

The Artists: Conductors

When a recording of Tchaikovsky's *Manfred* symphony was released with the Royal Liverpool Symphony Orchestra conducted for the first time on record by its new young star Vasily Petrenko, it was clear to critics and the classical collector that here was a very particular talent. 'We recorded the work in Liverpool Philharmonic Hall and what we tried to do is create something very special that gives a feeling of the monumental scale of Byron's poem and Tchaikovsky's symphony,' says Petrenko. The Naxos recording team reported back to Hong Kong that this was an exceptional recording, and before *Manfred* was released Petrenko and the RLPO had been invited, and had agreed, to do a Shostakovich symphony cycle over the forthcoming years. When the first volume came out, expectations were confirmed with high critical praise, awards and good sales. Naxos did indeed have one of the most exciting young conductors on its books.

This process was almost unique in twenty-five years of Naxos. It was the way the established classical record industry had worked since the early days of recording: look for stars and capture them. It was not the way Naxos, from its beginnings, had built its catalogue and its reputation. Naxos was a repertoire label. The composers were its stars. The role of the conductor was to direct performances on record that were sound, that would last, and that would, at the very least, stand up to scrutiny. If this appears to be damning with faint praise, it is not. Standing in front of the Slovak Radio Symphony Orchestra, or the Capella Istropolitana, the conductor had to be a master of his art and direct an interpretation that had character and verve, and was accurate and well balanced. And that is exactly what those Naxos conductors did. They were highly capable and experienced, giving successful concerts night after night; they may not have been conducting at the Salzburg Festival or in the Berliner Philharmonie but they knew the music and could perform it.

This relaxed pragmatism is typical of the conductors whose names appear again and again on Naxos covers dating from the label's very first sessions. There was a central core of conductors in the first decade who helped to build the world's largest classical catalogue in record time. Many remain busy even now, and although they are not often in the fashionable limelight, they know as well as any star how to conduct an orchestra and bring a symphony to life: Anthony Bramall, Béla Drahos, Stephen Gunzenhauser, James Judd, Adrian Leaper, Ondrej Lenárd, Barry Wordsworth, Antoni Wit, Dmitry Yablonsky, to name a few. Each has a place in the Naxos history.

Anthony Bramall was director of music at the Municipal Opera in Augsburg when he recorded Bizet's *Carmen* and *L'Arlésienne* suites with the Slovak Philharmonic Orchestra in Naxos's very first year; over 100,000 CDs have been sold and the recording is still available. And he is still in Augsburg. The Hungarian Béla Drahos has a broad Naxos discography. Heymann chose him to conduct the label's first one-conductor Beethoven symphony cycle (with the Nicolaus Esterházy Sinfonia) as well as nine volumes of Haydn symphonies, Hofmann flute concertos and the complete Vivaldi bassoon concertos; he is also the soloist in a selection of Vivaldi's flute concertos. Stephen Gunzenhauser has been conductor and music director of the Lancaster Symphony Orchestra since 1979 and was for a long time music director of the Delaware Symphony Orchestra in Wilmington. He was a Naxos house conductor for many years and was at the helm for the label's top-selling disc of all time: *The Four Seasons* played by Takako Nishizaki with Capella Istropolitana. Adrian Leaper, now principal conductor and artistic director of the RTVE Symphony Orchestra and Chorus in Madrid, took charge of a wide variety of repertoire for Naxos, including works by Eric Coates, Frederic Curzon, Elgar, Sibelius and Tchaikovsky, Chinese orchestral music, and Nielsen's symphonies. Ondrej Lenárd, Slovakian born, has a long list of recordings, including volumes of Strauss and Tchaikovsky; but he will go down in Naxos history as the man who conducted the world-premiere recording of Havergal Brian's Symphony No. 1 'The Gothic' (originally released on Marco Polo). He can wear that badge with pride. Barry Wordsworth, a stalwart with the Royal Ballet, Covent Garden, conducted the Capella Istropolitana in volumes of symphonies by Haydn, Mozart and Beethoven in the very first years of Naxos.

These were the conductors whose names, totally unknown to begin with, were imprinted on those white CD covers and became curiously familiar. Their faces may never have become famous, but their music-making can be found at the heart of millions of classical CD collections around the world.

Naxos has never set out to sign star conductors, though this is not to say that it doesn't have conductors of exceptional talent, charisma and personality. Throughout the Naxos years Heymann approached conductors of all ages, backgrounds and nationalities to take charge of a wide range of repertoire. Sometimes they came to him with specific projects. Always the proposal was repertoire-driven. In many cases the success of the Naxos label, and its ubiquitous availability, helped to promote the careers of the conductors themselves. Sometimes the conductors were disappointed that they were unable to commit to disc their own interpretation of a major classic because it existed already on the label (though on rare occasions Heymann relented); but they came to appreciate the Naxos philosophy and they worked hard for the projects they did have. Being a conductor is often not as glamorous as it seems. Sometimes the requirement is purely to focus on the task in hand, in which case it is relatively straightforward; but often the conductor is also the impresario, fundraiser, problem-solver and diplomat, and has to display a cool head and resilient attitude. Without Leonard Slatkin's championing (over a decade) of William Bolcom's *Songs of Innocence and of Experience*, the GRAMMY Award-winning recording would never have been made; Marin Alsop has brought untiring energy and resource to her Naxos projects, including, if the truth be told, convincing Heymann that he and Naxos did indeed need a Brahms symphony cycle conducted by her; and from the moment Peter Breiner met Heymann he has been juggling the roles of conductor and arranger.

As with the instrumentalists, each conductor has his or her own tale to tell of the relationship between the artist and Naxos. The one consistent characteristic shared by all these conductors, in common with Heymann himself, is a lack of pretension. Their podiums are the standard height above an orchestra. They are, above all, fine working musicians. Here are some of their stories.

Marin Alsop

No one who has seen Marin Alsop's fiery performances on the main concert platforms of the world, whether in New York's Carnegie Hall or at the BBC Proms in London, will forget her sheer dynamism. She inhabits the rostrum with an unquestioned star quality yet the focus is always on the music. This is why her musical ideas come across so forcefully on CD, and why her recordings for Naxos have become a key part of the label's catalogue. In the twelve years since making her first recording (Barber's Symphonies Nos. 1 and 2) her international career has grown steadily, leading to her appointment, in 2005, as the first female director of a major American orchestra, the Baltimore Symphony Orchestra. Significantly she acknowledged straight away the reciprocal benefit of her association with Naxos by programming Naxos recordings with the orchestra, including the Dvořák symphony cycle recorded live at the Joseph Meyerhoff Symphony Hall in Baltimore. Others have followed, including her widely praised studio recording of Bernstein's Mass, which brought her a *Gramophone* Award in 2010.

The Alsop–Naxos association began with a coincidence. Alsop had planned to record music by Samuel Barber while director of the Colorado Symphony Orchestra in the mid-1990s but it never happened. Then Klaus Heymann decided that he wanted to record Barber's main orchestral music, asked the Royal Scottish National Orchestra to do it, and was told that they had in fact recently appointed an American as principal guest conductor: Marin Alsop. So began the relationship. She had recorded for EMI and others, but it was with Naxos that she settled. 'The Barber cycle was a great project to start with: running to six strong CDs, it had a long life, and during that time I got to know Klaus quite well. We met a few times, and over the years have been in constant email and telephone contact – more recently on Skype, of course!'

Right from the start, Alsop encountered 'this very interesting stigma' about being a recording artist for a so-called budget label. 'Everyone said I shouldn't be with a budget label – that no one has ever heard of the artists on the label. I thought about it, but once I had spoken to Klaus it was clear to me that he was so outside the box and entrepreneurial in his thinking. He was looking at this industry from such a completely new and fresh vantage point. I really liked that. I could see the brilliance in his thinking and his willingness to take chances; and I could see that by going with Naxos I would be able to do a lot of things that otherwise I would not. It was really a win-win situation.'

The first Barber recording came out in 2000, a time when Alsop's career was beginning seriously to take off. It may have helped that she was a female conductor (still relatively rare), though that had no bearing at all on Heymann's decision to do the Barber cycle and then charge ahead with a variety of recordings. For him, they were simply exciting performances. The bonus was that until this point Naxos had not really had a conductor (or any artist) who was regularly appearing at the world's top concert venues. The Naxos roster included many musicians who recorded a lot, but very few who, like Marin Alsop, had a concert career at the highest level. Developing a close association with the Bournemouth Symphony Orchestra, which resulted in a string of Naxos recordings, Alsop became a familiar figure in the UK – and not only for conducting.

Alsop is far from a traditional maestro and her informal personality enables her to engage directly with audiences. A little like her mentor Leonard Bernstein, she found she was able to introduce works like Bartók's *The Miraculous Mandarin* in such a relaxed yet informative style that BBC Radio 3 decided to broadcast not only the music but her words as well – a rare occurrence. This facility for the spoken word enabled her to diversify into audiobooks; she recorded *The Story of Classical Music* and two volumes of *Famous Composers* for Naxos AudioBooks, titles that brought classical music to a younger audience. More accustomed to addressing adults, she nevertheless proved a natural raconteur for children, taking them through music from the early periods to composers whose work she conducted around the world – and composers she knew personally! This gave her a penchant for the speech studio, and she determined to fit in a session with Naxos whenever she could. On more than one occasion her schedule was so tight that it meant her flying across the Atlantic to London, catching a taxi straight to the Naxos AudioBooks studio, and recording words for children, or introductions to Takemitsu or Brahms or other imminent recordings, or various podcasts, before going to her hotel.

This remarkable stamina and energy is born of a keen sense of purpose. Alsop knew that in starting with Barber, even with Heymann's broad repertoire plans, there would be a danger that her recording activity could become stuck in an American niche. It was something she was determined to avoid, whilst acknowledging that American repertoire is natural fare for her. 'It was inevitable that I would do a lot of the American classics for Naxos because I had a good reputation for doing American contemporary music. I liked it and it remains important to me.' Some of her American recordings now form the backbone of the 'American Classics' series on Naxos: symphonies by Aaron Copland, Philip Glass and Roy Harris, for example. She even championed the work of a young American composer, Michael Hersch, recording his Symphonies Nos. 1 and 2. She points to this CD to demonstrate the remarkable eclecticism that Heymann is eager to foster even though Naxos is a budget label. She actually encouraged Heymann to take risks with other contemporary composers, including Michael Torke and the doyen of Japanese classical composers, Tōru Takemitsu.

In common with many conductors Alsop also wanted to record some of the mainstream composers; initially she ran into the problem that by this time (shortly after the turn of the millennium) Naxos already had most of the core works in the catalogue and Heymann was still not keen to repeat repertoire. However, he acknowledged that Alsop was respected for her interpretations of a wide range of music, and when she came to him with a project to record Brahms's symphonies with the London Philharmonic Orchestra he agreed. Made in the UK in 2004 and 2005, these were released with a cover design that

departed from the standard Naxos white frame and featured
Marin Alsop herself. The recordings demonstrated on CD what
her concert performances had shown for some time: that here
on Naxos was a distinctive interpreter of the central Viennese
classics. 'Brahms's music is especially close to my heart. His B
flat String Sextet was the first piece that emotionally affected
me, when I was about twelve years old, and I suddenly understood music's power to change lives and capture our hearts.
My only *goal* has always been to record music I feel passionate
about, and Klaus has been very open to that. My *hope* is that
people can hear the connection among the Brahms symphonies
over the four CDs. I feel that they are four planets in the same
solar system, inherently, organically, indelibly connected – yet
each unique and distinct in its own right. I hope that people
can feel the architecture of the Brahms cycle, not just the structure of each symphony.'

The commitment shown by Alsop (and by Heymann) has
paid off: since she took up the baton in Baltimore a stream of
important discs have emerged, including the Dvořák symphony
cycle recorded live in the hall that the orchestra knows so well.
'Dvořák, for me, is like an extension of Brahms. I admire those
same qualities in Dvořák that Brahms himself admired: incredible melodic inventiveness, long lines, unexpected variety. I also
like the fact that Dvořák was the underdog, being Czech and
remaining true to his inner self, promoting his heritage and
standing up for his country. I have tried to bring a balance of
beauty and authenticity to the performances. I love the primal
underpinnings in Dvořák's music and have tried to blend that
deeply human quality with the sophistication of the mature
Dvořák.'

Having started performing Bartók in Bournemouth (an
unlikely conjunction that nevertheless produced some spectacular results in concert and on CD), she continued in Baltimore
with the *Concerto for Orchestra* and *Music for Strings,*
Percussion and Celesta. She has also brought to Naxos one of

the most exciting operas of recent years: John Adams's *Nixon in China*, again a live recording taken from several performances. 'That was *insane*! It is *insane* to do live an opera as complex as *Nixon in China* and I must give unbelievable praise to the producer, Tim Handley ... that was really a *tour de force*!' A Prokofiev cycle, comprising concert and studio recordings from São Paulo, is among other forthcoming projects. 'It is hard to compare studio and live recordings. I think that the studio setting gets you a better recording technically but there is something about the live recording, with the audience there, that captures the flow and the living-in-the-moment. So I like parts of both. Perhaps my ideal is to have the live recording with a patch session just to pick up small slips.'

Alsop sees through the whole process of the recording. After some fifteen years she feels much at home with it. She listens carefully to the first edit. 'I listen on headphones – sometimes on my computer, though that is a terrible thing to admit!' She makes her comments and then listens subsequently to the final master. She is familiar with other areas of Naxos. 'I often use the Naxos Music Library as a resource: it is one of my key tools when I am programming. I also find out what Naxos has already got, which helps me when I propose new recordings!'

Marin Alsop and Klaus Heymann communicate regularly. 'We enjoy talking about music – and business. I like him and respect him a lot. There is no hierarchy in Naxos, there is no wheeling or dealing. I get paid just the same as some kid on the street. People could say that this is a cheap way to treat artists but I think it is a very honest way. Recordings are not about making money any more: they are about promoting your career and your orchestras and getting your ideas out there, and Klaus is the best partner I could hope for in doing that.

'I do have a non-exclusive contract with Naxos, even though I treat it like an exclusive contract. If I am going to record for another label I always ask Klaus and discuss it with him. My view is that I want to offer every project to Klaus first. When he is not interested in it, he is perfectly happy to have me do it somewhere else. It is very simple: I value being with Naxos. I am also thrilled to be embarking on an educational series. I feel that Naxos has done more to connect the public with classical music than almost any other entity. To be able to reach out to young people is a passion of mine and this opportunity brings together all of my interests: love of music, desire to demystify classical music, communication with audiences, offering possibilities to young people, and igniting their imaginations.'

Antoni Wit

The distinguished Polish conductor Antoni Wit has been recording for Naxos across almost two decades and now features on some 100 CDs that have collectively sold more than three million units (and that is not counting download sales). It is an achievement that, before 1990, he never would have thought possible. He was then the managing and artistic director of the Polish National Radio Symphony Orchestra in Katowice and had heard along the musical grapevine that a strange company was making a lot of CDs with orchestras in Slovakia. Then he heard that the label Marco Polo was doing some Szymanowski with another orchestra based in Katowice that he knew was not of the standard of the PNRSO. Contact was made, and within months Heymann asked Peter Breiner to travel to Katowice and record some of his arrangements with the PNRSO; the result showed the standard of the orchestra.

Wit takes up the story. 'We now had a chance to get in touch directly with Mr Heymann, and I said that we had an interesting Prokofiev project coming up for the centenary of the composer's birth, giving concerts with the five piano concertos played by the Korean pianist Kun Woo Paik. Klaus suggested that we record the concertos for Naxos. We made two discs and they won the Diapason d'Or and the Grand Prix de la

Nouvelle Académie du Disque in France. We could not have wished for a better start, and after that the collaboration became more and more successful.'

Heymann had been looking for a top-class orchestra to take on some of the big Romantic repertoire, and now he entrusted much of it to the Polish National Radio Symphony Orchestra: all the symphonies by Tchaikovsky, Mahler and Schumann, and many more. Most were conducted by Wit, though he shared the Tchaikovsky cycle with Adrian Leaper and the Mahler with Michael Halász. The stream of offers continued – and for a wide variety of music. There was core repertoire, with Wit and the PNRSO providing sensitive accompaniment on concerto discs: piano concertos by Brahms, Dvořák, Rachmaninov (twice – first with Bernd Glemser, then with Idil Biret) and Ravel; and violin concertos that included both of Bartók's (with György Pauk). There was also Smetana's *Má vlast*. 'It was one of our early recordings, and I didn't feel at the time that it was very special. But it sold 150,000 CDs, and the Polish National Radio Symphony Orchestra in Katowice was on the world musical map.' Wit and the PNRSO also recorded Messiaen's *Turangalîla Symphony* coupled with *L'Ascension*, which won a Cannes Classical Award at MIDEM Classique, 2002.

Wit remained at the Polish National Radio Symphony Orchestra until 2000, and in the preceding decade he began to record Polish music extensively for Naxos. 'The year Witold Lutosławski died [1994] Mr Heymann had the idea to record all the music that Lutosławski wrote for orchestra. I was particularly happy to do this.' The recording of the Piano Concerto remains unforgettable for Wit. It had to be recorded twice: the first pianist was replaced by Piotr Paleczny in order to achieve a more satisfactory result – a rare event in Naxos's history. (The problems did not end there: the disc appeared with Paleczny's name correctly displayed but with a photo of the first pianist, which raised a few eyebrows, not least because the gender was wrong!)

Wit brings a special authority to his Naxos recordings due to his close personal associations with principal Polish composers of the second half of the twentieth century. He studied composition with Krzysztof Penderecki at the Academy of Music in Krakow and was keen to record Penderecki's main orchestral works, including the symphonies and the violin concertos. 'Penderecki changed so completely his way of writing music. What he was writing forty years ago is so different from what he is doing now. It is true of all the Polish composers, but with Penderecki you can see the greatest change.' Wit particularly appreciated Penderecki's presence at the sessions. 'Penderecki would always come to the recordings when he could. It was very stimulating for the orchestra, and interesting for me to discuss the music with the composer himself. I have also had the pleasure of conducting the music of Lutosławski and Messiaen with the composers present. They are all so different! Penderecki can write a metronome marking of 90 and he conducts at 60. When I asked him why he doesn't amend the score and do metronome 60, he said that maybe someone in the future will do metronome 90.'

Lutosławski was a total contrast. 'I worked with him in concerts and recordings for Polish Radio and Polskie Nagrania. One year before his death he wrote his Fourth Symphony for a premiere in Los Angeles but asked if he could come one month earlier to do a recording of the work, which would be held in abeyance until after the first performance. I was pleased to assist him on his symphony and work with him closely. He was very deep in his thought, and in everything he wrote. He never wrote anything casual. If you take the score of No. 4 you will see at the beginning the metronome marking crotchet 55. This is unusual for a metronome marking because you have 54 or 56, not 55. Maybe you will not believe me, but I have a recording of Lutosławski himself doing No. 4 and the metronome is exactly 55.'

Wit had a similar experience with Messiaen. 'We recorded

the *Turangalîla Symphony* in Katowice in the 1990s, after Messiaen's death. But I prepared *St Francis* in Katowice with him some years earlier: he came and attended five rehearsals. To satisfy him meant that you had to know really well what is in the score, but also you had to develop things in the score.' Not surprisingly Wit took the Naxos recording of the *Turangalîla Symphony* very seriously. The two-CD set was recorded in 1998 in Katowice's Grzegorz Fitelberg Concert Hall, in two blocks of four-day sessions – an unusual undertaking for a budget label.

When Wit took up the post of managing and artistic director at the Warsaw Philharmonic Orchestra in 2002, the Naxos commitment moved with him. It was business as usual. The Penderecki programme expanded to include the *St Luke Passion*, *Seven Gates of Jerusalem* and *Utrenja*, important choral works which had made an impact worldwide. Wit also undertook a Szymanowski series, encompassing symphonies, choral works and both violin concertos. And for the 150th anniversary of Chopin's death, Wit conducted new recordings of the piano concertos with the Uzbek pianist Eldar Nebolsin.

Circumstances had changed, however. Wit points out that while Poland had been under a communist regime, and there had been a black market, the Naxos fee had been extremely attractive to musicians. 'The Naxos fee was worth five times more!' The development of democracy put paid to that advantage and if the Warsaw Philharmonic does a recording it has to be subsidised slightly by the orchestra itself. 'But it is important to promote Polish music abroad.'

In 2005 Heymann asked Wit to travel to Weimar and record *An Alpine Symphony* by Richard Strauss with the Staatskapelle Weimar. 'It was one of the first CDs they had ever made, I think, so it was something special for them. They were very keen and passionate and they love this music without anyone having to explain that it is beautiful.' He went on to record more Strauss there: *Metamorphosen* and *Symphonia domestica*.

Antoni Wit is a conductor very much in the central European style. He speaks Polish, German, French, Spanish, Italian and English; he is comfortable conducting around the world and enjoys seeing his Naxos recordings wherever he goes. 'I am sometimes asked by other companies to do a concerto disc but mostly I am happy with Naxos. I did two discs of Szymanowski for EMI but I never see these discs. But when I go to Australia or São Paulo or even to a small city in Spain or elsewhere and I go to a shop, I see many of my Naxos CDs. This is very important to me.' His work for Naxos continues. He still looks forward to the release of his recordings and is clearly not jaded by the number he has done. He feels that his recent recording of Penderecki's *Credo* is special, though he knows it will never compete with his top-selling disc: Górecki's Symphony No. 3, which has sold nearly 250,000 CDs. Among other recent recordings are two CDs of music by Janáček, choral works by Brahms, and two CDs of the Polish composer Mieczysław Karłowicz, who died at the age of thirty-three in 1909. He has enjoyed working with many of Naxos's soloists, including the pianists Idil Biret and Jenő Jandó. 'All the soloists Klaus has suggested have been very good.'

Despite more than two decades of collaboration, Wit and Heymann have met only twice: once when Wit was on tour in the Far East and Heymann went to see him in Taiwan, and once when Heymann invited the PNRSO to Hong Kong for a week's music festival. Other than regular phone and email contact – and Wit is another who marvels at Heymann's rapid response – they have not met for fifteen years.

Dmitry Yablonsky

Dmitry Yablonsky is unequivocal. 'I owe my conducting career to Klaus Heymann and Naxos,' he declares. Given that he has conducted on more than sixty CDs for Naxos, covering a very wide range of music, it is almost too easy to overlook the fact that he began his concert career as a highly gifted cellist. Only recently he recorded for Naxos Popper's *High School of Cello Playing*, a collection of forty studies which, without question, are among some of the most difficult and demanding pieces in the instrument's repertoire. Just how he came to record them, when most of his time is now taken up by conducting rather than playing, is typical of a musician who combines bravura and talent with a touch of adventure.

'I suggested it to Klaus because so many of my friends were saying that I was no longer a cellist, just a conductor. But to be honest, if Klaus had said no, I wouldn't have learned them. They are incredibly difficult. I have recorded them all but I still don't have them under my fingers. Ask any cellist and they will say that these studies are impossible to play. I recorded five at a time, eight sessions in all. I can't tell you how difficult it was. Sometimes I was shaking as I went into the studio because I didn't know what to expect. It is like Schubert's *Arpeggione*: if you are not on the money, you just fall apart.'

With Maria Kliegel having been given the lion's share of the cello repertoire, recording opportunities on Naxos for a player of Yablonsky's accomplishment were inevitably going to be limited; he has, however, recorded Khachaturian's Cello Concerto and Concerto-Rhapsody, Shostakovich's Cello Sonata and other chamber music – and, of course, Popper's *High School*, which for cellists comes first! 'Klaus is a very straightforward man. He gives me compliments as a cellist but says, "You don't have a career as a cellist, but as a conductor." And in a way that is true. If I play fifteen recitals a year, that is fine – there are certain people who don't want to do 100 Dvořák concertos every year.'

Yablonsky established himself as a cellist first and foremost, both as a gifted child in the Soviet Union, and from 1977 when he emigrated to the US with his mother, the pianist Oxana Yablonskaya. He went to The Juilliard School, studying with

Zara Nelsova, but he always maintained his interest in conducting. It was actually through his mother that he made his first contact with Heymann and Naxos, via the intermediaries Victor and Marina Ledin, San Francisco-based producers and advisors to Naxos. (Yablonskaya herself went on to record concertos by Glazunov and Khachaturian, and several albums of the Naxos Liszt edition.)

In the early 1990s Heymann had extensive plans to record Russian, Scandinavian and Baltic music, particularly for Marco Polo. These included works by two Latvian composers: symphonies by Jānis Ivanovs and orchestral works by Jāzeps Vītols. Having learned that Yablonsky had an association with the Latvian National Symphony Orchestra in Riga, he offered him both projects. On paper it was a perfect match and so it proved in the studio. A selection of orchestral works by Vītols was recorded in the Great Concert Hall of the Riga Recording Studio in August 1994 and the first of the Ivanovs symphony programme six months later. On hearing the results, Heymann offered Yablonsky an ambitious list of around sixty discs. 'He is a great cellist, a musical conductor and a good businessman,' Heymann comments. He went on to entrust Yablonsky with some key recordings for Naxos, including violin concertos by Tchaikovsky and Bruch, and piano concertos by Tchaikovsky and Rachmaninov.

Yablonsky's particular contribution to Naxos and Marco Polo has been his ability to take on little-known repertoire and give a strong, distinctive performance. In fact musical politics intervened right at the start of the Marco Polo programme, when another conductor attempted to take over the Naxos offer with the Latvian National Symphony Orchestra. Heymann demonstrated his commitment to Yablonsky by helping to engineer a switch to Russian orchestras, including the Moscow Symphony Orchestra and the Russian Philharmonic Orchestra. Only then did the stream of recordings get underway, rising to as many as fifteen in a year. There was music by

Amirov, Arensky, Balakirev, Glazunov, Kabalevsky, Karayev, Lyapunov, Myaskovsky and Tishchenko; and, later, Japanese composers, including Ifukube and Ohzawa. Interspersed was more central repertoire: Shostakovich's Symphony No. 7 'Leningrad', his film score for *Hamlet*, and the *Jazz Suites*. A particular commercial success was Tchaikovsky's complete music for *Swan Lake*.

'It was really challenging to record all those CDs of unknown repertoire. You jump into the studio and do something you have never done before. I was a relatively inexperienced conductor and your brain has to work at 250 miles an hour. Everything was learned from scratch, and there were many occasions when I was working from a score written by hand. I think I am quite quick at learning scores, but until you actually hear it played by the orchestra it is quite difficult to know what it is really like. And problems arise: wrong notes, wrong rhythms ... so sometimes we lost a lot of time in the studio because of mistakes by copyists. Sometimes I tried to arrange concerts beforehand, so we could get to know the works (I was guest conductor of the Moscow Philharmonic from 2000), but if it is an unpopular work the orchestras don't want to programme it.

'Some of the music was very difficult to source. Take for example Arensky's *Egyptian Nights*, the music for a ballet by Fokine for Diaghilev's Ballets Russes. I found out that there was a handwritten score by somebody in St Petersburg. I called the Mariinsky Theatre and the Kirov Theatre, and they wanted $10,000 for the score. So I used my channels, and I got it for $1,000. We have libraries and librarians!'

Yablonsky certainly champions some of the works he has recorded for Naxos. 'Glazunov's piano concertos should be in the repertoire, not only Rachmaninov's concertos! Richter used to play Rimsky-Korsakov's Piano Concerto and that should really be heard in the concert hall more often – as you can hear if you listen to our Naxos recording with the wonderful

Chinese pianist Hsin-Ni Liu – though I suppose it needs a famous person to bring it back into popularity. And Lyapunov's Violin Concerto is a gem.'

Such was the pace of recording from Yablonsky that there were times when the session tapes were lost on Naxos shelves! The third disc of Ivanovs' symphonies (Nos. 8 and 20) and the disc of Arensky's suites were both originally scheduled for Marco Polo but were released only years later, on Naxos.

'It was an unforgettable time, particularly those first years. There was so much to do. Economically it was quite difficult – the last years of the Soviet Union – and Naxos didn't pay very much; but it paid enough for the orchestral musicians to eat. Now the situation is much better.'

With so many recordings, conductor and label owner have been in regular contact, though they have only met a couple of times – once in Paris at the start of the relationship and then at MIDEM some years later. 'For fifteen years it was "Mr Yablonsky" and "Mr Heymann", then one night it was "Klaus" and "Dmitry". And we exchange ideas. He came to me with Shostakovich and with Prokofiev's *Alexander Nevsky*. And I recently suggested some Croatian piano concertos – not something you would think up over breakfast, but I know a very good Croatian pianist, Goran Filipec, and Klaus seems very excited about it.' Yablonsky is co-artistic director of the Qabala Music Festival in Azerbaijan and professor of cello at the Baku Academy of Music, so he is getting to know the country's music. 'There are some fantastic things here that nobody has heard of.' A CD of Azerbaijani piano concertos – by Amirov and Adigezalov – will appear on Naxos.

Yablonsky lives in the French Pyrenees, on the border with Spain. He has 330 old olive trees and harvests them himself. He calls the place his 'Catalan dacha'. And he still, occasionally, appears on Naxos as a cellist, in chamber as well as solo music. His recording of Rachmaninov's piano trios that he made with two friends (Valeri Grohovski, piano and Eduard Wulfson, violin) in England's Potton Hall studio – a world away from his customary place in the Mosfilm Studio in front of the Russian Philharmonic Orchestra, conducting Lyapunov – shows how much he still enjoys simply playing music.

Michael Halász

As a busy conductor working in the heart of Europe, for more than thirty years in leading opera houses (including a decade as resident conductor of the Vienna State Opera), Michael Halász was able to bring a wealth of experience to Naxos. At the same time, Naxos was able to offer him a substantial recording profile, which otherwise – in a culture dedicated to highly promoted artists singled out as the darlings of the major labels – may not have been open to him. From this association sprang a series of fine recordings on Naxos and Marco Polo of both central repertoire and lesser-known works – performances which would enhance any label at any price, as many of the reviewers agreed. In particular, Halász's day-to-day work in the opera house brought him into contact with some of the finest up-and-coming singers of the day; his expertise in this area resulted in some truly outstanding recordings of Mozart operas.

Hungarian born, Halász is a large personality – a strong, clear, practical musician who is highly capable in the recording environment. He remembers one week in Budapest with the Failoni Orchestra. 'Klaus asked me to do Schubert Symphonies Nos. 1–4, No. 6 and the Joachim transcription of the *Grand Duo*. I had already done Nos. 5 and 8 and the *Rosamunde* overture. Well, it happens in life that if you prepare something well, sometimes it goes easily. It all went well and I realised that we would have a clear day and a half in the schedule, so I rang Klaus in Hong Kong and said, "What next? Shall we do the Ninth?" He said "Yes!" I didn't have my score in Budapest, so they brought me a score from the orchestral library. I had done it in concert many times and I had a clear imagination of it, and as we had spent the week playing Schubert it was very easy work!' At 9 a.m. he picked up his baton, the horn call sounded, and off they went. It turned out to be an excellent recording, idiomatically Viennese, and it is still in the Naxos catalogue fifteen years later. 'We just played Schubert. When you are in the studio for six or seven hours a day, you don't think about what an historical moment it is, that you are recording one of the greatest works in the symphonic repertoire. You are just caught up in this glorious music. Now and again I thought about my feet, because I was on my feet for a very long time.'

The association between Halász and Naxos has spanned nearly twenty-five years; the Schubert symphony cycle is one of its highlights, though it began in more obscure territory. Heymann and Halász first met in 1985 in Bratislava when Takako Nishizaki recorded Rubinstein's Violin Concerto with the Slovak Philharmonic Orchestra for Marco Polo. Mutual respect meant a constant stream of subsequent recording commissions. In the following year Halász recorded Goldmark's Second Symphony and the overture *Penthesilea* with the Rhenish Philharmonic Orchestra. It was the first of a number of world-premiere recordings that Halász conducted for Marco Polo, the ideas for which, he acknowledges, generally came from Heymann. 'At that time Klaus was looking for the gaps, for what had not been recorded. I think he was sleeping with the *Musik in Geschichte und Gegenwart*, looking for the holes. He drove me almost to insanity to make me do Myaskovsky symphonies. I asked him, "Who wants this stuff?" He said, "The Myaskovsky revival is coming." I am still waiting for it, but I did the Seventh and Tenth Symphonies anyway.'

Other orchestral repertoire that Halász recorded for Marco Polo includes ballet music from Rubinstein's operas, Schmidt's Symphony No. 1 and *Notre Dame*, and Richard Strauss's Symphony No. 2; and it was for Marco Polo, not Naxos, that he first brought his operatic expertise into play. Since 1978 he had been general musical director of the Hagen Opera House and, just before leaving to take up the post of resident conductor at the Vienna State Orchestra, he proposed to Heymann Schreker's *Der ferne Klang*. It was the most ambitious project yet undertaken by Marco Polo, though just the kind of world premiere that Heymann wanted. It was only possible because Halász had already programmed it at Hagen, so all the rehearsals and preparation had taken place. Quite a coup for the label, it was released in 1991.

'The tasks Klaus gave me for Marco Polo meant that I learned things I wouldn't have known. They were worth doing because they were world premieres – though to be honest we didn't really know how they would turn out. The Goldmark is not the best symphony because it is so programmatic and the Strauss symphony is not a very notable piece because it is not the Strauss we know; but just because it is not Dvořák doesn't mean that it is unimportant. They were worth doing – though I am *still* not sure about Myaskovsky!'

By the early 1990s Halász was also busy recording more popular works for Naxos. There was a steady outpouring of repertoire that included ballets by Tchaikovsky (*Swan Lake* and *The Nutcracker*), overtures by Beethoven and even Beethoven's Symphonies Nos. 3 and 6. 'When Klaus asked me to do the Third I did wonder if I should. There are so many recordings of Beethoven's "Eroica" – who is waiting for the "Eroica" conducted by Halász? Doing it in a concert is a different thing, but the 150th "Eroica" on record? Then I thought, ok, if the world can take Myaskovsky's symphonies, they can take Halász's "Eroica"! I did it, and I think it is a decent thing.'

Other works included Mozart's C minor Mass and Brahms's Symphony No. 4; cello concertos by Elgar and Dvořák with Maria Kliegel; and part of the Mahler symphony cycle, shared with Antoni Wit (Halász recorded Nos. 1, 7 and 9, as well as *Das Lied von der Erde*). Though based in Vienna, Halász remains very respectful of the orchestras with which he worked. 'The Slovak Philharmonic was an excellent orchestra; it was only because it was in Bratislava that it was not regarded as a leading orchestra, like the London Philharmonic. They could do almost everything. It was just because they were behind the Iron Curtain at this time that they were not so well known in the West.'

His appointment to the Vienna State Opera came at a time when Heymann was ready to risk new digital recordings of opera on a budget label. The margins were tight, but with an opera conductor of Halász's standing he did not need to worry about the result. Heymann wisely left the choice of singers to Halász. 'I was working with good singers all the time, and it was better that I chose them than agents pushed singers on to Klaus.' The first Mozart opera he recorded for Naxos was *The Magic Flute* – in the Italian Institute in Budapest with the Failoni Orchestra. The soloists were Herbert Lippert as Tamino, Elizabeth Norberg-Schulz as Pamina, Hellen Kwon as the Queen of the Night, Kurt Rydl as Sarastro, and Georg Tichy, who hit the comic mark with his Papageno. When the recording was released in 1994 *Gramophone*'s complimentary review began, 'Naxos has done it again'.

The recording sessions went well, but it could so easily have foundered in the editing studio: 'I always like to be with the people when they edit, sometimes even in the first edit. It was particularly important to be there for *The Magic Flute* because there is so much spoken dialogue, and some of the singers did not have very good German. We also had to mix in some sound effects – the magic flute, the thunder and the roaring lion. It was lucky that I was there. I was sitting in the edit studio when we were mixing the thunder before the Queen of the Night's first entry. The engineer put it together and I listened back, and I felt there was something not quite right. I said to the engineer that the Queen of the Night was suddenly a half-tone higher. He said it was not possible. I said I do not have absolute pitch but it seems to be not only higher but faster. When we checked it we found that the high note of the Queen of the Night was now not F but F sharp. It was a fact! We were totally puzzled. We didn't know why. The original recording was at the right pitch. So we started to read the manuals to the digital editing system that was being used. The engineer didn't have very good English, and although I could read the English I wasn't an engineer and didn't really understand the technical data! But thinking it through, I came to the solution that the sound-effect sample of the thunder was at 48 kHz and everything else was at 44.1 kHz. By picking up that sound effect and placing it before the Queen of the Night, it took her higher. I said, "Ok, what can we do?" The solution we came to was not in the manuals, but we made it work: we put in one millisecond of digital silence between the thunder and the Queen, and this allowed the Queen of the Night to play at 44.1. I was very proud of that millisecond.'

Beethoven's *Fidelio* was recorded in 1998 and *Don Giovanni* two years later, both in the Phoenix Studio in Budapest with the Nicolaus Esterházy Sinfonia; and he was back there in 2004 for *The Marriage of Figaro*.

Now in his mid-seventies, Halász looks back at his many years of recording for Naxos with a sense of satisfaction and affection. It was not as overtly glamorous as his work in the opera houses, but it was a sustained thread. 'I have often underestimated what it has meant to be on the label. I recorded in Bratislava or Budapest, but Klaus was selling Naxos all over the world. I found that a lot of people knew me in parts of the earth that I could never imagine I would be known. I was surprised. I know I can record well because I have a good feeling for tempo and editing, though I don't like to listen to my recordings now because they remind me of the development I have been through. But some I am proud of: Mahler 9, a lot of the Schubert symphonies, perhaps the Ninth, the Second and Third. As for opera, I think *The Magic Flute* – all the Mozarts –

and *Fidelio*, too. But I did not do all these recordings for the money, or for my immortality. I love conducting good pieces.'

Jeremy Summerly

Jeremy Summerly, a conductor and lecturer, is head of academic studies at the Royal Academy of Music in London, a broadcaster for BBC Radio, and an editor for Faber Music. He founded the Oxford Camerata choir in 1984 and was conductor of the Schola Cantorum of Oxford from 1990 to 1996. He has conducted music spanning nine centuries on more than forty recordings for Naxos, and has also conducted at the BBC Proms and the Berliner Philharmonie.

Summerly is very precise about his first contact with Naxos. 'I was woken up the day after celebrating my thirtieth birthday, 28 February 1991, by a man called David Denton. He said, "You may not have heard of the company, Naxos." But I had, because I had heard the Schumann and Brahms piano quintets, which was a glorious recording. He said he had heard me on Radio 3 (it was on *Record Review*) reviewing recent Renaissance choral music, and he presumed I had my own choir. I told him I did, the Oxford Camerata, and I sent him recordings of concerts we had done.

'Shortly after that he rang me again and said, "We are looking for five recordings of Renaissance choral music, more or less as soon as you can do them." By the summer we were up and running and we did the first five in fifteen months. Our first recording was the collection of *Lamentations* by White, Tallis, Palestrina, Lassus and de Brito. We recorded it in New College, Oxford, where I had been an undergraduate myself. It was the summer, so I managed to get in there quite easily and it meant that I was recording in a building I knew well with singers I knew well, and I chose the repertoire, which I also knew very well. We followed that pattern and stuck with what we knew. After the *Lamentations* we recorded Palestrina's *Missa Papae Marcelli*, Masses by Byrd, Victoria and Tallis, and some motets. We were within our comfort zone to get out these five recordings as quickly as we did. When an opportunity like that happens, you either move or you don't!'

However, things were not quite as simple as they sound. Summerly and the Oxford Camerata had to move from recording at New College for practical reasons. 'We went from New College to Dorchester Abbey then back to New College, then to Hertford College, Oxford, where we ended up doing most of our recordings because it is very quiet – there is no through traffic. That is very important when you are working with small forces – in our case, fifteen *a cappella* voices. You can't afford to have any extraneous noise at all. Every time the session has to stop for noise you lose a bit of the magic, by which I also mean your temper. In the end, we built a real relationship with this small chapel. Hertford College wasn't chosen for its architectural surroundings but it has really intimate acoustics and it became our recording home.

'I hadn't really thought what was going to happen after the first five were made. Since we'd started in 1984 we had been going along in a gentle way, doing concerts as and when the opportunities arose; but recording for Naxos forced us to become a proper group. It was fortunate that I had worked as a sound engineer for the BBC between 1982, when I graduated, and 1989, and I had also done some freelance production. So I was completely comfortable in the whole recording environment. Actually, the *Lamentations* was my second recording because I had made a CD with the Schola Cantorum of Oxford for a small English label. This meant that when I needed a fully fledged choir for Naxos I could turn to the Schola Cantorum, keeping the Oxford Camerata for Renaissance music.'

The Oxford Camerata's recordings sold remarkably well: *Lamentations* has topped 100,000 and Palestrina's *Missa Papae Marcelli* more than 150,000. They were also widely praised and helped to set the standard not only for Naxos recordings of early music but for the label's improving musical standards in general. This was especially important because, though the group emanated from England and was drawing on the excellence of the English choral tradition, its repertoire was international.

After those first five recordings, David Denton asked simply, 'Well, what's next?' Summerly suggested Gesualdo's five-part music, which conveniently fitted onto one disc. 'It was not music we knew well, and so for the first time we moved slightly out of our comfort zone and into music I hadn't thought of recording before. But this was an opportunity to broaden our range, and from that moment there seemed few barriers. I didn't have to plan, because Naxos started to request specific music from us, such as Fauré's Requiem, which as it happened I was performing with Schola Cantorum. Then came Bach and Vivaldi. It was quite an organic process. It burgeoned in a way I hadn't expected it to do. Actually, I hadn't considered myself a specialist in Renaissance music when we started so I was very happy when the brief expanded back to the medieval period and then up to the Baroque and the nineteenth century.'

Being an academic as well as a conductor, Summerly was able to contribute to Naxos in other ways. 'It never occurred to me that there was a restriction in recording for a budget label: we were being paid a professional fee and we were not doing a budget job. But we did feel that what was provided in the booklet with the CDs could be improved by heftier liner notes, texts and translations. When I mentioned this, David simply suggested I send them to him and they would be printed! It was so straightforward! Fortunately, we had a number of people in both choirs who were very reliable in a variety of languages, not least Latin, so we did it all in house and Naxos paid for them. So with this kind of relationship it never occurred to us, though our reputation was growing, that we could do better by going to EMI or Deutsche Grammophon. There would have been so many more constraints on what we could do.'

Summerly began to discuss future projects directly with Heymann, and he recalls that it was Heymann himself who was the prime mover in taking Summerly's recordings beyond the Renaissance area. They first met when the Oxford Camerata was invited to sing at the company's tenth-anniversary London concert in 1997. 'He described us as Naxos five-star artists.'

The music that Summerly was now conducting stretched back in time to Hildegard of Bingen, Machaut and Gombert, and forward to John Tavener. Summerly formed the Oxford Camerata's own instrumental ensemble for the recording of Fauré's Requiem but used the Northern Chamber Orchestra for Bach (including the *Magnificat*) and Vivaldi. He continued to feel that he had artistic freedom. 'It suited us down to the ground. The wonderful thing about the association with Naxos is the lack of artistic meddling. Klaus said he wanted Fauré's Requiem, and I said I would like to do the fantastically beautiful original version without violins. His reply was simply that that was our call.'

Of the many recordings that Summerly has now made for Naxos he highlights two in particular. 'Perhaps the most special for me was Purcell's Anthems with the *Music on the Death of Queen Mary*. It is English music and we are a quintessentially English choir. In the recording sessions I remember we didn't want to move on. We would get to the end of a piece and the producer would say, 'Let's move on,' and we really didn't want to. We wanted to do it just once more . . . we almost couldn't bear to say it was a wrap on any one track.' Especially memorable too was the recording of *Spem in Alium*, Tallis's forty-part motet, a unique jewel of Renaissance choral repertoire. 'We recorded *Spem in Alium* for the twentieth anniversary of the Oxford Camerata in 2004. The producer was Andrew Walton and the engineer was Mike Clements. Of course we needed forty voices. In these early music groups, singers have a very useful window of about a decade before their voices mature and they start to become soloists, and so the makeup of the choir constantly changes. With *Spem* we were able to get people back and have a wonderful time. But I will also never forget it because we recorded the piece in the round, which I had never done before. I remember standing in the middle of the huge circle in the large nave of All Hallows, Gospel Oak, doing this wonderful piece. Wherever I looked in this huge circle of forty singers I could see a really good friend. It was both a most extraordinary musical and a most extraordinary emotional experience for me. Even now, I can't listen to it because it moves me too much. I know each one of those forty voices, and I was slap bang in the middle of it. It was unforgettable.'

Summerly has recorded for Naxos for over twenty years: what started as performance in the highly specialist area of Renaissance music expanded beyond all expectations. He has conducted Tavener's *Lament for Jerusalem*, *The Christmas Story* by Schütz, Portuguese Masses by Lobo and Cardoso, and Handel's Coronation Anthems (including *Zadok the Priest*). He even recorded a wordless version of thirty seconds of the Agnus Dei from Fauré's Requiem for a car advertisement on television (the producers were going to use the Naxos recording but decided it was not appropriate to use sacred words, so the choir was recorded afresh without them). As a teacher at the Royal Academy he could identify gaps in the catalogue of available choral music recordings, and he found Heymann receptive when he explained the need for a good recording of music by Machaut, for example.

Easter Week of 1993 was particularly packed. 'That was my busiest week. Most of the choir, being church musicians, had had Holy Week, which is massive, then Easter Day, and we had barely left church for seven days. Then we moved up to Oxford, where for two days we recorded Lassus' Masses for Five Voices. A day off ... then two days of English madrigals and songs, having had to fit in the rehearsals for it the week before Easter. I will never forget that. People were absolutely exhausted but they just got better and better through the Lassus disc, and it shouldn't have been possible to make that English disc. But we did and it sounds excellent!'

Summerly and his groups now make fewer recordings, though he still appears regularly on new releases: he must be one of the most anthologised conductors on Naxos. His recordings, largely of sacred music, have appeared on *Classical Meditation, Chill with Bach, A Bride's Guide to Wedding Music, Classics Go To War, Mystic Voices, 101 Classics – The Best Loved Classical Melodies, Caravaggio: Music of His Time, Adagio Chillout, Music to Die For*, and many more. Summerly is not at all precious. 'I am flattered! It doesn't matter where the music ends up. If it gets into someone's home and on someone's CD player or computer that's fine!' – very much a Naxos message.

Helmut Müller-Brühl

For more than fifteen years the Cologne Chamber Orchestra (CCO), under the baton of Helmut Müller-Brühl, has recorded exclusively for Naxos, building a discography of over sixty discs. It was an important association, as the orchestra set a certain style of performance for the central eighteenth- and nineteenth-century works that it covered on the label, drawing on its unusual history. Formed in 1924 by Hermann Abendroth, it switched to period instruments in 1976 and for a decade was prominent in historical performance. In 1987 Müller-Brühl decided on a return to modern instruments, but with a continuation of period-performance techniques. Although it is now commonplace, this approach was novel at the time. There were various practical reasons that contributed to Müller-Brühl's decision, some concerning the size of concert halls; but there were musical reasons as well.

'To achieve the correct period style it is far more important to observe historical performance practice and information than to use so-called original instruments; and by observing historical performance practice, including reading the material correctly, an historically informed interpretation can be achieved even with modern instruments.'

The change was successfully managed, and by the mid-1990s the CCO with Müller-Brühl was well established as a leading German chamber orchestra, no longer using historical instruments. It was at this point that Müller-Brühl met Klaus Heymann, whose own predilections towards performance favoured the CCO's approach. The environment of the first meeting, Müller-Brühl remembers, was not particularly auspicious: 'We met at the Airport Hotel at Frankfurt Airport in 1996 during a flight transfer.' But there was an immediate understanding and within months the CCO was recording for Naxos, starting with oboe concertos by J.S. Bach, played by Christian Hommel. It was a declaration from both Müller-Brühl and Heymann that period style and the faithful presentation of a Baroque or Classical composer was possible in conjunction with the benefits of modern instruments. Müller-Brühl is unequivocal in his belief that the series of recordings devoted to orchestral works by J.S. Bach opened a new chapter in recording. 'They were the first convincing recordings on modern instruments and are today, as a set of complete works, second to none,' he declares confidently. The Beethoven recordings were made with a similar conviction. 'There are many Beethoven symphony cycles on the market, but ours, in addition to being highly developed, freshly interpreted and in an historically informed performance style, is also one that can actually be heard! I am glad that the release of the Ninth Symphony completes our cycle in time for the twenty-fifth anniversary of Naxos.'

The sixty-plus recordings made by the CCO encompass works by J.S. Bach and Vivaldi, eight volumes of Haydn symphonies, three volumes of Mozart symphonies, and many concerto discs – including discoveries such as the violin concertos by Vanhal and Saint-Georges, recorded with Takako Nishizaki. Müller-Brühl is particularly pleased with the disc of Telemann's 'Darmstadt Overtures', which won a Cannes Classical Award in 2001. 'This was such an event, since no other group playing Baroque music on modern instruments had won this award before. To me it was a breakthrough which showed that the validity of Baroque music performance is primarily achieved though an historically informed interpretation and not merely through the use of historical instruments.'

Throughout the sixteen years of his recording for Naxos Müller-Brühl has been involved in frequent discussions with Heymann over repertoire. 'At the beginning most of the suggestions came from Klaus Heymann, such as the Telemann and many Haydn symphonies. Bach, Mozart and Beethoven are my gods. The more unknown musical treasures are the result of our cooperation in choosing repertoire. I was always impressed by the high quality of the Naxos recordings and was happy to see that this high standard of quality was available to the public at an attractive price. The close relationship I have had with Klaus Heymann and Naxos counts among some of the best experiences of my life and I am forever grateful for this.'

Takuo Yuasa

The Japanese-born Takuo Yuasa has an impressively diverse discography on Naxos. On more than thirty recordings he conducts music that includes violin concertos by Vieuxtemps and Lalo, Schoenberg's *Verklärte Nacht* and a selection of Webern, and works by Rubbra, Glass and Arvo Pärt; while in his home country he is known especially for helping to bring back into musical awareness a host of Japanese composers, including Yamada and Yashiro.

In many ways, his Naxos recordings mirror his personal musical journey. At the age of eighteen he left Japan to study first of all in the US and then in Europe (with Hans Swarowsky in Austria, Igor Markevitch in France and Franco Ferrara in Italy) before he became assistant to Lovro von Matačić, working in Monte Carlo, Milan and Vienna. He remembers the start of his Naxos journey very clearly. It was 1996 and he was scheduled to conduct the Hong Kong Philharmonic Orchestra. Shortly before he arrived he received a letter from Heymann, the opening of which he can recall even now.

> *Dear Mr Yuasa,*
> *I want to record with you.*

'That was the first sentence. He didn't introduce himself. He came straight to the point. That is so Klaus. Then he said would I be exclusive!'

They met when Yuasa arrived in Hong Kong, and a year later he made his first recording: *Veni, Veni, Emmanuel* and *Tryst* by the Scottish composer James MacMillan. Having conducted the BBC Scottish Symphony Orchestra for some years (he still has a flat in Glasgow), Yuasa was familiar with MacMillan; but it was still a challenging start. The recording was made with the Ulster Orchestra in the responsive Ulster Hall – Yuasa became the orchestra's principal guest conductor in 1998, which was the start of a long, amicable association – and went on to sell 20,000 copies worldwide. It was a very respectable figure for Scottish contemporary music.

Yuasa initially concentrated on British music. He recorded Tavener's *The Protecting Veil* and *In Alium*, which turned out to be another contemporary music hit and sold 40,000 copies; and he went back to the BBC Scottish Symphony Orchestra to record Britten's Violin Concerto (played by Rebecca Hirsch) and Cello

Symphony (played by Tim Hugh). Both these recordings were released in 1999. The following years saw more British repertoire, including Rubbra's Violin Concerto and two recordings in the 'British Piano Concertos' series (Harty and Rawsthorne).

Yuasa had to learn all these works specially for the recordings but he was comfortable with that, having always been able to get to grips with a new score quickly. 'This was thanks to my background in theory and composition with my professor, Hans Swarowsky. Most of the lessons were taken up by score reading, so now I have a very clear method in my approach to the score.' His most testing time in this skill was when he came to record *Inflight Entertainment*, *Powerhouse* and other works by the Australian composer Graeme Koehne with the Sydney Symphony Orchestra. Yuasa was conducting in Oslo and at short notice was asked to fly to Australia to do the recording. The score arrived just two days before he boarded the plane, but he was in command of the music by the time he walked into Sydney Town Hall. 'Fortunately, it was a very clear score and musically it wasn't complicated!' That was in January 2001. Circumstances meant that despite the urgency in the making of the recording, the CD was not released until October 2004 (which gives just a glimpse of another side to the record business).

As time passed, Yuasa's contemporary music discography expanded. He recorded Philip Glass's Violin Concerto and Michael Nyman's Piano Concerto (made from the film score of *The Piano*); and Arvo Pärt's *Tabula Rasa* (with *Collage über B-A-C-H* and Symphony No. 3), which has sold 60,000 copies.

Yuasa points out that being Japanese but having trained in Europe, there was not an obvious musical route for him to take. 'Klaus asked me what I wanted to record, and if I was Finnish I could have said Sibelius.' Yuasa suggested the Second Viennese School, because he had spent so many of his younger years steeped in that European tradition: his recording of music by Webern, including *Passacaglia*, *Symphony* and *Five Pieces*, remains an important one for him. Perhaps surprisingly, he values equally his disc of music by Honegger, which includes the Symphony No. 3 'Liturgique' and *Pacific 231*.

During 2001 his Naxos career took an unexpected turn. 'I remember when Klaus approached me right at the beginning, he mentioned – it was just a hint of a suggestion – that one day I could do some Japanese music. It didn't really stay in my mind, until a few years later he called me in Tokyo one day and he said he wanted to start recording Japanese repertoire.' Naxos had not gained as strong a presence in Japan as Heymann felt it should have done (after all, the country is one of the largest markets for classical music), so he had decided to do some Japanese symphonic repertoire that he had heard about, despite its being little known outside the country.

Yuasa was entrusted with these works, and made the world-premiere recording of Yamada's Overture with the New Zealand Symphony Orchestra. 'The Overture dates from 1912, and was written in the style of Weber or Mendelssohn. Yamada's next work, Symphony in D "Triumph and Peace", was in a slightly later style; but, by the following year, two tone poems showed that he'd had contact with Richard Strauss – Yamada had travelled to Europe and heard Strauss conduct.'

'Japanese Classics' developed into an ongoing series that initially explored pre-Second World War symphonic music, showing that Takemitsu did not emerge from nowhere: he was building on a Western-influenced but Japanese classical tradition. Although some of these works had been recorded before, Naxos's series, put together by the musicologist Morihide Katayama, gave the label the presence it was looking for in Japan. There are now some twenty recordings, half of which have been conducted by Yuasa. Many of the volumes – featuring composers such as Yashiro, Ohki, Moroi and Mayuzumi – were made with Western orchestras, including the Ulster Orchestra and the New Zealand Symphony Orchestra; this was regarded as a bonus for Japanese CD buyers, who were pleased that their music had travelled abroad.

The commercial success of the recordings brought the music to a wider Japanese audience than ever before. 'Naxos should get credit for many Japanese people becoming interested in their own repertoire. Nowadays you can often find orchestral concerts including Japanese repertoire, much more than before the Naxos series came out.' It also had the effect of establishing Yuasa's reputation as a conductor in Japan. For decades he was a Japanese export to Europe, but the recordings led to his conducting more frequently in Japanese cities. He currently divides his time between Europe, Osaka and Tokyo, where he also teaches at the Tokyo University of Fine Arts and Music. This has a professional orchestra and a recording faculty, and Yuasa organised the most recent 'Japanese Classics' release, Hashimoto's Symphony No. 2, to be recorded there. 'These Naxos recordings have made me known to the musical audiences in my own country.'

Leonard Slatkin

Ever since the first performance in 1984 of William Bolcom's *Songs of Innocence and of Experience*, based on the poems of William Blake, Leonard Slatkin had wanted to record it. He had conducted it a few times in concert but, as the years rolled by, the prospect of a recording seemed to become increasingly distant: lasting nearly three hours and calling for huge forces (orchestra, chorus and soloists, as well as musicians from outside the classical milieu: nearly 500 performers in total), it was just too big, too demanding and ultimately too costly to take into a studio. But in 2004 Slatkin saw his opportunity emerge. It was the twentieth anniversary of the work's premiere, and the University of Michigan, where it had originally been performed, was able to provide the players and even find sponsorship – after all, Bolcom himself was on its composition faculty. Slatkin found himself in the right place at the right time: he was just taking up a new appointment as director of the nearby Detroit Symphony Orchestra and was keen to make contact with the university, aware as he was of its high standard of music-making. He was prepared to volunteer his services and he knew that many of the soloists would do the same: this was a special work.

He knew that Naxos already had a relationship with Bolcom so he approached Heymann. 'I hadn't met Klaus at that point, but of course, having bounced around from record company to record company over the years, I was following the industry as much as I could. It was clearly changing but I was one of those people who thought that Naxos was doing exactly the right thing – offering repertoire that was unusual or familiar at prices that most people could afford. So I suggested doing the Bolcom, and he agreed.' It was decided to capture a live performance and use that as the basis for the recording (with an inevitable patch session afterwards); in the event, it was not quite so simple. For two months the university music faculty made the work a priority, preparing for the concert on 8 April 2004. Slatkin moved in to work with the musicians two weeks beforehand, which is an unusually generous amount of rehearsal time with the conductor for an event of this kind. He was impressed by the musicians. 'If you didn't put on the cover that it was a university chorus and orchestra nobody would know that it wasn't professional. That is the level of young musicians these days: it is so high.' The concert was a huge success and the musicians prepared for the post-concert patching session. 'We knew we would have to get rid of some audience noise, and because of the logistics of the piece it wasn't practical to take some of it from the concert: the forces were disposed all over the stage, with chorus and chamber pieces. Some sections would have to be recorded separately.' In the end, it proved impossible to use recordings from the concert performance because of balance issues created by amplification in the hall. It was all re-recorded in the succeeding day and a half, including some hours immediately after the concert.

There was an extraordinary, unanimous agreement for nearly everyone to stay on site until the recording was completed. Production control was in the hands of the experienced Naxos producer Tim Handley, with the engineer David Lau and the whole team working late into the night. The sessions continued the following day, the musicians and the recording team working for nearly nine hours non-stop to finish everything. It was a momentous challenge, one to which a youthful, vigorous and talented university team can perhaps rise better than most. The spirit of it came through on the three-CD set. It was released worldwide in October 2004 to widespread acclaim, and in February 2006 it scooped four GRAMMY Awards: Best Classical Album, Best Choral Performance, Best Classical Contemporary Composition, and Producer Of The Year for Tim Handley. It justified Slatkin's belief in the project and his ability to bring it together. 'Bill and I were students together in 1964 in Aston. I have played a number of his pieces over the years, commissioned one of his symphonies and recorded another. I love doing his music – it is so off the wall, such great fun.'

Winning the first classical GRAMMYs for Naxos, the recording cemented the relationship between conductor and record company. Regular releases of both American and European repertoire appeared in the following years, including John Adams's Violin Concerto played by the young English violinist Chloë Hanslip and the Royal Philharmonic Orchestra. Slatkin's tenure as chief conductor of the BBC Symphony Orchestra (2000–04) made him a familiar figure in the UK, which paved the way for further Naxos recordings there in addition to those in the US. In 2005, following the death of Kenneth Schermerhorn, conductor of the Nashville Symphony, Slatkin stepped in as music advisor. Naxos of America was based in Nashville and had an established relationship with the Nashville Symphony, so it was no surprise that in June 2006 Slatkin found himself in the Laura Turner Concert Hall recording works by another composer friend, Joan Tower. The CD contained the *Concerto for Orchestra*, but of special interest were the premiere recordings of *Made in America* and *Tambor*. The disc won two GRAMMY Awards in 2008, including Best Classical Album.

By the time of the award ceremony Slatkin was already deep in his next project for Naxos: the complete music by Leroy Anderson. 'Anderson is one of those composers whom a lot of people don't know by name but once they hear his music they know exactly who he is. I suggested to Klaus that for the centenary of Anderson's birth [2008] we should record as much as we could of what we know exists in his catalogue. It turned out to be five CDs and I think out of those there are perhaps nine pieces which have never been recorded before.' Slatkin chose to record the Anderson collection in London with the BBC Concert Orchestra (which he had conducted in the BBC Proms); it was perhaps a surprising choice, but the orchestra is known for its facility with light music. 'The players have a really good feel for the style and the requisite sense of humour. They didn't know all the music but they knew how to play it.'

Slatkin's appointments as music director of the Detroit Symphony Orchestra and of the Orchestre National de Lyon mean that both orchestras appear in future plans for Naxos. He has started a Rachmaninov symphony cycle with the DSO and regards the first disc – Symphony No. 2 coupled with *Vocalise* – as one of the best he has ever done. His work in Lyon will bring more Berlioz and Ravel onto Naxos, as well as the world-premiere recording of Gabriel Pierné's *The Children's Crusade* (although a major twentieth-century work, it has never been recorded before).

Slatkin has worked for many record companies – EMI, RCA, Vox, Telarc, Decca, Philips and Chandos – but his association with Naxos is what he wants now. 'With Naxos, I don't feel under pressure to record things just because they will sell. There seems to be a real commitment to the music that the label is producing. Yes, the money is tight but I am not doing it for money. Also, at this point in my life I don't have to record anything I don't want to. That is a good feeling. I don't have to worry about how I am being perceived. I have found that Klaus loves the things that are unusual like Bolcom or Pierné. And with Klaus, just when you think there is a change in the industry that is going to sink Naxos, he always comes up with some new way to rethink the industry itself. He is a good businessman, very easy to talk to, and very direct.'

Robert Craft

For nearly two decades the conductor and writer Robert Craft has been methodically recording the major works of the two composers with whom he has been so closely associated for most of his life: Igor Stravinsky and Arnold Schoenberg. From 1947, when he first came into contact with Stravinsky, Craft found himself catapulted into a milieu of music and the contemporary arts that was one of the most exciting and creative of any age; he met many of the greatest figures of the post-war period in Europe, America and the Far East – not only composers but artists, poets and 'makers of the twentieth century'. In 1950 Craft met Arnold Schoenberg, who was then in the last year of his life. A highly able musician himself, Craft proved to be indispensable to Stravinsky; he conducted and organised many performances and recordings of his music both during the composer's last two decades and after his death.

The purpose of Craft's assiduous and energetic recording programme, undertaken in the face of some obstacles, was simply to create a special archive, a legacy of a musical view of these two composers from someone who 'had their confidence'.

Craft has handpicked the orchestras and soloists and been extraordinarily diligent where the editions are concerned: he has often clarified details that he knew concerned the composers but perhaps were never documented; and he has brought out features that he is sure they would have wanted. These two archives have never been compromised by insufficient funds since Craft created a foundation that could allow the highest artistic standards. The recordings feature top orchestras in the US and the UK (Orchestra of St. Luke's, Twentieth Century Classics Ensemble and Fred Sherry String Quartet in America; Philharmonia Orchestra in England); they took place at leading venues, such as London's Abbey Road Studios; and immense care was taken over technical issues in their recording, editing and mastering.

Among them is the world-premiere recording of *The Firebird* in its complete original version, which reinstates the presence of two long, valveless trumpets, each playing a single note that stands out above the entire orchestra. It is a thrilling effect and is, in all likelihood, heard on this recording for the first time since 1910.

The collection so far contains fourteen discs of Stravinsky and eleven discs of Schoenberg, 'the two giants of twentieth-century music', as Craft puts it. There are also two discs containing the main works of Anton Webern, and Naxos offers the complete works of Webern in three volumes, which Craft recorded in 1957, to download or stream online. While Craft sees all these recordings as an important legacy, he makes no claim that they are definitive (he is far too aware of the range of possibilities when it comes to interpretation); but he does feel that the composers themselves would approve of the performances. Together they form 'The Robert Craft Collection'.

When Craft began this momentous task the recordings were released by two American labels: Music Masters and Koch International Classics. As time passed, these labels were unable to continue their commitment, and the ownership of the masters reverted to Craft. He sought a label that could match the dedication he was making to the music of these three composers, and the collection found its home at Naxos, starting in 2004.

At the time of writing, Robert Craft is eighty-eight and still actively seeing recent programmes through the editing stages as well as planning new recordings. 'The collection is the greatest pride of my musical life. The musicians on these recordings, like the Philharmonia, give marvellous performances, at a level that has never been achieved before. They have been cooperative and they are able to handle the technical problems in a way that was not possible at the time so much of this music was written.' Craft knows so well the music he is conducting that he even asks in advance for certain orchestral musicians to play in specified works. 'I give notes in advance that, for example, I would like a particular oboist to play in Stravinsky's *Symphony in C*: the second movement is almost like an oboe concerto! This careful choice is especially important with singers. The most musical singers are not always the singers with the best voices. I must have singers with good ears who can manage the dissonant intervals – the large intervals going to remote notes – but who also have a keen musical sense of rhythm and very little vibrato. This is important in modern music because we care about the pitches so much.'

Craft also enjoys taking advantage of the improvement in the technical side of recording since the early days, when generally only one microphone was used – though he acknowledges that this used to give a very real perspective of a work. 'You do get a balanced orchestra: we don't really care about the second contrabassoon in *The Firebird*. But now, using many microphones, you can give certain instruments more volume, more power; you can have close-ups of passages that would not be heard by a single microphone.'

He feels his recordings of Schoenberg serve a special purpose. 'Ninety-five per cent of Schoenberg's music is unknown to the general musical public – most of the works are never heard in the concert hall. But it is the kind of music that needs to be heard frequently. That is why I wanted these recordings to be with a record label that would keep them available to the public.' Of the Schoenberg discs he has a particular affection for the *Gurre-Lieder*. 'The performance is wonderful because it shows the hidden Wagnerism in me. There is that side of me that has not been able to come out through Stravinsky's music. I would have liked to record *The Ring*.' Of his Stravinsky recordings he singles out *The Rake's Progress*, played by the Orchestra of St Luke's. Craft first met Stravinsky on the same day that Auden delivered the completed libretto to the composer; he was immediately involved in the composition, helping with the pronunciation, vocabulary and rhythms of the English text.

In 2006 Naxos published in hardback a fascinating collection of thoughts and memoirs by Craft called *Down a Path of Wonder*. Many major figures of the twentieth century make an appearance within, including George Balanchine, T.S. Eliot, W.H. Auden and Aldous Huxley – as well as Stravinsky and Schoenberg.

James Judd

With the Heymann family having maintained a home in New Zealand for many years, it was not surprising that Naxos established a relationship with the New Zealand Symphony Orchestra. When the English conductor James Judd arrived in Wellington in 1999 to take up the post of music director, the relationship had temporarily halted and one of Judd's intentions was to revive it. 'The NZSO is an incredibly versatile orchestra, one where the musicians read very fast, like in London. You can put the red light on straight away and start recording. I was keen for the orchestra to work again with

Naxos because while it had done some recording and a little touring, it was really a secret in the musical world. But it was a terrific jewel of an orchestra.'

The NZSO is a very cosmopolitan group, with musicians from Europe and the Far East, but it also has a nucleus of homegrown players who have benefitted from the country's high standard of music education. It had never had a music director before Judd, working instead with many conductors and playing a wide range of repertoire in an equally wide range of styles. 'The musicians understand what a Brahms sound is, or a Mozart sound ... but they were also accustomed to recording contemporary works, especially the music of New Zealand composers, for small labels.'

As music director of the Florida Philharmonic Orchestra Judd had recorded Bernstein's Symphony No. 2 and the Symphonic Dances from *West Side Story*; it was logical, therefore, that his first few Naxos discs with the NZSO should contain American repertoire: Copland's Symphony No. 3 and *Billy the Kid*, followed by Gershwin's *An American in Paris* coupled with music from *Porgy and Bess*. More Bernstein followed, but Judd was keen for the orchestra to branch out. English music was an obvious step.

'I wanted to do English music because I felt we would do that especially well, but by then – 2002 – Naxos already had quite a lot! I particularly wanted to do Elgar, and we started with smaller pieces, both of *The Wand of Youth* suites and a volume of marches. Eventually I asked Klaus to give us a list of things he wanted, which opened up a very fruitful dialogue.' Vaughan Williams's Fantasias with the *Norfolk Rhapsody* was an early recording. Those which followed included Beethoven's incidental music for *Egmont*, Zemlinsky's *Die Seejungfrau* ('The Mermaid') and *Sinfonietta* (Judd had been performing Zemlinsky in concert), and two versions – one English and one German – of Mendelssohn's complete incidental music for *A Midsummer Night's Dream*; a few years later, Naxos added the spoken text, read by English and German actors, to form a world premiere.

The NZSO was also keen to record music by New Zealand and Australian composers. The chief executive of the orchestra, Peter Walls, had always programmed contemporary works by national composers in concerts, and Heymann, living in the region for part of every year, was committed to supporting its music. In 2003, under Judd's direction, the orchestra recorded *Earth Cry* and the Piano Concerto by one of Australia's most prominent composers, Peter Sculthorpe, and followed this a few years later with John Antill's music for the ballet *Corroboree*. For its first twentieth-century New Zealand music disc, Naxos again turned to an established figure, featuring orchestral works by Douglas Lilburn, described by Judd as 'the elder statesman of New Zealand classical music'. Judd was particularly impressed by the music of Lyell Cresswell – born in New Zealand though resident in Scotland – and recorded *The Voice Inside* with other works. 'That music is quite unique and unusual. Cresswell is a composer who I think should be better known. It is challenging to record contemporary music, when the composer is there. But it is important because Naxos, with its outstanding distribution, can take the music around the world.'

Judd has always maintained an international career – he is now conductor emeritus with the NZSO – and has recorded extensively in the UK as well. He suggested Bax to Heymann, and the Symphonic Variations coupled with the *Concertante* for piano left hand was recorded with the pianist Ashley Wass and the Bournemouth Symphony Orchestra. Wass joined him again, this time with the Royal Liverpool Philharmonic Orchestra, for Vaughan Williams's Piano Concerto, which was released with *The Wasps* and other works.

'I love the process of recording. What I am trying to do is to get something that is not just slick and clean but something that lives, where you can hear the hearts of the musicians pulsing hard on the page. I do find it a painful business listening back to the edits, and though I don't like doing it I do take it seriously. Fortunately I can trust the producers I work with – Andrew Walton and Tim Handley.'

Eleven

Composers of Our Time

There are many commercial reasons why a classical label selling at budget price should exercise caution when approaching contemporary music, or simply music in copyright. It comes down mainly to a question of margins. A royalty on all recordings sold – whether bought as physical CDs, downloaded or streamed – goes to all living composers, and then to their estates for a specified period after their death: seventy years in the EU and the United States (with some variation); fifty years in most other countries. The level of royalty is calculated according to the dealer price (the price at which the distributor sells to the shop). It means, in effect, that a recording of music in copyright generates between 20 per cent and 50 per cent less for the label than one of music in the public domain. In addition to this so-called mechanical royalty, many publishers demand a substantial upfront rental for the use of their scores and parts in the recording, a charge many record companies consider to be double-dipping. The other key factor, perhaps peculiar to classical music, is that recordings of contemporary music generally sell far fewer than those of Bach, Beethoven and Brahms, because the majority of classical music lovers often find music of their own time unappealing. There are many exceptions, of course, but on the whole this is true.

Naxos initially focused on public-domain repertoire and among the first 100 releases only one title was in copyright: Orff's *Carmina Burana*. Klaus Heymann's personal attitude was divided. On the one hand, he was a collector who had started with Marco Polo, a label designed for world premieres; what's more, his first recording was of his wife Takako Nishizaki playing a contemporary Chinese violin concerto. On the other hand, he was a businessman and Naxos was a business proposition. He realised that if he wanted to build a comprehensive catalogue of classical music he had to record the essential masterworks of twentieth-century and contemporary music. Within two or three years the die was cast: Naxos was becoming a fully fledged record label, which meant that this music must be included, whether it was Stravinsky (leading to the ambitious project of the complete orchestral works conducted by Robert Craft), Schoenberg or Shostakovich; or leading figures in twentieth-century musical iconoclasm such as John Cage (music for prepared piano), Edgard Varèse or Conlon Nancarrow (with his complex rhythms). Somehow Heymann would have to make the numbers add up, by attracting sponsorship or doing deals or selling far more records than past experience predicted or, in the final instance, swallowing the loss through success in other areas of repertoire. He tried never to make a recording that was guaranteed to lose money, but there were occasions when he approved a project while looking the other way.

In considering the music of our time that is available on Naxos and the composers who have been highlighted, it is interesting to note how methodical the coverage has been, with some clear national threads. The compositional line can be followed from the end of the nineteenth century to the beginning of the twenty-first. There seems to be an almost academic design. Heymann cannot say that it was planned that way; it happened somewhat organically, culminating in the works of key contemporary composers who, on the whole, have been delighted to find their music available at a low cost so that listeners can be adventurous in their choice. The collection is not comprehensive (that would be impossible); but after twenty-five years of Naxos recording there are interesting discernible threads, notably American, Polish and English. In addition, Naxos documents other developments that are less well known, such as the fascinating growth of Spanish and Japanese classical music – the latter represented in recent years by Tōru Takemitsu and Toshio Hosokawa. Many other composers of our time appear in the Naxos catalogue, though perhaps on only one or two recordings: figures as different as Gian Carlo Menotti and Luciano Berio. Naturally the catalogue is growing all the time: György Ligeti was represented only by Idil Biret's recording of the Études for piano until 2010, when the Parker Quartet's performance of his quartets was released. (It went on to win a GRAMMY Award in 2011.) Naxos now records more contemporary and twentieth-century music than any other record label, major or independent.

United States

The 'American Classics' series has been central to Naxos in America and now contains more than 360 recordings, many of which cover the leading symphonic composers of the twentieth century. Recording such a list for release on a budget label has been a risk and would not have been possible without support from many organisations, including The Copland Trust, which has helped with funds for musicians and composers. The giant figure of Charles Ives was crucial in releasing American music from European dependence, and when Naxos embarked upon his orchestral works (the symphonies and the *Orchestral Sets*) it was with the new critical editions. The liner notes explain the musical choices made by editor and conductor, and show the tremendous care taken with these recordings. This is why Symphony No. 4 has not been recorded yet: Heymann is waiting for the new approved edition to be finished. The complete songs appear on seven CDs and also use new editions. Then there are the musical surveys of William Schuman, Samuel Barber, Roy Harris and Leonard Bernstein (from chamber works such as the Clarinet Sonata to major choral works – *Chichester Psalms* and the Mass – to his most flamboyant musical signature, *West Side Story*).

A deeper look reveals a much wider and more challenging spread. There are the five string quartets of Elliott Carter, one of the major figures of twentieth-century American avant-garde, played by the Pacifica Quartet; and his Symphony No. 1, coupled with the Piano Concerto. Nine discs are devoted to works by George Rochberg and six discs to the music of Ned Rorem. Rorem is another key figure in twentieth-century American music; these recordings begin with a collection of his songs (sung by Carole Farley, accompanied by the composer) and include the three symphonies as well as a variety of concertos and chamber music. There are also two useful discs of George Crumb, another figure who used experimental techniques and pushed music on through the second half of the twentieth century, developing a distinctive American voice.

Then come the succeeding generations, who dominate the scene today. William Bolcom, John Corigliano and Joan Tower were all born in 1938 and their different musical paths have been reflected on Naxos. The label has even issued a recording called *The Class of '38*, featuring music by Bolcom, Gloria Coates (who also has two full discs, one of string quartets and one of symphonies), Corigliano, John Harbison, Frederic Rzewski, José Serebrier, Joan Tower and Charles Wuorinen (who has five full discs of varied music).

William Bolcom

William Bolcom's first appearance on Naxos was as a pianist rather than a composer: he recorded piano pieces by his teacher George Frederick McKay as a form of tribute. His wife, the soprano Joan Morris, also performed on the CD. It opened a Naxos connection, which led to a volume of his songs (on which he accompanies Carole Farley), his complete cello music and his four violin sonatas. But it was the premiere recording of his massive song cycle *Songs of Innocence and of Experience*, scored for soloists, choruses and orchestra, that won four GRAMMY Awards and made an unforgettable impact.

Ever since the first performance in Stuttgart in 1984 there had been discussions about recording *Songs of Innocence and of Experience*, but the practicalities proved to be beyond any record company. The University of Michigan, where Bolcom had taught since 1973, had mounted a performance of the work shortly after the Stuttgart premiere, and it was the composer Michael Daugherty, also on the teaching staff, who suggested another performance to mark the twentieth anniversary of that occasion. The university raised considerable funds to realise the idea, involving its top-class music students, local choirs and the university orchestra, with professional soloists, under the direction of Leonard Slatkin. It was at this point that Slatkin and Bolcom approached Heymann and suggested recording the concert, with some patching afterwards. Although momentarily daunted by the size of the project, Heymann agreed.

Bolcom was there throughout the preparations, the concert and the recording, and even years later his memory of the event is clear. 'It was an amazing thing. The whole of the school had turned its energies to the piece for two months to prepare. Leonard had conducted it twice already, and some of the soloists, like my wife, had also done it before; but many were coming to it for the first time. I had worked with the Naxos producer Tim Handley before and he was one of the most informed and best-prepared producers I have ever had to deal with – an amazing, interesting character with a fantastic pair of ears. And David Lau, the engineer, was excellent too. But to use the concert would have required too much equalisation, so we recorded it again. I am amazed at how it happened. We didn't do it in order: we did all the chorus sections together, then all the soloists together, so once you set up the mikes you didn't worry about changing them all the time. That was the most practical way of handling it. But for some reason the energy had been so positive that it felt like a live performance – to the point that when Leonard got to the first dub he wondered where the applause was at the end! Of the twenty or so performances of the work I have heard over the years, this was one of the very best.'

More music by Bolcom has been recorded for Naxos, including all his *Gospel Preludes* for organ, played by Gregory Hand.

John Corigliano

John Corigliano has developed a close relationship with Naxos in recent years and has a growing discography on the label, his music featuring on ten CDs to date. 'I am at every session that I can get to. I was a record producer at Columbia Masterworks in the 1970s and I know what I want, and my being there makes a big difference. In fact I co-produced the Naxos recording of *Mr. Tambourine Man* and we received two GRAMMYs for it in 2009 – one for the piece and the other for the best classical vocal performance. Being there means everything to me.'

One of the most widely recognised American composers, Corigliano works in many genres – from opera to concert music to film scores – and this is illustrated by his recordings. The music that originated as the film score for *The Red Violin* emerges in four different recordings, one in the form of a violin concerto played by Michael Ludwig with the Buffalo Philharmonic Orchestra conducted by JoAnn Falletta (coupled with *Phantasmagoria*, incorporating music from his opera *The Ghosts of Versailles*); the hauntingly beautiful Chaconne and the technically challenging Caprices each appear in two versions.

In *Mr. Tambourine Man* Corigliano set himself a tough challenge: to take Bob Dylan's poetry, which already had a musical existence, and give it a totally new musical life. Just how well he succeeded can be heard in the recording with the amplified soprano Hila Plitmann. The inclusion of a work like this indicates the boldness of the 'American Classics' series. It was preceded by the recording of another work in which Corigliano set famous words: *A Dylan Thomas Trilogy* (incorporating *Fern Hill*, *Poem in October* and *Poem on His Birthday*). This was given a bravura performance by the baritone Sir Thomas Allen with the Nashville Symphony conducted by Leonard Slatkin.

The most recent recording shows another side of Corigliano, involving adventurous writing for a large concert band. *Circus Maximus* was composed with a special production in mind that involved a stage band, a surround band and a marching band. The dramatic conception is realised by The University of Texas Wind Ensemble conducted by Jerry Junkin, and the CD was given a suitably striking 3D slipcase by Naxos. It is another recording for which the composer participated closely in the sessions, and it was eventually re-released as the first Naxos Blu-ray audio disc (BD-Audio).

Corigliano himself writes the liner notes for almost every Naxos recording of his music, often outlining the personal background to the works. It indicates the close relationship he has with the label, and with Heymann. Corigliano explains: 'I was a big fan of Naxos before being recorded by them. I loved their combination of unusual repertoire and savvy marketing: for example, there was always a huge display of Naxos recordings in every record store – no other company did this. So I asked my publisher [G. Schirmer] if I could have a meeting with the head of this company if he ever came to New York. It happened that Klaus was making a New York trip, and Schirmer asked him if he would meet with me. He not only agreed but came over to my apartment to talk. I told him of my experiences with other major labels: how they would spend a fortune producing a record and then fail to promote it; how you couldn't find my new releases in record stores because of distribution fiascos. I knew Klaus was aware of these things, but I wanted him to understand why I wanted to be on Naxos. We shared a fine white wine I brought back from Mendoza (Klaus ordered a case the next day), and I began to think that Naxos could be my next recording company.'

Corigliano's works are recorded by many labels, but he himself takes an active role in creating a link with Naxos. 'There is a partnership now, between orchestras and record labels, and I try to steer any orchestra interested in my work to the Naxos label.'

Joan Tower

Joan Tower, though born in New Rochelle, New York, spent her early years in South America and has always felt that this has influenced her music. Overcoming prejudice as one of the relatively few female composers, she held positions as resident composer with the St. Louis Symphony, Orchestra of St. Luke's and the Pittsburgh Symphony Orchestra which helped to establish her reputation. In 2001 a consortium of regional American orchestras received sponsorship from the Ford Motor Company Fund to commission a new work from a composer to be played by orchestras in each of the fifty states in America. The scheme was called 'Made in America'. Tower was commissioned by the consortium and wrote a fifteen-minute work that she called *Made in America*; it was played, as planned, throughout the country by no fewer than sixty-five community orchestras. Then it was recorded for Naxos by the Nashville Symphony conducted by Leonard Slatkin (coupled with *Tambor* and *Concerto for Orchestra*) and won three GRAMMY Awards, including Best Classical Contemporary Composition, in 2008.

From composition to recording, *Made in America* was one of the most unforgettable experiences for Tower. The first big step was the work itself. 'I began to think about these sixty-five orchestras – different communities, different sizes and different cultural interests. I wanted them to connect and I thought: "What do they all know? They know *America the Beautiful*", which is one of my favourite tunes (I think it should be our national anthem). "I am going to take this tune and weave it in and out of my music so that people will have an immediate reference in this new piece" – because a lot of these people hadn't heard anything by a living composer so I didn't want to frighten them off. It turned out to be a really good choice on my part. I had to write the piece so that a community orchestra could play it, and I am very pleased to say that all the orchestras did play it. I conducted some of the performances.'

When it came to the recording, the Nashville Symphony was asked to play, partly because of its reputation for American music and partly because of its affiliation with Naxos. The new Laura Turner Concert Hall in Nashville was nearing completion, and Alan Valentine, the enterprising CEO of the orchestra, decided to record in the hall even though it wasn't quite finished. He even held a concert of the three Tower compositions for all the construction workers, architects and others who had worked on the hall: 2,000 people, all with hard hats, filled the seats.

John Adams and Philip Glass

Minimalism has proved one of the most pervasive styles in contemporary music, and two of the leading American exponents (though their works venture into other areas as well) are represented on Naxos: John Adams (born 1947) and Philip Glass (born 1937), both especially well cared for by Marin Alsop. She conducts Symphonies Nos. 2, 3 and 4 by Glass, though it is the Violin Concerto played by Adele Anthony with the Ulster Orchestra conducted by Takuo Yuasa that tops the sales figures: this has sold more than 100,000 copies.

Many aspects of John Adams are represented on five discs. *Nixon in China*, arguably his operatic masterpiece, appears as a live recording conducted by Alsop; and his more recent opera *I Was Looking at the Ceiling and Then I Saw the Sky* is conducted by Klaus Simon. Alsop also conducts a collection of his best-known shorter pieces, including *Shaker Loops* and *Short Ride in a Fast Machine*; and Ralph van Raat plays his complete piano music. Unfortunately Adams has been less than gracious about the Naxos contribution to his discography. In an interview with *Newsweek* he was asked about the Naxos recordings and commented, 'Yeah, they do [all right], but their product is so mediocre. They must have made … seven or eight CDs of my work. They're poorly produced. In some cases the performances are ok, and in some cases the performances are disgraceful. It's like going to Costco and buying toilet paper with no brand on it.' The *Newsweek* reporter asked, 'Which recordings would you steer people away from?' Adams replied, 'Well, I wouldn't say it for the record.' His publisher later apologised to Klaus for his outburst.

Michael Daugherty

In 2011 the Nashville Symphony's recording of *Deus ex Machina* by Michael Daugherty won a GRAMMY Award for Best Classical Contemporary Composition. The *Metropolis Symphony*, Daugherty's lively homage to the American love of Superman and the comic genre, headlined the disc; but the award went to the more searching *Deus ex Machina* for piano and orchestra.

Daugherty (born in 1954) was co-chair with William Bolcom of the University of Michigan's music faculty until Bolcom retired in 2005; he then became chair. He has always combined the popular with the esoteric, a trait that was nurtured by his varied musical education. His family background was in popular music – including drum and bugle corps and, later, rock bands – and he has always retained a strong sense of his American roots; but his extremely varied range of studies included time at the IRCAM in Paris (Pierre Boulez's highly influential centre primarily dedicated to electro-acoustic music) and he became involved in the European avant-garde scene. Both these threads are evident in *Deus ex Machina*, vibrantly realised for Naxos by pianist Terrence Wilson and the Nashville Symphony conducted by Giancarlo Guerrero.

Daugherty comments: 'I grew up in the 1960s, which was about integration. The races had been segregated and the music was segregated, but in the time I grew up in, things were being integrated. So it has always seemed a natural thing in my music to integrate things – integrate art forms, integrate different aesthetics. In the twenty-first century it is natural to look at everything the world can offer, and that includes music. We have all different kinds of music. I have played rock and jazz and classical, jammed with ethnic music, and done electronic music and all those things. If you look at art and cinema it is very eclectic. Painters use different styles – it is wide open. Music tends to be the most conservative, ironically, but I am from a generation where it is not a big deal to mix things together, and that is what I have been doing.'

Speaking about the GRAMMY Award-winning disc, he says, 'The Nashville Symphony commissioned *Deus ex Machina* and they performed and recorded it with the incredible pianist Terrence Wilson. Then they decided to make a complete CD of my music and that is what we have now. The performances are amazing and I hope everyone will be very excited to hear it.'

Naxos has three other major Daugherty recordings in its catalogue. Contained on one disc are *Fire and Blood*, *MotorCity Triptych* and *Raise the Roof* – the three key works to emerge from his position as composer in residence with the Detroit Symphony Orchestra (2000–03). These are played by the DSO conducted by Neeme Järvi, with violinist Ida Kavafian as the soloist in *Fire and Blood*. The first Daugherty disc released on Naxos has the Colorado Symphony Orchestra under Marin Alsop playing *UFO* (written for percussion soloist Evelyn Glennie, who plays it on this recording) and *Philadelphia Stories*. Alsop conducts her European orchestra, the Bournemouth Symphony Orchestra, on a third disc of Daugherty's works. His standing as a composer is attested by his discography on various labels; Naxos's recording of *Metropolis* is not the only one, but the disc earned him his first GRAMMY Award.

Eric Whitacre

Eric Whitacre (born in 1970) is one of the most performed contemporary choral composers in the United States. He writes in a wholly approachable and graceful style, making the most of his melodic gifts. Although his music had already appeared on various Naxos collections, the first dedicated Whitacre disc was released on the label in 2010: choral music performed by the Elora Festival Singers, conducted by Noel Edison. In their accessibility the works lend themselves to performance by groups of all standards and thus demonstrate an important, participatory aspect of music-making in the US.

Poland

The Naxos commitment to Polish music emerged from a combination of Heymann's personal interest in the music of Szymanowski (which initially appeared on Marco Polo) and

Antoni Wit's championing of particular composers. It was certainly fortunate that Wit knew personally the outstanding twentieth-century Polish composers, having studied with Penderecki and worked closely with both Lutosławski and Górecki as well as figures less well known such as Wojciech Kilar. So the musical picture of Poland in the twentieth and early twenty-first century presented by Naxos has a particular air of authority.

Karol Szymanowski

In the first years of Marco Polo, Heymann identified Karol Szymanowski as one of the composers whose orchestral music he wanted to feature. He recorded the symphonies, ballet, choral–orchestral and chamber music, and eventually even added the opera *King Roger*. The rich, bold orchestral palette was just right for Marco Polo and naturally Heymann turned to Polish musicians for its performance, beginning with the Polish State Philharmonic Orchestra (Katowice). This laid the foundations for developing a Polish theme, in terms of performers as well as composers. History describes a clear lineage.

Witold Lutosławski

In the same year (1937) that Szymanowski, director of the Warsaw Conservatory, died of tuberculosis, Witold Lutosławski received his composition diploma there. He was twenty-four. Lutosławski was another composer admired by Heymann, and when Naxos began a strong relationship with the Polish National Radio Symphony Orchestra and Antoni Wit, he had the musical forces he needed. From the mid-1990s Wit recorded the symphonies, *Concerto for Orchestra*, Double Concerto for oboe and harp, Cello Concerto and much more, eventually recording every orchestral work of the composer.

Krzysztof Penderecki and Henryk Górecki

Krzysztof Penderecki and Henryk Górecki were both born in 1933, twenty years after Lutosławski. At first it was Penderecki who generally made a stronger musical impact in the Western world, with *Threnody for the Victims of Hiroshima* and then particularly with his deeply committed choral works such as the *St Luke Passion* and *A Polish Requiem*; but it was Górecki's Symphony No. 3 'Symphony of Sorrowful Songs' that became a totally unexpected worldwide hit, and the Naxos recording by the Polish National Radio Symphony Orchestra under Antoni Wit took it to an even wider audience. The same forces recorded Symphony No. 2 'Copernican', coupled with *Beatus Vir*, in 2001. This regular recording programme in Poland with Wit, who knew both composers extremely well, put Naxos in an ideal position to provide truly authentic performances. In fact Lutosławski, Penderecki and Górecki have all discussed the performance of their music with Wit before rehearsals, performances and recordings. Heymann has made a commitment to record all of Penderecki's orchestral and choral–orchestral works – an ongoing project, since the composer is still composing!

United Kingdom

The UK was the first Naxos territory to record methodically the music of its major national composers using its own musicians: the intention was to create the first budget-price CD catalogue of British music. After a relatively quiet nineteenth century there emerged a raft of composers born in the late nineteenth and early twentieth centuries, including Arnold Bax, Frank Bridge, Arthur Bliss, Ralph Vaughan Williams and William Walton. They led to the generation that would dominate the post-Second World War years up to the early 1970s, represented by Benjamin Britten and Malcolm Arnold. The Naxos recordings, which supported the revival of interest in these composers, were more than just reliable: bold statements were being made. The repertoire of Britten on Naxos has benefitted from the absorption of recordings from the defunct Collins Classics label but there are fine original Naxos recordings too, including the Violin Concerto coupled with the Cello Symphony, featuring the violinist Rebecca Hirsch and the cellist Tim Hugh; the Maggini Quartet recordings; and the *War Requiem*. The Naxos commitment to the music of Malcolm Arnold has been considerable, with all the symphonies, the string quartets, and the chamber music for wind being released over a period of ten years.

Attention has also been paid to the succeeding generation of composers. The UK found that success by other labels at full price did not preclude an opportunity for Naxos at budget price; in fact many listeners welcomed the Naxos recordings.

Sir John Tavener

Sir John Tavener (born in 1944) has had two undisputed hits: *The Protecting Veil* for cello and orchestra and the choral work *Song for Athene*. The Naxos recording of the former by cellist Maria Kliegel, with the Ulster Orchestra and Takuo Yuasa, has sold over 40,000 copies since its first release in 1999; and sales of *Song for Athene* and other works sung by the Choir of St John's College, Cambridge, directed by Christopher Robinson, have exceeded 60,000 since the CD's release in 2000. Naxos didn't stop there. More choral works were recorded as well as a CD of piano music; and *John Tavener: A Portrait* marked his sixtieth birthday. This was a special release, with music (including the world-premiere recording of *Prayer of the Heart*, a piece written for and sung by the Icelandic pop singer Björk), an extended biography and a recorded interview with the composer. 'The Icelandic pop singer Björk asked me if I would write something for her and the Brodsky Quartet. I'd heard her voice, and I liked also in her this raw, primordial sound. I thought of the ejaculatory prayer they call the "Jesus Prayer", "Lord Jesus, have mercy on me", and I set it in three languages: in Coptic, in English and in Greek. And I thought the way she sang it was quite wonderful. It couldn't possibly be sung by anybody else but her, or someone with a voice very, very similar to hers.'

Sir Peter Maxwell Davies

Perhaps the most unique contribution Naxos has made to contemporary music has been the *Naxos Quartets*, a cycle of ten string quartets commissioned by the label from Sir Peter Maxwell Davies (born in 1934), Master of the Queen's Music. Heymann explains, 'When the opportunity arose to commission ten string quartets from one of the greatest living composers, not only in England but internationally, we were of course very excited. We wondered whether he would be able to stick to the schedule, but he did, and what we have is a cycle of quartets that responds to the natural environment where he lives, in Orkney, but also sometimes comments on the wider events of his time. It has been a landmark in Naxos's history.'

Certainly the *Naxos Quartets* were a huge part of the life of Maxwell Davies himself between 2002 and 2007. No. 1 was premiered on 23 October 2002 in London's Wigmore Hall and No. 10 was finished in 2007, the final recording being released in 2008. The composer says, 'Right from the outset I viewed this as some kind of novel in ten chapters where they would all be part of a cycle and thematically interconnected. I live in Orkney. I have lived there for well over thirty-five years and I spend a lot of time just walking on the beach. This is a wonderful environment in which to just think. It's not silent, but the sea makes a wonderful noise: it is always changing, it is exciting, it is soothing. This is the background to all of the quartets but particularly No. 5 'Lighthouses of Orkney and Shetland', because from my house you can see the North Ronaldsay light and from just around the corner you can see the light from four lighthouses, and I just love the rhythms.' He attended almost every recording session. 'I didn't need to say very much because I had my say at the first performance, but I like to be there. Occasionally I have made last-minute changes to chords or something, just to improve the sonority.

'I have often said that writing for string quartet is like dancing naked in public. There is nowhere to hide. You have four voices there and you can't hide behind them. If you are writing for larger forces, you can write brass chords, or something for percussion if the interest flags a bit (which I hope it doesn't!). But with a string quartet you are totally exposed. Writing this cycle of quartets would have been much, much more difficult had I not had the constant rapport, exchange of ideas, constant encouragement, even corrections sometimes, from the Maggini Quartet.

'Quartet No. 10 is much better than Quartet No. 1 in that I understood much more about writing for string quartet by the time I came to do the last one. Of course I had written a string quartet many years before, and I had studied them, particularly a lot of Haydn; but when I came to No. 2 I knew a bit more, and No. 3 a bit more than that, and so on right the way through.' There was an extra political edge to No. 3. 'The Third Quartet started off being fairly well behaved. An ordinary string quartet with an *Allegro* first movement. But then the Iraq war started. I was right at the head of that huge crowd that protested in London. This anger got into the music but I think it is the function of music to represent everything you believe to be right and true, and to make statements no matter how they might offend politicians, for instance. The war was very much uppermost in my mind at that moment and it erupts into the music with cold fury.' Naxos has also released *Peter Maxwell Davies: A Portrait*, and will release, over time, all his Collins recordings.

James MacMillan

The choral works of the Scottish composer James MacMillan (born in 1959) are among the most challenging on Naxos; his large and uncompromising composition for percussion and orchestra *Veni, Veni, Emmanuel* was undoubtedly an important work of the 1990s. Coupled with *Tryst*, and played by the Ulster Orchestra under Takuo Yuasa, it was released on Naxos in 1998 and emphasised the kind of work that the label wanted to include in its coverage of contemporary music. It was followed by *Seven Last Words from the Cross* with other choral works, a disc which was particularly commended by MacMillan himself: 'It has been an enormous thrill hearing my music being performed by The Dmitri Ensemble. This excellent, young ensemble brings a breath of fresh air to music-making in this country, and they are fortunate in their director, Graham Ross – one of the most exciting new musicians to appear on the radar. I am honoured that they are choosing to mark my fiftieth birthday with this disc on Naxos, bringing together a number of different choral works from 1993 to 2005.'

John Rutter

The music of John Rutter (born in 1945) is completely different from that of MacMillan or Maxwell Davies but also rightly claims a presence on Naxos. He is unquestionably the contemporary choral composer whose music is most frequently sung in the UK, his mellifluous style proving highly attractive to choirs, even those further afield. He has his own full-price label, Collegium Records, for which he records his music with his own choir; yet he has welcomed new recordings of his most popular works on Naxos and has even been actively involved in the sessions as producer. He offered to produce the recordings of both his Requiem and the *Mass of the Children* (both performed by The Choir of Clare College, Cambridge under

Timothy Brown), convinced that these discs would bring his music to an even wider audience.

Other Contemporary Voices

There are many other iconic works from composers of our time to be found in the Naxos catalogue. Olivier Messiaen has a growing section led by the imposing *Turangalîla Symphony* (played by the Polish National Radio Symphony Orchestra under Antoni Wit, who had himself worked with Messiaen) and strengthened by two CDs from the Orchestre National de Lyon and the *Quartet for the End of Time* (one of the greatest twentieth-century chamber works). Paul Jacobs's recording of the *Livre du Saint-Sacrement* won the 2011 GRAMMY for Best Instrumental Soloist Performance (without Orchestra). Staying with France, there is Idil Biret's remarkable recording of the piano sonatas by Pierre Boulez; and, from the following generation, several recordings of music by Laurent Petitgirard (born in 1950), including two of his operas.

The distinctive Estonian voice of Arvo Pärt (born in 1935), sacred yet modern, is represented by five full discs covering his most important pieces for orchestra (including *Tabula Rasa*, Symphony No. 3 and *Fratres*) and the choral works *Passio* and the *Berliner Messe*. Heading further east to Japan, we find the equally recognisable voice of Tōru Takemitsu (1930–1996). Four discs present a good cross-section, with orchestral works such as *A Flock Descends into the Pentagonal Garden* and chamber music with flute.

Rediscovered scores come to Naxos too. The English conductor Mark Fitz-Gerald and Naxos production manager Peter Bromley, who keeps an up-to-date discography of Dmitry Shostakovich, have worked with Shostakovich's widow to bring some forgotten music to the studio. This includes the film scores for *The Girlfriends* and *Odna* ('Alone'); and, from 1945, his initial idea for the opening movement of Symphony No. 9 (which bears no relation to the eventual work).

Peter Breiner – Arranger

Most unusually, Naxos has its own arranger: the Slovakian-born but North American-resident pianist, conductor, composer and arranger Peter Breiner. When he suggested to Heymann that he arrange some of the biggest hits of The Beatles in the style of Handel and Bach for chamber orchestra, he met with scepticism. Surely those days of classical Beatles had gone? 'Ok, but if we sell 3,000 I will be surprised,' Heymann told Breiner. Twenty years later *The Beatles Go Baroque*, played by Peter Breiner and His Chamber Orchestra, has sold nearly 150,000 CDs (and thousands more downloads) and still sells well. It has the questionable distinction of being one of the most pirated works in the Naxos catalogue (a back-handed compliment of a kind) and it has even been illegally covered by a Ukrainian orchestra.

The association between Breiner and Heymann covers some three decades, stretching back even before Marco Polo. They *think* Breiner's first arrangement might have been some Malaysian folksongs for the early Heymann company Pacific Music, but neither can quite remember. Since then he has produced more than 1,000 arrangements, from Chinese pop songs for violin (for Nishizaki) and orchestra to a critically praised set of orchestral suites drawn from Janáček's operas.

'The first CD I did for Naxos as arranger and conductor was of Haydn and Boccherini cello concertos played by Ludovit Kanta – I wrote the cadenzas – and it is still available,' comments Breiner. His closest association with a Naxos performer is with Takako Nishizaki: over the years he has arranged numerous pieces for violin and orchestra, for both concerts and recordings; her recordings of Chinese folk, pop and classical music have sold hundreds of thousands of CDs. The two have had a lot of MOR ('middle-of-the-road') fun over the years with O Sole Mio – Classic Love Songs for Violin and Orchestra, Russian Romance, Tchaikovsky: None but the Lonely Heart (a programme of Tchaikovsky's songs arranged for violin and orchestra) and many more. He has also arranged music for other Naxos artists: his version of Granados' Spanish Dances for guitar and orchestra recorded by Norbert Kraft proved an enduring bestseller for the label and showcased the virtuoso skills of the Canadian guitarist.

In 2006 Heymann proposed a more unusual project: a set of orchestral suites taken from operas by Janáček. Jenůfa is one of Heymann's favourite operas. 'I felt that Janáček's music should be known more widely, and a set of orchestral suites would bring him to a wider audience,' said Heymann. Breiner was also keen. 'Janáček is my favourite composer; I was born on the same day and we are countrymen!' The resulting set of three CDs, with Breiner conducting the New Zealand Symphony Orchestra, appeared in the top ten classical discs of the year in the Chicago Tribune in 2009.

The most ambitious, ongoing and breathtaking project Breiner has undertaken is the unique boxed set of The Complete National Anthems of the World, which aims to keep up to date with the anthems of all countries. Since the moment Heymann came up with the idea in 1995, it has been a wonderful headache for Breiner. The first set of six CDs of popular national anthems played by the Slovak Radio Symphony Orchestra came out the following year on Marco Polo. Then Heymann realised that international sporting events – all the way up to the pinnacle of sport, the Olympic Games – needed a reliable source of national anthems for medal ceremonies. No such up-to-date set existed. It proved to be one of Naxos's greatest logistical challenges.

Each national anthem, reduced to a running time of a minute, had to be arranged and recorded, and then played to the Olympic committee of the particular country to be approved for use in international events. It is a continuing process, for countries change, anthems change, and views on arrangements change. Mixing music and politics is a world of mirrors and quicksand. 'I could fill a book with anecdotes of responses from sports committees,' smiles Breiner. 'I sent my arrangement and recording of the Polish national anthem to the Polish national sports committee. They replied that they couldn't give approval. They wanted me to record the anthem again: "Make it more like a march," they insisted. "It is not enough like a march!" My response was: "It is never gonna be a march unless you grow a third leg, because the anthem is in *three*. It is a Mazurka!"'

The organisers of the Athens Olympics were impressed by the set and agreed, as 2004 approached, to use it as the official source of anthems for all medal ceremonies. A total of 202 anthems – the number of nations participating in the Athens Olympics – would be needed. It was unlikely that the anthem of Andorra or Palau would ever be heard in a medal ceremony, but Naxos couldn't take the risk of not having it ready.

Many had to be rearranged and recorded: anthems alter with curious frequency. Extra sessions had to be booked with the Slovak Radio Symphony Orchestra in Bratislava. Every anthem had to be checked afresh. Shortly before the Games started, a member of the Athens Olympic Committee finally got to meet the Russian ambassador and cultural attaché at the Russian Embassy in Athens. They listened carefully to the recording of their national anthem and proclaimed it an excellent performance. Then a Russian cleaning lady who was polishing the windows piped up. 'Excuse me, Sirs, I am sorry to interrupt but I think you will find that our government changed the national anthem last week. We have a new one now.' And she was right. Breiner arranged and recorded it in time for the first medal ceremonies.

All the anthems played in Athens were accurate, but Breiner encountered his fair share of controversy when some American commentators dubbed his arrangement of *The Star-Spangled Banner* 'a Europe-friendly version': according to some fervently patriotic Americans, the anthem was not sufficiently 'chest-thumping, butt-kicking'. Fortunately Breiner was living in Toronto at the time. For the most part, however, his orchestrations were admired.

The sheer volume of music written by Breiner over the years is enormous. He used to keep the archive in two rooms in his home in Toronto but when he moved to New York in 2007 it was transferred to Naxos of America in Nashville for safe keeping. It filled an enormous truck and weighed 1.6 tonnes. Now it is archived carefully at the Naxos headquarters in Hong Kong. New pieces still arrive there on a regular basis – arrangements of operatic medleys for violin and orchestra, more operatic orchestral transcriptions, songs, new anthems ... they cover an extraordinary range of music. 'Music is a borderless land for me,' says Breiner.

One of the most public illustrations of Peter Breiner's work for Naxos involved his arrangements and performances of the national anthems and the scandal over the Beijing Olympics in 2008. In the years leading to the Games, Heymann approached the Beijing Organizing Committee on many occasions, trying to ensure that Marco Polo's national anthems were used (it would be particularly satisfying for a company based in Hong Kong). Surprisingly the authorities declined, deciding to give the commission for preparing the set of anthems to the Beijing Symphony Orchestra. Disappointed though he was, Heymann suspected that it would be an almost insuperable task.

After the very first medal ceremonies, questions began to be raised in the close-knit world of national-anthem specialists about the provenance of the music. Some of the arrangements sounded familiar – too familiar. Suspicions were aroused, then alarm bells began to ring. Some of these anthems sounded very like Peter Breiner's arrangements – published by Naxos and in copyright – though they were clearly played by an orchestra inferior to the Slovak Radio Symphony Orchestra. It transpired that some of the Marco Polo anthems had been 'borrowed' in one way or another, as *The Washington Post* reported. There were 204 participating countries and fifty-four of them won gold medals: fifty-four national anthems were played at the venues from the complete set provided by the Beijing Symphony Orchestra.

At first, the Beijing Organizing Committee denied that some of these were Breiner's arrangements. It had commissioned the Beijing Symphony Orchestra to record them, and in an interview in the *Beijing Chronicle* Mr Tan Lihua, music director of the BSO, said that it had been difficult to source the 212 anthems originally needed (though only 204 countries eventually took part). Apparently some scores came from the International Olympic Committee and others came from a variety of other sources 'including transcriptions from audio material'. This suggested quite openly that somebody had listened to the CDs and copied the arrangements, which were then played by the BSO.

Getting reparation for copyright infringement was not an easy task in China, even though the country was trying to clean up its reputation for music piracy. Doggedly Heymann pursued the issue, eventually approaching the International Olympic Committee. In the end, it was determined that some 100 Marco Polo recordings had been used in the Chinese set of anthems supplied to the Beijing Organizing Committee – some as sources for re-recording. A settlement was negotiated. 'It is very likely that the BOC had no idea that the orchestra copied our orchestrations,' concludes Heymann.

Twelve

Naxos and Its Labels

The simple line is this: Naxos is the world's leading classical music label. Actually it is far more than that, and there is no better illustration than the catalogue itself. It has 200 dense pages in small type; by a miracle of concision the Contents section is contained on one page. However, it does not encompass all the things that fall under 'Naxos'. The website, www.naxos.com, gets closer but even that is not all-inclusive. The problem is the sheer amount of material: thousands of recordings – some straining the 'classical music' description and others, frankly, venturing way past it, however you define 'classical'.

In truth it is the life's work of one enthusiast who, over the years, has been happy to stray into other territories, maintaining only a tenuous link with the world of Mozart and Beethoven. In the past twenty-five years he has created sublabels to realise his own ideas; formed new labels with some of the enterprising people whom he has met (sometimes using the name Naxos, but not always); and taken over other labels, occasionally letting them keep their names but often absorbing them into the mother ship. At various times he has gone outside the central classical recording territory into publishing (text, music and audiobooks) with an eye to education, or diversification, or complementing his business, or simply because it seemed like a good idea at the time. Here is a survey of the main parts of Naxos.

The Naxos Catalogue

In just a quarter of a century Naxos has created a catalogue comprising the largest number of individual works and the widest available repertoire of any classical label since the beginning of the recording era. It is a remarkable achievement, all the more so because it happened at a time when the record industry was at its most unstable and going through a period of dramatic change that brought many established labels to their knees. Some 7,000 titles have come onto the Naxos label. By far the majority of these have been recorded by, or for, Naxos itself. Some were originally recorded for Marco Polo and eventually transferred to Naxos, and a few were bought in from other labels. But Naxos as a large classical catalogue is the creation purely of Klaus Heymann: most of the recordings were set in motion by him, and certainly every single one of those recordings has been finally approved by him.

As with Marco Polo before Naxos, Heymann established a long list of works that had to be recorded – music that would form the centre of any record label. At the end of each of those early Naxos years the list became longer, not shorter, because the continuing success enabled Heymann to think more ambitiously. He readily acknowledges the suggestions and advice that came from members of his growing organisation across the world. In England David Denton set the English repertoire and recording schedule rolling, and this was continued and expanded by Anthony Anderson at the Naxos UK company, Select Music; in Scandinavia Håkan Lagerqvist, running Naxos Sweden, made a major contribution by recording Scandinavian music as well as launching some hugely successful television campaigns that promoted the label; in the US, Victor and Marina Ledin and then a committee of scholars helped to build 'American Classics'; in Hong Kong, A&R Director Edith Lei put together the complete Liszt and Scarlatti piano projects and the 'Laureate Series'. Many Naxos musicians – conductors and instrumentalists – have suggested a lot of repertoire over the years, and there have also been several individual enthusiasts who have plied Heymann with ideas. So while the detailed content of the Naxos catalogue was not entirely down to Heymann, the core, the architecture and the final choice certainly were.

Building the catalogue has been a most extraordinary journey, from producing a tight group of thirty popular classics at budget price to offering a range of repertoire that is unmatched by any other single label. Getting to that position has not been free of challenges and problems. Naxos certainly had its opponents, from both without and even within: several existing labels publicly denigrated the recordings and used their influence to try (unsuccessfully) to halt Naxos in its tracks; some people within the company itself questioned the wisdom of broadening out into more specialist areas, be it the piano sonatas of Boulez or obscure American symphonic music. Many within and without wondered, and still wonder: where has the character of Naxos, once so tightly defined, gone? Yet none can deny the success of the label, or the fact that no one has picked up the beacon of classical recording and run with it so boldly and so far.

The statistics are stupendous. All the 7,000 music recordings on the various Naxos labels (and for Naxos AudioBooks the total exceeds 700) are available digitally, with the vast majority also available on CD. On the Naxos main label alone there are approaching 5,000 titles, most having been specially recorded and relatively few having been bought in. This amounts to a steady average of 200 releases per year, a schedule that no other classical label, certainly of today, can get anywhere near. These include not only single CDs but many multi-CD sets (such as a two-CD set of Bach's Cello Suites or a four-CD opera set) and boxed sets (either popular compilations or specialist sets such as *The Complete Haydn Symphonies*).

It is not just the numbers: the range and variety are simply breathtaking and entailed relatively early on the creation of sections and series within the catalogue. However, the central classics – those works which any music lover building a collection would want to have – remain at the core of the label. These form the spine of Naxos.

The 2011 paper catalogue, an impressive document through which to browse, runs to 226 pages. It is a serious catalogue for the collector: the careful attention paid to detail takes it far past the budget-label tag. Recordings singled out for special praise by critics across the world are marked by different symbols (for a GRAMMY in the US, a Diapason d'Or in France, a *Gramophone* 'Record of the Month', a starred review in *The Penguin Guide*, and so on) and it is salutary to note how often these appear.

The Central Classics

From the label's early days the intention was to provide just one recording of each major classical work, in order to create a basic library. Heymann still likes to follow this policy, even with a wider repertoire (and great historical recordings are not regarded as directly competitive or comparable!), but as time passed and opportunities presented themselves it became clear that to stick to it rigidly would be perverse. Some of the early recordings were adequate but could be bettered. Sometimes a proposal landed on Heymann's desk which it would have been unwise to ignore. Occasionally there was a clear marketing reason – a new young player with something particular to contribute, perhaps. Nevertheless, every new proposal for a recording that would duplicate what is already in the catalogue is seriously questioned, and the vast majority of works – even popular ones such as Mozart's piano concertos – are still represented by the original recordings (and in the case of Mozart those are Jenő Jandó's sparkling performances, which remain a joy to listen to). The set of Beethoven's piano concertos recorded in the 1980s by Stefan Vladar, with the Capella Istropolitana conducted by Barry Wordsworth, also remains the only one in the catalogue. By contrast, the recording of the symphonies played by the Nicolaus Esterházy Sinfonia under Béla Drahos, made in the 1990s, replaced an earlier set (and now there is yet another, with the Cologne Chamber Orchestra under Müller-Brühl); and Heymann deemed that the early recording of the cello sonatas played by the Hungarian musicians Csaba Onczay and Jenő Jandó was worth keeping, though Maria Kliegel went on a decade later to record all of Beethoven's music for cello.

In Naxos's first decade Heymann often tended to entrust a composer's output in a particular genre to one musician or group of musicians. This was partly due to practicality, as there was so much to do in so little time; but the relatively few re-recordings to date make it clear how astute the choice often was. The Kodály Quartet's recordings of the complete Haydn string quartets will remain industry contenders for years to come when recordings are compared, as will Jandó's performances of the piano sonatas by Haydn, Beethoven and Schubert. Haydn's symphonies were recorded over a longer period and are shared between a number of orchestras, but they are not duplicated.

There are, perhaps unexpectedly, two sets of Brahms's symphonies: the early set with the BRT Philharmonic Orchestra conducted by Alexander Rahbari and the later recordings with Marin Alsop conducting the London Philharmonic Orchestra, which attracted a lot of critical praise and attention. There are also two recordings of Brahms's Violin Concerto: the early one played by Takako Nishizaki, coupled with Bruch's Concerto No. 1, and Ilya Kaler's recording coupled with Schumann's Concerto.

Central to the development of Naxos is of course the playing of Nishizaki, and all her recordings of the main concertos are available. Her very first recording for Naxos, in July 1987, of Vivaldi's *The Four Seasons* coupled with *Concerto alla rustica* retains its place in the current catalogue. It was not until 2006 that another recording of this most popular of classical works came into the catalogue: Cho-Liang Lin plays with Sejong, a virtuoso group of young musicians directed by Anthony Newman. The performance displays a more Baroque style but is still outsold year on year by its predecessor.

Heymann made a declared commitment to Georg Tintner for Bruckner's symphonies, which resulted in a cohesive set, even though it was shared between the Royal Scottish National Orchestra, the National Symphony Orchestra of Ireland and the New Zealand Symphony Orchestra. The Viennese conductor, who died in 1999, also recorded selected symphonies and orchestral works by Mozart, Schubert, Richard Strauss and others: his work has been collected into a 'Tintner Memorial Edition' series, which represents a unique accolade for an artist on Naxos.

Lieder – especially that of Schubert, and more latterly Schumann – has also been fostered with particular care by Heymann. Sensitive to lieder recordings made by non-native German singers, who are less equipped to convey a meaningful interpretation of the text, he entrusted the *Deutsche Schubert Lied-Edition* to the pianist Ulrich Eisenlohr, who selected German-speaking performers. Released in individual volumes between 1999 and 2010, the Edition features no fewer than thirty-nine singers, five pianists and six instrumentalists; with around 650 songs plus many in alternative settings or versions, it is the most comprehensive edition available. It was released as a boxed set in 2011.

It was not long after the start of Naxos that its catalogue extended beyond the brazenly popular. The bestselling works by the likes of Tchaikovsky, Schubert, Schumann, Grieg, Dvořák, Liszt and Rachmaninov came first, of course, followed by Mahler and Elgar; but Handel, Byrd and Tallis were also present. Within the first few years, chamber works such as the violin sonatas by Grieg showed that Heymann had his sights on a more broad-based classical label.

There was a form of master plan at the start, emanating from Hong Kong and covering core works; but in the early 1990s the repertoire being recorded had become subject to many other influences (suggestions from musicians, requests from distributors, demands from the market), some of which were totally unexpected. It was a music lover at the helm, not just a businessman. So there developed, almost undetectably, a bolder recording policy that took Naxos into the arena of the classical collector: chamber music, instrumental music, choral music. Even its early forays into contemporary music unexpectedly reaped both musical *and* commercial rewards. Another label's full-price recording of Górecki's Symphony No. 3 achieved popularity and hit the charts: would there be room for a budget version? The performance by the Polish National Radio Symphony Orchestra under Antoni Wit, recorded for Naxos in 1994, reflected more closely the voice of the composer's homeland than did the original Nonesuch version that had created a stir. It was widely praised and sold more than 250,000 copies. The same forces went on to record Symphony No. 2.

The film *The Piano* was a commercial success helped by Michael Nyman's soundtrack. Why not record the Piano Concerto that Nyman had formed from the film score and release the first budget version? It sold over 60,000 copies. Neither Arvo Pärt's *Tabula Rasa* nor John Tavener's *The*

Protecting Veil needed film support: they reached similar sales figures on their own merits. The Naxos pattern, which showed that people were prepared to try new music at a budget price, was continuing. These recordings may have appeared opportunist moves at the time because they followed successes achieved by the majors and the independents, but they were more than that: as good recordings at an affordable price, they helped to show that Naxos was fast becoming a serious classical label. This battle has now been won, but it had to be fought. An even more astounding success, given the nature of the music, was Idil Biret's recording of Boulez's Piano Sonatas Nos. 1–3; released as early as 1995, it has sold more than 40,000 copies. This was not repertoire that Heymann had ever expected to include on one of his labels. It just seemed to be the right thing to do at the time.

By the middle of the 1990s Naxos had clearly broken away from its initial purpose of providing affordable popular classics. It was spreading in all directions. There were many 'complete' series underway: Liszt's piano works, Reger's organ works, Glazunov's orchestral works (which had started on Marco Polo and shifted to Naxos), Rodrigo's orchestral works (ten volumes), Scarlatti's keyboard sonatas, Soler's harpsichord sonatas and Shostakovich's symphonies (originally recorded by the Slovak Radio Symphony Orchestra under Ladislav Slovak but now being recorded again in an award-winning manner by the Royal Liverpool Philharmonic Orchestra and Vasily Petrenko; both cycles are available). Heymann's pronouncements on the direction of the catalogue had to be constantly revised. What was the goal of Naxos? 'To record everything,' he said at one point.

One way of conveying the breadth of music covered by Naxos is to outline a page or two of the printed catalogue. Here, taken more or less at random, is the 'H' listing. On one double-page spread we get:

Haydn, Franz Joseph The end of the final column of his works, headed 'Vocal and Choral', including the oratorio *Il ritorno di Tobia*; and, from Naxos Educational, *The Life and Works of Haydn* written and narrated by Jeremy Siepmann.

Haydn, Michael A Divertimento (coupled with oboe quartets by Stamitz).

He, Zhanhao *The Butterfly Lovers* (Takako Nishizaki's recording that has sold millions in China).

Headley, Hubert Klyne A twentieth-century American composer represented here by his Piano Concertos Nos. 1 and 2, Symphony No. 1 and *California Suite*.

Heggie, Jake *For a Look or a Touch* (an excerpt from his stage work).

Heifetz, Jascha Transcriptions for violin and piano.

Helfman, Max *Di Naye Hagode* and other works from this Polish–American twentieth-century composer.

Helps, Robert Another twentieth-century American, with *Shall We Dance* for piano, and other chamber works.

Hely-Hutchinson, Victor An English twentieth-century composer represented by *A Carol Symphony* – his orchestral work based on Christmas carols.

Henze, Hans Werner Guitar music and the Violin Concertos Nos. 1 and 3 from this major twentieth-century figure.

Herbert, Victor Edwardian light music, including the *Irish Rhapsody*.

Hermann, Friedrich Chamber music from this nineteenth-century German composer.

Herrmann, Bernard The film composer is represented on four CDs that include his music for *The Egyptian*.

Hersch, Michael A young American composer championed by Marin Alsop, who conducts his Symphonies Nos. 1 and 2.

Hidalgo, Juan Volume 1 of *The Guerra Manuscript* – seventeenth-century secular Spanish vocal music.

Higdon, Jennifer A selection of chamber music by this American twentieth-century composer, including *Impressions* played by the Cypress String Quartet.

Hildegard von Bingen Two discs of this musical visionary, from the Oxford Camerata.

Hill, Alfred A prominent figure in Australian twentieth-century music, with three volumes of string quartets included here.

Hindemith, Paul The symphony *Mathis der Maler*, of course, but also chamber music.

Hoffmann, Johann A mandolin player and composer of the Classical era; two sonatas are included here.

Hoffmann, Melchior A Baroque composer represented by the cantata *Meine Seele ruhmt und preist*.

Hoffmeister, Franz Anton String quartets and double bass quartets from this Classical German composer and music publisher.

Hoffstetter, Roman String quartets good enough to have been attributed to Haydn for many years.

Hofmann, Leopold Five discs of attractive concertos from this Classical composer, the scores having been rediscovered and published by Artaria Editions.

Moving on to another section chosen at random, where the letter 'S' gives way to 'T' …

Szymanowski, Karol Piano music (four volumes), songs, sacred music, string quartets, two recordings of the violin concertos, *King Roger* and more.

Tabakov, Emil The twentieth-century Bulgarian conductor–composer directs his own piano and flute concertos.

Takemitsu, Tōru A generous selection of music from this leading twentieth-century Japanese composer.

Tallis, Thomas All the major works.

Talma, Louise A French-born American composer, whose music here includes Variations on *13 Ways of Looking at a Blackbird* for tenor, oboe and piano.

Taneyev, Sergey Ivanovich A torch first taken up by Marco Polo, Taneyev's works now on Naxos include string quartets and symphonies.

Tansman, Alexandre Two volumes of chamber music.

Tartini, Giuseppe Violin concertos (and the 'Devil's Trill' Sonata!).

Tárrega, Francisco Principal guitar works on one disc.

Tate, Phyllis Her *Triptych* forms part of a disc entitled *British Women Composers*.

Tavener, John Five CDs that of course include *The Protecting Veil* and *Song for Athene* as well as piano works and *Lament for Jerusalem*; also a special two-CD portrait of the composer from Naxos Educational.

Taylor, Deems The American composer's opera *Peter Ibbetson*.

Tchaikovsky, Boris A twentieth-century Russian composer ('I consider him a genius': Mstislav Rostropovich), no relation to Pyotr. Three CDs that include the Piano Concerto, Clarinet Concerto and the cantata *Signs of the Zodiac*).

Tchaikovsky, Pyotr Il'yich An entry which completes the page and runs on through both columns of the next.

This kind of page-by-page examination prompts amazement – even bemusement. The alphabetical listing of composers forms the first part of the printed catalogue and gives a kaleidoscopic picture of the label. There is method here, and a story behind most of the CDs. But after you pass

Zimmermann, Anton

Ziporyn, Evan

Zwilich, Ellen Taaffe

the picture changes.

The Collections part shows a totally different aspect of running a classical label. Heymann prefers to have one-composer CDs because they are so much easier to catalogue but this is often neither possible nor advisable. Anthologies are very popular and many have been produced. It is therefore necessary to give them their own section, which proves to be just as surprising as the A–Z composer listing. It starts with *Alphorn Concertos*: you may think it a specialist title (it does include Daetwyler's *Dialogue avec la nature* for alphorn, piccolo and orchestra, which caused no end of balance problems in the studio) but since 2002 it has sold a respectable 12,000 copies on CD alone. Next is *Classic American Love Songs*, performed by Carole Farley with John Constable, piano.

Here also are found some of the highly successful lifestyle and introductory compilations. Formally called 'catalogue exploitation', these are major revenue earners though they sometimes make the dedicated classical collector go pale. A typical example is the one-CD 'Best of' series: *The Best of Bach*, *The Best of Beethoven* etc. (all the way down to *The Best of Ziehrer*, which shows that Naxos does have a sense of humour). The series did well in the market so a sequel was required: a two-CD 'Very Best of' series. More compilations are found in the 'Chill with' series, which covers most of the same composers – Bach, Beethoven, Chopin, Mozart (100,000-plus units sold) ... down to Tchaikovsky – but has high-design covers.

In fact the printed catalogue shows only the tip of the iceberg when it comes to regional compilations, for many distributors across the world also release the 'Best of' series (and other variations) in their own languages. The enterprise of these distributors has contributed greatly to Naxos. In the US, a classical series called 'Listen, Learn and Grow' targeted at babies sold some 150,000 units, and when transported to the UK a further 40,000. Few could match the imagination of Naxos Sweden, which, engaging with a population of just 9.25 million, produced a string of hit CDs through television campaigns. (It began with a three-CD set *Klassiska Favoriter*, a compilation of popular classics, that sold a phenomenal 275,000 boxes.) Among the international campaigns with respectable results was *Voices of Angels* (music by Palestrina, Hildegard, Allegri, Byrd etc.), with global sales of 110,000.

Another regular marketing theme is Christmas. There are as many as thirty Christmas-themed collections in the Naxos catalogue (indicating the inventiveness of the marketing departments): *A Classic Christmas*, *Christmas Piano Music*, *Christmas Concertos*, *A Danish Christmas*, *Christmas Chill* etc. Remaining at 'C' in 'Collections', we find twelve volumes of 'Cinema Classics' (plus *The Very Best of Cinema Classics*), twelve volumes of 'The Classics at the Movies', and other cinematic compilations. There are pages of early music, easy listening, flute music and funeral music. Heymann has also supported light music, from orchestral 'salon' favourites to *Vintage Broadway*. There are operatic collections, *English String Miniatures*, *Finnish Orchestral Favourites*, *French Festival* and *Macabre Masterpieces*.

On a more serious note, there is a wealth of organ repertoire on Naxos, not only the volumes of Bach or Buxtehude but interesting and well-considered collections of English, French and German organ music. The piano is similarly well served, from 'Romantic Piano Favourites' (ten volumes) to 'Easy Listening Piano Classics' (more than ten volumes, divided by composers). In fact most of the main instruments (flute, clarinet, violin, viola, cello) have their own sub-sections in 'Collections': a glance under 'T' shows that there are five volumes of 'The Art of the Baroque Trumpet' as well as other selections for the instrument. 'Vocal and Choral' starts with *Abide with Me and other favourite hymns*, and among other highlights are *Pigs Could Fly* (children's choral music), *Psalms for the Spirit*, *Psaumes de la Réforme*, *Russian Divine Liturgy* and *Spirituals*. A closer look at this section unveils many more extremely thoughtful and useful anthologies. Moving on, there are a few collections of wedding music (including *A Bride's Guide to Music for Civil Ceremonies*) though the first one has outsold all others by far: *Wedding Music* has reached 140,000 units since its release in 1993.

It is on naxos.com that the most up-to-date and comprehensive information can be found. In the 'Sets/Series' section there are no fewer than twenty-nine divisions, focusing on particular aspects of Naxos and classical music. These include 'Early Music Collection' (125 titles), '19th Century Violinist Composers' (25 titles), 'Greek Classics' (10 titles), 'Italian Classics' (27 titles) and 'Spanish Classics' (75 titles). Laying the ground for the future is the task of the 'Laureate Series' (60 titles): recordings by prize-winners of various instrumental competitions around the world. Here are young musicians (principally guitarists, pianists, violinists and cellists), generally with impressive virtuosity on display, showing why they were laureates. However, also among these so-called 'Sets/Series' are to be found other significant parts of the Naxos catalogue.

Opera Classics

Opera has come to play a central and growing role on Naxos with the rise of the DVD, but recordings on CD remain popular and Naxos has made a helpful contribution to recorded operatic repertoire. There are now more than 100 titles in the Naxos opera catalogue, some of which, as usual, are unexpected (especially so given their low price). The recording programme began with Mozart (six operas to date, including *Don Giovanni* and *The Marriage of Figaro*) but swiftly moved on to cover other opera composers: Donizetti (six, including *Lucia di Lammermoor*), Rossini (sixteen, including *Il barbiere di Siviglia*), Verdi (seven, including *Aida* and *Rigoletto*), Wagner (six, including the *Ring* cycle) and Puccini (eight, including *La Bohème* and *Madama Butterfly*). There is Beethoven's *Fidelio*, Bizet's *Carmen*, Mascagni's *Cavalleria rusticana* and Leoncavallo's *Pagliacci*, Meyerbeer's *Semiramide*, Britten's *The Turn of the Screw* and *Albert Herring*, Berg's *Wozzeck* and Bartók's *Bluebeard's Castle*.

There are two operas by John Adams, including the one considered by many to be his masterpiece: *Nixon in China*. A further look reveals those by Lully, Rameau, Handel, Pacini, Massenet, Schoenberg (*Moses und Aaron*), Korngold, Schreker and Szymanowski, and operettas by Johann Strauss.

Many of these were Naxos-funded recordings, the casts chosen in association with the conductors; some were co-productions; and others were the results of licensing arrangements with radio stations or festivals. The cost of recording opera is so daunting that often it can be done only through joint productions with opera houses or broadcast organisations. Whatever the routes have been, the end result is a varied and satisfying opera catalogue.

American Classics

If there is any single area of Naxos that was the most unexpected, and is perhaps the most innovative, it is its championing of American classical music from the early nineteenth century to the present day. Many American composers are familiar names in classical music: Samuel Barber, Leonard Bernstein, Aaron Copland, George Gershwin, Charles Ives, and even those generally represented by just one or two works, such as John Philip Sousa, Walter Piston and Virgil Thomson. What Heymann set out to do with 'American Classics', which he began in 1999, was to create an unmatched catalogue of music by the greatest American classical composers, including those alive today, in order to awaken Americans to their own heritage as well as to show the musical world, through the Naxos international distribution network, that here was a body of work worth getting to know. In a decade of dedicated and carefully planned recording, with a release schedule that tried to keep up, 'American Classics' developed into a 360-title (and still growing) display cabinet for American music.

Initially Heymann turned to the producers and agents Victor and Marina Ledin (referred to by Heymann as 'the Encores', following the name of their company, Encore Consultants) for advice regarding repertoire. He subsequently assembled a formal advisory board with such luminaries as the eminent musicologist Wiley Hitchcock, the musicologist of the Library of Congress Wayne Shirley, and the highly regarded author and musicologist Joseph Horowitz. Together, after often animated arguments, they drew up a master plan for the project. Some of the recordings were world premieres – increasingly so as the years went by; but many were new, digital recordings of important orchestral music that had been unavailable on record for many years. Among the early releases were Victor Herbert's *Babes in Toyland* coupled with *The Red Mill*, the first volume in a series of piano works by Charles Griffes, and a disc of Leo Sowerby's works for organ and orchestra. Having decided on the repertoire approach, Heymann moved ahead rapidly, recording and releasing works by established American figures such as Piston, Ives, MacDowell, Barber and even John Cage: his *Sonatas and Interludes* for prepared piano went on to sell over 40,000 CDs. Important projects included the complete orchestral works of Barber, conducted by Marin Alsop (the Violin Concerto sold over 40,000 CDs); the complete music for wind band by Sousa, masterminded by Keith Brion (many of the scores had to be recreated using material gathered from a variety of sources; it was a major undertaking); the published symphonies of William Schuman, conducted by Gerard Schwarz; the complete orchestral works of Bernstein; and the first recording of the complete songs by Ives, in cooperation with Yale University. The music of other established twentieth-century composers such as Howard Hanson, Roy Harris and Leroy Anderson benefitted from being under the umbrella of 'American Classics': Anderson's *Orchestral Evergreens* sold over 40,000 CDs.

Equally important have been recordings of the younger generation of composers, including John Adams (*Shaker Loops*, the Violin Concerto, *Nixon in China*) and John Corigliano (seven CDs that include Symphony No. 3, the Violin Concerto *The Red Violin*, and music for string quartet). The biggest single endorsement of the whole enterprise came in 2006 when William Bolcom's *Songs of Innocence and of Experience* conducted by Leonard Slatkin won four GRAMMY Awards. A challenging work, its presence, in truth, did more for 'American Classics' than for the sales figures: it underlined the unwavering purpose of the series.

Many titles have sold only a few thousand CDs, despite being large orchestral works, but the momentum generated served the genre and the label. In total, sixteen GRAMMYs have been won by 'American Classics'.

Spanish Classics

Manuel de Falla, Isaac Albéniz and Enrique Granados, along with Joaquín Rodrigo, may be the best-known representatives of Spanish classical music but, as with most European countries, there is a wealth of other music known only within the country itself.

Apart from works by Renaissance Spanish composers such as Tomás Luis de Victoria, and by the eighteenth-century Juan Crisóstomo de Arriaga, the most important Spanish music was composed in the Romantic nationalist period; in its frequent reliance on regional folk melodies and rhythms it reflected the approach of well-known nationalist composers such as Dvořák.

In order to select the most important composers and their works, Heymann joined with Isabel Gortázar (editor, writer and businesswoman) to form the company Marco Polo and Naxos Hispánica SL in 1999. Her connections with several important orchestras in Spain and knowledge of the music itself made her the ideal person to develop 'Spanish Classics'. Over the next decade Heymann and Gortázar developed a list of around seventy-five titles that would reflect the country's variety of music, most of which did appear on Naxos or Marco Polo.

Following the nationalistic pattern, the collection started with what is to this day the most important series of Basque music ever recorded. Two Basque operas, *Amaya* by Jesús Guridi (1886–1961) and *Mendi mendiyan* ('High in the Mountains') by José Maria Usandizaga (1887–1915), were recorded in the original Basque language. *Mendi mendiyan* was a world-premiere recording. Guridi's zarzuela *El Caserío* ('The Homestead'), sung in Spanish, his *Sinfonía pirenaica*, and his most popular work, *Ten Basque Melodies*, were also included.

Francisco Escudero's oratorio *Illeta*, written in 1953, is also an important piece of the Basque collection. The Bilbao Symphony Orchestra (founded in 1922) was conducted by Juan José Mena in all the orchestral music and *Mendi mendiyan*; *Amaya* (released on Marco Polo in 2000) was conducted by Theo Alcántara.

Some of the bestsellers, not surprisingly, feature Rodrigo. The *Concierto de Aranjuez* is on the second volume of his 'Complete Orchestral Works', together with the well-known *Fantasía para un gentilhombre* but also with *Concierto Andaluz* for four guitars and orchestra, a lesser-known jewel. The guitar soloist is Ricardo Gallén, playing with the Asturias Symphony Orchestra conducted by Maximiano Valdés. (Released in 2002 it has sold nearly 60,000 units, which, considering the number of available recordings of the famous *Concierto*, including Norbert Kraft's bestselling version still in the Naxos catalogue, is no mean feat.) The commitment to record all Rodrigo's orchestral music being such a major project (aided by the composer's daughter, Cecilia Rodrigo), the recordings were shared among three different Spanish orchestras.

The Castile and León Symphony Orchestra (founded in 1991) recorded three of the Rodrigo discs and, more importantly, produced the first recording of the *Sinfonía castellana* by the largely forgotten Antonio José (1902–1936), a composer from Castile who was executed during the Spanish Civil War. The coupling is a Suite from *El mozo de mulas* (an opera still awaiting its first recording).

The Madrid Community Orchestra (founded in 1984) made seven recordings for 'Spanish Classics', including a contribution to the Rodrigo cycle, a bestselling *Preludes and Choruses from Zarzuelas*, and the premiere recording of the Symphony in D minor by Ruperto Chapí (1851–1909).

It fell to the Asturias Symphony Orchestra (founded in 1937) and Maximiano Valdés to record Manuel de Falla's *El amor brujo*, *El sombrero de tres picos* and *La vida breve* (as well as six of the Rodrigo volumes). In the spirit of the collection, which intended to 'resurrect' forgotten composers, the orchestra also recorded works by Julián Orbón (1925–1991).

Last but not least, a relatively small Catalan orchestra, El Vallès Symphony Orchestra, recorded various interesting works by Joaquim Serra (1907–1957).

Italian Classics

From the earliest days of the Marco Polo label, Heymann was keen to represent the growth of Italian orchestral and chamber music from the later nineteenth century and the first half of the twentieth century, a time when composers were determined not only to modernise the Italian opera tradition, with its excessive reliance on melody, but to re-establish non-operatic Italian music. It was an area of music neglected by record companies. Ottorino Respighi's *Sinfonia drammatica* received its world premiere on the label in the mid-1980s, as did the symphonies of Gian Francesco Malipiero in the 1990s (now on Naxos). In the first decade of the twenty-first century Naxos embarked on the complete orchestral music of Giuseppe Martucci, the foremost Italian orchestral composer of the late nineteenth century.

Heymann's long-standing plans – coupled with ideas from Naxos production manager Peter Bromley, a specialist in this area – are producing an unmatched range of Italian music from those years, written in a style that is generally late Romantic, sometimes neo-classical, yet progressive, distinct and often strikingly individual. Within it is a growing list of works by Alfredo Casella (1883–1947) (including his symphonies and concertos), two volumes of the complete *Shakespeare Overtures* by Mario Castelnuovo-Tedesco (1895–1968), orchestral works and chamber music by Ildebrando Pizzetti (1880–1968), and a two-disc survey of the complete piano music of Giorgio Federico Ghedini (1892–1965). There are many world-premiere recordings among the works on these discs: sixteen for Malipiero, thirteen for Ghedini, eleven for Castelnuovo-Tedesco, four for Casella and two for Pizzetti.

Interestingly, the works have not always been recorded with Italian orchestras and musicians. Those represented include the Orchestra Sinfonica di Roma conducted by Francesco La Vecchia playing Martucci, Casella, Malipiero, Busoni, Petrassi and Ferrara; and Massimo Giuseppe Bianchi playing Ghedini's piano music on a Fazioli piano in Perugia, with scores based on manuscript sources provided by the composer's daughter, Maria Grazia Ghedini.

However, also contributing to this series are the Thessaloniki Symphony Orchestra conducted by Myron Michailidis, playing Pizzetti, and the West Australian Symphony Orchestra conducted by Andrew Penny, playing Castelnuovo-Tedesco. Some of the recordings from the earlier Marco Polo days, including the complete published symphonies by Malipiero, were made with the Moscow Symphony Orchestra under Antonio de Almeida. World-premiere recordings of a number of Malipiero's earliest works, including *Pause del silenzio*, *Impressioni dal vero* and *Sinfonia degli eroi*, have also been made by the Thessaloniki Symphony Orchestra and the Orchestra Sinfonica di Roma.

Guitar Collection

There is a worldwide community of people who love the classical guitar. There are similar communities for many other instruments, but particularly so for the guitar because it is, largely, a solo instrument. The Canada-based guitarist–producer Norbert Kraft has since 1994 been serving this community through Naxos; and, with nearly 100 titles, he has created a lively but comprehensive catalogue of guitar recordings. It began with his own recordings of popular repertoire, made in the UK; but once he had established his own studio and editing suite in Canada the 'Guitar Collection' began to grow substantially. It is now the biggest single catalogue of classical guitar recordings in the world.

All the major figures are represented. Quintets by Luigi Boccherini, sonatas by Ferdinando Carulli and the works for violin and guitar by Nicolò Paganini open the Classical repertoire for the instrument, though there are transcriptions from the Baroque period too. There are fifteen CDs devoted to the music of Fernando Sor, four volumes of works by Napoléon Coste (1805–1883), as well as the *Spanish Dances* and *Escenas poeticas* by Enrique Granados. But it is the twentieth-century music for the instrument that forms the bulk of the series. This is considerably varied: from Europe, Mario Castelnuovo-Tedesco, Joaquín Rodrigo and Hans Werner Henze; and from Latin America, Agustín Barrios Mangoré, Heitor Villa-Lobos, Antonio Lauro and Astor Piazzolla. The 'Guitar Collection' also draws on new recordings made by winners of guitar competitions across the world.

Organ Encyclopedia

Fans of the organ form a similarly defined community and the Naxos 'Organ Encyclopedia' set out to cover the main ground. There is now a catalogue of nearly 100 titles presenting music spanning 500 years, from the early Renaissance to the present day. There are five volumes of the early Baroque composer Heinrich Scheidemann and seven volumes of the mid-Baroque Dietrich Buxtehude. Wolfgang Rübsam has also recorded the major works of Bach, though these appear in the main Naxos catalogue.

The Romantic era's Joseph Rheinberger is best known for his many fine solo organ sonatas, eight volumes of which appear in the Encyclopedia and are played by Rübsam; and Felix Mendelssohn contributed six worthy sonatas of his own to the organ literature that are also included here. Of equal note are the works by the influential Belgian organist and composer César Franck; Eric Lebrun plays two volumes of these.

The music of Louis Vierne, Max Reger and the prolific Marcel Dupré (thirteen volumes on Naxos) represents the late Romantic and early modern era's penchant for harmonic complexity and virtuosity. The bracing music of twentieth-century composers Jehan Alain and Jean Langlais straddles tonality and is somewhat more determinedly modern in conception. One of the most recent releases in the 'Organ Encyclopedia' is the GRAMMY Award-winning recording from Olivier Messiaen specialist Paul Jacobs of *Livre du Saint-Sacrement*, played on the organ of the Church of St Mary the Virgin, New York City. Recordings of Mendelssohn and Pachelbel are among the bestsellers.

Amadis, Donau, Lydian and Linz

In the first decade of Naxos, as CD manufacturing became more competitive, there emerged a need for super-budget labels selling at below the Naxos price and it was to meet this that Heymann started four new labels: Amadis, Donau, Lydian and Linz. These CDs were sold in outlets that would not take Naxos, and the repertoire was sometimes licensed by bookshops and other chains that wanted to create their own classical CD brands. Around 180 recordings were made and, despite their target audience and the tight budget involved, some of them turned out very well. Once more, it was central repertoire: symphonies by Beethoven, Schubert, Schumann and Brahms; piano concertos by Mozart, Beethoven and Chopin; the popular violin concertos; *Famous Waltzes*; and piano works by Chopin, Grieg and Mendelssohn. But there was some unexpected repertoire as well, including Shostakovich's Quartets Nos. 2 and 4, sonatas by Rossini for wind quartet, and harpsichord music by Rameau. These recordings now have a new life online.

Naxos Jazz

A Naxos jazz label, to be born in the West but to draw from different traditions, seemed an obvious possibility. It would be based on the same Naxos principles of high musical standards but low cost. The search began for players who had a following but lacked an existing record deal. The label was launched in 1997 with a varying group of releases, from the New York Jazz Collective's *I Don't Know This World Without Don Cherry* to *Havana Flute Summit* – the latter with some charismatic Latin flautists, including Richard Egues and Orlando 'Maraca' Vallé. On the whole they were well received critically, and the label moved energetically forward with the intention of a global perspective. *On the Other Hand* features German–Australian drummer Niko Schäuble; various Scandinavian groups include the Finnish jazz punk Lenni-Kalle Taipale Trio with *Nothing to Hide* (the single top-seller on the label); and the Germany-based sextet Ugetsu comprises players of Russian, German, American and Australian origin, led by bassist Martin Zenker.

The mastermind behind the label was Australian jazz pianist Mike Nock, whose brief was to record leading-edge jazz from around the world. Over a period of four years around sixty albums were released, generally to a very positive critical reception. But the culture of jazz proved too different from that of classical. There is a dependence upon star performers, or at least performers who are widely known; there is an incredible diversity of jazz forms, making it difficult to focus on a specific audience; and the Naxos distribution network had its own limitations because those who were good at getting music into shops and promoting it were specialists in classical, not jazz. New releases stopped in 2001, though with sales of more than 500,000 it was not a wholly unsuccessful venture. Many of the titles continue to sell in modest but regular amounts.

The main reason for the label's collapse was that in the world's biggest jazz market, the United States, non-American jazz does not sell well. In addition, the contemporary cover art did not work for a genre in which artist pictures were the rule; and the label did not have a champion within the company who could push subsidiaries and distributors to pay attention to it.

Naxos World

A similar story is reflected by the Naxos World label. Hopes were high in 2000 that the many traditions in world and folk music could become a part of Naxos. It certainly covered the globe from the start, beginning with a volume of sitar music by Irshad Khan (who was establishing himself as a fine player, moving well beyond being just the son of a distinguished father, Imrat Khan) and encompassing, in the very first year, music from China, Colombia, West Africa and Thailand. One of the bestsellers on the label came also in 2000: *Bhangra Beatz*, involving a group of musicians from India and the UK playing a very lively contemporary fusion of traditional and modern, mixing the Punjab tradition with reggae, R&B, rap and dance music. It sold over 30,000 units and was welcomed by Heymann for the way in which it took the Naxos label so emphatically into a totally new musical area. Dave Swarbrick, England's most well-known and distinctive folk violinist, plays his own compositions on the label and the sound could not be more of a contrast.

The most successful recording came from a very different musical heritage: Tibet. The recording of monks from Sherab Ling Monastery, living in exile in India where they maintain their traditions of worship, made a striking impact; it features their characteristically low chanting, which makes the most of overtones, accompanied by cymbals. Also present are the Tibetan oboes (their continuous sound made possible by the players' circular breathing) and the long, sonorous horns. This recording won the first ever GRAMMY Award for Naxos and sold more than 40,000 copies.

However, the specialist nature of world music, as of jazz, proved difficult to maintain and develop as a continuing thread within the Naxos label. Once again, this was partly due to the genre's emphasis on individual performers rather than repertoire or types. It didn't help that world music in the twenty-first century was, paradoxically, ever changing: it was, in a way, closer to pop than classical. Again, too, the label lacked an effective advocate inside the company. After forty releases, which also took in Slovenia, Russia, Cameroon and Iceland, the label was closed in 2003. Many of the recordings are still available on CD and all have a digital life, usefully broadening the musical base of the Naxos platforms.

Naxos Historical

As a collector Heymann was well aware of the legendary recordings made in the first half of the twentieth century, though perhaps his personal interest lay more in repertoire than in performance. Despite requests from some of the distributors, including Richard Winter at Gramola in Austria, he resisted for some years the idea of starting a section within Naxos devoted to historical recordings. 'I had been reluctant to get into the "historical" business because, with so many different versions of the same performances already in the market, I didn't have a unique angle. I only got interested when I was approached by the English producer–engineer Jonathan Wearn, who told me that he had access to the original masters [transcription discs] of historical broadcasts, which would offer us a distinctive quality advantage. Once we had started releasing these historical broadcasts, I was approached by Mark Obert-Thorn, widely regarded as one of the finest transfer engineers in the world, and he suggested that we also release restorations of commercial recordings. We started with Rachmaninov playing his own concertos and we were all surprised by the demand.' That was in 1999. 'To date, the recording of Piano

Concertos Nos. 2 and 3 has sold over 120,000 copies on CD alone.'

Few of the early historical releases matched this enormous sale but the response was generally very positive. 'I gave the green light to Mark to go ahead at full speed. Eventually he couldn't cope by himself and he suggested bringing in Ward Marston, another leading transfer engineer. The big advantage both have is that they are not only technicians but musicians as well, so their technical work is informed by their musical instinct.'

The range grew rapidly. Heymann was heartened not only by the sales but also by the critical reception, which bordered on the extreme: some reviewers said of quite a few releases that they sounded better than they had ever done – even better than when they were first released. This is partly due to the skills employed in the transfers. It is an issue of both skill and taste in deciding how much to reduce the surface noise on an old tape, or 78, or whatever the original material may be: too little and the crackling is intrusive; too much and the individual sound, even the character, of the performer is lost. The success was also due to the diligence that Obert-Thorn and Marston employed in searching for the finest original sources they could lay their hands on. Often they would use two or three different original sources and bring the best sections together, though this can take hours of painstaking work. As central 'historical players', well networked within the rarefied world, they knew who was likely to have a pristine copy of a relatively obscure recording by Jussi Björling or Alfred Cortot.

Heymann, Obert-Thorn and Marston initially aimed at the more commercial titles but it rapidly became clear that a longer-term strategy was required, and development of this resulted in the pattern that exists today. With a few exceptions, Naxos stopped releasing restored broadcasts. Titles that were thought to be essential for Naxos Historical's list began to be restored from the best available recordings sourced by the engineers.

In 2000 the historical recording division expanded with the creation of Naxos Jazz Legends, Naxos Nostalgia and Naxos Musicals. Other transfer engineers who specialised in these historical genres came on board, including David Lennick. This kind of non-classical repertoire was not a totally new departure for Naxos as it already had a substantial film music catalogue, a contemporary jazz label and even audiobooks, but it was still a surprise to find Nat King Cole, Noël Coward, Cole Porter or the Ink Spots crooning under a Naxos banner.

After more than a decade of releases Naxos Historical has taken a secure place in the overall Naxos catalogue, with nearly 1,000 titles having sold a combined total of six million CDs. The balance remains in favour of classical titles, which number over 600 (including both single CDs and boxed sets) and have achieved sales of well over four million. Jazz Legends, Nostalgia and Musicals, as well as a smattering of blues (including Bessie Smith), are represented by 340 titles, with sales of nearly two million. The continued expansion of the historical list has been limited by US copyright law: the United States is the only country in the world in which sound recordings never enter the public domain (at least they won't until 2067) because they are covered by state common-law copyright and not federal law. This is why all Naxos historical recordings, of any genre, are forbidden from being sold in the US. As a large part of the world market, especially for jazz and nostalgia, exists in the US, Naxos is restricted in what it can viably bring out. The release schedule is therefore much more restrained than it once was.

Nevertheless, Naxos Historical is an extraordinary archive library, in terms of both sound and content. The classical section is unrivalled for its quality and title selection. The focus of historical recording is, of course, on performance, which is why most of the well-known and often most important recordings are arranged according to instrument, in the 'Great' series. 'Great Violinists', 'Great Cellists', 'Great Pianists' and 'Great

Singers' carry the foremost instrumentalists of the twentieth century up to 1960; and 'Great Conductors', 'Great Opera Recordings' and 'Great Operetta Recordings' complete the series (apart from 'Great Violists', which at the time of writing has just one example: the English viola player William Primrose playing *Harold in Italy* and Walton's Viola Concerto!).

There is also a highly specialist biographical series that includes *The A–Z of Conductors* and *The A–Z of Pianists*, each comprising 300 artist biographies, four CDs and a dedicated website with more examples of the musicians featured. *The A–Z of Singers* and *The A–Z of String Players* are in the pipeline.

It is remarkable how durable some of these artists are – that years after their death, when the sound of the original recordings cannot match twenty-first century fidelity, they are still in demand. The 'Great' players include: Pablo Casals (his performance of Bach's Cello Suites has sold in excess of 100,000 copies), Sergey Rachmaninov, Glenn Gould (his performance of Bach's *Goldberg Variations* sold 25,000 copies in five years), Artur Schnabel, Vladimir Horowitz and Edwin Fischer (sales of his set of Bach's Forty-Eight Preludes and Fugues have reached over 40,000 copies). Among the violinists, Yehudi Menuhin's early recording of Elgar's Violin Concerto coupled with the First Violin Concerto by Bruch has sold more than 35,000 copies but is topped by the 1939/40 recording of Jascha Heifetz playing concertos by Brahms and Beethoven, which has achieved sales of 45,000 copies.

But did anyone ever think there would be, on a budget label, the five-volume complete edition of the Polish pianist Ignaz Friedman, or thirteen volumes of Benno Moiseiwitsch, or three volumes of *Women at the Piano: An Anthology of Historic Performances* between 1926 and 1954? What gems are hidden in there!

Topping individual sales among the 'Great Singers', perhaps unexpectedly, is the Swedish tenor Jussi Björling: the CD of his opera aria recordings between 1936 and 1948 was a hit all over Scandinavia, selling more than 60,000 copies. There are other standards too, such as Kathleen Ferrier's immortal recording of *Das Lied von der Erde* with Bruno Walter. What about Maria Callas? Her recordings continue to have appeal, as do those of Beniamino Gigli (who is represented by the ultimate fifteen-volume complete edition), Elisabeth Schwarzkopf and Kirsten Flagstad (heard with Lauritz Melchior in the rapturous 1936 recording of *Tristan und Isolde* conducted in London by Fritz Reiner).

Showing how fashions change, there is also the 1956 recording of Peter Cornelius' *The Barber of Baghdad* with a stellar cast of Oskar Czerwenka in the title role plus Elisabeth Schwarzkopf and Nicolai Gedda, with Erich Leinsdorf conducting – that is on a budget label with a superb transfer, excellent notes, and Weber's one-act opera *Abu Hassan* thrown in for good measure! Every one of these historic recordings is presented with the level of care applied to all Naxos releases, carrying all the relevant documentation and notes.

Leinsdorf features among the 'Great Conductors' in his own right, along with Wilhelm Furtwängler, Thomas Beecham, Erich Kleiber, Richard Strauss (conducting Beethoven) and many more of the twentieth century's great names, including the controversial Karajan. There is even the inimitable Stokowski conducting his own transcriptions (though he probably would have had mixed feelings to discover that José Serebrier's modern recordings of them, on the Naxos main label, have sold more).

Naxos Historical teems with legendary opera recordings: three of *La Bohème* (de los Angeles/Björling, Tebaldi/Prandelli and Albanese/Gigli), four of *Madama Butterfly*, two of *Tosca* (one with Maria Callas), and one of *Turandot*; there is Callas again in *Il Turco in Italia*, Gedda/Schwarzkopf in *Die Fledermaus*, and Schwarzkopf again in both Johann Strauss II's *Der Zigeunerbaron* and, not to be missed, Richard Strauss's

Ariadne auf Naxos. By way of musical contrast, the classic per-formances of Gilbert and Sullivan by The D'Oyly Carte Opera Company can also be found, among which *H.M.S. Pinafore* (sales of 20,000 copies to date) and *The Pirates of Penzance* particularly sell year in, year out.

Heymann admits that for him the recordings on Naxos Historical have been quite an eye-opener. 'The biggest discov-ery of all was that the interpretations were far more personal and that the artists took a lot more freedom with the works than would be acceptable today. But they also played with more feeling – sometimes in a style that would now be called "bad taste". And the biggest surprise in the vocal titles was that people sang with very little, if any, vibrato.' While he knows that the reputation for the high standard of these Naxos recordings has made them highly collectible for the committed buff (even one who already owns previous versions), he hopes that the budget pricing will open the door for a more general buyer, who, he is sure, will be at times astonished by the per-formances.

Of course, Naxos Jazz Legends, Naxos Nostalgia and the collection of Naxos Musicals are studded with household names. *That Christmas Feeling: 21 Vintage Seasonal Hits (1932–1950)* tops the sales charts at over 45,000, carrying as it does everything from *White Christmas* (Bing Crosby) to *Winter Wonderland* (Perry Como). Among others are leading crossover figures of their day: John McCormack, Richard Tauber, George Gershwin and Marian Anderson. Then there are some from different genres again, whose popularity sur-vives the passage of generations, such as Florence Foster Jenkins, Victor Borge and Larry Adler (whose recordings show even now what an exceptional virtuoso he was). The list is truly international: Mario Lanza, Gertrude Lawrence, Dean Martin, Lawrence Tibbett, Charles Trenet (*La Mer* is a top-seller), Paul Whiteman and Eartha Kitt. And Ezio Pinza singing *Some Enchanted Evening* – nostalgia indeed.

Jazz Legends has some surprises. Django Reinhardt tops the sales charts, Volume 1 selling over 35,000 copies and Volume 2 not far behind with 25,000. Stephane Grappelli, a one-time Reinhardt partner, has two CDs. Many other great names are here too: Duke Ellington, Sidney Bechet and Benny Goodman, Count Basie, Bix Beiderbecke, Billie Holiday, Louis Armstrong, Sarah Vaughan, Glenn Miller and Art Tatum; even Miles Davis from the 1940s (*Early Milestones*) and early 1950s (*Boplicity*).

The historical series grows month by month, albeit at a steady pace. As the years roll on and various copyrights expire, more performers – both popular and lesser-known – are added to the catalogue.

Naxos DVD

In 1990 Heymann found himself with a growing classical catalogue and began to look for new ways in which he could use those recordings. In Hong Kong and the rest of the Far East, VHS was increasingly a part of home entertainment, as was the continuing format of Laserdisc. So he set up a video team, based in Switzerland, with the brief to travel to the most important towns and tourist areas of Europe, taking films of the main sites: these could later be edited into attractive travelogues shaped around appropriately chosen classical music taken from Naxos and Marco Polo. Each classical work chosen formed the script on which the shooting schedule was based. It was a deft idea and Heymann invested considerably. It was neither easy nor cheap, and it had to depend on the VHS videotape format which by then had won the battle against Betamax to become the dominant home video medium.

Nearly 100 'Musical Journeys' were made and it was certainly an adventurous enterprise. The team travelled to St Petersburg and Helsinki in the north, Sicily in the south, Uzbekistan in the east and England in the west; the filmmakers took pictures of castles, churches, landscapes, palaces, civil buildings and flowers. Back in the Swiss studios, footage was edited with the music of Bach to result in *Germany, A Musical Tour of Bach's Homeland*; French music was the basis of *Chateaux of the Loire*; Czech music shaped *Prague: A Musical Tour of the City's Past and Present*; and Albinoni, Corelli and of course Vivaldi underlined scenes of Venice. In the musical tour of Uzbekistan – against visuals of mosques and madrassas of Bukhara, Khiva and other stops along the Silk Road – there was Rimsky-Korsakov's *Sheherazade* and *Sadko*.

Alas, in a way, the series fell between two technical systems. DVD was being developed but it did not really make a significant impression in the market until the turn of the century, and it was not until 2003 that DVD sales overtook VHS. These 'Musical Journeys' were more suited to a format that offered a fast and competent search facility. Heymann had, by then, long stopped production of the series, though it has since been released on DVD and is at last recouping some of its investment. Ever mindful of the Naxos base in China, Heymann more recently commissioned ten DVDs devoted to some of the finest sights in the country, including Beijing, Shanghai, Xi'an, Hangzhou as well as Tibet, though these came well after the main series had finished. In the case of these Chinese programmes, the footage came first and appropriate music was added later.

It became clear that DVD was going to make a significant contribution to classical music. Although this was a different area from classical audio recording, and very much the domain of companies with a background in television, Heymann brought to his new Naxos DVD label as many programmes as he could find.

There are operas and concerts, both classical and jazz. Opera festivals were keen for their productions to have a longer life than the live performances and a few TV airings: DVD was the ideal answer and opportunities appeared. On Naxos DVD now are operas by Donizetti (three, including *Lucrezia Borgia*), Rossini (including *Il Turco in Italia*) and Verdi (including *Luisa Miller* from Teatro La Fenice) as well as Wolf-Ferrari's *La vedova scaltra* (also from La Fenice) and Berlioz's *Benvenuto Cellini* (from the Salzburg Festival). There seems additionally to be a growing demand for films of concerts that include core classical repertoire.

An important addition to the DVD catalogue came in the mid-2000s from a remarkable American jazz series called 'Jazz Icons', which contained material from European television archives. It turned into a bestselling series, presenting as it did Woody Herman, Oscar Peterson, Sonny Rollins, Nina Simone, Sarah Vaughan and many others.

One of the most recent and unusual releases is *Cello Master Class* from Maria Kliegel, the distinguished Naxos cellist.

Deletions

A deletion policy is part and parcel of most sizeable classical labels, judicious pruning being advisable for both commercial and marketing reasons. It is pointless for dead titles to take up space in a warehouse or tie up money that can be used for new products. However, the advent of downloads has remedied the situation: there is no reason why specialist repertoire, which attracts very little interest, cannot now sit on a website for the handful of people who are interested in it. In fact Naxos has always operated a very modest deletions policy. Every few years there will be a slight cull, but in a quarter of a century fewer than 10 per cent (actually closer to 5 per cent) of recordings on CD have been deleted. Some have migrated onto less expensive labels, the most obvious examples being the Marco Polo recordings that have moved to Naxos; but Heymann sees his label as an archive for the collector, just as he did in the very beginning.

Thirteen

Marco Polo

Marco Polo started out as 'HK Marco Polo' in 1982. Heymann had begun recording Chinese orchestral music for his HK label in the late 1970s with the Hong Kong Philharmonic Orchestra and the Singapore Symphony Orchestra, but their musical directors did not want to be restricted to Chinese music: they were keen to record Western repertoire as well. Heymann realised that there was no way he could sell Mozart, Beethoven or Brahms performed by the Hong Kong and Singapore orchestras and decided to focus on world-premiere recordings, which collectors would purchase regardless of the orchestras, conductors and soloists performing on them. The initial releases carried the dual 'HK Marco Polo' stamp but very soon the 'HK' was dropped and the Marco Polo label was born.

From the start, Marco Polo was dubbed 'The Label of Discovery', for it was the first of the CD era to focus on world-premiere recordings: most of the releases featured works that had never been recorded before. In a way it was less of a commercial enterprise and more of a hobby for Heymann – his personal contribution to the music that had been a consistent inspiration during his time in the Far East, when he had otherwise been absorbed by business interests. He had always been drawn to Romantic and late Romantic music, and had been stimulated by venturing off-piste when collecting (and distributing in the Far East) Opus, Hungaroton, Melodiya and other similar labels. He found the kinds of works that he especially liked and, in reading around the subject in music magazines, music encyclopedias, old books and biographies, he realised that there were numerous composers active in the nineteenth and early twentieth centuries who had faded from concert-hall programmes (such as Anton Rubinstein, Joachim Raff, Franz Lachner and Vasily Sergeyevich Kalinnikov). Often they were just names in books and he didn't know what their music sounded like (because there were no recordings!). Consequently it was difficult to judge whether there really was worth in Myaskovsky or Garofalo or Čiurlionis; but once he had started he proceeded with a strong concept, determined to make Marco Polo a label of premiere recordings as well as one of discovery. There were many times when no one – apart from the conductor, sitting at home with a photocopied score from a specialised library in preparation for the recording's coming rehearsals – knew whether the work (in which a considerable amount had been invested) was any good at all.

Of course, most of the time Heymann made a shrewd judgement: sometimes he came across comments that contemporaries (critics and friends) had made about a composer's work; or he might know two symphonies by Raff and could judge that here was a serious and competent composer with something to say; or maybe he found that an established and more familiar composer, such as Respighi, Ippolitov-Ivanov or Cui, who was known by only a handful of popular calling cards, had a large repertoire languishing in obscurity. There were major names with sizeable works awaiting a recording premiere, or at least their first stereo recording, and some real gems were discovered. Rimsky-Korsakov wrote more than *Sheherazade*, and his *Night on Mount Triglav* and *Pan Voyevoda* received their first recording on Marco Polo. Perhaps there were also times in the studio when an able conductor, standing in front of an excellent orchestra in Moscow or Bratislava, was asked, 'Why are we doing this?' and could only answer, looking into his score, 'For a rich German classical enthusiast businessman in Hong Kong. We go from bar 65!'

Whether or not he was entertaining a personal enthusiasm, Heymann turned out to be more astute than many realised. An interest in these obscurities, and a market for them, did exist, consisting of men (and they were mainly men) who were on the same wavelength as Heymann and particularly intrigued by off-the-beaten-track repertoire. There were probably not many of them in any one country – the trick was to find them. One well-known supporter was an international star: the Australian comedian Barry Humphries, better known by his alter ego Dame Edna Everage. When Barry Humphries was invited to record the narration for Prokofiev's *Peter and the Wolf* for Naxos he waived any fee: all he wanted, he said, was a copy of every Marco Polo recording for as long as he lived. That was in 1996.

Thirty years after Marco Polo began it had notched up 1,000 new recordings, and sales (on various formats – LP, cassette, DVD but mostly CD) of around 3,750,000 units. Not bad for a personal enthusiasm.

The Marco Polo Catalogue

Chinese Classics

Marco Polo began with Chinese music on the HK label, Heymann realising that there was an opportunity for recordings of Chinese orchestral music written in a Western style (mostly since the end of the Second World War). It enabled him to acknowledge musically his Hong Kong home and to provide a service to Chinese music buyers. Piracy was undoubtedly an issue but the genuine sales were growing, and through persistence this category has sold millions of units over the years. It began with the most famous work of this genre, Chen and He's *The Butterfly Lovers*, featuring Takako Nishizaki as the soloist with her hometown orchestra, the Nagoya Philharmonic Orchestra. Over the years, Nishizaki recorded another seven versions of the work, in Japan, Slovakia and China (released in audiophile formats and on video as well as CD). Spurred by her constant touring and performances throughout China, the total sales reached several million units. There were other releases with good sales, including *Master of Chinese Percussion* featuring Yim Hok-Man, *Three Wishes of the Rose – Everlasting Chinese Love Songs*, Ding's *Long March Symphony*, Xian's *Yellow River Cantata* with other choral works (which has sold in excess of 30,000 copies), and Ren's *Colourful Clouds* with other Chinese orchestral favourites. Heymann also licensed a substantial number of recordings from China Records and these subsequently became available internationally for the first time.

Marco Polo Classics

'Marco Polo Classics' forms the central part of the label, with around 800 titles comprising possibly the most idiosyncratic repertoire of any independent classical calatogue. It began with an astute selection of forgotten overtures and marches by none other than Richard Wagner – *Polonia*, *Rule Britannia* and others, all previously unrecorded – played by the Hong Kong Philharmonic Orchestra. It was a typically smart Heymann marketing gesture, but it showed immediately a dedication to the task of bringing neglected music of substance onto LP – and soon CD. One of the next releases, Respighi's *Concerto gregoriano*, was another world-premiere recording and a very satisfying discovery for many. As the catalogue developed it soon fell into sections – orchestral, chamber, instrumental and opera – and as the years rolled by there came a handful of extraordinary ventures that gave the label extra dimensions. These included the complete music of the Strauss family, a stupendous undertaking that is approaching completion; and the 'National Anthems of the World', an unrivalled and constantly updated set that has become a boon to sports organisations worldwide, including the Olympic Games.

Opera

Unusual operas from the early nineteenth to the mid-twentieth century have been released regularly on Marco Polo. These include the world-premiere recording of Weber's *Peter Schmoll and His Neighbours*, Marschner's ghost opera *Hans Heiling* and Anton Rubinstein's *The Demon* from the nineteenth century; and from the twentieth century Franz Schreker's *Der ferne Klang* and *Die Gezeichneten*, and no fewer than ten operas by Richard Wagner's son Siegfried (including *The Man in a Bear's Skin* and *The Kingdom of the Black Swan*). There is Szymanowski's *King Roger*, Granados' three-act *María del Carmen*, Meyerbeer's *L'Étoile du nord*, Respighi's *Lucrezia*, Pfitzner's *Das Herz*, and even a contemporary Italian opera, *Divara – Wasser und Blut* by Azio Corghi.

Orchestral Music

The early showpiece of the label was undoubtedly the premiere recording of Havergal Brian's Symphony No. 1 'The Gothic', by virtue of its size as much as its musical content. But it could be said that here among the orchestral recordings is the heart of Marco Polo: a stream of discoveries by both the known and the unknown. There is plenty of music by familiar composers: Adam (two more ballets from the composer of *Giselle*), Arensky (*Egyptian Nights*), Balakirev, Bax, Bloch, Cui, Donizetti, Dvořák (opera overtures), Glazunov (four volumes of orchestral works, before the remaining sixteen volumes that were released on Naxos), Goldmark (Symphony No. 2 and

Penthesilea), Hummel, Humperdinck, d'Indy, Janáček (*Danube and Moravian Dances*), Korngold (Violin Concerto, coupled with Goldmark's), Respighi (many works, including the *Sinfonia drammatica*), Rimsky-Korsakov, Salieri (overtures), Smetana, Spohr, Stanford, Szymanowski and Zemlinsky.

Even more impressive, in a sense, is the collection of rarely heard or largely unknown composers who in Heymann's estimation have written works that are worth a place on CD and in the digital archives of today. A brief list scarcely scratches the surface: Bantock, Berners, Boulanger (both Lili and Nadia), Braga Santos (six volumes of this key Portuguese composer), Brian (eight volumes of symphonies and other orchestral music), Čiurlionis (*The Sea* and other atmospheric tone poems), Devreese, Emmanuel, Enescu (his complete orchestral works, licensed from Romania), Furtwängler (four volumes of symphonies and the Piano Concerto), Garofalo, Glière (four volumes including the three symphonies), Grechaninov, Hill (three volumes of symphonies), Ippolitov-Ivanov (three orchestral CDs), Ivanovs (four symphonies; two more were subsequently released on Naxos), Koechlin (including the distinctive *Le Livre de la Jungle*), Lachner (four orchestral CDs), Lajtha (all nine symphonies of this Hungarian composer), Liadov, Lyatoshynsky (five symphonies), Malipiero (all the symphonies), Markevitch (seven volumes of the complete orchestral music), Moyzes (all twelve symphonies), Myaskovsky (four volumes of symphonies so far but Heymann hopes one day to have a complete set), Pfitzner (Piano Concerto), Poot, Raff (all eleven symphonies), Rubinstein (the largest collection of orchestral works available anywhere, including five piano concertos), Schmitt (including *La Tragédie de Salomé*), Spohr (the complete symphonies), Taneyev, Tournemire and Vītols.

Light Music and the Strauss Project

Despite its seemingly serious purpose, Marco Polo has always been open to light music. The British light music series, though consisting of just twenty-four titles, has proved popular: Ketèlbey's *In a Monastery Garden*, Coates's *The Dam Busters* march, Coleridge-Taylor's *Hiawatha* and Tomlinson's *First Suite of English Folk-Dances* all sold well; Binge's *The Watermill*, with the *Scottish Rhapsody*, *Elizabethan Serenade* and others, was a surprise top-seller. The total sale of 130,000 CDs from twenty-four titles has been very respectable.

In the heart of the light music series are the first eleven volumes of waltzes, polkas, mazurkas and more by the Danish composer Christian Lumbye, music director and composer at the Tivoli Gardens in Copenhagen for nearly thirty years. That was in the mid-nineteenth century but his music is still hugely popular in Scandinavia. His complete orchestral works was a tall order for Marco Polo fans to absorb but Heymann was committed to it. He still hopes that some day he can complete the project: there are at least another thirty volumes to go.

But it is as nothing, at least in terms of logistics, when compared with the Strauss project. This is simply immense. Anyone else looking at the numbers, the prospects, the whole project, would probably call it reckless. It involved a huge amount of painstaking research in the beginning; many of the scores and parts had to be handwritten for the sessions because published editions did not exist. The complete Johann Strauss II Edition runs to fifty-two CDs. It began in 1991 and was concluded in 1996. The complete Johann Strauss I Edition runs to seventeen CDs so far and will eventually number twenty-four. The complete Josef Strauss Edition runs to twenty-six CDs. It is a stupendous project that is unlikely ever to be repeated. It could only have been imagined, planned, implemented, manufactured and released by the owner of the company.

Chamber Music

The nineteenth century produced an enormous amount and variety of chamber music, much of which is now forgotten. The Marco Polo contribution to rediscoveries, which are fashionable now but were less so in the early 1980s when Heymann started, draws on music truly from around the world. There are string quartets of the Slovakian Ján Bella, the Piano Quartet and Piano Trio of the French composer Léon Boëllmann; the Piano Trio in E and String Quartet in D by the Spaniard Tomás Bretón; and the delightful, very French salon piano trios by Félicien David. There is a useful collection of English cello sonatas by Ireland, Moeran and Rubbra, and three volumes of varied chamber music with piano by the American Arthur Foote that has resonances of Schumann and Dvořák. Piano trios and string quartets show Alexander Grechaninov to be rooted in the Russian Romantic tradition, though he died in New York in 1956. The two volumes of violin sonatas by Camargo Guarnieri, born in São Paulo, are similar in character to the music of Braga Santos and Villa-Lobos, while d'Indy's piano and string quartets take us firmly back to France. All the works for flute by the American twentieth-century composer Robert Muczynski fit neatly on one CD, which features the composer on the piano and, if you look hard enough in the catalogue, the doyen of French flautists Jean-Pierre Rampal playing flute duets with Alexandra Hawley. Not a lot of people know that Rampal is a Marco Polo artist. The English composer Buxton Orr used twelve-tone techniques so it is a bit of a mystery how his Piano Trios Nos. 1–3 got onto Marco Polo at all, but they are sound works. There are also two piano trios by Christian Sinding, part of the generation after Grieg. Ildebrando Pizzetti was part of the Italian *Novecento*, which Heymann has been keen to represent; Marco Polo has released two volumes of his works, including two string quartets. Heymann also felt that Franz Schmidt had been unjustly neglected by the recording fraternity and the catalogue now offers his two main chamber works for clarinet: the A major and B flat major Clarinet Quintets, played by Hungarian musicians.

Perhaps the strongest single representation of a composer's chamber music oeuvre on Marco Polo is the still-growing list of complete string quartets by Louis Spohr: fourteen volumes so far (there are thirty-six quartets in all). It shows the range of a composer who is so often sidelined into second or third rank. With much the same effect, Marco Polo showcases Spohr's seven string quintets.

Piano Music

The Marco Polo alphabetical piano listing starts appropriately with Charles-Valentin Alkan, the neglected giant of French piano music, ripe for Marco Polo promotion: there are five volumes played by Bernard Ringeissen and Laurent Martin that cover the major works. 'B' is for Bach – an unexpected inclusion bearing in mind the purpose of the label, but this is a CD of Busoni's transcriptions played by Sequeira Costa. Bartók also made transcriptions of seventeenth- and eighteenth-century music (less well known than Busoni's) and the Hungarian pianist Ilona Prunyi presents a selection. Continuing the theme, Daniel Blumenthal plays Hans von Bülow's piano transcriptions of Gluck, Wagner and others; and opera transcriptions by the Hungarian composer Ferenc Erkel are played by István Kassai. A more characteristic Marco Polo discovery is the Lithuanian composer Mikolajus Konstantinas Čiurlionis, who wrote appealing miniatures for the piano, and within the two volumes played by Múza Rubackyté are some haunting gems – as there are among the volumes of piano sonatas and other works by Robert Fuchs, who was praised by Brahms.

The Spanish pianist Jordi Masó has recorded two volumes of piano works by the twentieth-century Spanish composer Joaquim Homs and all the piano music by Homs's teacher Roberto Gerhard (which conveniently fits on one disc). Gerhard's Argentinian contemporary Luis Gianneo is represented by three CDs of piano music, from his Suite of 1933 up to the Sonata No. 3 and Six Bagatelles of the 1950s. There are also two discs of another Argentinian, Alberto Williams, played by Valentin Surif.

Major sets feature strongly. Tatjana Franova plays the complete piano music of Alexander Glazunov on four CDs, and Konstantin Scherbakov presents the first ten volumes of piano music by Leopold Godowsky, which makes staggering demands on any pianist. The works of another, though earlier, piano virtuoso, Sigismond Thalberg, appear on five CDs, including his variations on operas by Rossini for which Francesco Nicolosi is the agile performer. The piano music of Paul Hindemith on four volumes is performed by Hans Petermandl, the Austrian pianist who is particularly comfortable with the style, having played Hindemith's Piano Concerto under the composer's own direction.

On an English note, the pianist Rosemary Tuck plays two volumes of music by Albert Ketèlbey while Alan Cuckston takes care of music by Edward German. Edward MacDowell was similarly well known during his lifetime in his own country (the United States), and his piano music, played by James Barbagallo, is contained on four CDs (a fifth is filled with his songs).

Other Marco Polo regulars, such as Korngold, Lajtha, Liadov, Lyapunov, Myaskovsky and Rubinstein, have their piano repertoire included too.

Marco Polo Film Music

In the first fifty years of film, accomplished composers wrote outstanding scores. During that period, there was no snobbish division between film music and 'serious' concert music: composers were writing to order just as they had always done at some time in their lives. So making new digital recordings of some of the great scores of Honegger, Vaughan Williams, Herrmann, Khachaturian, Bliss, Auric, Waxman, Steiner, Shostakovich, Tiomkin and others seemed like a good idea – especially as they would be sold with the poster art from the original movies.

Michael Halász at work in the Vienna State Opera

The distinguished Polish conductor
Antoni Wit, one of the most prolific
conductors on Naxos

James Judd, former music director
of the New Zealand Symphony
Orchestra

(Photo credit: Juliusz Multarzynski)

A star of the younger generation: the Chinese violinist Tianwa Yang

Dmitry Yablonsky sustains an unusual double act for Naxos, as both conductor and cello virtuoso.

(Photo credit: Lluis Costa)

The spectacular recording of Tallis's motet *Spem in Alium* by the Oxford Camerata conducted by Jeremy Summerly

The discography of the Hungarian pianist Jenő Jandó is one of the pillars of the Naxos catalogue.

John Corigliano, one of the foremost American composers, who takes an active role in Naxos recordings of his music

(Photo credit: Henry Fair)

Naxos released Robert Craft's recordings of twentieth-century classics and published the conductor's book *Down a Path of Wonder*.

Ulrich Eisenlohr, who directed the *Schubert-Lied-Edition*

Juliet Stevenson reading
Jane Austen's *Emma*

Neville Jason still looking fresh after
completing the unabridged recording of
War and Peace

David Timson, who has read *The
Complete Sherlock Holmes* and
directed Shakespeare and Goethe
for Naxos AudioBooks

Kenneth Branagh, who plays
Richard III for Naxos AudioBooks
and reads Chekhov short stories

(Photo credit: Andrew MacPherson)

Michael Sheen plays Oedipus and reads
Dostoevsky and *Great Poets of the
Romantic Age* for Naxos AudioBooks.

Anton Lesser, one of the most popular
readers on Naxos AudioBooks, with
unabridged Dickens, Sterne, Homer and
Hamlet among many achievements

Andrew Walton, Naxos producer and MD of K&A Productions

Conductor Mark Fitz-Gerald and Naxos production manager Peter Bromley present Irina Shostakovich, the composer's widow, with the Naxos premiere recording of *Odna* in Paris.

The producer of numerous recordings made in Hungary, Ibolya Tóth

The face behind the Naxos
liner notes and much more:
Keith Anderson

The Toronto-based
Naxos recording team:
Bonnie and Norbert
Kraft (Photo credit: Cameron Ogilvie)

Jim Selby, CEO of Naxos
of America, in the Franklin
warehouse that stocks 2.3
million CDs and 225,000
DVDs from 150 labels

The Naxos Pyramid was one of the most striking shop fittings, devised by Naxos Deutschland.

An immensely successful Swedish TV campaign contributed to sales of more than 250,000 boxed sets, and decades later the product is still selling.

Anthony Anderson, MD of Select Music, with the *Gramophone* Award for Label of the Year in 2005

The Naxos White Wall in Montreal!

Some forty-six titles were recorded over a period of ten years, many with the Moscow Symphony Orchestra conducted by William Stromberg in the Mosfilm Studio in Moscow – often a big orchestra was needed in a space where sound effects, too, could be created with aplomb. Considerable research and preparation were involved to source the film scores, and in some cases a score needed to undergo detailed restoration (even total reconstruction) before the orchestra could go into the studio. It was a labour of love for the composer John Morgan.

The series began in 1990 with Arthur Honegger's music to *Les Misérables* and *Napoléon*, played by the Slovak Radio Symphony Orchestra conducted by Adriano. But by the mid-1990s the project had become more ambitious with the declared intention to work from only careful restorations. These were hugely expensive and time-consuming. Furthermore the films were deliberately chosen for their scores, not because they were box-office hits. Korngold's *Captain Blood* is on one CD coupled with Steiner's *The Three Musketeers*; it was recorded by the Brandenburg Philharmonic Orchestra conducted by Richard Kaufman and has sold in excess of 10,000 CDs. Steiner's *King Kong*, recorded by Stromberg in 1996 and released in 1997, was another bestseller, chalking up a similar quantity.

That level of sales, alas, was the exception. Despite the enormous effort that went into realising these recordings, they did not make a sufficient impact on CD buyers, and the last Marco Polo Film Music CD – Korngold's music to the 1938 film *The Adventures of Robin Hood*, conducted by Stromberg – was released in 2003.

Yellow River and Middle Kingdom

These two Chinese labels were established in the 1990s, Heymann wanting to look east for the Naxos label as well as west. With the Naxos headquarters in Hong Kong, which was shortly to be returned to China, it was part of the musical and commercial strategy to provide special recordings for the home market.

Yellow River began in 1992 with orchestral works based often on traditional themes and melodies. Among these are *The Legend of Shadi-er* and other pieces played by The Shanghai Conservatory Chinese Orchestra, and *Wild Geese on the Sandbank*, featuring solos by Chinese traditional lutes (the sanxian and the ruan). Also represented are compositions written during the communist era (such as the ballet *The Red Detachment of Women*, which tells the story of personal sacrifice for political success) and modern revolutionary Peking operas – for example, *Taking Tiger Mountain by Strategy*. There are some sixty recordings in total, all produced in mainland China.

Middle Kingdom was closer to the concept of a world label, with thirteen recordings presenting classical Chinese instruments (including the pipa, the erhu, the suona and the dizi) and featuring leading Chinese performers.

Postlude

Throughout the first decade of the twenty-first century the Naxos label expanded its coverage of specialist repertoire, not only by re-releasing Marco Polo titles at a low price but also by continuing to issue a wide range of music and world-premiere recordings. Market forces brought 'The Label of Discovery' down from full price to mid-price and the role of Marco Polo was redefined, so that now it is mainly the vehicle for the large series of light music works by composers such as the Strauss family and Lumbye. It has come a long way in thirty years.

Fourteen
Publishing

Naxos AudioBooks

Naxos AudioBooks was founded by Klaus Heymann and
Nicolas Soames in September 1994 with the defining line
'Classic Literature with Classical Music on Cassette and CD'.
It was a period of sudden expansion by book publishers into
the arena of spoken word, the genre having been dominated
previously by classical record companies selling spoken-word
LPs and cassettes into record shops. Heymann was keen to
open up a new area of expertise for Naxos and to use his
wealth of recorded music in ever-differing ways.

Naxos AudioBooks established its ground from the start by
recording not just popular classics (in abridged versions) but
the high end of literature, too. Behind the literary choice was
the confirmed Naxos intention: to make the classics as accessible as possible to the widest range of people. Among its first
recordings were Milton's *Paradise Lost*, in a three-CD abridgement read by Anton Lesser, one of England's leading classical
actors (a decade later he added his unabridged reading, which
is one of the finest recordings on the label); *The Death of
Arthur* by Sir Thomas Malory, read by Philip Madoc; Shelley's

Frankenstein shared between three actors; *Orlando* by Virginia Woolf, read by the young actress Laura Paton; and Dostoevsky's *Crime and Punishment* read by Michael Sheen, now a Hollywood star but then just out of drama school.

Three other recordings in those initial months set the pattern. The first was a remarkable four-CD abridgement of James Joyce's *Ulysses* read by Irish actors Jim Norton and Marcella Riordan. This won one of the main audiobook prizes, which established, in the label's launch year, its credentials for outstanding recordings and its ability to make the most difficult works in world literature approachable for all. The second and third pivotal recordings showed the intention of Naxos AudioBooks to serve classic literature for children as well, and both of these have been bestsellers ever since. Grimms' *Fairy Tales*, read endearingly by Laura Paton, was enhanced by classical music, which simultaneously introduced young children to delightful popular repertoire. It was followed by the first newly commissioned text for the label: teacher and writer Edward Ferrie retold some of the most popular Greek myths in *Tales from the Greek Legends*, and, through a widely praised and engaging reading by the young actor Benjamin Soames, introduced a younger generation to Perseus and Medusa the Gorgon, Theseus and the Minotaur, and many others.

Within a year Naxos AudioBooks was taking shape, with some fifty recordings divided into categories. 'Classic Fiction' was starting to cover a good range, from Hugo's *The Hunchback of Notre Dame* and Dickens's *Great Expectations*, to Melville's *Moby Dick* and Verne's *20,000 Leagues Under the Sea*, to Wilkie Collins's *The Moonstone*. Poetry was a growing thread, from Homer's *The Iliad* and *The Odyssey* (read by Anton Lesser) to compilations including *Popular Poetry, Popular Verse* and *Great Poets of the Romantic Age* (read by Michael Sheen). Even *Whale Nation*, the moving 'green' poem on whales (written and read by Heathcote Williams, with music again playing a particularly imaginative supporting role), was an early release. 'Classic Non-Fiction' was also there from the start (with T.E. Lawrence's *Seven Pillars of Wisdom*, and *Composers' Letters*) and there was the first step into drama with *Great Speeches and Soliloquies of Shakespeare*, a compilation that featured, among others, the young Simon Russell Beale, who is now established as one of the UK's leading actors on the classical and modern stage.

As the months and years went by, and Naxos AudioBooks became a regular prize-winner on both sides of the Atlantic, it broadened its scope and settled into a regular release schedule of fifty new titles per year. Readers are key to audiobooks, for the character of a voice and the approach to the performance can totally change a recording. Buyers follow readers as often as they do authors or genres. Some actors began to be strongly associated with Naxos AudioBooks. As early as 1995 Juliet Stevenson read Virginia Woolf's *To the Lighthouse* in abridged form, and her remarkably well-judged classical delivery became instantly recognisable. She went on to record most of Jane Austen's works in abridged and unabridged form, making them one of the most internationally appreciated parts of the label. Neville Jason, a reader of urbane poise, made a similar impact with two massive projects. The first was Proust's *Remembrance of Things Past*: it began with Jason's own abridgement of the first part, *Swann's Way*, moved on to *Swann in Love*, and as the years went by it continued inexorably to the final part, *Time Regained* (in his own translation). Even abridged the whole thing ran for thirty-nine CDs, but as with the abridgement of *Ulysses* it has served thousands as an introduction to a major twentieth-century novel. Then Jason settled into the studio for some twenty-five days to read Tolstoy's *War and Peace* in unabridged form. It was released on fifty-one CDs and is a startling achievement of sustained reading, the myriad of characters clearly delineated.

Another reader closely associated with Naxos AudioBooks is David Timson. When he read a three-CD collection of Sherlock

Holmes stories in 1998, including *The Speckled Band*, neither he nor Naxos AudioBooks had any idea that it was the start of the whole canon. Ten years later he went into the studio to read the final stories from *The Casebook of Sherlock Holmes*. Longer than *War and Peace*, *The Complete Sherlock Holmes* was released as a sixty-CD boxed set and features an absolutely extraordinary range of characters and accents from one of the most versatile readers England has ever produced. In typical Naxos AudioBooks style it contains an extensive booklet with Timson's explanatory notes on every story. It even includes a new Sherlock Holmes story written by Timson, which he reads with suitable flourish.

While all this was taking place, both Jason and Timson were also involved in directing a range of unabridged Shakespeare plays for the label. Jason directed the first one, *Hamlet* (with Anton Lesser in the title role), as well as *A Midsummer Night's Dream*. Timson directed *Twelfth Night*, *Othello*, *Henry V* and *Richard III*. The production of *Richard III*, with Kenneth Branagh in the title role, was unusual in that it went from the initial suggestion over the telephone from Branagh's office to the first day in the studio in just over a week. Branagh had been keen for some time to work on the play but had to fit it in between a series of blockbuster films. The cast was agreed and gathered quickly; and the recording, across three days in the studio, buzzed with excitement.

The single bestseller of the Shakespeare plays is *Romeo and Juliet*, featuring Kate Beckinsale and Michael Sheen – who plays Romeo and also directed. The highly individual Irish actress Fiona Shaw directed *Macbeth* while also playing the part of Lady Macbeth. Both Shaw and Sheen, directing an audiobook production for the first time, produced extremely vivid Shakespeare.

The next big step for the Shakespeare series was through the distinguished former BBC producer John Tydeman, who brought Paul Scofield into the Naxos AudioBooks studio to play *King Lear*. Scofield, celebrating his eightieth birthday year, headed one of the finest casts ever assembled for an audiobook drama production, with Emilia Fox as Cordelia, Kenneth Branagh as the Fool, and Alec McCowen as The Earl of Gloucester. Tydeman also directed *The Tempest* with Ian McKellen (fresh from his triumph as Gandalf) as Prospero. Finally, a three-way production between the Donmar Warehouse (one of the leading London theatres), BBC Radio 3 and Naxos AudioBooks brought the award-winning stage production of *Othello* to CD with Chiwetel Ejiofor as Othello and Ewan McGregor as Iago, directed by the Donmar's Michael Grandage.

There are other classic plays too, including Samuel Beckett's *Waiting for Godot* and Ibsen's *Hedda Gabler* (with two memorable performances – from Juliet Stevenson in the title role and Michael Maloney as George Tesman). A brilliant four-hour production of Goethe's *Faust* starring Samuel West in the title role and Toby Jones as Mephistopheles was released in 2011. This fully dramatised performance, directed by David Timson, was originally broadcast on BBC Radio 3.

Naxos AudioBooks marked the centenary of 16 June 1904, one of the most celebrated dates in literature (the day Leopold Bloom walked out in Dublin), with an unabridged recording of *Ulysses*, read by Jim Norton and Marcella Riordan. This twenty-two CD production was directed by Naxos AudioBooks's Joycean expert Roger Marsh and presented with extensive, helpful notes, a listener's guide written by Marsh, and a CD-ROM containing supplementary material. It has been praised by critics as one of the finest audiobooks ever produced. It is joined in the Joyce offerings by *Finnegans Wake* – in abridged form!

It was Marsh who directed another pillar of the label: the unabridged recording of Dante's *The Divine Comedy* in a sparkling new verse translation by Benedict Flynn, read by the idiosyncratic playwright, actor and author Heathcote Williams. Flynn went on to translate for Naxos AudioBooks *Beowulf* and *Gawain and the Green Knight,* and to write modern versions, for younger listeners, of *King Arthur and the Knights of the Round Table* (read by Sean Bean, it is the single 'Junior Classics' bestseller) and retellings of Homer, *Robin Hood* and Irish myths.

Naxos AudioBooks was the first audiobook company to offer all its titles on CD and remained at the technological forefront in being the first to offer its own download site within naxosaudiobooks.com (designed and maintained by the freelance IT consultant Arthur Ka Wai Jenkins). It offers all its titles for streaming as part of the Naxos Spoken Word Library, a unique resource that enables people to listen to titles on demand and even read the texts online at the same time.

The label expanded its range to include key religious works from Christianity and Buddhism, and philosophy texts (Plato, Lucretius, Descartes, Nietzsche and others). It also established a reputation for outstanding original works that introduced classical music to adults and children. *The History of Classical Music* and *The History of Opera,* written by Richard Fawkes, were followed by *The Story of Classical Music* and *Famous Composers,* written by Darren Henley and read by both the Naxos conductor Marin Alsop and Aled Jones. This series grew fruitfully into other 'Histories', covering *Theatre* (written by David Timson), *Literature* (Perry Keenlyside) and *Poetry, Science* and *Western Art* written by the versatile Peter Whitfield.

Yet Naxos AudioBooks has continued to serve fiction. In the first years of the twenty-first century the growth of downloads and the availability of MP3 players have resulted in an increasing demand for unabridged recordings. Thirty hours of recording is considerably more manageable physically in the MP3 format than on CD. Many of the classics have therefore been re-recorded in unabridged form, and the label is aiming to have in its catalogue all Dickens's major novels in unabridged form by the 200th anniversary of the writer's birth in 2012 –

read principally by Anton Lesser, Sean Barrett and David Timson.

Naxos AudioBooks now has more than 700 titles and it continues to grow. It is a world leader in classic literature but has made an impact in the contemporary field too, notably with the Japanese writer Haruki Murakami (his major novels on the label include *Norwegian Wood* and *Kafka on the Shore*) and with the American Pulitzer Prize-winner Cormac McCarthy (Rupert Degas's atmospheric reading of *The Road* and the Irish actor Sean Barrett's highly praised Texan performance of *No Country for Old Men* feature strongly). It also remains perhaps the only label worldwide that is consistently commissioning new texts specifically for the audiobook medium. There are non-fiction junior programmes, varying from *Great Explorers of the World* by David Angus and *Great Rulers of Ancient Rome* by Hugh Griffith to *Stories from Shakespeare* by David Timson; and new titles for adults (*A Guide to Wine*, *The History of the Olympics*, and a broad range of subjects in the introductory 'In a Nutshell' series, such as *Napoleon*, *Cathedrals*, *Afghanistan* and *Confucius*).

Over nearly two decades Naxos AudioBooks has developed one of the most distinct and accomplished spoken-word catalogues in the world, and been one of the most innovative labels in its field.

Naxos Hörbücher

Audiobooks in German command the second-strongest market after those in English, and in 1998 Klaus Heymann set up a German audiobook label with Sören Meyer-Eller. It began, as did Naxos AudioBooks, with the intention of producing classic literature, though it was decided to concentrate on unabridged works where possible. Schiller, Hoffmann, Heine and Goethe started the list, followed by Kleist, Grillparzer and Kafka. Its most marked commercial success came with a series of CDs by the German performer and storyteller Lutz Görner; he toured Germany and accumulated handsome sales for the label. Naxos Hörbücher branched out to include translations: of children's classics such as Lewis Carroll's *Alice in Wonderland*; of Alexander Pushkin, Alphonse Daudet, Robert Louis Stevenson and Guy de Maupassant; even of Arthur Conan Doyle's *The Hound of the Baskervilles*. It has some 130 titles in the catalogue.

Naxos Educational

There was an educational purpose to Heymann's involvement in classical recording before Naxos began: the Budget Classics cassette line in the early 1980s was designed to introduce classical music to a new audience, and a substantial booklet containing an introduction to the subject (written by Keith Anderson) was offered free to collectors of the whole series. Even Naxos itself was partly targeted at first-time classical buyers.

It didn't take long, after the initial rush of the label's early years, for specific educational projects to appear. They took various forms but unquestionably the most successful were *The A–Z of Classical Music* and *The A–Z of Opera*: massive two-CD and 250,000-word projects with composers in alphabetical order, again written and compiled by Anderson. Despite the huge booklets (printed in China and slipcased with the CDs, making a very chunky package) these were sold at a normal Naxos two-CD price around the world; consequently they were seen as an absolute bargain. Even bookshops sold them in the front of their stores. The profit margin was tiny – just a few pence – but as far as Heymann was concerned the educational value and the broadening of Naxos's profile made it worthwhile.

There were other similar projects, which led to the establishment of Naxos Educational shortly after the millennium. The label then began promoting its educational activities more specifically. With the audiobook histories on classical music produced by Naxos AudioBooks behind him, Heymann could see a more particular opportunity for music to be presented in this way and he commissioned a number of composer audiobook biographies from writer–broadcaster Jeremy Siepmann. Each release in the 'Life and Works' series was designed as a four-CD set; Siepmann's narration was interspersed with letters and writings (of the composer and of those who played a part in his life) that were read by actors. Woven into the whole was music. The listener learns about the life, meets the composer through his own words, and hears some of the most important works. It is an ideal format for a composer biography and one not widely developed on CD. Eleven composers are featured in the series.

The second major audiobook strand brought into Naxos Educational was 'Classics Explained', with a sister series, 'Opera Explained'. In 'Classics Explained' Siepmann throws the spotlight on particular works, going through them step by step. There are eight titles (each of two CDs), ranging from Schubert's 'Trout' Quintet to Stravinsky's *The Rite of Spring*. The intention is to open up a work for the non-musician; few technical terms are used. Each of the single-CD 'Opera Explained' titles focuses on a particular opera: the script by opera buff Thomson Smillie presents the background and storyline, and introduces the big arias and set pieces. These are read by Naxos AudioBooks actor David Timson (himself a singer), and with knowledgeable sound editing they provide an entertaining and informative introduction to the regular opera-house repertoire. There are now thirty in the series, from Monteverdi's *Orfeo*, Gluck's *Orfeo ed Euridice* and four of Mozart's operas to Verdi, Puccini and Wagner. Its most recent addition is the two-CD introduction to *The Ring of the*

Nibelung, written and narrated by Stephen Johnson: a flagship for the series.

Attractive though they are, the spoken-word productions did not sell particularly well and Naxos Educational began to focus more on CD packages with extended essays. 'Art and Music' is a series of single-CD titles with extended essays. It reveals how the major developments of art and music have not run in tandem (music developing half a century or so later). Many artists were touched by music in their life and work, and exploring both areas side by side also yields some fascinating connections. Artists include Canaletto, Rembrandt and Picasso. Written with authority and wit by Hugh Griffith, they are illuminating and at times surprising.

In the bold 'Portrait' series, contemporary music is put into the spotlight. Two CDs of a composer's key works, and sometimes a short interview with the composer himself, are supported by a long essay. Bartók, Maxwell Davies, Pärt, Prokofiev, Rodrigo, Shostakovich, Stravinsky and Tavener are the featured composers. In the same format were issued *The Story of British Classical Music* written by Anthony Burton and *The Story of American Classical Music* written by Barrymore Laurence Scherer.

The 'Discover' series also began life as a two-CD set slipcased with a 100-page booklet. The first five titles covered the established periods in music – *Discover Early Music* (Jenkins), *Discover Music of the Baroque Era* (Unger Hamilton), *Classical Era* (Johnson), *Romantic Era* (McCleery) and *Twentieth Century* (McCleery) – before specific genres were introduced: *Symphony* (Huth), *Chamber Music* (Siepmann), *Choral Music* (Hansell), *Film Music* (Riley) and *Opera* (Kimberley).

Naxos Books

In 2005, keen to extend its brand even further, Naxos moved into book publishing. It began with an enterprising project of music biographies that combined a book with two CDs and a dedicated website offering many hours of further listening. The 'Life and Music' series presents ten principal composers, each biography written in an accessible style by an established music writer. First to be published were *Mozart* and *Beethoven*, both written by Jeremy Siepmann, then *Chopin* by Jeremy Nicholas and *Mahler* by Stephen Johnson.

With Naxos's unequalled catalogue of American classical music recordings, it was possible to offer the same format (a book with two CDs and a website) for the first lengthy account of the subject, *A History of American Classical Music* by Barrymore Laurence Scherer. Naxos Books then underpinned its publishing credentials with *Down a Path of Wonder* – the fascinating personal view of twentieth-century music, musicians and art in general by Robert Craft, Stravinsky's protégé and heir. On the more compact side, Naxos Educational's 'Discover' titles covering the periods in music history were turned into attractive low-cost books with websites (some have also been issued in audiobook form).

Naxos Books has made its strongest impact on both sides of the Atlantic with two imaginative books about classical music for younger readers, by Genevieve Helsby. Lively illustrations and an informal yet informative text make *My First Classical Music Book* the perfect introduction to classical music, composers and instruments, for children between the ages of five and eight. It is accompanied by an audio CD full of the music mentioned in the book. *Meet the Instruments of the Orchestra!*, illustrated with hundreds of photographs, is aimed at an older age group; in addition to being a reliable and engaging guide to its subject, it has an accompanying CD-ROM packed with music as well as games and other historical information.

The distribution of books worldwide depends on a totally different network from that of CDs, and at times Naxos has struggled to gain a presence in bookshops. The children's books were instrumental in gaining the necessary foothold.

Naxos became one of the very first companies to bring together e-texts with music recordings, for both smartphone and tablet consumers, and to develop classical music apps. The 'Life and Music', 'Portrait' and 'Discover' series have been successfully converted for e-readers, while *My First Classical Music App* was released to broad approval. Once again, Naxos is at the cutting edge of technology.

Artaria Editions

One of the least-known and more specialist corners of Naxos, Artaria Editions is a boutique music publishing house devoted to rediscovering and publishing music of the Classical period – primarily the Viennese eighteenth century, though it has more recently expanded into the early years of the nineteenth century. Founded in New Zealand in 1995 and named after the original publisher of Haydn and Mozart, it was the brainchild of musicologist Allan Badley and Klaus Heymann. There still exists, Badley maintains, a wealth of music from the age of Haydn, Mozart and Beethoven waiting to be discovered. 'Performers welcome these ideas from the Classical era that appeal to audiences looking for something new but familiar.'

The Artaria venture was originally intended to provide new and unique material for Naxos's list of eighteenth-century repertoire but eventually it took on a life of its own. It now publishes more works in a year than Naxos can possibly record and release.

Artaria has published nearly 500 works by some thirty composers who have, for centuries, been mainly footnotes in musical history. These include thirty symphonies by Franz Ignaz Beck (1734–1809), who was born in Mannheim though spent most of his professional life in France, living through the difficult years of the French Revolution; thirty symphonies by the prolific Johann Baptist Vanhal (1739–1813), regarded by

Badley as one of the most talented composers of the period; and thirty-six works (symphonies, concertos, sonatas and a motet) by Leopold Hofmann (1738–1793), Kapellmeister at St Stephen's Cathedral in Vienna. Haydn's star pupil, Ignaz Pleyel (1757–1831), one of the most popular composers of the late eighteenth and early nineteenth centuries, is also well represented in the catalogue with important editions of symphonies, *symphonies concertantes*, concertos and chamber works. Artaria's ongoing publication of the complete works of Joseph Martin Kraus (1756–1792) promises to be one of the milestones of eighteenth-century scholarship, with editions of the complete symphonies, ballet music, keyboard music and violin sonatas already complete. One of the major initiatives in recent years has been the publication of the complete works for piano and orchestra by Beethoven's pupil Ferdinand Ries (1784–1838).

A growing discography has emerged from this publication programme; it includes concertos for oboe, violin, cello and flute by Hofmann; four CDs of sinfonias and the complete keyboard music by Kraus; symphonies by Christian Cannabich; and overtures by Domenico Cimarosa. There are also recordings of rare choral works, such as Masses by Vanhal and Johann Nepomuk Hummel.

Artaria's scholarly editions are intended first and foremost to be of practical use to the performer, although they contain detailed information about the sources used and reflect scrupulous editorial standards. As Badley explains, 'Autograph scores and authentic copies (those corrected by the composer) of eighteenth-century works are extremely rare and the reliability of the extant performing material is extremely variable. This can pose great challenges to the editor, particularly in instances where a work survives in a single copy; but it does have the advantage of simplifying the choice of sources used for the edition.

'Many of the compositions, however, survive in multiple

handwritten copies and preference is usually given to sources that are close to the composer or are associated in some way with his professional activities.' Even with all this research, Artaria does not publish 'critical editions' in the strictest sense of the term. The firm's objective is to produce clean, erudite scores and parts that as far as possible faithfully represent the composer's intentions as transmitted by the source or sources being used. 'More often than not, one has to be content with a clear, professionally copied set of parts as the working source material and hope that most of the notes are there! Occasionally we need to do some fairly advanced reconstructive surgery on the pieces. I've become pretty adept at writing missing parts over the years and pride myself on the fact that my additions are undetectable in performance, although they are scrupulously marked in the score.'

Artaria moves outside the central European focus from time to time. It offers seventeen chamber works by the English violinist and composer William Shield (1748–1829), a friend of Haydn; overtures and the opera *Polly* (a sequel to *The Beggar's Opera*) by another English composer of the period, Samuel Arnold (1740–1802); violin sonatas by Pietro Locatelli (1695–1764); and symphonies by the Walloon composer François-Joseph Gossec (1734–1829).

Fifteen
Behind the Scenes

A&R, New Recordings and the Release Schedule

Naxos releases are unquestionably more numerous and ambitious in repertoire than those of any other company in the world. In the twenty-five years of Naxos and Marco Polo together, it has regularly released more than 300 recordings in a year – a staggering number given the international complexity of its recording schedule and the worldwide spread of its operation.

The management of this is remarkable, all the more so because much of it goes through the hands of just one man: Klaus Heymann. In the early years of Naxos, when he was consciously building a catalogue, all repertoire and artist choices were his. Much of it was carefully planned, with lists of works and priorities. As the label grew, the confidence of his planning grew with it, until within five years it was very clear to him that he was building a world-class classical library with major repertoire. He proved himself adept at both creating a catalogue of works and choosing artists to perform the music. From his base in Hong Kong he read proposals, listened to

DATs and to people, and with the support and advice of Takako Nishizaki he came to definite conclusions. He was not afraid or shy to say 'no' as often as he said 'yes', or to say 'yes – but not that repertoire'.

A quarter of a century later, he seems not to have lost his touch. Instinct, information, an openness to ideas, a commercial nose and risk-taking have created Naxos. This is his A&R method, though it is not one that any conventional corporate entity could stomach. He has made a few mistakes but more often than not he has turned them to his advantage, converting a loss into an eventual gain.

Nowadays, while he still approves all new recordings, ideas and offers flow in from many different sources: agents, musicians, conductors, orchestras, impresarios, scholars, even individual collectors and classical music enthusiasts. All of it is coordinated by his director of A&R, Edith Lei (formerly general manager of the Hong Kong Philharmonic Orchestra), who also reminds him of the production costs when he considers a recording that she thinks will not sell sufficiently. In addition, he evaluates suggestions and projects proposed by the Naxos subsidiaries. The UK and USA are most active, with recording programmes that dwarf many independent labels; but there are ideas constantly put forward by other territories – from Scandinavia, Greece and Spain to Japan, New Zealand and Australia. He filters the repertoire and the artists carefully. He may mix and match, approving the repertoire idea but preferring it to be done by another orchestra for musical or marketing reasons; he may decline the repertoire because it is already in the pipeline or is too marginal (even for him) but want to work with the artist or orchestra – in which case he may come up with a counter-suggestion.

All these ideas go through to a master file that is maintained by Lei in Hong Kong and called, with refreshing and characteristically Naxos simplicity, 'Recordings in the Pipeline'. This consists of a regularly updated spreadsheet of twelve separate pages, each with the current number of scheduled recordings in a particular category. At the time of writing, this was the picture: Orchestral 176, Concertos 73, Chamber 163, Instrumental 139, Vocal and Choral 76, Miscellaneous 31, English 64, Ballet, Opera & Stage 32, American 90, Other Regions 42, Blu-ray Audio 11 and Artaria (the publishing house) 10. This document does not include the book wing (incorporating Naxos Educational, Naxos AudioBooks and Naxos Books), which is run as a separate division. It is for regular new Naxos recordings, as well as finished recordings accepted from individuals and those previously released on labels such as Delos or Collins Classics.

It is a massive, well-organised operation. In previous years there were times when Heymann's enthusiasm was so extreme that a project could be confirmed without being entered in the system: the first that the staff would know about it was when the master turned up. Surprises like that were not infrequent in the 1990s and a huge backlog of masters built up on the shelves at K&A's mastering suite in Potters Bar, UK.

All masters go to K&A, and production information (the label copy) is entered into the Naxos production schedule maintained by Peter Bromley. As production manager he has the task of scheduling these releases into months, in detail for the coming two months and in general for further ahead. The construction of this schedule is a complex if fascinating job, for many factors need to be considered.

The sheer number of releases is always a problem. Salesmen worldwide do not like having to present an unwieldy Naxos release schedule, and often there are around thirty titles in a month. Certain dates dictate placement: anniversaries and concert tours, for example. There may be contractual reasons established at the start which state that a recording must be released at a particular time. Then there are planned campaigns (some international, some regional), often prepared far ahead for a specific reason. The balance of repertoire each month is important. The aim is to include: one blockbuster (big orchestral or choral–orchestral or opera recording); a concerto; an orchestral recording; one early music or Baroque recording; one guitar or lute recording; a chamber music recording; a keyboard recording; a national recording (other than 'American Classics'); one 'American Classics' recording (if the other categories do not include works by American composers); an opera recording (if the blockbuster is not an opera); one choral recording (if the blockbuster is not a choral–orchestral recording) and every other month a lieder/song recording. Despite his collector's instinct, Heymann asks that no more than 25 per cent of each month's titles are what can be described as specialist releases. Only too often, this is not possible.

Other priorities that contribute to the selection process are: core repertoire; recordings by key artists; the continuation of series; commitments to competitions (guitar, violin, cello or piano); long-term commitments to festivals; projects brought by subsidiaries; and the bank of finished masters simply awaiting release! In addition to all this, there must be a balance of music from different periods and a variety in terms of nationality – not too many American classics or English orchestral music, for example, which may be indigestible for other territories. Smooth scheduling can be complicated by a number of scenarios: unexpected problems may arise with masters or notes or permissions; a year may be full up, but suddenly an important contract is signed with an orchestra that stipulates early release of a number of recordings (which could not only challenge the number of releases but cause a repertoire clash); a recording may just have been made that is considered to be of exceptional, award-winning standard – can it be rush-released to make it in time for the GRAMMY Awards? And so on.

Managing the Naxos release schedule is an ever-changing juggling act that connects closely with recording, editing and artwork production, not to mention sales, marketing and promotion, and other commercial demands.

In January each year the Naxos distributors interact and meet customers at MIDEM in Cannes, but their main focus is the day of Naxos presentations in a hotel conference room. The highlight of this is the start, when the coming year's releases are put on a big screen and Klaus Heymann takes his distributors through those recordings which he thinks are most important or interesting. It is the moment when all aspects of the company's production work come to one point. Each month may have around thirty releases, but he will focus on five or six and play excerpts from just one or two. These do not include local crossover campaigns based on back-catalogue exploitation or promotion of a particularly local artist: it is the international new release schedule that is in the spotlight, the backbone of Naxos, by which it stands or falls. When Heymann unveils these plans each year, he takes the floor for around thirty minutes, without notes, and you can hear a pin drop.

Recording, Producing and Editing

It takes Andrew Walton and his K&A production team about four hours to set up the equipment for a Shostakovich symphony recording with the Royal Liverpool Philharmonic Orchestra and Vasily Petrenko in the city centre's Philharmonic Hall. Phil Rowlands, the engineer, likes to use a matched pair of AKG 414 microphones as a main system, together with Schoeps outriggers, then individual cardioid mics at the head of each string section and for the woodwinds. Depending on the symphony, he places spot mics for the brass and – it being Shostakovich – for the percussion.

Hundreds of metres of cabling between the control room and studio have to be neatly laid, and the mixing desk and computers have to be organised: there is a back-up system but the recording goes straight into the SADiE software on the computer (the same software that will later be used to edit it). Walton and Rowlands will be in the studio for four three-hour sessions over two days – or for five sessions over two and a half days if the music is particularly challenging, in terms of either playing or recording. It can be a tense time, with everyone working at full concentration for long periods, and technical hitches or blemishes are the last thing that anyone wants.

Before the first session the producer and conductor will already have had a discussion about the work itself. Walton will know the score well and be aware of the difficult spots, and his task is to enable Petrenko to realise his interpretation. Petrenko will highlight bars where, perhaps, he wants to bring out an inner melody, or push on the tempo, or is aiming for a particular balance between woodwind and strings. As it happens, Walton himself was a professional violinist before he turned to producing so it is an added benefit that he knows the work from a player's point of view. The relationship between producer and conductor is crucial and can make or break a recording: some of the finest recordings in the history of the record industry have come from a special understanding between these two figures; when the relationship falters – or, even worse, breaks down – the sessions can turn into a nightmare for everyone.

'As producer, you never go into a recording session thinking that you are going to put your own ideas of a work across,' says Walton. 'You may disagree with what the conductor wants, but it is his or her recording. Empathy is really important. On the other hand, you have to be open and say when you think something is not working, and suggest ways of getting what you think the conductor is after.'

Walton marks the score as he goes, noting the takes and bars that have worked and the sections that need improving. Producers work in different ways; some even have a system of coloured pencils for successive takes, though Walton keeps it fairly simple. However, he aims to leave the sessions with a relatively clear plan of preferred takes marked on the score, so that when he starts to edit there is a good roadmap to follow.

Back in the K&A studios in Potters Bar he will start by observing the initial editing plan he made at the sessions, though he will listen to other takes to see if perhaps there was something a bit better that he hadn't noticed – maybe a detail that was clearer. He will produce a first edit to which the conductor will listen and make comments; Walton will try to implement these when he makes the second edit. He reckons that by the end of the editing stage he has listened to more or less everything again twice. It generally takes four or five days before the recording is ready to be mastered. This is the general process that lies behind all Naxos titles: a considerable amount of expertise, care and detailed work goes into just one, which can be showered with awards and sales, or dismissed in one trenchant line by a critic.

The basic pattern has changed little since Marco Polo and then Naxos started, though technology for both recording and editing has moved on considerably. Many Marco Polo recordings were made in two centres, Bratislava and Budapest; and when Naxos began, Heymann relied on a recording team based in Heidelberg that had been put together by Teije van Geest, with producers Martin Sauer and Günther Appenheimer. Their names are on the back of numerous Naxos CDs dating from the early years. On 10 July 1987 Appenheimer left Heidelberg in a van packed with his recording equipment. By the morning of 12 July he was set up in the Concert Hall of the Slovak Philharmonic, ready for the first session of *The Four Seasons* played by Takako Nishizaki and the Capella Istropolitana, conducted by Stephen Gunzenhauser. (He was a producer who was happy to set up the microphones and engineer the recording himself – as are some Naxos producers even now.) It took nearly a week, because the sessions had to be slotted within the normal work of the musicians and use of the concert hall. So for the recording team there was quite a lot of waiting! When the sessions finished, Appenheimer returned to Heidelberg where the van Geest team (a busy independent company) edited and mastered the recording. On 10 October 1987 Appenheimer was back in Bratislava to record the Capella Istropolitana, conducted by Wolfgang Sobotka, playing Mozart's *Eine kleine Nachtmusik*, *Serenata notturna* and *Lodron Night Music*. The recording is still available and sales are approaching 250,000 CDs. This process continued for some years, though the rapid expansion of Naxos (and Marco Polo) meant that recordings were made in many other centres too, and were produced and engineered by teams all over Europe, from London to Moscow as well as in the US, the Far East and New Zealand. Generally the edited DATs went to Heidelberg to be mastered.

The success of the label began to put the spotlight of critics and consumers not only on the performances but also on the technical aspects of the recordings. While most were acceptable, Heymann realised that Naxos had to achieve a greater consistency of standard. There was an equally urgent need for a central studio to collate and organise the hundreds of tapes flooding in from all over the world. Heymann decided it was time to set up a dedicated Naxos production facility. In 1995 David Denton, who was initiating many recordings in the UK, introduced him to Andrew Walton, then a young but keen producer who was dividing his time between his passion for record-making and freelance work as a professional violinist. He had long been fascinated by the recording process and was spending an increasing number of hours in front of a mixing desk rather than a conductor. It was Walton who produced the first private recordings made by the Maggini Quartet, which led to the group's contract with Naxos. Those recordings also led to a complete change of career for Walton. He spoke on the phone with Heymann (in Hong Kong), who had heard the recordings and could judge their quality; and even before the two met, Heymann invited Walton to form a joint venture company and provided funds to rent premises, buy equipment to set up a state-of-the-art studio, and hire staff. Most contact with Heymann was via fax during this period as he was in either Hong Kong or New Zealand, but after some two months the process distilled into the creation of the company that Heymann named 'K&A [Klaus and Andrew] Productions', its primary purpose being to set up a mastering house to consolidate and raise the technical quality of Naxos and Marco Polo CDs. Despite going into business together, Heymann and Walton didn't actually meet until they both attended a sales conference in Germany later in the year.

K&A's task involved the careful auditioning of every recording that was sent to Naxos for release – checking it against the score for performance mistakes, audible edits, noises, unequal levels and the many other problems that can spoil an otherwise good recording. Sometimes extensive corrections needed to be made. Walton remembers that for those first few years he was surprised at the varying standards of recordings submitted by producers. Part of the problem was simply the number passing through the hands of producers and editors: Heymann's ambitious plans – provoked by both enthusiasm and consumer demand – had put the system under strain. Each recording was now put through a meticulous quality control. There were times when Walton requested the re-recording of material because problems could not be fixed by his team; sometimes he even recommended that recordings should be discarded because they did not meet the labels' high standards. Copies of such examples would be sent from Potters Bar to Hong Kong, where Heymann and Nishizaki, reluctant to lose a whole recording, would listen to them. Almost always they accepted Walton's advice.

It was a very busy time in Potters Bar. Between July 1995 (the month that the fledgling company took wing) and the end of the year, 211 recordings were mastered. In 1996 the total grew to 515, which reflected the continuous activity by Naxos musicians all over the world. It stayed at that 500 level for nearly a decade. In 2004 it shot up to 752. By this time K&A had expanded within the Potters Bar building and had at least six mastering engineers working full time. The recordings covered the gamut of the Naxos enterprise: new recitals, orchestral music, chamber music and opera; and a huge number of historical recordings, most of which had been expertly transferred from 78s by Mark Obert-Thorn and Ward Marston on the other side of the Atlantic but still had to have the track points inserted, be checked generally, and then be mastered. In 2005 the total rose to 898; 2007 was the top year, with 950 recordings, before the number settled down to a more manageable average of 700.

The pace of Heymann's recording programme meant that there was inevitably a backlog: sometimes there were as many as 600 recordings sitting on the shelves, logged and with paperwork, waiting to be mastered. The volume of work was such that some recordings were delayed in their release for years. In the first fifteen years of K&A some 10,130 recordings were checked and mastered, and many of them were edited too. In addition, its high standards had become recognised by other record labels and the company found itself in demand by both majors and independents for its services. 'We wanted to make a product that was technically and musically from the top drawer, regardless of price,' declares Walton. The regular editing commissions from award-winning labels and producers were the proof that this aim was being achieved.

Of course the days of editing with tape and razor were over: everything was digital. For the first few years K&A used Sonic Solutions, an editing software system based on the Apple Mac. Then it switched to SADiE, a PC-based system that it still uses today. Initially everything was mastered from DATs but gradually CD-Rs came in. The nature of the work and the ever-changing technical environment meant that Walton was constantly investing in the latest equipment. He was fortunate to have in Heymann a partner with a background in studio equipment who knew how important it was to be at the forefront of technology. In fact, regardless of its budget price, Heymann wanted Naxos to put out its top new recordings in the latest format of the day, and this has led to the label being a trail blazer in new formats, be it DVD-Audio, SACD or BD-Audio. Recent years have seen a rapid expansion of classical DVDs, and K&A has added DVD and Blu-ray Disc authoring to its roster of activities.

The initial purpose of K&A was to be a mastering house, with quality control its main function; but less than a year after the company started, it was in charge of recording sessions as well. Paul Myers, the distinguished former CBS and Decca producer, had started to work for Naxos but in 1996 became ill during a recording session in Bristol of piano music by Wilhelm Stenhammar, played by Niklas Sivelöv. Walton and his team stepped in, and within a short time they were equally busy recording as well as mastering. Walton has always preferred to work with a sound engineer, so that he can concentrate on producing and working with the musicians. In the following years he and his team travelled all over the world, recording for Naxos and Marco Polo. Many discs of French, Spanish, Japanese and Portuguese music were made by them, involving long hours of driving or flying, usually transporting their own recording equipment. The symphonies of the Portuguese composer Joly Braga Santos, conducted by Álvaro Cassuto, took Walton to Lisbon, Dublin, Bournemouth and the Algarve; Guridi was recorded in Bilbao, Hanson in Nashville and Yashiro in Japan. One of the most challenging but rewarding tasks was recording the ten *Naxos Quartets* by Peter Maxwell Davies, played by the Maggini Quartet in Potton Hall, Suffolk.

Walton feels privileged to have recorded for Naxos the entire series of nineteenth- and twentieth-century English choral music with the Choir of St John's College, Cambridge directed by Christopher Robinson (with repertoire ranging from

Stanford to Rubbra and Tavener). He has also been responsible for recording live concerts, directing the necessary patch sessions after the audience's departure. He has encountered and dealt with most glitches that can bedevil a recording: musicians who come to the session unprepared, traffic noise, rain from holes in the roof, fluttering pigeons in the roof space, having to pay off street vendors who make too much noise outside the recording studio, and musicians who arrive late. He was recording the *Spitfire Prelude and Fugue* and other pieces for the Naxos series of William Walton's orchestral music when a bassoonist, needed for one work, was forty minutes late. It meant that in order not to overrun and incur very expensive overtime, the English Northern Philharmonia and Paul Daniel had time for only one take of *March for 'A History of the English Speaking Peoples'*. They nailed it with eight seconds to go.

However, the international nature and the sheer size of the Naxos recording programme has meant that the bulk of the recording work has been done by other teams. One of the most important contributions made over many years is by the producer Ibolya Tóth in Budapest, with the engineer János Bohus. Tóth was a student (composition and conducting) at the Liszt Academy at the same time as Jenő Jandó, András Schiff and Zoltán Kocsis, and as their playing careers developed she moved into production, first of all in radio and then, in 1980, with the Hungarian national record company, Hungaroton. She was already working there when Heymann began his association with the company: it recommended musicians and recorded on his behalf for Marco Polo and – in the very early days – Naxos. In October 1987, when still with Hungaroton, Tóth worked on István Székely's recording of Chopin's Ballades and Scherzi, made for Naxos at the Italian Institute in Budapest. The contact with Naxos was to change her life.

By the end of the decade Tóth was producing regularly for Naxos as Hungarian musicians provided much of the Viennese repertoire. In two groups of sessions in May and June 1989 she recorded Mozart's Piano Concertos Nos. 20 and 21 ('Elvira Madigan') with Jenő Jandó and Concentus Hungaricus, conducted by András Ligeti: it was to be the start of the complete cycle. In 1990 Tóth left Hungaroton and started her own recording company, Phoenix Studio, though she continued to record at the Italian Institute and the United Reformed Church in Budapest. 'Hungary was very backward at the time, though we could make very good records!' she says. 'We had no fax machine at the start, and I remember sitting and watching the first fax come through, and I really couldn't believe it.'

There were further Jandó discs made in 1990 (including Liszt's B minor Sonata); Tóth was in the producer's chair when Jandó recorded most of his major cycles, including the complete Mozart sonatas and concertos, the Haydn sonatas, and Bartók's piano music. She produced the Kodály Quartet's recordings of the complete Haydn, Beethoven and Schubert quartets as well as the Éder Quartet's complete Mozart string quintet cycle; and she produced Béla Drahos and the Nicolaus Esterházy Sinfonia's recordings of Beethoven's symphonies (she herself founded the Sinfonia in 1992).

In 1995, the same year in which K&A started, she took the bold step of designing Phoenix's own large, purpose-built recording studio in Diósd on the outskirts of Budapest. This is where all her recordings were subsequently made, including Mozart's operas for Naxos. Phoenix became the leading independent classical production team in Hungary and, although it recorded for others, Naxos was for many years its major client. Tóth recorded, edited, worked with the musicians to arrive at a final edit, and sent the recordings to K&A to be mastered. Such was the standard of her work that there were rarely any problems.

Other Naxos regular musicians started to come to Hungary to record, including the cellist Maria Kliegel and the pianist Christopher Hinterhuber, whose C.P.E. Bach discs were recorded in Budapest. Over the years, Tóth has produced more than 350 Naxos recordings, which have sold in excess of three million discs. 'The producer is a mirror to an artist,' she remarks. 'The musician never knows the reality of what they are doing until they hear it back. So in the recording, the musician is the inner ear and I am the outer ear.' After hundreds of recordings – and her CD covers on the wall include Hungarian folk musicians as well – it is clear that neither her passion for music nor her respect for many of the musicians whom she records has diminished. Jenő Jandó is one example. 'Jenő has an ability to learn music quickly, but his true talent is that he absorbs it so naturally, so instinctively, that it sounds as if he has been playing it for years. Even when he was recording such a lot of music for Naxos in such a short time, it was always fresh and idiomatic. He doesn't think of what he can do with it or how he should play it: the music is immediately expressive. And at any one time, he has twenty-five or thirty piano concertos in his head.'

The team of Norbert and Bonnie Kraft in Toronto has been similarly active for Naxos. The success of the Krafts' productions, which began with guitar CDs, led to a wider recording brief. They began to take on more ambitious projects, from period performance of key orchestral works, such as Handel's *Music for the Royal Fireworks* and *Water Music* with the Aradia Ensemble directed by Kevin Mallon, to full Baroque opera and oratorio. The largest recording was of Berlioz's Requiem with 400 musicians, which was quite a challenge. Yet they were equally comfortable recording Ilya Kaler's solo violin discs of Bach and Ysaÿe. The Krafts became the primary production team for Naxos's solo and chamber music in North America and started to attract Naxos musicians from all over the world: the Vermeer Quartet recorded Bartók, the New Zealand String Quartet recorded Mendelssohn, Boris Berman recorded Cage's *Sonatas and Interludes* for prepared piano, Patrick Gallois recorded French flute music, and Takako

Nishizaki came from Hong Kong to record the final group of Mozart's violin sonatas. At one point, the Krafts were producing as many as thirty recordings a year – recording, editing and mastering. In two decades with Naxos they have made nearly 250 recordings.

One of the most prolific producer–engineers of the past decade is the UK-based Tim Handley. Since the turn of the century he has travelled the world, working on everything from solo discs to recordings of the largest scale. He generally works on his own, happy to produce and engineer, and has made over 200 Naxos recordings, including two huge 'live' projects: William Bolcom's *Songs of Innocence and of Experience* conducted by Leonard Slatkin and John Adams's *Nixon in China* conducted by Marin Alsop. These live recordings place considerable pressure on the producer, who has to work fast and immediately identify sections for the patching sessions that follow: there is very little room for error. But most of Handley's work has been in studio conditions. In July 2008 he was with the Nashville Symphony, again with Leonard Slatkin, working on the *Abraham Lincoln Portraits* disc. A couple of weeks later he was in France with the Orchestre National de Lyon and Jun Märkl recording Messiaen's *Poèmes pour Mi*, *Les Offrandes oubliées* and other works. Then came a volume of Roussel in Glasgow with the Royal Scottish National Orchestra conducted by Stéphane Denève; just over a month later he was in New Zealand to record symphonies by Sibelius with the New Zealand Symphony Orchestra and Pietari Inkinen; then it was back to Glasgow for more Roussel. In between this travel, he returned to his studio in London to edit.

There are many other producers around the world regularly working on Naxos projects. Michael Ponder has produced numerous solo and chamber music recordings in the UK, and Günther Appenheimer is still producing for Naxos after decades. The production team of Karol Kopernicky and Otto Nopp continues to look after the mammoth complete Johann

Strauss I Edition with the Slovak Sinfonietta Žilina conducted by Christian Pollack and the late Ernst Maerzendorfer in Slovakia, one of the most extraordinary Marco Polo enterprises.

From the very first Marco Polo discs, Klaus Heymann ensured that the recording details were accurately printed on the back of each CD and he saw no reason why this should not be continued on Naxos, despite its budget status. As a record collector himself, he knew the contribution made by the producers and engineers: he was always intrigued as to when a recording was made, by whom and where. Most of the musicians know how much is owed to the technicians who work on a project, and this is acknowledged on Naxos and Marco Polo, with care taken over details.

Recording Speech

While all the music recording was happening, Naxos AudioBooks was steadily producing its catalogue of classic literature. Most of its recordings are one-voice productions, but speech recording is a different discipline, involving special microphones and a studio with little, or no, natural ambience – unlike music recording, which requires a more lively acoustic. With some works running to thirty or even forty CDs (*War and Peace* unabridged was fifty-one) it means that the reader and producer can be working together for as long as three weeks, virtually on a daily basis. The producer is crucial to the recording: he must know the text intimately and will have reached clear decisions on the pronunciation of esoteric names and places. Roy McMillan, who has produced many of the major unabridged classics (including *Middlemarch* read by Juliet Stevenson and *Nicholas Nickleby* read by David Horovitch), will discuss with the actor the tone of the work and the interpretation of the protagonists, and this can influence the character of the whole performance.

Recording classic plays, with a large cast, music and sound effects, makes considerable technical demands – in the studio as well as in the long process of editing: both the Battle of Agincourt in the fields of France and the death of Juliet in the tomb in Verona must sound equally realistic.

Editing speech is a specialist skill, as is mastering. For classical music a wide dynamic range is the requirement; for speech the priority is that all the words can be heard wherever the recording is being listened to – in the car, on a train, or in a quieter environment at home. If the dynamic range is too wide, the quieter speech cannot be heard while the louder speech can come as a sharp shock to the listener. Putting music to speech is also a particular skill; it has to be done with sensitivity.

For the first few years Simon Weir of the Classical Recording Company oversaw many of the Naxos AudioBooks recordings. For the last decade the principal editor has been Sarah Butcher. She has edited hundreds of hours of recordings, from *The History of Opera* by Richard Fawkes (with all its musical excerpts), read by Robert Powell, to Anton Lesser's reading of *Our Mutual Friend* by Charles Dickens. As a professional cellist, she has been able to use her knowledge to select appropriate accompanying music and place it with exceptional skill.

Contracts and the Organisation of Recordings

Recordings have to be organised, and organised well. Fixing the hall, booking the musicians, getting the music to the right place at the right time, scheduling the sessions – these are administrative issues that require not just organisational ability but an intimate knowledge of music, and often language skills.

At the heart of the Naxos recording operation for most of its life has been the Slovakian musicologist Ivan Marton. Helped by his background in music and an ability to work in English, French, German, Polish, Russian, Hungarian, Italian and Dutch as well as his native Czech, Marton ensured that the recording programme in the first decade and more was kept on the rails, no matter how frenetic the pace. He became the Naxos fixer and contract manager. During the mid-1990s he was looking after as many as 200 recordings a year from his small office in Bratislava, sometimes with one assistant but often on his own. It could be a sonata programme involving just two musicians or a full opera involving orchestra, chorus and twenty or more soloists: all the details and the principal organisation would go through his hands.

He first met Klaus Heymann in the mid-1980s when he worked for Slovart, the state export–import business that handled all commercial affairs for arts organisations in the Slovakian part of Czechoslovakia. 'We met at MIDEM, and I was very excited because Klaus said he wanted to make forty recordings of popular repertoire.' In the summer of 1987 the Slovak Philharmonic Orchestra started to record the CDs and Marton remembers it as a very busy time. 'It was the communist period and Klaus Heymann brought the musicians work, money and hope! They were doing two and sometimes three sessions a day – and these were four-hour sessions, not three hours like today.'

The project encountered political problems within the communist regime and the work shifted to the Czecho-Slovak Radio Symphony Orchestra, but Marton continued to work closely with Heymann. In May 1989, just before the Velvet Revolution, Marton left Slovart and joined Naxos. The expansion of the recording programme meant that Naxos needed a full-time administrator and A&R advisor. For nearly a decade he organised all the recordings that happened in Eastern Europe, including Russia, the Ukraine, Poland and Hungary. He went to many of the sessions in the Czech Republic, Slovakia and Budapest, and advised on new orchestras to record, as and when they were needed.

The opera recording programme, which Marton started in Bratislava, was particularly demanding administratively. 'We had to make a very detailed plan so that the singers knew exactly when they were required: they had busy schedules which meant that as soon as they had sung their arias they would leave immediately for their next job.' Marton worked closely with the relevant conductor and scheduled the sessions to the minute. They had to decide how long a scene would take to record and ensure that all the singers would be there at the right time. There was very little room for error. 'We knew that if we got seriously behind, we were unlikely ever to make it up!' The pressure was considerable. 'It was exciting and exhausting.'

From the late 1990s, as Naxos began to record more regularly in Western Europe and elsewhere around the world, much of the A&R administration went to Hong Kong, where it is now looked after by Edith Lei. Marton's work concentrated on the contracts. Clear contracts have been the bedrock of Naxos, right from the beginning. Each musician must have a signed contract in place before the start of any recording so that there are no misunderstandings at a later stage. After more than two decades Marton continues to work from Bratislava, doing all the key contract work and advising on certain specialist projects, such as the recording of Martinů's Piano Concertos by the Bohuslav Martinů Philharmonic Orchestra with pianist Giorgio Koukl, released in 2010.

Booklets and Designs

Every Naxos and Marco Polo CD and download recording comes with booklet notes (or 'liner notes', as they are often referred to in the trade). Their existence is so ubiquitous that they are an expected part of the CD package. But they have played such an essential part of the Naxos story that they have become, in their way, extraordinary. Their existence in the very early days demonstrated that although this was a budget label there was no need to stint on giving the customer the basics that he or she would expect from any good classical label. This helped enormously as Naxos closed the gap on the majors, showing that this budget company from Hong Kong provided everything that the full-price labels did. The trouble was the presentation of the notes: they simply didn't look impressive enough. They were laid out in the simplest of typefaces in the simplest of ways, with little attempt at interesting design. Clarity was the watchword. There were between 1,000 and 1,200 straightforward words of information about the composer and the work, plus something about the performer. And that was that.

The early Naxos releases concentrated, of course, on the most popular classical works; neither critics nor collectors who picked up the CDs were likely to feel newly informed about the background to *Eine kleine Nachtmusik* or Tchaikovsky's Piano Concerto No. 1. Heymann was often told that notes were not really needed, that money could be saved here; but he had his eye on his main customers – the newcomers to classical music who wanted to build up a basic classical CD collection, and the students who were eager to learn. They were being given exactly the right amount of information at the required level. So he persisted.

Within a relatively short time, there started to appear works slightly off the beaten track. Suddenly the notes were being read even by collectors, who couldn't quite recall the provenance of the piano quintets by Schumann or Brahms, for example, and found themselves usefully and reliably enlightened.

For followers of Marco Polo this was nothing new. For more than five years they had been reading and relying upon the notes accompanying those recordings. Many of the composers were relatively obscure and the works even more so. There were several composers from Eastern Europe and the Baltic;

and even when well-known composers were represented, it was by works that were just lines in the history books. Collectors of Marco Polo would put on the LPs (and then CDs) before turning straight to the liner notes for information – and there they were: at least 1,000 words of clear, informative text explaining how the works came to be written, in what context and when. At the bottom was the bland line, 'Notes by Keith Anderson'. They were always by Keith Anderson. When Naxos began producing hundreds of recordings a year, that line was still there: 'Notes by Keith Anderson'. For years and years it was the same. So who was, or is, Keith Anderson?

He is a short, quietly spoken classical music writer, teacher, one-time violinist, viola player and pianist, and a descendant of Sir George Grove, founding editor of *Grove's Dictionary of Music and Musicians*. Anderson ended up in Hong Kong in the 1970s – by a circuitous route from Oxford, via Ankara – playing the violin in film sessions and broadcasting as a member of The Ensemble of the Chinese University. It was here, at a concert, that he met Klaus Heymann. Anderson was as much an academic as a performer. After winning a classics and music scholarship to Lancing College (where Benjamin Britten and Peter Pears were then frequent visitors) he had gone on to study *Literae humaniores* at Wadham College, Oxford. This was followed by various jobs (including private tutor to the conductor Benjamin Zander) before he moved to Turkey, where he taught English in Ankara and tutored one of the sons of the Prime Minister. In 1973 he arrived in Hong Kong and lived there until 1996. In the early years he made his living partly through playing, partly as a music critic for various papers, including the *South China Morning Post*, and partly through teaching at the Chinese University and subsequently at The Hong Kong Academy for Performing Arts and Hong Kong Baptist University.

So when he met Heymann sometime in 1973, Anderson was a proficient writer and academic who could speak English, French, Spanish, Italian, German, classical Greek, Latin and

Turkish. He also had a smattering of Cantonese. With Heymann's background of linguistics it was a perfect match. When Heymann launched his first classical label (Budget Classics – the introductory-level cassette series) he turned to Anderson for the notes. There was also the bonus of a free extended brochure on classical music for those who bought the whole series. His ingenuity was more sharply tested with Heymann's next enterprise: HK, a label designed to record and release Chinese 'Western' classical music. Works such as *The Butterfly Lovers*, *Yellow River Cantata* and *Fisherman's Song of the East China Sea* all needed notes. At least Anderson was in the right place and knew the right people to ask for information.

This was merely a warm-up for an even greater test to come, however: the start of Marco Polo in 1982. To write about popular classics, even Chinese ones, was relatively uncomplicated, but suddenly Anderson was required to write authoritatively and accurately on forgotten, neglected corners of music, when living in Hong Kong. In 1,000–1,200 concise yet accurate words he had to introduce and explain the forgotten works of Joseph Joachim or Anatol Liadov or Nikolay Myaskovsky or Kurt Atterberg or Wilhelm Furtwängler. He did have his own copy of the 1945 *Grove Dictionary of Music and Musicians* at his home and there was the university library that he could access, though it meant time-consuming visits. Later Heymann bought a copy of *Die Musik in Geschichte und Gegenwart* ('MGG') which was kept in his business offices, and fortunately Anderson could read German. But would these sources be sufficient for 1,200 words on overtures by Wagner that had never been recorded before? What did they sound like? They were rarely, if ever, played in concert. And what about Azio Corghi's opera *Divara – Wasser und Blut*?

Anderson recalls the difficulties and the pleasures. Remembered now as a conductor, Furtwängler also wrote symphonies, choral works and concertos, and Heymann was keen to bring them to CD. That meant notes – lots of them. Anderson found commentaries on the works by Furtwängler himself but they were written in a tortuous philosophical language that foxed even native Germans in Hong Kong. Gleaning meaning was a tough task. He will never forget the struggle. On a different note, he clearly remembers, when researching for the notes to *Tonadas*, being warned by the composer Joaquín Nin-Culmell not to believe everything that his sister, Anaïs Nin, had to say. But Anderson was stimulated to find out more about Franz Schreker when Marco Polo made the world-premiere recording of *Der ferne Klang*. Similarly his musical curiosity made delving into the operas of Siegfried Wagner, son of Richard, an enjoyable task – even if the talent had been diluted down a generation.

By the time Marco Polo was established, Anderson had moved from Kowloon to a traditional Chinese village (without roads) in the New Territories called Siu Lek Yuen. It had some telephone communication but there were times when weather cut it off from Hong Kong. Anderson would sit in his small room with his Brother typewriter and pour out the words on Tournemire's Symphony No. 6 or all eleven symphonies by Joachim Raff. There must have been times when he lauded Heymann's completist instincts, and times when he was less impressed. Information came to his village room in a variety of forms – including photocopies of scores and articles from learned European musical journals, which he then had to translate – and was supplemented by his own discussions with conductors or musicians or agents.

In the early 1990s Naxos was well underway. If obscurity was not such an issue, volume was. The number of releases threatened time and again to overwhelm him, but Anderson heroically remained the solitary writer for years. He would write one note a day, and deliver them every few days by making the journey to the Naxos offices in Kowloon, the industrial part of Hong Kong. For years Klaus would take them home with him, read them overnight, make any slight alterations necessary, and return them to the offices. They would be typeset, and proofs would go to Heymann and Anderson for checking before the booklet was released. Being multilingual, they were both sticklers for the correct diacritics on the host of different names and words. On the whole, the notes were in English only; but if it was thought that a release would have a strong German or French or Spanish sale then translations were made, and both Anderson and Heymann would check those too. This continued almost to the present day (though there are many more people involved now). The amount of words that were written and read is incalculable. Anderson himself has no idea. 'Only the Almighty knows,' he says, not meaning Heymann, who also doesn't know – though he once wondered whether Anderson was the most published writer in the world in terms of the quantity he has produced over decades. For not only was Anderson responsible for the notes, but he also wrote two massive anthologies: *The A–Z of Classical Music* and *The A–Z of Opera*. Each was released in a slipcase with two CDs in the late 1990s and sold hundreds of thousands of copies; they sold once more in massive quantities when revised, and enlarged versions were published a few years later.

In 1996 Keith Anderson left Hong Kong and settled in a small Welsh village. Now, in his eighties, he lives in Northumberland in the northeast of England. He was an early adopter of computers, owning one of the first Apple Macintosh Classics, and continues to write notes, proofread and deal with the stream of queries that come his way. One recent task that landed on his desk was to solve the identity of a poem translated by Stefan George and apparently misattributed to Baudelaire; it was typical of the varied odds and ends that Naxos sends his way.

Anderson's achievements have not gone unnoticed through the years. *Fanfare*, the American music magazine, started to comment regularly on his notes when reviewing the discs. 'Keith Anderson's notes are good. Naxos's sound is a bit grey...' says one; 'Faulknerian' was another epithet. A different American critic remarked: 'To add to the excellent presentation, Keith Anderson's booklet notes are written to his usual high standard.' Heymann salutes his work, pointing out with some satisfaction that no one has ever picked up a mistake in it – an almost unbelievable fact given the volume. He has also called him 'one of the fathers of Naxos'. This may have added significance in that Anderson's son, Anthony, joined Heymann's company after university and is now part of the senior management team, holding wide responsibilities in the international business while also running Select Music, Naxos's UK distribution company.

During the first half of the 1990s the job of production manager – overseeing all the booklets and the covers – was done in Hong Kong by Anthony Anderson. Coordinating these and assimilating the detail was becoming an immense task, but finding personnel in Hong Kong capable of doing the necessarily specialised work was proving increasingly difficult. More and more aspects of Naxos started to transfer to the UK, especially when Anthony returned in 1997 to become managing director of Select Music. One of the first changes that he instigated was an upgrading of the label's logo. The famous Naxos pillars, instead of being black on white, were given a more stylish look, becoming white on blue. In 1999 a new production manager, Peter Bromley, was appointed to oversee all the covers and booklets of releases, now numbering as many as 300 in any one year.

By the end of the twentieth century Naxos and Marco Polo had grown so fast, the recording schedule was so large, and the commissioning was so adventurous and spontaneous, that the labels were operating three months behind schedule. Matters were further complicated by the international nature of the design and production operation, with designers and editorial staff working on different continents. This situation was later facilitated by email and it is the norm now; but at a time when fax was still prominent it was ambitious, to say the least. With so much investment in new recordings their release was a priority, and less effort was devoted to backing-up and archiving; but an emerging need to prepare everything for Internet development meant that this area of activity was increasingly important. The considerable task of creating a proper, accessible archive was one of Bromley's first. Naxos and Marco Polo CDs were being pressed by CD manufacturers in different continents, and sourcing old graphic files and dealing with lost artwork films were vital, if less glamorous, jobs than designing packaging for the latest symphony release.

The front cover and the overall booklet design and content had all remained much the same through the first decade. For Marco Polo, putting a picture of the composer on the front had been an obvious solution, though Heymann had quickly realised that this meant a lot of older men with beards. For Naxos, from the start, he had employed the simple solution of a painting or other artwork, finding these where he could. By 2000 Naxos was working more formally with standard picture libraries across the world, at closely negotiated rates because the volume was so high.

The range of releases had become so wide that to clarify the Naxos catalogue for consumers it had become necessary to create series. The variety only grew with time, and for each of the many labels and series (be it 'Complete Piano Music of Liszt', 'Naxos World', 'Very Best of', 'Wind Band Classics' or 'Guitar Collection') a design had to be created by Bromley and his production team. Sometimes the decision was to stay close to home with the white Naxos look, especially for the national labels such as 'American Classics' or 'Spanish Classics'; sometimes, where the subject demanded a bolder approach, such as Film Music or Naxos Nostalgia, it was decided to break away from that framework. The system has remained the same for the last few years: each release has to be coordinated with the editors who are working on the sound files and will provide the track points and timings; and each release has to have its introductory 'blurb' for the back, written by marketing staff but overseen by Bromley. Naxos is still the only label in the industry to provide this basic information about each recording on the rear inlay card, something Heymann has considered essential. A cover image has to be chosen for each release, the notes commissioned (with translations where required) and edited, and all the basic information about the recording collated: venue, date, engineer, producer, editor and more. Naxos may have started as a popular budget label but it had its roots in Heymann's personal interest as a collector – and collectors want this information.

Broadband Internet access has meant that the production team is international and largely freelance, working from home. In general one designer – in the UK, New Zealand, Italy, Hong Kong or Manila – will work on one release from start to finish. However, sometimes a cover may be created in Manila and the rest of the booklet designed in the UK. Designers with specialist classical interests are used whenever possible, and it is important that they are aware of diacritics on names: the international nature of the musicians and composers means that accuracy with Czech or Hungarian or Polish names is paramount.

Opera libretti and sung texts add another layer of complexity. For orchestral and instrumental releases the layout was very straightforward but for opera, lieder, chansons and other song releases, as well as sacred music, booklets burgeoned. It was up to Bromley's department to source these texts and reproduce them – initially the sung language only but increasingly translations as well. There was no problem with out-of-copyright libretti, other than working with considerable amounts of texts in a variety of languages. However, there was often great difficulty with copyright owners who, accustomed to being paid handsomely by full-price labels, did not appreciate that the Naxos margins were slim. The aim was, and still is, to provide the best possible recordings for the price, but where negotiations failed more detailed synopses were commissioned instead.

Bromley has also overseen general style developments, including the introduction of a greater variety of fonts and other design elements. There has been an increasing use of full-bleed covers for particular repertoire and an introduction of slipcases for the most important releases, all to make those CDs stand out and appear more substantial, even within a Naxos white wall. The back inlay was redesigned, with a panel to enclose the recording details.

There are times when one recording is released in a number of different formats with slightly different specifications: the European release, the US release, the Far East release ... It can be complicated because often each manufacturing plant has slightly different requirements in terms of measurements or layout. The designer looking after these various versions has to pay great attention to detail.

The growth of download sales and the drop in CD sales have also had an effect on design. A cover must now work in thumbnail size – with very clear titling – as well as look attractive on the shelf. Some titles are 'pre-released' in digital format before being put into the international CD release schedule, in which case there is a half-way design stage: a basic design is employed before the eventual CD cover design supersedes it.

Coordinating this is a considerable logistical enterprise. With designers and now note writers in many different countries, the Naxos production team works from a central FTP site that is accessed twenty-four hours a day. A decade of work is on that site, so that Naxos subsidiaries around the world can download a cover or notes if they are needed suddenly for a campaign. It has become a key resource.

Sixteen

Naxos on the Web

Developing the Digital Services

The Naxos presence on the Internet has been one of the most innovatory and effective parts of the company. It indicated as far back as 1996 that this was much more than a budget classical record company. Naxos was intent on providing a long-lasting and comprehensive classical music service; its purpose was, ultimately, to go far beyond the confines of one specific classical label. Heymann wanted to expand the reach of Naxos and make it a classical music provider in the richest and broadest sense, taking in audio, video and a wealth of other media: in short, a one-stop digital source of classical music.

Heymann is the first to admit that this wasn't a clear strategy back in the mid-1990s when the Internet was beginning to make a serious impact. Living in Hong Kong, he was aware before most in the classical music world of the Internet's growth; and when approached by his warehouse manager S.K. Wong, an amateur computer enthusiast, to set up the first site he responded positively. Initially he rejected Wong's advice to register the domain names 'naxos.com' and 'marcopolo.com' and went ahead with just one website under the name of the parent company, 'hnh.com'. It was a mistake that was later rectified. Nevertheless, in 1996 the fledgling hnh.com appeared with basic information about Naxos and Marco Polo. It was slow, simple and a bit confused. But it did stream one track of every new release in RealAudio and Heymann saw its potential.

By 1999 the website had been completely revamped: it was faster, with clearer information, and most importantly visitors could stream in Windows Media Audio (WMA) format any of the complete Naxos or Marco Polo albums. It was now called 'naxos.com'. This was a real innovation – the first site, classical or pop, to offer all its titles for listening online, track by track. It meant streaming, not downloading, but it brought music via the Internet directly into the home. The quality was basic, 20 kbps being the only realistic option in the dial-up era, but it was a huge step forward in classical marketing. In fact it was also a massive risk. Within the company, many distributors warned that this was a highly dangerous step. Piracy was already beginning to have an effect on pop. Surely, the doubters said, Heymann was *inviting* theft of his recordings. He did not agree. Firstly he saw it as an ideal marketing tool which would attract sales; secondly the quality was so low that although it was good enough for judging the performance, no real classical music lover would be content to have the music at that bitrate. In any case, Naxos CDs were cheap and Heymann did not believe that people would go to all the trouble of stealing the music (not easy to do at the time) when they could have the CD itself for a relatively small amount.

This bold step was to have far-reaching consequences. It put Naxos in the forefront of classical music presence on the web, and it meant that the company suddenly found itself with its own Internet department. In a growing number of rooms in the warehouse offices in Hong Kong, there were young and keen IT experts ripping CDs and creating digital files of the contents; and, just as importantly, musicologists compiling all the metadata (background information) required by the database that drove the website. What was being created was a digital source which, at the click of a mouse, would supply all information relating to all 2,500 CDs – including the notes. It was a remarkably prescient operation, and perhaps only possible because the company was based in Hong Kong, where computer technology was at the cutting edge.

Only too often, however, Heymann paid the price for being at the cutting edge. He can no longer remember how many times the website and the entire, and rapidly expanding, catalogue has had to be redigitised. As Internet speeds became faster, 20 kbps was no longer acceptable and everything had to be brought in at a higher bitrate. Tracks had originally been streamed in the RealAudio format but, as Windows Media Player had started to dominate the market, the format had been converted to WMA, and was subsequently converted to Flash. Heymann decided that there was no need for DRM (digital rights management) as the risk of people recording the streams was not very great. There were also concerns within the company that the money being invested in the whole Naxos Internet activity far outweighed any likely commercial reward. Heymann pressed on. From where he was sitting, in Asia, he had personal experience of the rapid improvement of Internet service and speeds. He was actually better placed to judge than his distributors in his main markets in the USA or Europe.

At the turn of the century came a totally new venture which used this digitised sound archive. In 2001 Heymann toured his main markets with a hard drive – then the size of a box – and held it up in front of the salesmen. 'This contains all our recordings,' he said enthusiastically, and he explained his concept. Top hotels around the world would subscribe to the Naxos classical music catalogue, paying an annual subscription that would enable them to offer all guests a wide choice of classical music to be piped into their own rooms. He said that it would only take around 1,000 hotels paying a reasonable amount to double the income of the company, and there would not be the expense of pressing CDs. The immediate response of the salesmen in the US was to go pale at the thought of that hard drive getting into the wrong hands and being copied. Surely, they thought, if Mr Heymann is going around the world with all the Naxos recordings in his briefcase, he needs a bodyguard. Heymann exhorted his distributors to pursue subscription customers – hotels, hospitals, restaurants and numerous other avenues. In the end, this didn't really take off; but it was the first step towards arguably the most innovative and useful Internet classical music provision, and one that has proved itself of inestimable educational value: naxosmusiclibrary.com.

The Naxos Music Library was launched in 2002. Its purpose was to provide educational and musical establishments with an unmatched classical music resource. The 'NML', as it is generally called, was designed as a streaming service for schools, universities and music conservatories. It was quickly adopted by others: orchestras, music societies (for preparing programmes), arts organisations, public libraries, and even commercial companies involved in the use of classical music for film and advertisements. It was also attractive to individuals wanting the freedom to access music of their choice at any hour of the day or night. Initially, because the streams used up a lot of still-expensive bandwidth, the idea was to provide the music to subscribing institutions on a hard drive so that only the search took place through the Naxos Music Library site. Very soon after the service was launched, however, the cost of bandwidth dropped dramatically and it became possible for subscribers to stream the music from the main server in Hong Kong.

The content now offered as a streamed provision is, in short, the largest and most comprehensive collection of recorded classical music available (with a foot in the door of other genres, including world and jazz). This came about because, although it is called 'Naxos Music Library' and at its heart is the extensive Naxos catalogue, Heymann's idea from the start was that it should include all other classical labels. He invited and sometimes coaxed other labels to join. Those which were already distributed by Naxos were more open to it than those which still harboured a residual reserve towards the 'budget' label. It did mean that the labels had to place their own content into the hands of a rival, which naturally made some hesitate; but a fair revenue share, transparent reporting and clear contracts ensured that the number of labels grew month by month. What's more, the site was designed so that no priority was given to Naxos recordings: a search for a work with multiple recordings on the NML from different labels displays the results in the order generated by the Google algorithm. Before too long the Naxos Hong Kong office was inundated with CDs (and, later, hard drives) from other labels, ready for conversion into the required formats.

In the first decade of the twenty-first century, downloading (and illegal file sharing) was all the rage. Little attention was paid to streaming but Heymann judged that in the near future, as fast broadband became more universal, streaming would be of equal or even greater importance. Access rather than ownership was the key, he felt. As a catalogue owner, however, he appreciated that the business model had to offer security above all, as well as a meaningful revenue to label owners. He did not think that the advertising path (payment by share of advertising revenue) was reliable or appropriate. In his opinion, the subscription model, aimed initially at institutions and companies, offered the best chance of a worthwhile business for all. The owners of the recordings would be paid for every microsecond their recordings were accessed.

A basic subscription model already existed in the classical music world for editorial projects such as *Grove Music Online*. However, it had not yet been applied to recorded music, largely because it needed an agglomeration of labels to make it viable and no one had ever achieved this before on the scale that Heymann was proposing. It certainly wasn't an easy task. Labels were very cautious – even suspicious. Independent labels, naturally, were more flexible and gradually joined in droves, while the major labels put their collective heads in the sand and declined to join. As the years went by, the attitude of the majors became less important because of the range and depth of repertoire achievable by Naxos in combination with the independents. From a repertoire point of view, all works could be accessed, studied and appreciated. (Heymann's initial aim was to have at least one recording of every work ever recorded.) The majors were important from a performance point of view – they had the stars; but for the needs of the institutions at which the NML was principally aimed, repertoire was more important than performance.

Certainly this was the attitude taken by universities and music academies, which began to join and then renew their subscriptions on a regular basis. The Naxos sales teams around the world had to learn to work within academic environments, which were very different from retail circles. It was quickly seen by universities and others that subscribing to the NML was economically more sound than investing in one CD copy of each work: the CD could be used by only one student at a time and could be lost or damaged; but, with just ten or twenty subscriptions, music students throughout the university could access the NML and study any of the works at their leisure.

It was not just about the music itself. Musicologists around the world – in Hong Kong, Manila, the US and the UK – were engaged in providing further background information about the works, instead of purely creating metadata. It was a momentous task. Heymann wanted students and musicians to be able, at a mouse-click, to find out the performers, the length of the work, the history of the work and the composer, the recording details, and even the instrumentation and information on the publisher. The goal was, in Heymann's words, to make it an unrivalled total music resource.

Within five years it was already by far the global market leader in this kind of provision, having overtaken other attempts to create something similar. Daily updates to the content indicate the sustained pace of growth. By the end of 2010 the NML contained 50,000 albums with 750,000 tracks. By the end of 2012 this is expected to rise to 70,000 albums with one million tracks.

The growing success of the NML prompted Heymann to develop a spoken-word sister site. He had a successful and growing series of classic literature recordings on Naxos AudioBooks which gave him the content he needed. The Naxos Spoken Word Library (NSWL) was another unique enterprise: from the very beginning it offered, where possible, the texts as well as the recordings, enabling the user to listen and read simultaneously. This has been particularly useful for English language and literary studies.

In 2005 a new Naxos office was opened in Manila: it was to concentrate on Internet activity, and much of the work in Hong Kong was relocated there. It used to its advantage an English-speaking IT workforce and available musicologists. For the next five years it was the hub of Naxos's Internet presence until another change of personnel and direction divided the work again. Much of the back-office updating of the websites continued to take place in Manila, with other IT work in Hong Kong; but in 2010 the principal IT development projects were shifted to Naxos of America in Nashville, nearer the world's biggest online music market.

With the NML happily underway, Heymann turned his attention to downloads. By 2007 the situation regarding classical downloads was steadying into a pattern. The MP3 format was becoming largely accepted; iTunes was the dominant player in classical music downloads, with eMusic and Amazon following. There were others but they were not significant. With the growing NML content, it seemed that it would be relatively easy to provide a top-quality classical music download store with a sophisticated search engine, specially developed for classical music. It was clear that subscribers to both naxos.com and the NML wanted the facility to buy the digital files, and this made a download store an obvious development.

In 2007 ClassicsOnline (COL) was launched. It was decided to adopt a neutral name rather than stamp it with the Naxos provenance, not least because the Naxos label would be just one among many. Downloadable tracks were first sold at a bit rate of 128 kbps (the NML was streaming at the same rate) but subsequently the rate was increased to 320 kbps, producing a quality of sound more in line with the expectations of classical music enthusiasts. COL started steadily and attracted a regular custom, but by 2010 it mirrored the situation of downloads worldwide: sales had begun to plateau rather than expand. Nevertheless it was another revenue stream for the participating labels.

The growing significance of classical DVDs in the market was a clear indication that a classical specialist online video platform was needed. Once again, Heymann put his faith in the streaming medium and in 2009 launched the Naxos Video Library (NVL). The spread of fast broadband worldwide made this viable and the subscription model had proved its worth. Having become the dominant distributor of classical DVDs, Naxos had the relevant expertise to move into this area; and considerable growth in the field generally – opera and ballet companies, orchestras and concert promoters were becoming increasingly keen to film their events for TV and DVD sales – meant that an Internet presence was timely.

The Platforms

Naxos Website (naxos.com)

For the Naxos labels, naxos.com is the main marketing window on the world. It has evolved considerably over the years and is now a comprehensive source of information regarding Naxos that is updated on a daily basis. An international platform, it is managed by an international team: news and new-release information flows in from all the Naxos centres and is coordinated in Hong Kong, web updates are handled in Manila by a team of three, and advertising and reviews are organised in Hong Kong. Until relatively recently the revolving banners were all approved by Heymann himself, who set the tone and the design. It has some 300,000 non-paying subscribers who can stream 25 per cent of each track, and a smaller number of paying subscribers who can access all complete tracks. Membership is truly global.

It is a large site that also acts as an information base for those working within the company. It takes some diligent investigation to journey into the many different corners of the business and there are several surprises along the way. First and foremost it has information on the existing catalogues of the audio and video labels owned or distributed by Naxos. Then there are the various series within Naxos that are carefully documented. This 'Sets/Series' section helps to highlight corners of the label that would otherwise be in danger of getting lost in the main catalogue.

Artists and composers also have their own sections. There are extraordinary details here that can be teased out of their digital corners. The 'Composers' section, which includes birth and death dates for each composer, takes you from Aagaard, Thorvald (1877–1937) to Zyman, Samuel (b. 1956), and a huge amount of content is available. For each composer there is a biography, information on the main works by genre, and a discography. For example, the J.S. Bach discography contains some 1,800 titles. Click on any one of those titles and the full, recorded information appears: the works, the performers, the track times, the release date, and often the notes and much more. There are even quick links to the biographies of key composers and general essays on genres and periods.

There is a newsletter archive, a news archive, a reviews archive, information about distributors around the world, information on how to buy the CDs, and the essential key-word search to take you directly to the object. The amount of information on the site is breathtaking.

Naxos Music Library (naxosmusiclibrary.com)

Most music students around the world will know and speak highly of the Naxos Music Library. Many will have used it for research or just for listening throughout their student years. It is a well-functioning music library that is always at one's fin-gertips. This has literally been the case since 2010, when the introduction of the NML app enabled the subscriber to access the library's music from a coffee shop. It is in using the app that one really appreciates the capabilities and growing flexibility of the streaming technology.

The NML has close to 400 labels in its database, encom-passing classical and folk music, jazz, blues, nostalgia, spoken word and even relaxation music. New albums are added daily – almost too many for the listener to keep up with. EMI was the first major to join, bringing 6,500 classical and jazz titles in 2011. It was followed by Warner Classics. The rich character of the NML and the wide variety of repertoire is underpinned by many independent labels, large and small.

Every monthly update on naxos.com is automatically reflected in the NML, but in addition there are all the monthly updates from the independent labels. There is a 'Recent Additions' button that provides a weekly or monthly overview, but even this is often a long list in itself.

The 'Playlists' function has become indispensable for many subscribers. Professors and individual students can create playlists within the library so that works being studied can be conveniently accessed again. They can be bookmarked, and even accessed and altered via the NML app.

The whole site is searchable by composer, by work, by label or by genre and there is a huge amount of information accessible about each individual recording. For example, the website entry for Bach's Cantata *Jauchzet Gott in allen Landen!*, BWV 51 includes the tracks themselves, the performer details, biographies and discographies for each individual performer, as well as details of the work itself: composer, lyricist, instrumentation, publisher, duration, period and genre. The listing also includes an electronic reproduction of the notes that appear in the CD booklet and a list of all the available recordings of the work in the NML.

There is also an 'Advanced Search' function that allows searching of the database by many different criteria, including playing time. This is very useful for professional musicians and anybody involved in programming. For example, a conductor can search for a fifteen-minute piece of nineteenth-century Spanish orchestral music by entering '14' and '16' into the 'Duration' fields, 'Spain' into the 'Country' field, '1800' and '1899' into the 'Year Composed' fields, and 'Orchestral' into the 'Genre and Music Categories' field, and will get the results instantly together with details on the instrumentation and publishers of all the works.

There are other useful sections to the NML. The 'Study Area' offers specially commissioned texts on music history and theory that are presented according to the specific requirements of the education systems in North America, the UK, Australia and other countries. 'Resources' includes a section cross-referencing all the pieces listed on the UK's ABRSM syllabus for the upper grades of violin, piano, cello, guitar and flute (and some for Trinity Guildhall too). The 'Pronunciation Guide' covers the majority of composers' names, spoken by native speakers. 'Glossary' and 'Fundamental Terms' give definitions of a wide range of musical words and phrases. There are many opera libretti, such as *Carmen, Il barbiere di Siviglia* and all the operas of Richard Wagner. Copyright issues restrict these libretti to public-domain texts, but it is still an impressive selection.

The NML has proved a ground-breaking resource and it continues to expand as more content and new features are added. There is also Naxos Music Library Jazz, which has a growing number of labels and currently consists of 5,000 albums and 50,000 tracks.

ClassicsOnline (classicsonline.com)

With the download site ClassicsOnline, Naxos was entering an Internet area already served by some established sites (the world leader iTunes, but also eMusic.com and others). Nevertheless Heymann felt that Naxos, with its outstanding reputation for web services, should have its own download facility, and he set about creating one specifically for classical music. Drawing on the resources in the Naxos Music Library, he had the technical advantage of not having to start a classical website from scratch.

ClassicsOnline was intended from the start to cater for all classical buyers, including the dedicated collector. Its selection, of course, was key to this and expanded rapidly; to date, the site contains one million tracks from some 50,000 CDs and represents almost 400 labels. Each track can be sampled and the music is offered DRM-free.

The great benefit to the classical connoisseur is the advanced search facility, which enables a precise search – year of composition, genre, nationality etc. In addition there are 'classical-friendly' features that highlight new labels, recent releases, critics' picks and COL exclusives. It is the Harrods of classical download sites.

Naxos Video Library (naxosvideolibrary.com)

The Naxos Video Library (NVL) is the most recent subscription-based streaming site. With a rapidly growing repertoire of more than 1,000 titles, it draws on Naxos's involvement with DVDs over the past decade. With some thirty labels contributing to the database, it offers a wide range of videos: opera, ballet and concerts, as well as documentaries, educational programmes and travelogues. Opera is the predominant genre, with a varying selection: five productions of *Macbeth*, three each of *Madama Butterfly* and *La Bohème*, three of *Siegfried* and four of *Tristan und Isolde*, in addition to operas by Donizetti, Rossini, Mascagni and others; but there is also Janáček's *Jenůfa*, Berg's *Wozzeck*, Bernstein's *Trouble in Tahiti* and Sallinen's *The Palace*. Subtitles included on the original DVD are available here and libretti are also provided in different languages, so that users are able to see subtitles in the original language with the libretto in another language, and vice versa. Ballets include multiple productions of the popular Tchaikovsky works as well as modern ballets from the Netherlands Dance Theatre and the Alvin Ailey American Dance Theatre. Among the documentaries are some historic films of Leonard Bernstein, Karl Böhm, Sergiu Celibidache (in rehearsal and performance), Nathan Milstein and Itzhak Perlman; a master-class with Júlia Varady; and 'Global Treasures' – a series of travel documentaries, from Budapest to Borobudur.

The Naxos Video Library is still in its early stages but as a classical video resource it is expected to become increasingly important.

Naxos Spoken Word Library (naxosspokenwordlibrary.com)

The majority of this site consists of the 700 titles from Naxos AudioBooks. It is an outstanding resource primarily for English classic literature but it also offers many European classics in English, from Plato to Dante and Hugo to Tolstoy. The design of the site enables quick access to individual chapters of books, or individual poems, or an act in a Shakespeare play. It also contains a collection of German classics from Naxos Hörbücher, including works by Goethe, Fontane, Heine, Hoffmann and others, as well as German translations of other European classics, such as those of Chekhov, Daudet and Lewis Carroll. A limited number of French texts are available too. The playlist facility, with bookmarking, means that recordings and texts can be accessed and revisited with ease (also available on the deft NSWL app).

As with the NML, the NSWL is adopted mainly by institutions but is attracting a growing interest from individuals.

Naxos Web Radio (naxosradio.com)

Naxos Web Radio was one of the early online services of the company, offering music from the catalogue streamed at 48 kbps. Perhaps the least known of the Naxos services, it performs the straightforward task of bringing classical music into the home or workplace twenty-four hours a day, seven days a week. There are more than eighty pre-programmed channels, covering all the genres of the Naxos labels (from 'Early Music' to '21st Century Classics', 'American Classics' to 'Chinese Classics', 'Film Music' to 'Melodies of Love', 'Piano' to 'Guitar & Lute' etc.). It is free of advertising and the subscription is very low.

Seventeen

Distribution: The Growth of an Empire

Distribution has played an unexpectedly crucial role in the expansion of the company. Klaus Heymann did not plan to organise a worldwide distribution network when he started first Marco Polo and then Naxos. He was interested in the music and wanted to concentrate on developing the labels, to invest in catalogue building not in distribution. He had previously developed a network of distribution companies and licensees in Asia, which he sold to BMG in 1989, and he remained the distributor of Bose audio equipment in Hong Kong and China until 2003. Finding distributors for Marco Polo was not very difficult because it was a full-price label focusing on world-premiere recordings. Naxos was a different matter. Even though it was the first budget classical CD label to have new digital recordings, finding distribution was a challenge. Established distributors of classical labels did not want to touch 'a classical CD budget label from Hong Kong' (although there had been successful classical budget LP labels such as Vox-Turnabout and Vanguard). So in the beginning Heymann was forced to work with outsiders.

His first German distributor was a small company that

parallel imported Denon hi-fi equipment into Germany. It started to import Naxos CDs because they were manufactured in the early days by Denon, and it sold them at full price. This missed the point of the enterprise, and Heymann soon changed distributor. In Australia he worked with another outsider who manufactured the label under licence; eventually the arrangement ended up in the courts and Heymann had to find a new distributor. In France the initial success in the hypermarkets made it difficult subsequently to find a distributor willing to sell Naxos to regular retail stores. In the UK the breakthrough came when Woolworths took on the label.

Eventually Heymann built a network of independent distributors, most of whom did not specialise in classical music. For various reasons most of them got into financial difficulties and had to be bailed out or taken over by the Naxos parent company in Hong Kong. Once he had established distribution subsidiaries in most major music markets, it became obvious to him that it was difficult to sustain companies that sold only his own Marco Polo and Naxos labels. He therefore decided to take on the distribution of other independent classical CD labels – and, beginning with Arthaus Musik in 2000, the distribution of independent classical DVD labels too.

As the business changed, with CD sales beginning to falter and globalisation advancing, the physical distribution of classical labels came to be concentrated in fewer hands. It made increasing economic sense to supply even individual shops across country borders from a central warehouse point, rather than for each country to maintain its own stock. Consequently Naxos of America now supplies shops in Canada, Naxos Sweden supplies shops throughout Scandinavia, and Naxos Global Logistics (NGL) in Munich supplies shops in France as well as Germany. The likelihood is that this pattern will increase. It is a model that also allows the national distributors to focus on sales, marketing and promotion rather than the maintenance of a big warehouse. The picture can appear quite complex, but Naxos now has five main regional logistics centres providing warehousing and distribution for a mixed domestic and export service: NGL, Naxos Sweden, Naxos of America, Naxos Far East and Select Music, UK.

Having been highly successful with its own distribution from the start, it was clear that the company knew how to do it. The leading independent labels chose to come to Naxos for distribution even though, at first, it must have seemed for them like entrusting their livelihood and business secrets to their greatest rival. A level of integrity was always maintained: advance knowledge of an independent's release plans was never misused for Naxos benefit. In fact it was of general benefit for Naxos to know what an independent was releasing so that clashes were reduced by negotiation. Success even resulted in the majors acknowledging that the Naxos distribution network was better suited than their own to distributing their back catalogue.

The real challenge for Heymann in buying into new distribution companies was always finding the right person to run them. The surprise is that there was no one model, no Naxos distribution managing director clone. Some of the managing directors have a strong classical music background: this is true of the UK, Germany and Australia. The MDs in both Sweden and the US have learned about classical music on the job (their background is in other forms of music). In Japan there was classical music knowledge but initially no distribution experience whatsoever. Somehow Heymann brought these various talents together to create the world's strongest international classical music distribution network, selling CDs and DVDs as well as marketing the group's subscription services and licensing its recordings.

Naxos Global Logistics

The first Naxos CDs were pressed by Denon in Japan, which was an important factor in the early success of the label because Denon had an outstanding reputation for quality. It was not very long, however, before the demand for the rapidly expanding label called for manufacturing and central warehousing to be nearer the main markets. This meant Europe. Germany, right in the centre, was the most logical location, and in 1991 Music and Video Distribution (MVD) was set up near Munich. It was a company with two purposes: to organise and coordinate all CD (and later DVD) manufacturing with European CD plants; and to provide an efficient distribution service for the Naxos distributors in countries around the world.

There were many pitfalls to be avoided. Careful stock management is crucial to the health of a label such as Naxos, and ruinous overstocks can quickly build up if individual distributors are holding a lot more than they need. Centralised CD production and centralised warehousing and distribution were the answer – most of the time. It was certainly true for the supply of territories in Europe, the Far East and Australia, where local demand only rarely warranted local pressing. It was more difficult for the US and Canada: some pressing had to take place there, especially for a title with particular regional appeal, either because of the repertoire or artist, or perhaps because of a special campaign.

The hub of manufacture and the warehousing for international distribution remained in Munich. In July 2008 a new company called Naxos Global Logistics (NGL) was set up by the Naxos Group and is headed by Mohamed El Wakil, who had worked at the previous distribution company as well as for Naxos Deutschland. The work there is complex and crucial to the welfare of the whole Naxos enterprise: NGL is able to offer a full range of services to the distributors and labels, including distribution to shops and to end consumers worldwide. Somewhere between twenty and forty new Naxos recordings are released each month and the staff at NGL check each title before shipping. Stock of the massive back catalogue must also be available in appropriate quantities: all this calls for clear management within the warehouse.

Then there is the distribution itself. In the early years, faxed orders – pages of them – came in from numerous countries around the world. Orders also came over the phone, from Hong Kong and the Far East in the morning, Europe during the day, and the US in the evening. Now most orders come in via email, and there are hundreds, large and small, every day. Container lorries packed with pallets bearing thousands of classical CDs travel to Europe and beyond, and to ports and airports. There are daily, weekly and monthly shipments to the main classical territories – to Germany, the UK, the US or Japan. Regular, even frequent, orders come from other continents too, such as South America and Australia. NGL has dealings with more than fifty main international distributors, including quite a few unexpected ones, such as Lebanon and Kenya.

Rafael Schölermann, the international customer service manager who has been in this Naxos hub for twenty years, has seen the CD format peak and begin to diminish. In its heyday some six million CDs would go through the central warehouse, though now it is down to around three million. The speed and ease of re-pressing CDs means that initial print-runs can be quite low – between 1,000 and 3,000 – but Schölermann recalls that the first pressing of the tenth-anniversary sampler in 1997 numbered 250,000.

With nearly 9,000 CD and DVD titles in the Naxos and Marco Polo catalogues, plus those of other CD and DVD labels that are distributed by the Naxos network, NGL can supply stock of 33,000 titles at very short notice and generally has around three million units under its roof. This is necessary because the decline in CDs means that NGL is more frequently distributing CDs directly to individual shops throughout Europe: centralised delivery of this kind plays an increasingly important role. Communication and transport links are so good that NGL in Munich can supply shops in Budapest, Amsterdam, Bucharest, Rome, Warsaw and much further within twenty-four hours. Not surprisingly, all shops in Germany have for some years been supplied directly by NGL.

Naxos Distribution Around the World

United Kingdom: Select Music and Video Distribution

The growth of Naxos in the UK set an example for the company's expansion in many other territories. It reads in retrospect as such a rapid, confident upward surge on so many fronts that it could act as a prototype for other industries and illustrate a management manual. The reality was not quite as ordered and planned as the story suggests. It was a case of the right product being in the right place at the right time, but supported and driven by an enthusiasm and classical knowledge that went beyond mere corporate behaviour. There was a feeling that the classical establishment really could be challenged and bypassed – and, with the help of a few key turning points, it was.

Naxos first settled in the UK in the late 1980s as the house label of Woolworths, where each CD sold at £3.99. The low-price chain was in its final years as a prominent feature of Britain's high streets, but Heymann had shrewdly slipped Naxos in as the store's exclusive budget label (the CDs were clearly Naxos branded and had the white covers, which were already standard by then). Then, in 1989, Heymann read a review of some early Naxos recordings in *Classical Music* by David Denton, a Sheffield-based music writer. Denton described a selection of the CDs as good value for money but claimed that they were hampered by being enclosed within the doors of Woolworths; in order to expand, the label had to get out. Heymann contacted Denton and brought him on board with the purpose of giving Naxos a broader reach in the UK. He fully acknowledges the subsequent work of Denton – with his wife, Rona – as crucial to Naxos's development.

A new enterprise was launched by David and Rona Denton called Naxos Promotions, whose first task was to negotiate the label's exit from Woolworths' exclusivity. This was made relatively easy because Naxos was beginning to produce multi-CD sets which had to go into bigger cases, and Woolworths did not have the racking for them. Furthermore, there was repertoire coming through that Woolworths did not wish even to try to sell, such as Bartók's *Concerto for Orchestra* coupled with *Music for Strings, Percussion and Celesta*. So, a move beyond Woolworths was timely and appropriate. Denton signed a UK distribution deal with Harmonia Mundi, the French label that offered UK distribution to smaller classical labels from its London warehouse. The managing director was Graham Haysom. In 1990 Naxos began to appear in classical record shops up and down the country at the increased price of £4.99, which was still perceived as inexpensive. (It was to stay at that price level for fifteen years, until 2005.) It became a famous price point for the label and contributed substantially to its profile and its success: for years CD buyers were amazed that new digital recordings of decent quality could be so cheap.

Denton continued to proselytise with untiring enthusiasm at all levels – in shops, record clubs and the press – and found the response to be generally positive. The recordings had the tag of Eastern European orchestras but they were digital, sounded good, and few could deny that the music was reliably played at the very least. The word was getting around, and bulk orders started to come to Harmonia Mundi from retailers. David Blake, then sales manager at Harmonia Mundi UK and later sales manager at Select Music, remembers that after Harmonia Mundi had taken over, shops would ring up and ask for a few of each new title, and soon they were ordering 'ten of all the new titles'. Naxos was distributed by Harmonia Mundi for some eighteen months, and by the end many shops were buying a box (twenty-five CDs) of each new title. Some were ordering even higher numbers, and adding more boxes of back-catalogue titles. This was unheard of for a classical label. The fax machines could scarcely keep up as the rolls thundered round, page after page of orders spilling onto the parquet floor of the warehouse. The Harmonia Mundi staff struggled to cope. On the new-release mail-out day, the floor space was completely covered in boxes. 'Sometimes we couldn't help stepping on them,' remembered Blake. It was crazy. It was exciting.

The interest in Naxos was sparked by savvy marketing and a growing awareness that classical CDs did not have to be expensive to be good. From the Dentons' house in Sheffield, and later a small office, simple advertisements were designed and placed, press releases were written, and a review service was maintained. Denton and his wife visited record clubs up and down the country, promoting the Naxos message. There were interviews with Heymann in newspapers.

It was difficult to breach the wall of superiority maintained by the classical establishment, but chinks appeared as certain writers simply couldn't ignore public demand. People were keen to replace their basic classical LP collection with the new CDs, and felt that Naxos would more than serve. Soon Naxos exited from Woolworths and entered the main shops, including HMV, Our Price and Tower Records. Then came the affirmation from one of the UK's most respected music critics: Edward Greenfield, the classical reviewer for the *Guardian*, decided it was time to write a piece. Denton sent a box of Naxos releases to him at very short notice, and the resultant article, a large and well-displayed commendation of the label, its recordings and its price, gave Naxos the imprimatur necessary to raise its status. After all, Greenfield also wrote for *Gramophone*, the most respected review magazine, and *The Penguin Guide to Classical Music*: if he said the Naxos CDs were good, there was no question about it. Greenfield remembers his discovery:

'Originally, Naxos discs were sold exclusively in Woolworths, which meant that no critic took them seriously, and they were not sent out for review. Happily, my cousin bought a number from a cycle of the Beethoven piano sonatas played by a Hungarian pianist of whom few had heard, Jenő Jandó. I quickly realised that these recordings were remarkably fine, offering performances that were refreshingly direct and straightforward. I then used my record column in the *Guardian* to write about Naxos, and I am flattered that Klaus Heymann attributes something of the early expansion of the company to what I wrote!'

Harmonia Mundi was even more swamped with orders. It was still only 1991. The majors responded with the accusation that Naxos exploited Eastern European artists. Heymann and Denton countered it but already they were beginning to plan the next stage: recording in the UK. Naxos was offering fair fees and most orchestras had no basic objection to working for a budget label. One or two majors (and even an independent or two!) tried to stop this by saying that any orchestra or artist who worked for Naxos would never be welcomed back to them; but, regardless, a number of orchestras came on board, including the Bournemouth Symphony Orchestra, Royal Scottish National Orchestra, Northern Sinfonia, BBC Scottish Symphony Orchestra, City of London Sinfonia, English Northern Philharmonia and BBC Philharmonic. They were joined by a group of capable freelance recording engineers who were all given due credit on the CDs: Andrew Walton, Tim Handley, Chris Craker, Gary Cole, John Taylor and Michael Ponder. They were all needed, too, because the UK was becoming an important recording centre for both standard repertoire and specifically English music (broadened, from time to time, to a 'British' music series).

The UK was a hive of Naxos activity. As 1991 progressed it was clear that Naxos was outgrowing Harmonia Mundi, whose French founder, Bernard Coutaz, looked in disbelief at some of the sales that his satellite company was achieving. He was less than happy to discover that a Hong Kong-based budget enterprise was outpacing his distinguished label. He instructed his company's UK directors, Graham Haysom and Fergus Lawlor, to discontinue distribution of Naxos, even though it made an important contribution to the company's turnover. Haysom contacted Heymann and informed him; but, confident that Naxos could be the label of the future, Haysom suggested that the three of them (Heymann, Haysom and Lawlor) set up their own joint-venture distribution company. Matters moved swiftly, and in October 1991 Select Music and Video Distribution Ltd began trading from an industrial estate in Redhill, Surrey, with the primary purpose of distributing Naxos and a broader aim of bringing other labels on board to enable greater economies of scale.

It was the right decision. Every year between 1991 and 1997, sales of the Naxos label increased dramatically. This was partly because the catalogue itself was growing with astonishing speed. Denton instigated a busy programme of recordings, at times with two a week somewhere in the UK. Helped by a good review and excellent sales of Elgar's First Symphony conducted by George Hurst, he had convinced Heymann that English music could sell. In a typically expansive manner, Heymann asked Denton to prepare programmes for his top 100 English music CDs and record them. (Denton notes that only in 2008 was this at last finished, the final recording being two volumes of Tippett's string quartets.) There was the Walton series from the English Northern Philharmonia; the Bax symphony cycle from David Lloyd-Jones and the Royal Scottish National Orchestra; a variety of Bliss recordings; and the series of English chamber music that was begun by the Maggini Quartet. With good reviews resulting from these recordings, Naxos was beginning to be respected specifically for its contribution to British music. It was a reputation that even travelled abroad to other Naxos territories and helped to feed the international profile of the company.

Denton also advanced the label's expansion into period performance. It was not of particular interest for Heymann, whose focus was the central classical repertoire played on conventional instruments. However, as with English music, he listened to Denton and agreed to trial a few recordings, notably those of the Oxford Camerata and the Rose Consort of Viols; these proved their worth commercially and musically. Denton and his wife went to concerts countrywide, searching out players who could record specific repertoire for Naxos. He only suggested to Heymann musicians whom he had personally heard (and vetted) in concert, and whose performances he felt assured could be replicated for the microphone.

Hand in hand with these imaginative A&R pursuits, which were totally unexpected from a budget label based in Hong Kong, went lively commercial development. Naxos CDs had originally been displayed variously in shops' general classical racks but people had started to search for the white label with the £4.99 sticker. So HMV began to rack Naxos on its own in long bins, and the spread of white covers resulted in what became known as the 'Naxos White Wall'. No other label was displayed like this and it established a strong brand identity. Sales followed. Customers would browse the Naxos White Wall and go to the tills with not just one or two but often a handful. They saw Naxos as a real bargain. This migrated to other retailers. Haysom remembers distinctly that in September 1993 Select Music received its biggest single order thus far: £250,000's worth of Naxos CDs sold to Our Price, one of the leading record chains, which had decided to stock the label in every one of its shops. It was the first time that Our Price had committed itself to a classical budget label in this way: it was recognising the demand.

Select Music was proving a success and other full-price labels decided to join the company, despite some apprehension about its link with a budget label. Of course it had started with its own full-price label, Marco Polo. Although Marco Polo was perhaps overshadowed by the sheer commercial success of Naxos, Heymann continued to invest in it, and its principal aim of providing premiere recordings of Romantic and late Romantic music continued. It was a label full of interest and still prized by collectors. Among those which joined it at Select was one of the finest in the UK: in 1995 Ted Perry decided to take a risk and came on board with his star classical label Hyperion. European labels such as BIS and CPO, and new initiatives such as Clarinet Classics, were followed by another leading English independent, ASV. By that time Select had already taken up the challenge of Naxos AudioBooks, distributing recordings of classic literature on CD and cassette into bookshops in the UK.

The company could clearly manage all these new ventures: it had proved profitable from the start and exceeded its budget every year. In 1996, for the first time, it sold over one million discs and had a turnover of £4 million. Naxos was the jewel in the crown, commercially speaking, and in the early years accounted for 80 per cent of its turnover. By 1997 this had balanced to 60/40, though the unit split weighed more highly in Naxos's favour. As the Naxos label consolidated itself, its UK market share continued to increase. Although prejudice persisted it was lessening with every year, as artistic enterprise, in the fields of both British and international repertoire, could not be ignored. Haysom and Lawlor started Select when distribution for independent classical labels had recently gone through an uneven period, with a number of companies appearing and then going to the wall. Select succeeded both because it was efficiently run and because it had its own top-selling record label to promote. It was a winning formula. Throughout the 1990s not only was turnover going up at least 20 per cent per annum but the budget was exceeded every year too. By the mid-1990s Naxos's market share of CD sales in the UK was approaching 13 per cent at a time when EMI's was around 30 per cent and Universal's (Decca, Deutsche Grammophon and Philips) was 30–35 per cent.

Naxos was everywhere – and not always under its own brand: for a few years, a selection of Naxos titles (some deleted and some new) appeared under the brand of the leading book-shop chain Dillons. Graham Haysom says, 'There is no doubt that during this time Klaus had upped his game, improving the standard of artists, the recordings, the production, the presen-tation and the promotion. This increase in the quality of the label is what made the success of Select possible in the 1990s.'

By 1997 a difference of approach had emerged between Haysom and Lawlor on one side and Heymann on the other. Haysom and Lawlor had ambitious plans to diversify: they saw Select first and foremost as an efficient distribution company which could, potentially, distribute anything that their target shops would buy. Haysom admits, 'I didn't want all our eggs in one [classical CD] basket, not least because the classical music world is relatively small.' Heymann, however, was keen to con-centrate on the distribution of purely classical music. It was another turning point for Naxos as a label because it under-pinned Heymann's principal goal at the time: to make Naxos into a sound encyclopedia of classical music without being dis-tracted by other money-making ventures, however attractive they might be. He had no idea, at this juncture, that the world of recording was soon going to be turned on its head by another advance in technology. The use of the Internet in the industry was beginning to appear, but classical music's future still appeared locked into the CD, despite glimmers of DVD and other formats.

In the autumn of 1997 Heymann took over control of the production and distribution activities in the UK. Haysom and Lawlor left Select, and at the same time David and Rona Denton retired (they had been concentrating on new recordings and they were ready to pass on the busy schedule). The UK had become possibly the single most important Naxos centre outside Hong Kong, with three strands to its activity: production, mastering (at K&A Productions, set up by Heymann with Andrew Walton in 1995) and distribution. Heymann needed someone to oversee it all and he turned to Anthony Anderson, then Naxos classical label manager who had been based in Hong Kong for eight years. A classics graduate with a wide knowledge of music (and son of Keith Anderson, the company's main writer of liner notes), Anthony Anderson returned to the UK in July of that year to become managing director of Select and represent Heymann in all other Naxos activities in the country.

It was a challenging appointment for Anderson: the company was by now the leading independent classical distributor in the UK; Naxos AudioBooks was winning awards but experiencing sales and distribution problems; the amount of mastering work going through K&A was increasing beyond all expectations; and the A&R centre, formerly in Hong Kong and briefly New Zealand, was moved to the UK too. 'My main memory of that time is that it was a tremendously hectic period, but I was also very driven by the new responsibility,' says Anderson. 'The basic aims were to keep a reasonable level of profitability and increase Naxos's market share. We increased the investment in the marketing of Naxos, including, for a while, advertising in the national press. From 1997 to 2000 Naxos CD sales increased by around 35 per cent and they reached their height in 2002.' That was the bottom line; but in the decade following his arrival Anderson had to encounter the widespread effects of enormous changes in the record industry itself.

In Select he found a well-organised distribution company that was still looking to expand. At its centre was Naxos, a label that was already exceeding its original brief of providing reliable recordings of central classical repertoire at budget price. In the release schedules could be anything from John

Cage and Pierre Boulez to Rameau on period instruments; Arnold, Bax or Stamitz; Korngold, Josquin Desprez or the complete chamber music of Poulenc; works by Einojuhani Rautavaara or waltzes by Johann Strauss II. Important also for many years was the Naxos Historical catalogue, with its highly praised transfers providing anew some of the finest classical and jazz recordings of the past. Naxos was fast becoming a label with the highest aspirations of any existing classical record company, though often it seemed an uphill task to convey this position to both the classical press and the classical collectors. The collectors got there first, voting with their purses and buying the new releases in bulk; but perhaps it was the very success of Naxos as a popular budget label that made it so difficult to shift the prejudices maintained by the established press, despite a handful of champions. Even well into the 2000s there still appeared the familiar line that damned with faint praise: 'Excellent recording for a budget-price CD.'

Anderson's recording schedule helped considerably to change Naxos's image in the UK. During his tenure at Select, most years have seen between fifteen and twenty new UK recordings produced under his aegis. These were not all of British music though the series was a continuing and important thread in the release schedule, incorporating both orchestral and chamber music. The Maggini Quartet recorded works by Alwyn, Rubbra, Rawsthorne and other composers; and the group's fifteen-year contribution to Naxos was crowned by the unique project of Peter Maxwell Davies's ten *Naxos Quartets* written specially for the label. Also significant was Anderson's work in bringing outstanding young English musicians into the Naxos studio. A good example is the pianist Ashley Wass. Anderson recalls: 'I first heard Ashley Wass in 1997 when he won what was then the World Piano Competition (by a country mile in my opinion). Part of the prize was the chance to make a recording for Naxos and he chose repertoire by Franck. A few years later he contacted us and we began talking about other repertoire, ending up with Bax and, subsequently, other British composers. I think Ashley may have been a bit reluctant to tackle British repertoire, much of which was almost unknown, for fear of being typecast as a performer of British music. However, through the process of living with the music and recording it, he has warmed to much of it. I believe now as I did in 1997 that he is one of the finest young pianists in our country.

'Ashley also featured in the British Piano Concerto series, which was born from an idea by the pianist Peter Donohoe. Initially a British Piano Concerto Foundation was established. However, when the Foundation ceased to be through lack of funding we continued the series (which is still a work in progress). I think the recordings have managed to get much music out there which wouldn't otherwise have been heard, and in that sense one of the Foundation's original objectives has been achieved.'

The strong English choral tradition had already been harnessed by David Denton (with Jeremy Summerly and his ensembles Oxford Camerata and Schola Cantorum of Oxford) and Anderson continued to foster it, bringing on board the Cambridge choirs of St John's College and Clare College. The most surprising commercial success was a new 'ensemble' version of John Rutter's Requiem with the Choir of Clare College, Cambridge conducted by Timothy Brown, which sold over 60,000 copies in the UK: it is one of the best-selling new 'homemade' recordings. Anderson comments: 'A large part of the success of that recording was due to John himself, who kindly produced it – particularly magnanimous as there was a risk that the Naxos release would cannibalise sales of the same work on his own Collegium label.' This unusual collaboration showed how a distributed label such as Collegium could work together with Naxos under the Select banner, to the benefit of all. These British recordings – Butterworth's *A Shropshire Lad*, for example, or Vaughan Williams's *Sancta civitas* and *Dona nobis pacem*, or the evergreen *Spem in Alium* – frequently featured in Select's monthly Top Ten Naxos recordings, having reached very respectable sales figures. The commitment to British music was deepened by the acquisition of certain recordings from the defunct Collins Classics label, notably music by Benjamin Britten and 'The English Song Series'.

Also from Select came a number of popular compilations that opened classical doors for a very wide audience. These 'lifestyle' and introductory concepts include the 'Best of' and 'Meditation' series as well as 'Chill with' (*Chill with Mozart*, *Chill with Vivaldi* etc.), a series of twelve titles that has sold over one million copies worldwide. For many years these popular compilations amounted to as much as 10 per cent of Naxos's turnover in the UK, and as they were based on existing Naxos recordings and were therefore very economical to produce, they were particularly worthwhile. These UK concepts were often picked up by Naxos companies abroad, from the US to Asia, and achieved further, considerable sales.

There were imaginative diversions into other popular areas, including titles aimed at a younger audience. *Peter and the Wolf* narrated by the actor Barry Humphries (in the voice of Dame Edna Everage) was the first of these. It was released with an entertaining cartoon cover design by the children's illustrator Tony Ross (best known for his work on the *Horrid Henry* books) and was among Select's bestsellers in the UK for many years, reaching over 100,000 copies. This highly successful children's series went on to feature Saint-Saëns' *The Carnival of the Animals*, with the late Johnny Morris reciting his own verses, and other titles narrated by such UK household names as June Whitfield, Brian Cant, Angela Rippon and Bernard Cribbins; it sold in its thousands both in the UK and internationally.

The most high-profile compilation may have been *The Sven-Göran Eriksson Classical Collection*, a three-CD set of tracks chosen by the manager of the English football team for a campaign in the run-up to the 2002 World Cup. It attracted considerable publicity, including a presence on peak-time television, and sold a healthy number. It followed the Naxos principle of taking classical music to a wider audience and it earned its keep in terms of exposure; but over-enthusiasm on the initial pressing as well as the early exit of England from the tournament in South Korea and Japan resulted in a lot of left-over stock. That is one of the dangers of boldly venturing beyond comfortable classical confines.

Despite the commercial success of Naxos over the first decade, it was not until 1999 that it made its mark on the *Gramophone* Awards, which were seen as the premier UK accolades for recordings: its British music series received an Editor's Choice award from James Jolly. Two years later came the first award from the *Gramophone* critics for a particular disc: the Maggini Quartet's recording of works by Vaughan Williams. In 2009 the Orchestral Award was won by Tchaikovsky's *Manfred* symphony played by the Royal Liverpool Philharmonic Orchestra under the charismatic Vasily Petrenko; and another Editor's Choice went in the following year to Bernstein's Mass conducted by Marin Alsop. Naxos was simply too big to ignore.

Shortly after his arrival in 1997 Anderson began actively and successfully to recruit additional important labels for distribution, starting with the composer–conductor John Rutter's Collegium label. Many others followed, including Chandos, Gimell, BBC Legends and Opera Rara, as well as house labels such as the London Philharmonic Orchestra, the Berliner Philharmoniker, The Sixteen (Coro) and the Monteverdi Choir and Orchestra (Soli Deo Gloria). Other composers followed John Rutter's example and brought their labels to Select too, including Michael Nyman and Carl Davis.

Of growing importance in the opening years of the new millennium was classical music video. Heymann had signed Arthaus Musik to a worldwide distribution deal, convinced that the main sales for classical video tapes and DVDs would be through classical music outlets rather than the video shops, as was generally presumed at the time. He was proved right, and Anderson developed Select into the leading supplier of classical music DVDs, including those of TDK, Opus Arte, The Christopher Nupen Films and EuroArts.

Independent labels came to realise that their fears of second-class treatment within Select would not materialise. In fact there were many advantages to being with a Naxos company, for as a label it was also having to deal first-hand with the dramatic changes that were taking place in the CD world. Many were deeply worried by the growth of downloads, witnessing the effect that not only piracy but also legitimate downloads were having in the pop and rock worlds. Would CDs be around by the second decade of the twenty-first century?

Running the Naxos labels in the UK while also representing many others, Anderson was perfectly placed to anticipate new developments. Perhaps unexpectedly it was the Naxos policy worldwide to involve the distributed labels in its plans for making the most of the new world – and a new world it certainly was. The Naxos label itself was actually hit hard by the drop of CD sales.

Anderson explains: 'Up to 2005 Naxos was prominent in retail and was often the only classical range in chains such as Andys, MVC, WH Smith and pop-dominated Our Price. However, from 2005 onwards most of these retailers disappeared from the high street. A large proportion of sales migrated from bricks-and-mortar stores to e-tailers, most notably Amazon but also classical specialists such as Presto and MDC. It happened quite rapidly. This shift has actually deprived Naxos of one of its distinct advantages: in-store visibility. The Naxos White Wall became a much rarer sight.' The 'impulse purchase' phenomenon prompted by the price, which even at £5.99 (from 2005) allowed buyers to experiment with an unfamiliar composer, work or performance, was disappearing. And with e-tailers making special offers on full-price labels as a matter of course, the famous Naxos price advantage became less distinct. Fortunately the label had reinvented itself by becoming the premier catalogue label for classical collectors, providing specialist repertoire as well as the core works, so it could compete on equal terms with any of the full-price labels. By 2010 it was the most prolific classical label, its budget price purely incidental.

The first decade of the twenty-first century saw Naxos take a leading role in digital distribution through the development of its own digital platforms and services. Heymann's foresight in pouring funds into the Naxos Music Library and the download store ClassicsOnline not only gave a future to Naxos as the premier specialist digital provider but paradoxically provided a lifeline to classical labels everywhere. In 2004 Select began selling Naxos Music Library subscriptions to educational establishments throughout the UK. By the end of the decade most music schools and music departments in the tertiary sector had signed up, as well as many music departments of secondary schools in both the state and private sectors. One of the crucial factors in the library's success is that it offers the catalogues of many other independent labels in addition to its own. It has become a resource unmatched by any other worldwide.

In the twenty years since Select Music was founded, and put Naxos into the driving seat of its own distribution in the UK, it has secured a position as the leading classical distributor in one of the most important classical music markets. It did this with particular success, joining with its main competitors – the finest of other independent labels – to present the greater efficiency of a combined service for the trade. This left the key competition to take place at the retail level. The approach has many benefits for individual labels and certainly for the Naxos labels themselves, which are not at the mercy of changeable distributors concerned only with the health of the bottom line. It is interesting to note that what has worked so well in the distribution of physical product is now being extended to the digital world.

United States: Naxos of America

Of all the major territories in which Naxos established itself, the United States proved the most difficult. It was a chequered first decade, when Naxos was initially distributed by various independent distributors and a licensee, until Heymann, following the UK success, decided that any long term future in the US would depend upon the formation of his own company. Begun in 1991 from offices in New Jersey, it ran for a few years, seemingly fulfilling the function of distributing the growing catalogue in classical circles. Nevertheless it failed to generate positive critical attention for Naxos and looked as if it would never break even, let alone make a profit.

In 1997 a drastic change was made. Two new, young but experienced music professionals, Jim Sturgeon and Jim Selby, were brought in with a brief to start afresh. Neither was a classical specialist, but both knew the record industry and they could see that the company needed some serious improvements in the logistics of CD distribution as well as better placement in the market. They started by taking the drastic step of moving Naxos of America to Franklin, Tennessee, which they felt to be a far more sensible location for a CD label, albeit classical. Franklin neighbours Nashville, which is a music town; and being situated in the centre of the US facilitated distribution of product. 'Within one day's drive we could reach 50 per cent of the population,' explains Selby. The office opened in 1998 despite some scepticism within Naxos, the Nashville environs being known far more for their country music than their classical. Actually there was the Nashville Symphony and Kenneth Schermerhorn, a conductor with whom Heymann had already worked in Hong Kong when Schermerhorn was the musical director of the Hong Kong

Philharmonic Orchestra. Furthermore, a new concert hall that would be ideal for recording was about to be built in Nashville: it was a fortunate coincidence that was to bear the fruit of many recordings in the coming years.

When Naxos of America opened its doors in Franklin, says Selby (now CEO), it represented mostly Heymann's labels: Naxos, Marco Polo, Naxos AudioBooks, as well as CPO and the affiliated Danish label Dacapo. It had an annual turnover of around $3.5 million. The target was to improve the logistics dramatically, re-establish relationships with retailers, raise the profile of the labels (especially Naxos), and increase the turnover. Ten years on, despite the most dramatic changes in market circumstances ever experienced by the music industry – the spread of digital piracy and digital sales, the consequent collapse of traditional retail outlets, and other factors – Naxos of America was becoming the leading classical distributor in the country, with a turnover of nearly $20 million, a strong reputation for its own American label, and a handsome collection of GRAMMY Awards to boot.

This extraordinary achievement was down to some far-sighted decisions made by Heymann in Hong Kong and developed by a relatively youthful US management team, au fait with technology; and the ability to innovate, which proved as important in classical music as it was in more popular genres.

Two new areas of growth emerged in the early years in Franklin. The first was commercial exploitation. 'Klaus started really pushing the concept of licensing music from the Naxos catalogue,' recalls Selby. It proved to be an area of rapid expansion, particularly because of Heymann's foresight when he set up the label in insisting that Naxos must own all the rights to its recordings. Music is constantly being licensed and used in innumerable ways: in films, television, premium giveaways, telephone switchboards, CD compilations for babies and even doctors' and dentists' surgeries. Licensing can be complicated, with many rights needing to be cleared – but not for Naxos. It became well known as a one-stop source for classical music. This developed quickly into a business that approached $1 million a year and continued to expand.

The second area of growth was musical. In 1999 Naxos of America released the first titles in its 'American Classics' series; these launched a regular release programme that presented music from all periods but specifically set out to champion the classical music of the continent. The 'American Classics' project was an ambitious attempt to establish Naxos in the US market and simultaneously bring American classical music to the world market. With Heymann aided by the producers and agents Victor and Marina Ledin and an advisory board of eminent American musicologists, the series went from strength to strength. Suddenly critics and writers were noticing the Naxos label for its musical offerings. Individual projects did not always meet with commercial success: there were quite a few recordings that did not pay their way, and in fact will never recoup their costs. But overall the series was profitable, and it was so evidently a service to American music that it reaped other benefits too. 'American Classics' put Naxos on the map in a way that budget offers and lifestyle compilations could never have done.

At the same time as there was new life in Naxos of America, market forces were beginning to challenge record labels. In 2004 Tower Records, with its 130 large shops around the country, went into Chapter 11, the start of its road to bankruptcy and closure. This had been signalled by the ever-growing size of its returns. A few large returns from Tower, a major account for Naxos of America, could prove crippling. Too great a dependence on Tower and Borders (another company that was showing early signs of suffering the bumpy retail road ahead) was extremely risky, yet paradoxically these were the easiest and most powerful routes to the core classical buyers. In common with all record labels, Naxos of America learned to dread the pallets of product arriving from these big retailers. It was also frustrating to find only too often that many of the boxes were still taped up, indicating that the CDs had never even made it onto the shop shelves: they had simply moved from the Naxos warehouse to the retailer's warehouse and back to Naxos again. The whole industry was creaking under business practices that were not sustainable for anyone, especially in this ever-changing environment. In 2006 Tower Records folded.

In the midst of this, Naxos of America was not only surviving but expanding, developing what were termed 'non-traditional outlets'. The licensing division was flourishing. In particular, in 2005, it moved strongly into the educational sector, working with important publishers such as W.W. Norton, Prentice Hall and McGraw Hill: it provided Naxos recordings to accompany text books and even went on to act as project manager for new text books, bringing in other companies as well. This was to prove an excellent revenue stream as multiple reprints brought in regular income.

Naxos of America also contributed to, and benefitted from, the success of the digital services. What had been regarded as a possible *coup de grâce* for the music industry was, by 2005, a reliable and growing source of revenue. However, the omens when digital downloads began to take off were not good. At the end of the twentieth century, digital piracy was beginning to have a serious effect on music sales and Selby was among those who wondered whether the recording industry would survive it. He was in his early thirties and familiar with technology – he knew how to download music and was aware of all the pirate sites – and he was concerned that this would be the end of the commercial viability of music. But Heymann's percipience and Selby's active interest in music in digital form was to give Naxos of America a lead over all its classical rivals.

It started in Hong Kong. By the millennium, naxos.com, based and maintained there, was already one of the most comprehensive classical record sites. As far back as 1996 Heymann had ensured that the complete back catalogues of Naxos and Marco Polo as well as the new releases were transferred into digital form, with all the necessary metadata. The complete recordings of the two labels were made available for streaming at 20 kbps, track by track and free of charge, for promotional purposes. In 2003 Apple launched its game-changer iTunes. Albeit for the US only, it was a stunning development. It was dominated by pop music but Naxos was the only classical label offering a broad range of repertoire: it had already made all its audio available digitally, so its entire catalogue had been relatively easy for iTunes to ingest. It was encouraging to see that customers of iTunes were eager to try out classical music in digital form. Naxos's prominent presence within iTunes, combined with its status as a well-known brand name in classical music, meant that it became the bestselling classical label in the store.

The growth of digital sales, Selby remembers, was staggering. 'Our first royalty cheque was $3,500, which was the equivalent profit of thousands of CDs – but for very little work. And no returns! And every month was better than the next. In those early days it grew 100 per cent month over month.'

Even though Naxos of America had all the digital files, a considerable amount of work was needed to meet the iTunes specifications. Up to this point all the digitisation within the Naxos group had taken place in Hong Kong, where naxos.com was based. With the emergence of iTunes and other US-based reputable digital outlets, it became inevitable that Naxos of America would need its own technical department to serve these digital service providers (DSPs). It was not as simple as handing over a hard drive with all the music on it: each DSP required a slightly different delivery spec. A new division was set up in Naxos of America, giving the company an important place in Naxos's digital structure. It rapidly became clear that this kind of digital-conversion-and-delivery service would be required by some of the third-party labels that Naxos of America was fast attracting for CD distribution: by 2005 it was the physical distributor for Analekta, CBC Records, Naïve and Pentatone Classics. The company was now in a position to offer this digital service to its labels, which was seen by all as a valuable part of a distributor's role in a future of declining CD sales.

Another major digital development in the early years of the twenty-first century was the label's own Naxos Music Library. This highly innovative subscription-based streaming service was being taken up by educational institutions all over the US, further enhancing the credibility of Naxos. Its reputation both as a serious classical music company and as a leading innovator in technology was confirmed. So just as Tower Records and other US retailers were under immense pressure, Naxos was already diversifying. The CD retail business remained absolutely key to the company's existence, and there were tense times as retailers went to the wall whilst holding Naxos stock (which was not always easy to retrieve); but Naxos of America was already far down the road in preparing alternative ways of reaching its customers.

By 2005 Naxos of America had a turnover of $16.5 million, $6 million of which came from physical CD sales. Another major slice came from its DVD wing. Over the previous five years, following Heymann's first foray into taking on DVD labels for international distribution, Naxos of America had become the leading distributor of classical DVDs in the US. It had Arthaus Musik, Opus Arte, TDK DVD, EuroArts and others. In fact there were one or two years when the DVD revenue exceeded the CD revenue.

Although the bricks-and-mortar retail structure of the US was collapsing, Selby was convinced that the core classical music buyers of CDs would still exist and that it was only a matter of finding where they would surface. He presumed that it would be on the Internet, and he began gearing his marketing operation towards Internet activity in the form of fan sites, blog sites and forums. NaxosDirect, a website offering directly to the consumer all the labels distributed by Naxos of America, was created. At the same time, Amazon, with its efficient services, was experiencing extraordinary growth. Amazon orders now flow in to Naxos of America every ten minutes via any one of six distribution centres around the US. Whereas in the past there could be thousands of copies of any one title sitting in stores (or unpacked in their warehouses!) around the country, fewer retail outlets now mean less excess stock – though this in turn raises other logistical challenges, such as shipping a large number of relatively small orders without any delay.

All the time that these commercial changes were taking place, the status of Naxos as a classical label was improving. 'American Classics' had made an impression in 1999, but it was relatively muted while the recordings were made in Slovakia. In 2000 Naxos issued Hanson's Symphony No. 1 'Nordic' and *Merry Mount* Suite, played by the Nashville Symphony under Kenneth Schermerhorn, and this immediately opened doors to unreserved critical acclaim. Many more recordings with the orchestra followed, including the Second Symphony of Ives, orchestral works by Chadwick, and Bernstein's *West Side Story*. Naxos increased considerably its roster of American artists to include other leading musicians, notably Marin Alsop and Leonard Slatkin.

The great and continuing success story of the GRAMMY Awards ensued. The first GRAMMY won by Naxos, in 2003, was Best Traditional World Music Album for *Sacred Tibetan Chant* sung by the monks of Sherab Ling Monastery; the recording was made by the Naxos World label, which had been started by Naxos of America. It was 2006 that saw the first classical GRAMMYs, when William Bolcom's *Songs of Innocence and of Experience*, conducted by Leonard Slatkin, won four of them. Sealing the 'respectability' of the budget label, it was a major coup for Naxos that resulted in a stronger profile and greater sales. In 2008 another title in the 'American Classics' series, Joan Tower's *Made in America, Tambor* and *Concerto for Orchestra*, won three GRAMMYs. In 2011 there was a notable success when five GRAMMY Awards came to Naxos, three for the recording of Michael Daugherty's *Deus ex Machina* and *Metropolis Symphony* played by the Nashville Symphony under Giancarlo Guerrero: Best Orchestral Performance, Best Engineered Classical Album and Best Classical Contemporary Composition (for *Deus ex Machina*, with pianist Terrence Wilson). The Parker Quartet, a young, talented New England ensemble, received its GRAMMY for Ligeti's String Quartets Nos. 1 and 2; and Paul Jacobs's recording of Messiaen's *Livre du Saint-Sacrement* won the first GRAMMY ever awarded to a solo organ recital. To date Naxos has received sixteen GRAMMY Awards, including a 'Latin' GRAMMY for piano music by Villa-Lobos.

A decade after the move to Franklin, Naxos of America had become one of the major players in classical music. By the end of 2010 it was the largest distributor of independent classical labels in the US; and in the number of CD sales it was second only to Universal (which depended upon crossover titles for its ranking). The 'American Classics' series, comprising some 360 titles, represents a major achievement; and the list of independent labels distributed (which includes one of the UK's leading labels, Chandos) is still growing. In 2010 one of the majors came into the fold for distribution: Warner Classics, comprising Warner Classics, Erato and Teldec. This became the second-highest seller on the distributor's roster after Naxos. The company remains the leading distributor of classical DVDs (it also acquired distribution rights to Jazz Icons, which proved a commercial hit).

Naxos of America is now playing a major role in Naxos's digital musical presence worldwide, liaising with the DSPs as well as managing the maintenance and continuing development of the Naxos Music Library and ClassicsOnline. The company is also responsible for the digital distribution of many independent classical labels. At the time of writing, its business is comfortably spread, with audio over 40 per cent, DVD sales touching 30 per cent, digital revenue nearly 20 per cent, and licensing 10 per cent. The US tends to lead the way in retail trends, and though Naxos of America is itself an industry leader it is also sufficiently flexible and light on its feet to accommodate change.

While business and commercial activities as well as 'American Classics' drove Naxos of America to its current position, a handful of close musical relationships were of immense benefit too.

The special association that developed between the Nashville Symphony and the Naxos label shortly after Naxos of America moved to the area in 1998 proved mutually beneficial. Both were ambitious and fast-growing companies. Alan Valentine, president and CEO of the Nashville Symphony, had recently taken over the reins when Naxos arrived, and had plans to build the orchestra into a prominent force in American music; to this end, he recognised the need for a recording series with a major international label. The orchestra's music director, Kenneth Schermerhorn, had already recorded for Naxos (*Finlandia* and other tone poems with the Slovak Radio Symphony Orchestra) and had a good relationship with Heymann. Schermerhorn had a particular interest in American music, especially the New England composers, so Nashville was an obvious place for Naxos to record some of the key works in its 'American Classics' series.

Hanson's Symphony No. 1 'Nordic' and *Merry Mount* Suite marked the beginning of the association. It was followed by Ives's Symphony No. 2 and *Robert Browning Overture*, using the new Ives critical editions; the orchestra's performance of the works in Carnegie Hall highlighted the forthcoming recording, which on its release was admired by the critics.

More than twenty discs followed over the years, covering a range of repertoire. Some of the ideas came from Heymann, such as Amy Beach's Piano Concerto and 'Gaelic' Symphony, and Bernstein's *West Side Story*. When Heymann asked the Nashville Symphony to record *West Side Story* Valentine characteristically took the idea further, joining with the Tennessee Repertory Theatre for a co-production in the city. It gave the project extra prominence and the recording itself became a Naxos bestseller. Not all the repertoire recorded in Nashville was for the 'American Classics' series; other requests from Heymann included important central classical works (such as Beethoven's *Missa solemnis*), which demonstrated the respect he had for Schermerhorn and the orchestra.

Ideas that came from the Nashville Symphony side included a disc devoted to John Corigliano (*A Dylan Thomas Trilogy* and other works), conducted by Leonard Slatkin and featuring the baritone Thomas Allen; and overtures and tone poems by Thomas Chadwick. The recording of Joan Tower's *Made in America*, sponsored by the Ford Motor Company Fund, was another special event in the Nashville Symphony's history. Coupled with *Tambor* and the *Concerto for Orchestra*, and again conducted by Leonard Slatkin, it went on to win three GRAMMY Awards in 2008.

The association between orchestra and label was given an extra boost by the opening in 2006 of the Laura Turner Concert Hall in Nashville's Schermerhorn Symphony Center, a hall that was designed to be ideal for recording; all the Nashville Symphony's Naxos discs have been made there since its opening. Alan Valentine believes it has made a real contribution to the quality of the recordings. 'You can hear the hall!' he says.

Valentine feels that the Nashville Symphony has two distinctive qualities which can be heard on all its recordings, whoever the conductor may be. One is specifically related to the performance of American music. 'The orchestra is situated

in Music City USA where lots of American music is made –
country music, R&B, a lot of pop music. When they have time,
many of our musicians play sessions as well here. This means
that they "get" the idioms of American popular culture, which
very often is fused into the music by American contemporary
composers writing for symphony orchestra. Take Leonard
Bernstein – his *West Side Story*, or *Dybbuk* and *Fancy Free* – or
Daugherty's *Metropolis*: the orchestra just gets that music
instantly. The playing is idiomatic and that comes through.

'The other thing about the orchestra is the string playing
that has developed beautifully in our new hall. It has a really
interesting quality. It was coming with that early recording of
Hanson's *Rhythmic Variations on Two Ancient Hymns*, and it
has become even more refined since.'

Valentine adds, 'The relationship between Naxos and the
Nashville Symphony has been good for both of us, but I have
to give a great deal of credit to Klaus and Naxos for the reputation we have been able to build. Frankly the incredible
trajectory of the orchestra's growth was helped by our relationship with Naxos because it sparked the imagination of our
community and our community leadership about what was
possible. Klaus has been a great partner.'

The last decade has also seen an increasing number of
recordings from two American conductors in particular, very
different in personality and style: Gerard Schwarz and JoAnn
Falletta.

For more than a quarter of a century Schwarz was music
director of the Seattle Symphony Orchestra. From that base
came numerous ground-breaking recordings, most notably
those featuring the music of William Schuman, Walter Piston
and Howard Hanson; and, through the Milken Archive of
Jewish Music, works by David Diamond and other Jewish
composers. Falletta has been music director of the Buffalo
Symphony Orchestra for more than a decade. She has, on disc
as in the concert hall, championed music by contemporary

American composers, including John Corigliano and Kenneth
Fuchs, as well as the works of Aaron Copland, Ernő Dohnányi
and Richard Strauss.

Now in his mid-sixties, Schwarz has had personal contact
with major American figures of the twentieth century, as a
trumpet player in his early years and later as a conductor. 'I'm
old enough to have been a friend of Samuel Barber and Aaron
Copland, and to have studied with Paul Creston, Milton
Babbitt, Jacob Druckman and Vincent Persichetti. Gunther
Schuller is a close friend, as was David Diamond. So when I
came to Seattle in 1985 I made a determined effort to promote
not only these composers but such masters as William
Schuman, Walter Piston and Howard Hanson, whose music at
that time was being almost completely ignored, thanks to the
rise of the avant-garde, and of serialism. Their more conservative music wasn't just neglected but actually looked down on.
It seemed people were no longer interested in the kind of well-
grounded, well-structured symphonies that Hanson wrote. It
was almost like there wasn't time for his music to gain a following because we had moved on, and become interested in
other things. Since then, though, two recording companies in
particular have made a major contribution to the fortunes of
American music. First came Delos, and now we have Naxos,
who have helped a huge amount. What Naxos is doing with
their American series is really tremendous. Fantastic. Still, what
we really need is for *everybody* to be doing it!'

For Naxos Schwarz conducted Hanson's important 1933
opera *Merry Mount* on a two-CD set, a recording based on the
performances given by the soloists and the Seattle Symphony in
1996 (the centenary of the composer's birth); he has recorded
the eight published symphonies by William Schuman, coupled
with other works, creating an important discography for the
composer; and he has recorded Piston's Symphonies Nos. 2, 4
and 6 as well as *The Incredible Flutist* and other orchestral
music.

With a total of nearly 250 recordings made over the years for a wide range of labels, Schwarz has cast his net far further than just American music. Recently he has undertaken a series of Rimsky-Korsakov recordings for Naxos. Among these works is, of course, *Sheherazade*; but he is pleased also to have conducted many lesser-known pieces, including various overtures and suites from Rimsky-Korsakov's operas. 'One album is devoted entirely to overtures, and I'm very excited about them all, quite frankly.' All these Rimsky-Korsakov recordings are played by the Seattle Symphony.

In 2009 Falletta's recording with the Buffalo Philharmonic Orchestra of music by John Corigliano – *Mr. Tambourine Man: Seven Poems of Bob Dylan* and *Three Hallucinations (from Altered States)* – won two GRAMMYs (Best Classical Vocal Performance, and Best Classical Contemporary Composition for *Mr. Tambourine Man*). The composer himself took an active producing role in the recording sessions of *Mr. Tambourine Man* at the Kleinhans Music Hall, Buffalo, New York, working with Naxos's own producer Tim Handley. Falletta went on to record Corigliano's Violin Concerto *The Red Violin* (with Michael Ludwig as soloist) and *Phantasmagoria* (a suite from his opera *The Ghosts of Versailles*), also with the Buffalo Philharmonic Orchestra. These Corigliano recordings have certainly been a highlight in the decade of association between Naxos and Falletta.

'Well, I must say first of all that throughout our association, Naxos has been just an unbelievable partner, with their continuing appetite for unusual music. They've encouraged us to seek out, discover and record all kinds of things, from an orchestral version of Schubert's 'Death and the Maiden' Quartet to a disc of orchestral music by Duke Ellington. They've opened the door to so many wonderful projects and maintained an untiring appetite for the unusual. One thing I particularly like is finding *old* works that haven't been played – Romantic repertoire that has somehow fallen through the cracks, for whatever reason. You know, people tend to think, "Well, if it were any good we would know about it already." I don't believe that. There are lots of reasons why music gets lost.'

Falletta has made two discs of Dohnányi that cover both violin concertos and *Variations on a Nursery Song*, and she has been rediscovering for Naxos the music of Josef Suk (Dvořák's son-in-law), including the Fantasy for violin and orchestra, a *tour de force* for the instrument. In April 2010 she travelled to The Netherlands to conduct a recording of Arvo Pärt's *Lamentate* for piano and orchestra. 'I was working with Ralph van Raat, a fantastic pianist who is particularly involved with new music and loves that vocabulary of sound. When we're dealing with someone like Pärt, the sound is very nuanced: it's intimate, and the vocabulary of the piano is greatly expanded by the tone colours he uses. *Lamentate*, like most of Pärt's music, is a very profound work. It has its roots in his spirituality, in his views on the pains of war, of our modern world, and the challenges that everyone faces; it deals with our individual confrontation with the pain and the tragedy that surround us, and how we make our way through that. It's not only profound, it is very beautiful music too.'

With Copland's *Prairie Journal* and *The Red Pony* Suite, Daron Hagen's opera *Shining Brow*, and works by Respighi, Jack Gallagher and Marcel Tyberg also gracing her discography, JoAnn Falletta has covered for Naxos a very wide range of music indeed.

Germany: Naxos Deutschland

The market share of classical records in Germany is the highest in Europe, at around 7.5 per cent. In a way, this makes it a particularly tough market to break into with something new: the audience is knowledgeable and experienced, but also largely traditional. The buyers know what they like. Certainly it was not an easy market for Naxos to enter. For the first six years Heymann struggled to get it away from the bargain bins in supermarkets. This may have been acceptable for the first couple of years of the budget label, but by the early 1990s Naxos had matured into a serious classical company. It desperately needed to make the move into the mainstream classical retail outlets, especially as Marco Polo, handled by the same distributor, was there too and rather uncomfortable in a cardboard bin.

One day in 1990 Chris Voll, chief salesman for a leading classical music distributor, Fono, decided he really should try out these cheap-looking CDs that he had been noticing in the bins for some time and he took two home with him. He put one in his CD player and went into another room: a distant background sample would probably serve, he thought. He became involved in something else, and it was fifteen minutes or more before he returned to that room and heard the music. He had totally forgotten what he had put on, but stood and listened. It was rather good, he concluded. He looked around for the case and was astounded to find it was a Naxos disc. He listened to the rest of it. Then he put on the second disc and was similarly impressed. Sadly, two decades later, he can't remember what the music was – but he knows he was astonished.

Shortly after this, he went to MIDEM Classique, the classical music trade fair in Cannes, for the first time. It was January 1991. He was walking through the Palais where the exhibition halls were and came across Naxos and Marco Polo. He made an appointment and met Klaus Heymann. They talked for a long time and found a lot in common, including contact with the Vox label, which had pioneered some of the ground Naxos was to tread. In the end, Voll offered to distribute Marco Polo. This was clearly a specialist label that would sit well in a company of Fono's reputation. He made no bid for Naxos because he didn't think it was available. Within two months he was distributing Marco Polo in Germany; it was scarcely more than another two months when he received a phone-call from Heymann in Hong Kong, who asked if Fono had supermarkets as its customers as well as the specialist music shops (of which there were hundreds in Germany at the time). 'Yes,' Voll replied. Heymann explained that he was seeking a replacement distributor for Naxos. Would Voll and Fono take it? 'Certainly,' said Voll. 'Ok,' said Heymann, 'you can take over next week.'

It was a big step for Naxos and for Fono. The distributor was challenged on all sides. 'We had to learn how to handle big quantities, to discuss prices, bonuses and incentives with super-market buyers,' Voll recalls. 'We were not used to this.' They also had to face prejudice from the classical world that they knew so well. 'We had to convince our serious and conservative specialist shops that "respectable" Fono hadn't made a terrible mistake taking on a label like Naxos.' Inroads were gradually made, and Naxos eventually became Fono's biggest label.

For five years Voll and his team at Fono worked on Naxos, before the growing strength of the label and the necessity of a change in distribution policy suggested a fresh direction. Klaus Heymann decided to form his own sales, marketing and distri-bution company, Naxos Deutschland. On 1 January 1997 Chris Voll, as managing director, opened the doors of the new company in Münster with a small team of three, including Ludger Diekamp as marketing manager. A former key member of the EMI team, Diekamp was a well-known figure in Germany's classical recording scene. These two were to direct the Naxos fortunes in Germany for the next fifteen years. With a four-man sales team, all ex-Fono, Voll set out to establish Naxos more firmly in Germany. 'Naxos was only one label in Fono. By calling our company Naxos Deutschland we were demonstrating the particular commitment to the label.' Nevertheless it was joined from the start by a small group of independent German labels, including Hänssler Classic and Preiser Records. It was, appropriately, the tenth year of Naxos.

The first campaign was intended to make an impact, and it

did. Voll and Diekamp designed a series of ten 'limited edition' five-CD boxed sets of popular and useful compilations. They were stamped 'Jubilee' to mark Naxos's first decade and included Beethoven's complete symphonies, Chopin's solo piano music, Vivaldi's most important concertos, and a set of classical guitar works. They were offered at a very low price, and some of them sold more than 100,000 units. The concept was so popular that there was clearly a strong demand after the year was up, and Voll told dealers that the offer would be extended to one more order per retailer. Large orders came in but the demand continued ... Voll admits that some of the sets are still available and sell to this day.

This campaign was followed by other ideas, such as the 'Trio' series: three original CDs in an attractive German-language slipcase (Albinoni's oboe concertos, Beethoven's piano concertos and *Festliche Barocktrompete*, for example). There were forty titles in the series, with the slogan '3 CDs for the price of 2': it is an overworked marketing tactic now but it was unheard of in the late 1990s, certainly in classical music. Some of them sold 50,000 units in Germany alone. Then there was the enormous success – mirrored throughout all the main Naxos territories – of *The A–Z of Classical Music*, in a German version, with one CD and a booklet of 1,000 pages. It was more of a gamble in Germany because there was the added expense of translating it; nevertheless it sold more than 250,000 units at an extremely competitive price (just a few pence above the manufacturing cost). For Naxos Deutschland it was as much a marketing tool with a small profit margin as a genuine product for sale.

The success of all these initiatives underpinned the growing presence of Naxos in the shops, and prompted such spectacular in-store presenters as the huge acrylic Naxos pyramid. Behind them all was the hard graft of establishing Naxos as a respected classical label in Germany. 'Our motto was: "Hohe Qualität – niedriger Preis" [High Quality – Low Price].' It was branded on all the displays, and low price it certainly was. When Fono took on Naxos, it sold each CD for DM9.90. When Naxos Deutschland started, the price continued. When, in January 2002, the euro was introduced, Naxos Deutschland kept the price low: €4.99. But it simply couldn't make a reasonable profit margin, and a year later raised it to €5.99. Other Naxos distributors in Europe and elsewhere raised prices as well, but few met with the kind of resistance that emerged in Germany. The big supermarkets said they would refuse to carry Naxos, and prepared to return all the stock. The independent sector was already in decline, and it now encountered opposition from customers who felt betrayed. Naxos Deutschland experienced much the same response. 'We had so many postcards from individuals saying that they had been a great fan of Naxos and had 180 CDs or more in their collections, but now they were going to say goodbye.'

On the positive side it was an indication of the success of the 'High Quality – Low Price' branding; but at the same time it was extremely difficult to turn those attitudes around. Voll started with the big shops. He realised that their main concern was not the price rise in itself but that the increase would start a price war on the high street. He prevented that by exercising judicious diplomacy, and no one undercut the suggested price. As for the record collectors themselves, time and the continuing expansion of the label healed the wounds. 'People were *very* sensitive about it,' Voll declares. It was a hard-learned lesson, and the price of a Naxos CD in Germany remains €5.99.

The label had in fact become too important for the collectors to ignore or sidestep. The special boxed sets appealed to one end of the market; but at the other end, collectors welcomed new recordings of German orchestras that were initiated by Naxos Deutschland, especially the Cologne Chamber Orchestra (with releases such as *Römische Weihnacht, Barocke Kostbarkeiten, Telemann: Darmstädter Ouvertüren* and *Mozart: Heitere Serenaden*) and the Leipzig Chamber

Orchestra. There were further specialist titles from Naxos Deutschland specifically for its market. These even encompassed a spoken-word series by musicologist Dr Stefan Straub containing explanations of classical music interpolated with music extracts: there was a discussion on the role of sonata form in Beethoven's piano music, a consideration of musical architecture, and a study of Shostakovich.

Naxos Deutschland's turnover peaked in the first years of the new millennium in a similar way to that of other European Naxos distributors. The market became tougher. Rivals appeared, some of very poor quality (including one called 'Nexus'); but they were no more than a temporary threat. The tactics of the major companies could not always be brushed aside so easily, for Germany was a prime classical battlefield and they were prepared to pour in considerable resources. Voll saw off more than he can remember, but one or two had some success and the competition is ongoing. The majors had some great advantages, including big-name artists from their back catalogues whom they could recycle, and the market strength to make special deals with record shops (involving pop as well as classical). Naxos could not compete specifically in either area. Instead Voll made the most of the growing repertoire base and the availability of a huge catalogue.

The issue of the CD boom, which also peaked at this time, was playing its part. When classical CD sales began to drop, the shops that sold them closed by the score, and, although online mail-ordering grew, the browsing-to-buy habit diminished. At the same time, download sales began slowly to make an impact, and other competitors surfaced.

However, there had appeared a new opportunity to promote classical music: DVDs. One day in 1999 Voll went into Diekamp's office and overheard a telephone conversation regarding the distribution of classical DVDs. Arthaus Musik, an important film and DVD company, was looking for a distributor for its classical DVDs. Voll went to see them and said he believed that Naxos Deutschland, with its specialist classical distribution and knowledge, was in a better position to look after the product than the film distributors they were currently with. They were persuaded and, after a conversation with Heymann, who saw a global opportunity, they gave world distribution rights to Naxos. The approach paid off. A few months later, Voll was approached by other major classical DVD labels, including EuroArts, asking if Naxos would take them on too. Naxos Deutschland was in a prime position to benefit from the rapid growth of the medium and became the absolute market leader in this field. By the end of 2010 DVD sales had grown to nearly 30 per cent of physical sales in Naxos Deutschland.

Since 2008 Naxos Deutschland has concentrated on sales, marketing and press, and the development of musical projects, leaving physical distribution to NGL.

In the twenty years since Voll first distributed Naxos, the German classical record market has changed beyond all recognition. Most sales now go through three big chains (which sell mainly electrical goods) and two big Internet retailers. There are scarcely forty specialist classical dealers left. Curiously, downloads have been quite slow to take off in Germany and they currently make up less than 5 per cent of classical music sales: it seems that Germans like their CDs too much! With this kind of diminished retail face, marketing and press become crucial for a distributor in providing information that a collector or potential buyer can browse. Despite all these changes, Naxos Deutschland has played a key role in establishing the label in the heart of Europe.

The Nordic Countries: Naxos Sweden

Naxos Sweden, led by Håkan Lagerqvist and Mats Byrén, made a special contribution to the development of Naxos in Scandinavia and the Nordic region through a series of bold, innovative television campaigns in the 1990s. These resulted in some exceptional sales, took classical music to a whole new public, and established the brand of Naxos as the most popular and well known in Sweden, with a dominant market share. Now, with some 300 classical labels in addition to Naxos on its distribution roster, Naxos Sweden as a distributor commands a remarkable 85 per cent share of the classical recording market in terms of units. Furthermore, it oversees distribution of these labels in the other Nordic countries via the sister companies Naxos Denmark, Naxos Norway and FG Naxos in Finland: it is the pre-eminent classical network in the whole area.

None of this could have been predicted in 1989 when Viva, a small Swedish Christian music distributor, agreed to represent Naxos in the country. Neither Lagerqvist nor Byrén, forming the sales team assigned to look after the label, had more than a cursory knowledge of classical music and they found the task challenging at the start. Lagerqvist remembers the two of them sitting with the catalogue, trying to prepare the first purchase order. 'We knew the name of Bach, so we thought perhaps we should order ten or fifteen of a title. But we had little idea about most of the names in the catalogue and really didn't know what to order.' Despite those shaky beginnings, Naxos was distributed by Viva for the next three years until the company ran into difficulties and closed in 1993. Klaus Heymann immediately invited Lagerqvist and Byrén to set up Naxos Sweden, which would focus on the Naxos label but also provide a distribution service for other independent classical companies. Based in Örebro, a town 200 km from Stockholm, it began in June 1993 with five employees. Within two years the classical market share of Naxos in terms of units jumped from 10 per cent to 65 per cent.

'We were profitable from the start, but the challenge was getting Naxos established in the large retailers and classical specialists,' explains Lagerqvist. Time and again, he and his team ran into overt prejudice against the label because of its Eastern European orchestras, conductors and instrumentalists. The buyers in shops were just too lofty to accept it. 'We found it difficult to break into the classical specialist stores and we therefore decided to put together a totally different strategy.' This was an 'authorised Naxos retailer' network, offering one retailer in each town exclusivity and special terms on three conditions: 1. That Naxos was racked separately; 2. That the whole catalogue was stocked; 3. That all new titles would be taken on a subscription basis. The bigger cities often had two or three authorised Naxos retailers, but each would have its own area to cover. It was established quite quickly. The next step was the development of a special four-CD boxed set, *Best of Naxos*, a popular compilation sold at a competitive price. Naxos Sweden then took out one full-page advertisement in the biggest national newspaper and carried the complete list of authorised Naxos stockists. Within a short time 20,000 sets had been sold – an exceptional result for a classical product – and they had made such an impact that independent classical shops and the classical departments in the big music stores could no longer ignore the label. By 1994 Naxos was being stocked by the bigger retailers, while the authorised ones were kept happy with special terms. Naxos Sweden was accumulating a tidy profit but Heymann and Lagerqvist decided to invest it straight back into the business and go for a larger share of the classical market. 'Klaus was very inspiring and supportive at this early stage and he was prepared to take a risk,' says Lagerqvist.

The following move certainly was a risk: a nationwide television advertising campaign, the first classical music campaign of its kind in the country. 'We invested all of our marketing budget in this one venture. The idea was to make an enormous impact,' Lagerqvist recalls. It worked. Terrestrial commercial television had recently started in Sweden, and Lagerqvist and his team, not being traditional classical distributors who were set in their ways, saw this as an obvious route. 'I saw the market as a triangle. The top 5 per cent were the knowledge-able classical consumers who knew their classical music. The next band, 25 per cent, were those who knew a little bit, maybe had one or two classical CDs in their collection. (I was like that. I remember as a teenager buying Vivaldi's *Four Seasons*, taking it home and listening to it all the way through, rather frustrated, because I was waiting for the one tune I knew in it. When I found it I was happy.) The largest band at the base of the triangle were the 70 per cent who knew nothing about clas-sical music. Obviously this was the best sector to aim at. How could we tempt this group of people to buy a classical CD set? We only had to ask ourselves the question: what would tempt *us*? We believed that everyone would like a bit of classical music and we had a slogan: "Everybody Loves Classical Music". It is all about helping people to find what they love.'

The product was a three-CD boxed set called *Klassiska Favoriter*. It was October 1994. For the thirty-second adver-tisement, Naxos Sweden developed a simple story. The scene was a noisy, colourful, chaotic children's party: the children had faces painted as animals, and the parents were struggling to keep it all together. The scene was then transformed into a painting of an idyllic paradise scene, with Adam and Eve sur-rounded by animals, and gentle classical music warmed the picture. Within months, the set sold 100,000 units. Fortunate timing meant that it peaked at Christmas. It was elected Christmas Present of the Year by the national TV news and it entered the overall top-selling music chart at position one, where it remained for three weeks. To date it has sold more than 330,000 units and it still sells a few thousand each year. For a young company, run by people with little classical music knowledge, it was an astounding success. As the cash tills were ringing, Naxos Sweden was preparing its second television campaign, which was very different though no less bold.

'Having opened the classical doors for the first time for

many people, we felt we should educate them a little, and we came up with the idea of a CD of specially recorded Swedish classical music played by the Helsingborg Symphony Orchestra.' The composers included Stenhammar, Söderman, Larsson, Alfvén and Peterson-Berger. They were not household names; and it was a one-CD set, so the revenue per sale was much smaller. In the event, the high cost of the TV advertisement could not be justified – not in simple financial terms. *Svenska Klassiska Favoriter*, released in spring 1995, sold 150,000 copies, which was impressive given the repertoire but hardly sufficient to recoup the marketing costs. Lagerqvist acknowledges that it may not even have paid its way to date. The benefit was in the exposure gained by the Naxos brand: its dedication to music, notably Swedish music, was broadcast far and wide. This was beyond the simple balancing of books and would pay dividends in the future. Undaunted, the company launched its third TV-promoted album – *Klassiska Favoriter*, Vol. 2 – in the autumn of 1995. The theme was an off-the-wall concept concerning a monkey, but it worked. This also sold 150,000 copies though the income was better as it was a three-CD set. It was followed a year later by *Klassiska Favoriter Opera*, which sold 120,000 copies and, in common with all these sets, continues to sell well.

In 1997 Naxos Sweden decided to change tack and approached the lifestyle market, with spectacular success. *Lugna Blå Timmar* ('Blue Hours'), a three-CD compilation of music suitable for 'blue moods', with a stylish cover, was the subject of a Nordic-wide television campaign and has reached sales of 300,000 worldwide. Other campaigns followed, but the company's marketing activities were not wholly based around TV advertising. A Christmas disc made in 1996 with the Göteborgs Domkyrkas Gosskör, a boys' choir, sold 40,000 copies with no TV advertisement and entered high in the overall top-selling music chart. This proved too much for the classical establishment. 'The majors who controlled the top-selling chart made a new price rule so that Naxos CDs could only be seen on the classical mid-price chart, which of course had only a small exposure and circulation. I guess they were thinking: if they can't beat them, restrict them,' says Lagerqvist. It was petty, and too late. Market research conducted by a Swedish university showed that by the end of the 1990s Naxos was the most well-known classical brand in the country. And if people didn't identify the brand itself, classical music still meant to them *Klassiska Favoriter*. The commitment to television had worked. What's more, those who knew the Naxos brand were ten years younger than the average classical music buyer.

The 1990s were peak years of growth for Naxos Sweden. In 1998, five years after the company had begun, the number of employees had tripled and the turnover had more than quadrupled. As in other territories it coincided with the CD boom and it was impossible to sustain in terms of CD sales. However, the company was also initiating more and more recordings of Scandinavian music. With the help of a classical music advisor, Lars Johansson (a former retailer), it put forward an increased number of recording proposals to Heymann and made nearly fifty recordings over the years. Prominent among these has been the Swedish Chamber Orchestra: its performance of symphonies by Joseph Martin Kraus, the 'Swedish Mozart', won a Cannes Classical Award at MIDEM Classique in 1999. Behind these special projects, Naxos Sweden was proving adept at the month-by-month release and distribution of Naxos and Marco Polo and the steady promotion of the rapidly expanding catalogues.

In addition to all this Naxos activity, the company was becoming the leading distributor of classical independent labels, both home-grown and foreign. Virtually all the independents from the Nordic countries, UK, France, Germany and even the US were looking to Örebro for their foothold in Sweden. Among them were BIS from Sweden, Hyperion (the first major independent label to join Naxos Sweden, in 1997) and Chandos from the UK, Harmonia Mundi and Naïve from France, ECM from Germany, Telarc from the US; and all the most important classical DVD labels. The dominance of Naxos Sweden was made possible by the majors' decision to withdraw from the field. (A majority of the majors themselves eventually decided to consolidate into one distribution network.) Naxos Sweden's list encompasses jazz, folk, Christian music and pop music as well as classical.

The changing face of classical recording made the first decade of this century a testing period for distributors in countries with small populations, and this was especially true of those in the Nordic region. Some kind of conglomeration was inevitable, though a clear route was not obvious in the beginning. The four countries of Sweden, Denmark, Norway and Finland have different languages and different traditions. For most of the twentieth century they had all sustained their own distribution networks, representing many of the same labels. (The very first distributor of Naxos in Europe, signed in 1987 by Heymann, was actually Olga Musik in Denmark, run by Birger Hansen.) Increasingly, because of the strength of Naxos, Lagerqvist was travelling around the region to advise and see how they could work together more closely, initially in the distribution and promotion of Naxos products but also in other areas, including logistics and even marketing. The natural drop in CD sales was not being compensated by a growth in the digital medium, at least not in commercial terms: the notorious success of The Pirate Bay (an illegal file-sharing website) created specific problems for Sweden and the Nordic area as a whole. Classical music suffered less than pop and other genres from piracy, but it was affected. (Such was the spread of The Pirate Bay's operation that the day on which the four key personalities involved were found guilty of assistance to copyright infringement, and given one-year prison sentences, Internet usage in Sweden decreased by 40 per cent.)

Heymann found that if he wanted reliable distribution in the

Nordic region, he had to dip into his pocket and invest in the independent companies that had distributed his labels in the 1990s. One by one, they became Naxos companies: FG Naxos in Finland had already been formed in 1995, and was followed by Naxos Denmark in 2002 and Naxos Norway in 2011. There was a growing benefit in consolidation. It was clearly no longer sustainable for each country to have its own warehouse and stock many independent labels, most of which were small. The Naxos Sweden warehouse in Örebro is now the central Nordic warehouse, and the Naxos offices in the individual territories provide mainly sales and marketing functions. The problems of language have been overcome: English links them all.

Naxos Sweden has grown and changed in other areas. In recent years it has been acquiring Nordic labels. These include Proprius, Prophone, Swedish Society and the Finnish label Ondine. 'We don't know how long the CD will be with us, and the importance is to have material rights, to have something to distribute in whatever format people may want,' says Lagerqvist. He sees a new, extended role for Naxos Sweden: as a service provider to classical labels. 'To our 300 labels we offer distribution, sales and marketing, but also we can help with product development, manufacture, artwork, digitisation, advice on recordings – even help with contracts.'

Although Naxos Sweden started with a strong Naxos focus, the label now accounts for only 25 per cent of its overall business. The company is crucial for Naxos itself because it is the distributor for the region, but Naxos Sweden has extended its activities beyond distribution. It has had to do this because it is apparent that it will take some years for the decline in CD sales to be matched by digital growth. The Naxos Music Library has secured a good foothold in academic institutions and public libraries – Sweden has perhaps the highest number of subscribers per capita – but, as yet, download sales are far from achieving a serious level.

Naxos Japan

It was ironic that although Japan was so much a part of Naxos right from the start – through the playing of Takako Nishizaki – it proved extremely difficult for the label to find a foothold in the country itself. This was partly because Japan was very traditional in its attitude to classical music, and put its trust mainly in the big stars marketed by the majors, such as Karajan or Solti, or figures of the past, such as Furtwängler or Toscanini. The very concept of a budget classical CD label was something of an anathema for Japanese collectors. So for the first years of Naxos, Heymann found no distributor willing to take it on.

Finally, in 1991, it was Heymann's brother-in-law Atsushi Nishizaki who stepped into the breach. He left his job in television and started Ivy, a distribution company based in the family's home town of Nagoya. It was not an easy job. Of course there was significant consumer prejudice to combat, but first of all he had to face the cartel that existed in classical distribution: even now there is one main organisation that dominates the distribution of classical recordings to record shops. In the end Nishizaki had to circumvent this standard route and distribute Naxos to the shops directly from his warehouse in Nagoya.

The next hurdle was gaining acceptance from the classical magazines, where again the label faced prejudice. The leading review magazine, *Record Geijutsu*, declined to carry reviews for some years, even when Naxos CDs were stocked in the main record stores, including both the HMV and Tower chains, and most of the Japanese chains and specialist stores. Nevertheless the prejudice of consumers began to dissipate: the public voted with its purse, and, as the decade rolled by, Naxos gained greater prominence in the stores. It didn't attain 'white wall' status as in other countries, but this was largely because most CD racking in Japan caused the CDs to be displayed side-on rather than face-out. Throughout the 1990s the Naxos presence in most record shops grew significantly. Most magazines could eventually no longer ignore the trend, and they started reviewing the label.

Sales were not bad as the new millennium approached, but Heymann realised that they were not heading for the level that he felt should be attained, despite the diligent work by Nishizaki (who had now been joined in the business by his son Hiroshi). Having seen the success of Naxos's special 'national' recording programmes, Heymann decided it was time to start 'Japanese Classics'. The ancient Japanese music traditions of *gagaku* (the court music) and performance of music for instruments such as the *shakuhachi* or *koto* still continued; but the Westernisation of Japan from the start of the twentieth century had extended to music, and there were several Japanese composers who chose to write in a Western symphonic style. Most of them were known only by name and their works were rarely heard in concert. With the help of one of the leading experts in this field, Morihide Katayama, a series of key orchestral works were chosen to be recorded. In 2002 'Japanese Classics' was born with the release of *Japanese Orchestral Favourites* (composers included Yuzo Toyama and Akira Ifukube) and it was to change the perception of Naxos in Japan. The CD was praised by reviewers in Japanese magazines. Mamoru Shima of *Stereo Sound* wrote, 'This ambitious project will introduce our cultural heritage to the world. To be honest, it's a shame that this is produced by an overseas company, but I assure you that it achieves a perfect ten in music, performance and sound. I hope that many people will enjoy this special gift.' Yuji Ito from *CD Journal* wrote along the same lines, adding, 'We can do no more than bow our heads to Naxos.'

It was followed in 2003 by the Violin Concerto and other works of Hiroshi Ohguri, played by the violinist Kazuhiro Takagi and the Osaka Philharmonic Orchestra conducted by

Tatsuya Shimono. This was recorded in the Osaka Philharmonic Hall and produced by Andrew Walton. At the beginning of 2004 a CD was released of orchestral works by Kôsçak Yamada, who was the first Japanese composer to write in a symphonic style (his Overture, which was a world-premiere recording on the CD, was written in 1912). By this time, the coverage given to 'Japanese Classics' had attracted such a broad public that in the same year a poll by a magazine found that Naxos was suddenly the second most respected classical label in Japan – second only to Deutsche Grammophon! It was a remarkable accolade.

The 'Japanese Classics' series has never sold in any real quantities internationally, but the sales in Japan alone were more than sufficient to recoup the investment. *Japanese Orchestral Favourites* has sold nearly 50,000 units, Tōru Takemitsu's *Toward the Sea* and other works has sold over 40,000, and many more have achieved figures in the region of 15,000. Even though a few of the twenty-five titles have only reached 10,000, the series established the whole catalogue in Japan. This meant, too, that *Record Geijutsu* took notice of the label, though after all these years the monthly magazine has never given Naxos a cover feature.

By 2007, having established Naxos firmly in the Japanese classical market, the Nishizaki family was ready to retire and to close Ivy. Since 2005 the Naxos digital and licensing business had been handled by Naxos Digital Japan, which was a Tokyo-based joint venture started by Klaus Heymann and Ryuichi Sasaki (an executive with an IT background). This company now took over the physical distribution of the Naxos label and became Naxos Japan. It had already been successful in the digital arena: the Naxos Music Library had found favour with an amazing number of individual subscribers in addition to educational institutions. To date, there are more individual subscribers to the NML in Japan than in the rest of the world put together. Already in the habit of listening to and downloading music on their phones, the

Japanese subscribers particularly welcomed the NML iPhone and Android applications.

Income from Naxos Japan is now divided into three equal areas: NML subscriptions, licensing (for games, publishing and other ventures), and physical sales. The CD is still very much alive in Japan; and with the initial plans for 'Japanese Classics' largely complete, Naxos is looking to a collaboration on new recordings with the Tokyo University of Fine Arts and Music.

Australia: Select Audio-Visual Distribution

For the first fifteen years, Naxos was distributed in Australia by independent companies – notably Sonart, which was managed by Les Hodge. Over a decade and more, he was responsible for establishing Naxos in Australia. In 2003 the sales, marketing and distribution operation was taken over by Heymann: a new company, Select Audio-Visual Distribution (SAVD), was formed, which was based in Sonart's former premises in Sydney. Six months later, Andrew McKeich, a veteran of the Australian classical record scene, having run his own label and worked for other companies, joined as managing director.

There are circumstances unique to Australia that present their own challenges to a company importing and distributing classical labels, even when, as with SAVD, it is the largest of its kind in the country. In common with other Naxos-owned distribution companies it represents many of the top independent labels (especially from the European market) as well as the Naxos labels. However, Australia is a large country with a small population, distant from classical music centres in Europe and the US, which means that rather different conditions prevail: there remains a healthy classical music retail sector, more so than in most developed countries, with some fine specialist stores. At the same time, Australian-based mail-order firms are few and far between, and downloads have yet to become a significant area of the business.

As McKeich points out, it is a highly competitive market for a label such as Naxos, with generally low retail prices for back-catalogue CDs, a growing list of other budget labels, and a state-run record label, ABC Classics, which releases and strongly supports Australian classical music on disc. There is also the increasing issue of importing through amazon.com (and even amazon.co.uk): when the Australian dollar is strong it can be economically beneficial, even factoring in postage, for consumers to order from the US.

When McKeich took over, the priority was to revive the distribution and general standing of Naxos in Australia, which had diminished in the last years of Sonart: retailers had lost faith in the efficient supply of Naxos CDs. The huge back catalogue was still in demand, especially for leading titles such as *Peter and the Wolf* (read by the Australian Barry Humphries) and Holst's *The Planets*. In addition, there was always interest from classical collectors in the new releases. In order to reach a wider audience, and counterbalance the specialist nature of these new releases, McKeich and his team developed with considerable success a range of popular compilations. *The Ultimate Opera Album* was a two-CD set containing many of the most popular arias, choruses, overtures and orchestral interludes from 400 years of the genre; but the masterstroke was the cover. 'We decided to go against the contemporary practice and we boldly put a large, traditional Wagnerian soprano on the front.' He was appealing to a particularly Australian type of humour and he clearly understood it because the set sold in the thousands. Five years on it was still a bestseller in the shop of the Sydney Opera House. After several months it was joined by *Extreme Classics*: a two-CD set of the best loud and aggressive sounds in classical music, beginning with Tchaikovsky's *1812* overture. This was another sales success.

McKeich brought these and other compilations together with a commercial television campaign called 'Experience the

Classics – all the classical music you will ever need', which resulted in strong sales. Other labels decided to follow suit, which forced the SAVD marketing initiatives to move into other areas, including the more precise targeting of collectors. The mass market for low-price classical CDs is still there, believes McKeich, but online discounting, parity with the US dollar, and the ease of purchasing abroad have caused a decline, and no one in this business can rest on his laurels.

As did other Naxos distribution companies, SAVD benefitted from the rise of the classical DVD. McKeich comments, 'As collectors found they have enough audio in their collections, they have been turning to visual material. The market seems more receptive now to opera and ballet DVD productions, even though they are usually higher priced than movie DVDs.' As for the digital market, although classical downloads are not making a significant impact in Australia, the Naxos Music Library has been established in educational institutions.

The strength of the Naxos position, once again, is that it is the house label of its national distributor: at around 35 per cent of SAVD's sales, Naxos is in pole position in the company. Even so, it is only part of the distributor's infrastructure: the broad base of SAVD is its safety net.

Naxos Far East

The strong interest in Western classical music in the Far East can be seen by the number of fine musicians coming from China, Japan, South Korea and neighbouring countries, and this is reflected in classical CD sales: there is a healthy market on Naxos's own doorstep. It has never been an easy market, however: Hong Kong is relatively small and the sale of CDs and DVDs into China has been bedevilled by piracy. Even a budget label such as Naxos can produce a profit for those determinedly engaged in illegal copying. On the other hand, limited quantities of regular CDs are imported by the China

National Publications Import and Export Corporation. Naxos has also been able to license some of its books, together with the accompanying CDs, to publishing companies in China.

Rick Heymann, Klaus Heymann's son, has run Naxos Far East since 2008. He specifically looks after Hong Kong, China, Taiwan, Singapore, Malaysia and Thailand; and, being able to speak the language, he regularly visits Japan, where he is on the board of Naxos Japan. Naxos Far East represents forty labels in addition to the Naxos group, including many of the main classical DVD labels (Arthaus Musik, Opus Arte, EuroArts and C Major). On DVD, concerts sell better than operas, perhaps because few DVDs offer Chinese subtitles; and Blu-ray is growing steadily. Among the CD labels distributed by Naxos Far East are Harmonia Mundi, BIS, Challenge Classics, OehmsClassics, Hänssler Classic and Audite.

'The market for audiophile labels in Hong Kong and China is huge, which is why First Impression Music and Reference Recordings are our top labels in revenue terms,' explains Rick Heymann. 'We get some very good orders for audiophile recordings, usually from our China partners. The number of rich people is increasing rapidly in China, and they are looking for ways to spend their money. So, they buy hi-fi equipment worth US$20,000 to US$60,000 in some cases, and purchase these audiophile CDs from us. These are people who buy cables that cost US$1,000-plus for their hi-fi equipment!'

The CD market is quite stable in Hong Kong. 'iTunes is not here yet, and there are no really successful download sites. Core classics, compilations and boxed sets sell well here and in Asia in general: boxed sets do especially well in Taiwan. As much as 99.9 per cent of our sales come from CD shops – we get very few mail-order requests. As in many countries, CD shops can no longer sustain their business by only selling CDs, and they are carrying other products: DVDs, video games, iPhone accessories, T-shirts and books. But we are also doing more with concert sales in Hong Kong and China.'

The bestselling titles in the Far East continue to be those of Rick Heymann's mother, Takako Nishizaki, whose star status in Hong Kong ensures continued popularity for all her CD and DVD recordings, particularly the violin concerto by Chen and He, *The Butterfly Lovers*.

Naxos Korea

The Naxos presence in South Korea is rather unusual. The physical side of the business (CDs and DVDs) is handled by an independent distribution company, Aulos Media; but the major source of revenue comes from Naxos Korea ('Naxos Global Distribution, Korea'), established in 2004 initially to sell Naxos's range of digital services and subsequently also to license Naxos recordings to all kinds of media. The company was the idea of Kai Czepiczka, who was born and educated in Germany. He studied German literature but in his twenties he became deeply interested in classical music and started collecting CDs. He has lived in Seoul, South Korea since 1994, and he used to teach in universities – until he met Klaus Heymann, as he explains:

'Around 1995 or 1996 I was looking for ten Marco Polo CDs at retail shops in Seoul but was told by the staff of the shop that they don't have them on stock and I should come back next week. This continued for a couple of months but the CDs never arrived. So I sent an email to Naxos in Hong Kong asking why it was not possible to purchase Marco Polo CDs in Seoul. I wrote to an address such as info@naxos.com or customer service – I don't remember – but it was not an address of a named individual. To my surprise I received an email from Klaus Heymann himself! He told me he was going to be on a business trip in Seoul a week later and I could tell him which CDs I wanted. I sent him the list and he told me to meet him at his hotel in Seoul. He gave me the CDs (for which I paid him in cash) and he invited me for a tea because he was curious about me as a customer and about the general retail situation in Seoul. So we talked for a while and later kept in contact. I told him that he was welcome to contact me whenever he had questions about the situation in Korea and he did this a couple of times. Many years later, in 2003, I was getting tired of my job at the university and I read that Naxos was looking for staff to hire in Hong Kong. So I sent an email to Klaus and asked him if he would be interested in setting up a Naxos branch in Seoul. After I sent him my business plan he agreed and I founded Naxos Korea in February 2004. Ironically, if I had had the chance to purchase the Marco Polo CDs from the shop eight years before, and if Klaus didn't look after this individual customer in the way he did, Naxos Korea wouldn't exist today.

'In 2004 Naxos was already working with distributors in Korea and had introduced the digital services, such as the Naxos Music Library, as well. As Korea has always been one of the countries with the best IT infrastructure [it has had perhaps the best broadband network in the world for quite some time and Wi-Fi is more widespread than in any other country], I focused on the digital business first. There was no reason to put the distributor out of business and they already had a distribution network for physical products. But the new, digital business promised a lot of opportunities. We started with selling NML, NSWL and later NML Jazz and finally the new NVL. We then also added licensing and the business with local DSPs [download service providers]. The business developed very well: in 2004 I started on my own from scratch and now we are four very busy people.'

Naxos Korea licenses Naxos recordings and texts to many different kinds of companies. Some of the more unusual deals have included: preloading tracks on mobile phones; preloading tracks on GPS systems; licensing video content to IP-TV operators; and setting up an educational music-streaming service with KBS (Korean Broadcasting System), the leading broadcaster in South Korea. The Naxos Music Library has also been sold very successfully: most Korean university libraries, and practically all those with music departments, now have subscriptions.

'It's an exciting business and often I feel that we are the only classical music company in Korea which is looking into the future with optimism,' says Czepiczka. 'The digital business moves forward very fast and we are lucky to have the content and (by now) the experience to run a successful business.'

France: Abeille Musique (an independent)

Naxos does not have its own distribution company in France and has relied on a series of local distributors. It is true to say that France has consistently proven one of the most challenging countries in Europe for the label, ever since its dramatic start.

Hypermarket chains in France sparked the very beginning of Naxos in 1987, with the opening spectacular order from a Hong Kong purchasing company, Fargo, of up to 5,000 units per title of the initial thirty-CD catalogue. They sold by the box-load. It was a dream start for Heymann. But the long-term future of Naxos in France was more of a nightmare. Yves Riesel, founder of Abeille Musique, a leading independent distributor which now represents Naxos in France, remembers that the concept of a budget classical label with serious ambitions was a contradiction in terms for French classical record buyers. He was a classical collector at the time, and knew and admired Marco Polo for its adventurous repertoire. In 1989 he began to work with Media 7, a distributor of pop music that was keen to get into classical, and he started to bring foreign independent classical labels to Media 7, such as Testament and Chandos. Marco Polo was already on the distributor's list, but he was more nervous about Naxos. 'The cultural set in France love to be pretentious and they understood full-price labels. But Naxos is completely unpretentious and I knew it would be a real battle to wipe out the early reputation in France of Naxos as a cheap, worthless, budget label only fit for supermarket shelves. However, it is my pleasure to fight with people who are pretentious.'

In the autumn of 1990 Media 7 agreed to take on Naxos. Virgin had just launched its first French store in the Champs-Élysées and wanted to stock Naxos exclusively. Riesel felt that this would be too restrictive and he persuaded the company to take 3,000 units of fifty selected titles to be repackaged on a label that would be exclusive to it, Espoir Classique. The name was chosen because the Berlin Wall had recently fallen, along with the Iron Curtain, and there was a new hope in the air (and Naxos had many Eastern European orchestras!). After Riesel reached a complicated but very quick agreement with Hong Kong, Espoir Classique was born and had French liner notes. The Virgin promotion went very well and was extended to other French stores that opened shortly afterwards.

Riesel's main task, however, was to establish the Naxos brand, and the task was difficult because of the label's history in France. He felt unable to go straight into the classical departments of record shops, to say simply that he was representing the label and here was the catalogue, because most of them would immediately reject any proposition that involved 'the supermarket label'. So he used a sleight of hand, offering a selected list of recordings that involved players who were already known and respected for a few recordings on Hungaroton or Sony (including the Kodály Quartet and the pianist Stefan Vladar). Riesel simply listed them on the new-release information without mentioning the record label. He used other similar devices to push recordings without revealing their provenance, and it worked. Dealers were interested in them and placed orders. When the CDs were delivered to their shops and they saw the Naxos name, they rang Riesel and claimed they had never ordered them. He told them they had: they could return the CDs, of course, but now that they had them, why didn't they give them a chance? Most dealers did, the CDs sold, and Naxos began a new life.

With bold, deft campaigns of this kind, Naxos began to find a foothold in France. French repertoire also helped. Releases such as the CD of violin sonatas by Saint-Saëns, Debussy, Ravel and Poulenc played by Dong-Suk Kang and Pascal Devoyon began to make Naxos more acceptable to French collectors and the general public. A giant stride was made when, to the surprise of everyone, the boxed set of Prokofiev's Piano Concertos Nos. 1–5, played by Kun Woo Paik with the Polish National Radio Symphony Orchestra conducted by Antoni Wit, won a Diapason d'Or. That was in the spring of 1992, and in the winter of the same year it was named *Diapason*'s Record of the Year. From now on, Naxos could no longer be dismissed as purely a budget label that sold for under fifty francs. Heymann came to France to give interviews and promote the label, and Riesel's efforts to make Naxos respectable were gaining ground.

Riesel started a special French Naxos label. It was called Naxos Patrimoine. He knew that on Marco Polo there were many attractive but rare recordings of French music, by composers such as André Caplet, Félicien David, Maurice Emmanuel, Benjamin Godard, Henri Sauguet and Charles Koechlin. 'Marco Polo was a dream label for so many collectors,' declared Riesel. 'I don't think Naxos would have been as strong as it became had it not been for Marco Polo, because music collectors with specialist knowledge and interests were in touch with Klaus in those early Marco Polo days and continued to suggest ideas to him for Naxos. Equally significant was the attitude of Klaus, who built the label with the enthusiasm of a real music lover – and not just pursuing opportunism as so many major labels were doing at the time.' Riesel had the idea of putting these French Marco Polo composers on a label just for France, and at Naxos price. Approval for Naxos grew.

By the mid-1990s Naxos was selling highly respectable quantities in France: one year, Riesel says, it sold 750,000 units. More French artists came onto the label. The French pianist François-Joël Thiollier recorded the complete piano works of Debussy and Ravel. Hervé Niquet and his outstanding choral group Le Concert Spirituel began a series of Charpentier discs that were unimpeachable in their scholarly and musical execution: French early music was now established in the Naxos catalogue.

Riesel then suggested something even more outrageous. He had heard Idil Biret playing the Second Piano Sonata by Boulez in the '70s and suggested to Heymann that they should ask her to record all three for Naxos. Heymann, always willing to take a risk and help a distributor, was slightly more cautious but ultimately agreed. They were recorded at Studio 106 in Radio France in January and February 1995. The disc went on to sell exceptionally well, and extended yet further the reputation in France (and elsewhere) of Naxos as a serious classical label. Riesel created and printed an amusing advertising campaign in all specialist classical magazines with the slogan: 'If you think that you don't like this music, now you will know why!'

It was a time of growth and excitement. In 1995 Riesel and Heymann set up a joint venture: Naxos and Marco Polo France. The purpose was for Riesel to concentrate on marketing and promotion for the two labels (with Media 7 he had other independent foreign labels in his portfolio as well) and for Media 7 to do the sales and distribution. Riesel also had a brief to develop more French recordings and other specifically French cultural products. The complete chamber music of Poulenc emerged from this period, as did the association between Naxos and the Orchestre National de Lille, which produced the widely praised recording of Debussy's *Pélleas et Mélisande* conducted by Jean-Claude Casadesus.

In 1997 Naxos's tenth anniversary was celebrated in France with a grand concert at Notre Dame de Paris; the 'Organ' Symphony by Saint-Saëns and the Organ Concerto by Poulenc were on the programme. The Archbishop stood up and praised

Naxos for putting on such a concert and contributing to French culture. It was *un moment incroyable* for the label. The live recording that was made of the Organ Concerto is still available on Naxos.

However, Media 7 was moving in a different direction and Heymann felt a complete change was needed in France. Naxos and Marco Polo France was closed and the marketing and distribution was moved to Naïve, a French label that also had a distribution network. After a few years it was switched again, this time to Intégral Distribution.

Meanwhile, Riesel had founded his own distribution company, Abeille Musique, which was looking after an increasing number of foreign, independent, full-price labels. In 2006 he and Heymann signed a sales-and-distribution contract for Naxos and Marco Polo. In 2009 this was modified to enable the current strategy, whereby Abeille Musique is responsible for sales and promotion, and the shipments for France are sent directly from the Naxos Global Logistics warehouse near Munich.

The retail presence for music recordings in France has contracted, as in most countries. It is dominated by one chain, Fnac, with a few independents that are under increasing pressure to survive. Mail order has become more important, it being for many the only way of getting specialist classical CDs; online, amazon.fr dominates the scene, though abeillemusique.com also provides the service. Revenue from downloads and streaming (from ClassicsOnline and the Naxos Music Library) is still relatively small. Riesel estimates that classical music sales in France divide into three equal parts between Fnac, Amazon and other retailers.

Eighteen
Naxos: The Future

The general view of classical recording is that it is a pretty steady sector of the entertainment industry. Out comes a new recording of Beethoven's Symphony No. 5; a dynamic young violinist, perhaps from China, plays Tchaikovsky; or an attractive blonde singer presents a volume of sparkling arias. Actually, this is only one small part of it. The truth is that the classical recording business, like the pop business, is fast-changing, driven partly by technology but just as much by the fashions, politics and economics of music. What is certain is that classical recording does not exist in the kind of protected bubble that it enjoyed for most of the second half of the twentieth century.

This is particularly true of a company such as Naxos, which for a quarter of a century has led the way in so many areas, and which prides itself on taking risks, being at the cutting edge, and trying to maintain the ability to change fast when the circumstances demand it. Naxos in 2012 is totally different from Naxos two decades ago: what began as a budget label focused on recording popular works has become a serious repertoire label offering the widest choice, the deepest catalogue, of any classical label in the world. It has had its crises of identity along the way, and Klaus Heymann has had many tough times in being assailed by differing opinions: 'More new recordings of well-known music played by a saleable performer,' insists a distributor; 'What about this set of seventeenth-century Bohemian sinfonias I discovered in a library in Slovakia,' cries a conductor. 'We can do this massive symphony for Blu-ray Audio as well as ordinary CD,' suggests a keen engineer; 'We will never get our money back if we press this recording on CD: just release it digitally and limit our losses,' says an accountant.

The pressures, the dilemmas and the complexities now facing a classical record company are greater than they have ever been, not least because so many musicians, of a very high standard, are prepared to fund their own recordings for labels to then release. The musicians view it as a promotional expense, but while labels are glad to have free masters they are also concerned that all these new titles are clogging up the market.

Where is Naxos – that is to say, Naxos the label and Naxos the distributor, Naxos online and Naxos the service provider – heading as the second decade of the twenty-first century unfolds? Heymann is often approached for his general view of classical music, whether it is by *The New York Times* or the *Financial Times* or *Gramophone*. His comments about where we are now, or predictions for the future, may be related to his own company, but at the same time he takes a world view. And people listen, because one of his great strengths is that he is forthright when he speaks. He says what he thinks, regardless of whether colleagues in Naxos feel he is being a bit indiscreet or giving away trade secrets; what's more, he is never afraid to say that his view has changed or that he was wrong, or that circumstances now dictate a different approach.

Take the fundamental Naxos ethos of regarding repertoire as more important than artists, and not featuring artists on the covers in a bigger typeface than that of composers: this principle built the character of the label for the first fifteen years, but gradually it became clear that, on Naxos as on full-price labels, a few artists had strong selling power and it was sensible that they should appear prominently on the covers. Heymann now acknowledges that there will be more of these 'artist-led' recordings, with the company developing an increasing number of relationships with outstanding musicians who become identified with the Naxos label. However, he is keen to see them record a balance of standard and rare repertoire. He chooses artists who display a natural interest in this direction, who can bring to the label some interesting works as well as their own musical insights and personality.

Heymann wants Naxos to continue being an adventurous label. He likes looking through the box of new CDs that arrives on his desk every month and seeing the mixture of extremely rare works sitting cheek by jowl with a couple of lifestyle compilations ('providing they are in good taste' is his only caveat).

With its distribution network and digital platforms Naxos is much more than a record label, but ironically this came close to not happening at all. It is not widely known but some eight years ago, feeling momentarily burdened by the responsibility of running the distribution network as well as the label, Heymann offered the main Naxos distribution companies to their respective CEOs. He proposed to guarantee that the Naxos label would remain with them for a specified period so that they would not lose the jewel in the crown. Interestingly, not one CEO picked up the offer. In a way, it was understandable: the growth of the digital medium was evident, so where, they asked, was the future? So the distribution remained with Heymann and he set about developing the network into even more of a powerhouse than it already was, and giving it a clear role in a digital world.

The distribution companies are now stronger than ever and are continuing to grow, fuelled by ideas from Heymann. This is partly because so many other independent labels have come to them for distribution. The CD may be said to be dying (though it seems to be healthier than everyone, including Heymann, predicted); but additional factors have seen the disappearance of many other classical distributors, so that the Naxos network could become the last one standing. Heymann's distributors have also been encouraged to reinvent themselves as service providers within the traditional classical music industry.

Heymann can see how online resources such as Wikipedia have brought information, education and entertainment together, with easy, instant access for the individual. He already has advanced plans for a comprehensive online encyclopedia of classical music and other online music appreciation pro-grammes. Naxos is ideally placed to serve the subject in a remarkably comprehensive way. The distributors no longer focus only on promoting and selling CDs, but also on promot-ing and selling online services and resources that can enrich those who are interested in classical music. The future indicates a balance between physical and digital activities.

At the heart of all this are Naxos, Marco Polo and the other labels owned by the company. This is why, when the distin-guished German classical label Capriccio ran into financial difficulties and needed financing, Heymann bought only the digital rights and not the CD rights. He noted that the Capriccio label filled many gaps that existed within the Naxos labels, such as music by C.P.E. Bach and Kurt Weill, and this was important for the streaming and downloading services such as the Naxos Music Library and ClassicsOnline.

He doesn't over-emphasise the current financial role that these online services, into which he has invested huge amounts, play within the company. While they pay their way, they do not yet match the income from the original business of CD sales – though they are expected to in the future. 'Naxos and other owned labels will continue to be the main revenue earn-ers, if not through physical sales then through downloads, streaming and licensing,' he affirms. 'In my opinion, the indus-try will look like this within five years: 25 per cent physical products, 25 per cent downloads and 50 per cent streaming on demand, including all-you-can-eat subscriptions. Downloads may actually account for a slightly higher percentage if we are successful with our various new digital products, texts with music, and texts with spoken word and music. Educational and other applications may also have a substantial impact on the download-to-own business model.'

At the height of CD sales, in the late 1990s, the Naxos group sold some ten million albums a year. Some of those were quite large boxed sets, which meant it was pressing more than twelve million CDs a year. Physical sales have declined, and although downloads and streaming have not yet caught up they are growing all the time. CD album sales seem to have settled at around three million, and many millions of tracks have been streamed or downloaded (the equivalent of hundreds of thousands of albums). There is no doubt that the business of selling classical CDs – those of Naxos and of its other labels – has declined along with the music CD business globally; but the worth of the company as a whole is still increasing, fuelled by the distribution network and other services.

It has been a long journey from the casual request of a Korean door-to-door sales company for thirty cheap, digital CD titles to the transformation of the international classical record industry. And the story continues. There is no sign that Klaus Heymann, at the age of seventy-five, is considering retirement: he still enjoys the cut and thrust of it all too much and is full of ideas that he wants to develop – that he believes will expand the audience of classical music.

In August 2010 *Gramophone* published an interview given by Klaus Heymann to Martin Cullingford in which he considered the future of the industry. It is fitting to conclude with that interview because, although in places it may have been coloured by time, it shows his bold attitude and clear views about the classical record industry on which he has had such an effect over the past twenty-five years. It is vintage Heymann.

Gramophone: Describe the challenges the rapid growth of online music has posed you.

Klaus Heymann: We have to be quite clear about the fact that there will be the CD – or a physical carrier – for many more years to come. The classical CD is not declining at the same rate as pop or rock. This year, if we look at various territories for the first four or five months, it's actually pretty stable – some are down, some are up, but on average I think CDs this year will be the same as in 2009. We don't have that rapid decline.

G: How would you explain that – is it the collecting aspect connected to classical music?

KH: I think we are basically down to the core collector. And I think that's at a stable level. Any changes in sales are more due to repertoire, or one-offs – like in Japan, where Harmonia Mundi sold 100,000 copies of Nobuyuki Tsujii [pianist, and Gold Medal winner of the Van Cliburn Competition]. These kinds of things can change it dramatically. But by and large I think we've now found a fairly stable market for physical product. Beyond that of course we all look at where will it happen online – what is there beyond the physical business? And it looks like downloads will not be it.

G: Why do you say that?

KH: Well, the growth in downloads has slowed down dramatically. There's a bit of growth, but it's not at the same rate. Again we're talking about classical music, but I doubt it will go above 20 per cent of total sales. And 80 per cent physical. Possibly a little higher than 20 per cent in the States, and the speed of development is different in different markets. I think the future of listening will be an all-you-can-eat formula where people pay a flat rate, per month or per year, and they can listen to as much as they want. This is the model of our music library, and now our video library, of the Spotify premium model, or Rhapsody. It will happen on TV as well – I think we will not be interested in searching 150 channels and looking for what might be on at that moment. But if someone wants to watch *Parsifal*, they want to watch it now, and they can watch it. We'll still see what we call linear channels, but more and more it will be an 'on demand' service. That will be the future. What form it will take – whether the service will be offered by broadband providers, ISPs, by telephone companies, by cable TV, electricity companies – nobody knows yet.

G: But for now, for you, it's still through a Naxos site?

KH: There is the Naxos Music Library, and the Naxos Video Library, but if anybody comes with a similar concept then we are happy to offer our content. I think there will be many different operators trying different kinds of formulae. And so if they want to download our content, and pay for its delivery on hard disc, here it is and see what they can do with it. If you look at when downloading first started and more and more sites sprang up, we thought 'we have to be on all of them'. But at the end of the day there are no more than 10 sites that can actually sell classical music. There's iTunes, there's Naxos Music Library, probably second now, there's eMusic, ClassicsOnline is probably fourth, then there's a bit of Rhapsody, a bit of Napster, there's ArkivMusic, there's Classical Archives. So instead of being on all the sites, it turns out that certain sites can sell classical music, and others cannot.

G: And what sells classical music online?

KH: I think the selection. The kind of traffic sites can generate. For example on our ClassicsOnline website the traffic is static and we're trying to figure out why. Our Naxos.com website has more traffic, so we're now considering putting

downloads on Naxos.com as well to see whether together
the two sites show growth. It's a lot of effort generating traffic – you know this. The conversion rate is very steady, 1.5
per cent of people who visit the site buy, but the traffic
doesn't grow. But the Music Library is showing very strong
growth.

G: When you started the Music Library it was very much
aimed at academic institutions, conservatoires, and so on.

KH: Well, it's still universities and music schools which
account for a large percentage of users. More and more professional musicians use it. If you talk to Marin Alsop or
Leonard Slatkin, they say they can't live without it any more.
They use it for making programmes and listening when they
travel. There's an iPhone application now, and we're working on Blackberry and Android applications – that's more
and more attractive to professional musicians. If a cellist is
building a programme of French cello music, and looking for
a piece that is 11 minutes long, he or she can type in '10–12
minutes', 'France', 'cello', click – and all the pieces come up.

G: So the functionality is specifically designed with that
audience in mind?

KH: That's right. And you can also find the publisher, and
instrumentation – we're building more and more features
into it. We have GCSE, A-level, Baccalaureate music programmes in there, we have a Canadian music programme in
there – we're building more and more into the site. We have
playlists of all the major exam boards – ABRSM, Guildhall,
and so on.

G: Are you going to create a new front end for a more general audience?

KH: Yes, we will have a consumer site. This will be integrated
with the download site. You can download, you can order the
CD or DVD, or you can buy a streaming subscription.

G: Last time we spoke you were talking about providing music for a car manufacturer. So you're in the position of being both content maker – A&Ring, recording etc. – and also the content provider, the seller. Not many labels work in this way.

KH: Well, they'd like to, but they don't know how to as they're too small. So we do the licensing for them. We have about 30–40 labels whose content we also licence. You need a representative who sells, so we have a sales force – we have one person here in the UK, two in the States, one in France, one in Germany, one in Sweden, so it takes active effort to sell. We are big enough to be able to offer our services to other labels. Naxos started out as a budget label, and now we're the major service provider to the industry – distribution service, logistics service, digital distribution for Chandos, BIS, for more than 60 labels, we supply their content to iTunes, to eMusic, we create metadata in Hong Kong and the Philippines. No label can do it on their own.

G: Metadata has been one of the problems with classical music online – very few get it right.

KH: That's right, and we're very good at that. I myself proof-read every entry – I don't proof-read the whole listing, but I proof-read what appears on screen, as one line, and make sure that's 100 per cent correct, and I sometimes look at others to check they're consistent. Spelling consistency is an issue – is it C major – capital C, lower-case 'major' – for example. iTunes has a formula which is not quite in line with musicology, so we basically keep two sets of data, our site which is [in the same style as] *Grove* and the *RED* catalogue, and another one which is the iTunes standard which they've set. Data creation is really very important – that's why we employ 13 musicologists in Manila, and another two in Hong Kong.

We're now working on an online music encyclopedia.

We've right now people who are cutting up all of our music notes into the sections that belong to individual works. Of course normally our music notes are for an album, three or more different works, and we're cutting apart those music notes for the album and attaching the music notes to each work. We've now 7,000 of those – and we have about 40,000, so there's still a way to go! Then we have lots of books on classical music, *The History of Opera*, *The History of Classical Music*, *The A–Z of Conductors*, so we cut all of that up. So if you just have all our own content, we have actually something as comprehensive as *Grove* – not as scientific, but *Grove* has no music notes, and no music. And every entry will have a link for listening.

G: How will you monetise that?

KH: You subscribe to the Naxos Music Library and you pay an extra five dollars to access the online encyclopedia.

G: How do you see tomorrow's music consumer? Let's look at labels – people used to identify with, and follow, certain labels. Is that changing?

KH: Well, I think, the major labels don't have a lot of label loyalty. People don't go into a shop and ask for the latest EMI, or DG – they will ask for the artist. Whereas the label loyalty is with the indies – people who buy Hyperion, people who buy Harmonia Mundi – labels which stand for certain things, have a well-defined image. And Naxos is I think the only label which is sold in shops as a label. I've never seen Hyperion stands, or EMI stands, but there are a lot of Naxos stands around the world. Because the label is based in Hong Kong, we don't have a natural identity – so in England we're an English label, in America an American label, with the American classics – we've had a few lucky breaks in that respect.

G: In terms of the recordings you still make, what do you look for? What drives your A&R policy?

KH: Amazingly, we're still filling gaps in the repertoire, that's still our No. 1 guide. Then we produce for specific markets – so here in England it's very much driven by Select, so the English Song Series, English Piano Concerto series. In America we produce a lot for the American market – it's our biggest investment, and it's also our biggest market. Our house artists need to be kept busy! Marin Alsop, Leonard Slatkin, have a list this long [of things they want to record]! We also now build [new] artists. We will still continue filling gaps in the catalogue but our oldest recordings are now almost 25 years old, so I think we could now justify doing some standard repertoire again. If you want to sign successful artists, you have to offer them the standard repertoire also. So we're now doing Shostakovich with Petrenko, and the next big thing is a Mahler cycle.

G: Who is conducting that?

KH: We haven't decided yet. But this may be the future. Beethoven symphonies, Mozart symphonies – we don't need another Brahms cycle, Marin has done that – Schumann symphonies, a Tchaikovsky cycle, that is also 20 years old. I have a few pet projects I want to do – Pfitzner's *Palestrina*. That's something I will do for my private pleasure. I would like to record the complete Pfitzner – he is one of the most underrated composers.

G: How aware are you of the demographic of your online listeners?

KH: It's a much younger audience than who goes to concerts. It's a little bit distorted by the demographic of the Naxos Music Library, which is obviously sold to an audience of 18–24 – we now have entire school districts in the United States, where all schools have the Naxos Music Library, and it's growing. And that means the audience now goes down to six years. We hope to equip schools in China with MP3 players, because many rural areas don't have broadband – it's not ideal sound, but you can reach young people. There are a lot of people who don't know that we make CDs! We went to a library convention, and we had a stand – and our guy had a stack of CDs, and the Music Library next to him with a screen, and many music librarians came over and said 'I didn't know you also made CDs!'

G: What will the industry look like in 10 years time?

KH: Actually I think it will not look too much different. Physical sales will be there, we will probably reach a point where it's just a hard-core [of collectors] we're selling to. And then there will be high-end people demanding the ultimate in sound – and I think that will be Blu-ray, or high-end downloads, studio masters, but this will be relatively small. I think those downloads will go back down once there is an established high-end physical product out in the market. And then you will have all kinds of subscription services – there will be the equivalent of iTunes as a streaming service – iTunes doesn't want to do streaming, not yet, but my guess is they will change their mind. There will probably be a jazz streaming site, there might be a world music site, and several classical sites, we don't know, it depends on how much content they amass. And that will be pretty much the market. But there are now things we never thought would happen – you can now watch opera in the cinema. There is enough content now to mean that each city could support one or two cinemas showing only high-definition music content. That's a whole new business, and we're gearing up to have one sales person per subsidiary who can do that business.'

With thanks to Gramophone *for kind permission to reproduce this slightly edited version of the interview with Klaus Heymann, which first appeared in the August 2010 issue.* *www.gramophone.co.uk*

When I am asked the secret of my success, I reply:
1. I didn't read music.
2. I didn't play an instrument.
3. I hadn't worked for a record label.

Klaus Heymann

Appendix: Awards

Although the early reputation of Naxos was founded on new, reliable, digital recordings at budget price, the label began garnering more sophisticated musical plaudits from the 1990s onwards. Here is just a small selection of awards and critical approbation from leading magazines and music critics.

GRAMMY Awards

Sacred Tibetan Chant 76044-2
Best Traditional World Music Album
46th Annual GRAMMY Awards

Bolcom: Songs of Innocence and of Experience 8.559216–18
Best Classical Album
Best Choral Performance (Soloists, Michigan University Choirs, Slatkin)
Classical Contemporary Composition
Producer Of The Year, Classical (Tim Handley)
48th Annual GRAMMY Awards

Tower: Made in America / Tambor / Concerto for Orchestra 8.559328
Best Classical Album
Best Orchestral Performance (Nashville Symphony, Slatkin)
Best Classical Contemporary Composition (Made in America)
50th Annual GRAMMY Awards

Carter: String Quartets Nos. 1 & 5 8.559362
Best Chamber Music Performance (Pacifica Quartet)
51st Annual GRAMMY Awards

Corigliano: Mr. Tambourine Man / Three Hallucinations 8.559331
Best Classical Vocal Performance (Hila Plitmann, soprano)
Best Classical Contemporary Composition (Mr. Tambourine Man)
51st Annual GRAMMY Awards

Daugherty: Metropolis Symphony / Deus ex Machina 8.559635
Best Orchestral Performance (Nashville Symphony, Slatkin)
Best Engineered Album (Classical)
Best Classical Contemporary Composition (Deus Ex Machina)
53rd Annual GRAMMY Awards

Dorman: Concertos for Mandolin, Piccolo, Piano / Concerto Grosso
    8.559620
Producer Of The Year, Classical (David Frost)
53rd Annual GRAMMY Awards

Ligeti: String Quartets Nos. 1 & 2 / Andante and Allegretto 8.570781
Best Chamber Music Performance (Parker Quartet)
53rd Annual GRAMMY Awards

Messiaen: Livre du Saint-Sacrement 8.572436–37
Best Instrumental Soloist Performance (without Orchestra) (Paul Jacobs,
    organ)
53rd Annual GRAMMY Awards

Gramophone Awards

British Music Series
Editor's Choice, 1999

Vaughan Williams: Phantasy Quintet / String Quartets Nos. 1 & 2
    8.555300
Chamber Award, 2001

Naxos
Label of the Year, 2005

Tchaikovsky: Manfred Symphony / Voyevoda 8.570568
Orchestral Award, 2009

Bernstein: Mass 8.559622–23
Editor's Choice, 2010

Cannes Classical Awards

Beck: Symphonies 8.553790 – 1998
Franck: Piano Quintet / Chausson: String Quartet 8.553645 – 1999
Kraus: Symphonies, Vol. 1 8.553734 – 1999
Vanhal: Symphonies, Vol. 1 8.554341 – 2000
Telemann: Darmstadt Overtures (Suites) 8.554244 – 2001
Howells: Requiem / Take Him, Earth, for Cherishing 8.554659 – 2001
Messiaen: Turangalîla Symphony / L'Ascension 8.554478–79 – 2002

International Classical Music Awards

Shostakovich: Symphony No. 8 8.572392 – 2011

Penguin Guide Awards

These include only the Penguin Guide Rosettes – the highest awards – not all the recommended recordings, which are numerous.

Bach, C.P.E.: Complete Flute Concertos 8.555715–16
Balada: Orchestral Works, Vol. 2 8.555039
Barber: Symphonies Nos. 1 and 2 / Essay for Orchestra No. 1 8.559024
Bax: Symphony No. 6 8.557144
Brahms: Hungarian Dances Nos. 1–21 8.550110
Copland: Rodeo / Prairie Journal / The Red Pony Suite, Letter from Home 8.559240
Dohnányi: Complete Piano Works, Vol. 1 8.553332
Dohnányi: Serenade / Sextet 8.557153
Donizetti: Double Concerto, Flute Concertino, Clarinet Concertino 8.557492
Fauré / Ravel: String Quartets 8.554722
Linde: Violin Concerto / Cello Concerto 8.557855
Liszt: Années de Pélerinage, Vol. 2 8.550549
Manfredini: Concerti grossi 8.553891
Ockeghem: Missa l'homme armé / Alma redemptoris mater / Ave Maria 8.554297

Piston: Symphony No. 4 / Three New England Sketches / Capriccio 8.559162

Piston: Violin Concertos Nos. 1 & 2 / Fantasia for Violin and Orchestra 8.559003

Prokofiev: Peter and the Wolf / Britten: The Young Person's Guide to the Orchestra / Poulenc: The Story of Babar the Elephant 8.554170

Puccini: La Bohème 8.111249–50

Rochberg: Symphony No. 5 / Black Sounds / Transcendental Variations 8.559115

Rutter: Requiem 8.557130

Soler: Sonatas for Harpsichord, Vol. 1 8.553462

Soler: Sonatas for Harpsichord, Vol. 2 8.553463

Soler: Sonatas for Harpsichord, Vol. 3 8.553464

Soler: Sonatas for Harpsichord, Vol. 4 8.553465

Soler: Sonatas for Harpsichord, Vol. 5 8.554434

Soler: Sonatas for Harpsichord, Vol. 6 8.554565

Soler: Sonatas for Harpsichord, Vol. 7 8.554566

Soler: Sonatas for Harpsichord, Vol. 8 8.555031

Soler: Sonatas for Harpsichord, Vol. 9 8.555032

Soler: Sonatas for Harpsichord, Vol. 10 8.557137

Soler: Sonatas for Harpsichord, Vol. 11 8.557640

Soler: Sonatas for Harpsichord, Vol. 12 8.557937

Soler: Sonatas for Harpsichord, Vol. 13 8.570292

Tallis: Spem in Alium 5.110111 (DVD-Audio)

Tallis: Spem in Alium 6.110111 (SACD)

Tallis: Spem in Alium 8.557700 (CD)

Telemann: Viola Concerto / Recorder Suite / Tafelmusik 8.550156

Tomkins: Consort Music for Viols and Voices 8.550602

Vaughan Williams: Phantasy Quintet / String Quartets Nos. 1 & 2 8.555300

Vivaldi: Cello Concertos, Vol. 3 8.550909

Weber: Symphonies Nos. 1 & 2 8.550928

Diapason d'Or Awards

Regular Naxos Titles

Benevolo: Missa Azzolina / Magnificat / Dixit Dominus 8.553636

Berwald: Symphonies Nos. 1 & 2 8.553051

Berwald: Symphonies Nos. 3 & 4 / Piano Concerto 8.553052

Boulez: Piano Sonatas Nos. 1–3 8.553353

Britten: Rejoice in the Lamb / Hymn to St Cecilia / Missa Brevis 8.554791

Britten: String Quartets Nos. 1 and 2 / Three Divertimenti 8.553883

Ego sum Resurrectio – Gregorian Chant for the Dead 8.553192

Elgar: String Quartet in E minor / Piano Quintet in A minor 8.553737

Guarnieri: Piano Concertos Nos. 1–3 8.557666

Guarnieri: Piano Concertos Nos. 4–6 8.557667

Ives: Symphony No. 1 / Emerson Concerto 8.559175

Lutosławski: Symphony No. 4 / Violin Partita / Chain II / Funeral Music 8.553202

Muffat: Concerti grossi Nos. 1–6 8.555096

Muffat: Concerti grossi Nos. 7–12 8.555743

Offenbach arr. Rosenthal: Gaîté Parisienne / Offenbachiana 8.554005

Penderecki: A Polish Requiem 8.557386–87

Prokofiev: Piano Concertos Nos. 1, 3 & 4 8.550566

Prokofiev: Piano Concertos Nos. 2 & 5 8.550565

Roussel: Bacchus et Ariane / Symphony No. 3 8.570245

Schenck: Nymphs of the Rhine: Vol. 1 8.554414

Schenck: Nymphs of the Rhine: Vol. 2 8.554415

Shostakovich: Symphony No. 10 8.572461

Szymanowski: Songs with Orchestra 8.553688

Szymanowski: Violin Concertos Nos. 1 and 2 / Nocturne and Tarantella 8.557981

Various: Lamentations 8.550572

Naxos Historical Titles

Busoni and His Pupils 8.110777

Caruso – Complete Recordings, Vol. 4 8.110719

Caruso – Complete Recordings, Vol. 5 8.110720

Caruso – Complete Recordings, Vol. 6 8.110721

Caruso – Complete Recordings, Vol. 7 8.110724

Caruso – Complete Recordings, Vol. 8 8.110726

Cortot – Chopin: Ballades Nos. 1–4, Nocturnes 8.111245

Cortot – Chopin: Piano Sonatas Nos. 2 & 3 / Polonaises 8.111065

Curzon/Budapest String Quartet – Brahms / Dvořák: Piano Quintets 8.110307

Ferrier – Brahms: Alto Rhapsody / Schumann: Frauenliebe und -leben 8.111009

Ferrier – Mahler: Kindertotenlieder / Symphony No. 4 8.110876

Friedman – Chopin: Mazurkas 8.110690

Friedman – Mendelssohn: Songs without Words 8.110736

Gieseking – Beethoven: Piano Concertos Nos. 4 & 5 8.111112

Gigli Edition, Vol. 1: Milan Recordings 8.110262

Gigli Edition, Vol. 2: Milan, Camden and New York Recordings 8.110263

Gigli Edition, Vol. 3: Camden and New York Recordings 8.110264

Gigli Edition, Vol. 4: Camden and New York Recordings 8.110265

Gigli Edition, Vol. 5: New York Recordings 8.110266

Gigli Edition, Vol. 6: New York Recordings 8.110267

Gigli Edition, Vol. 7: London, New York and Milan Recordings 8.110268

Gigli Edition, Vol. 8: Milan, London and Berlin Recordings 8.110269

Gigli Edition, Vol. 9: Berlin, Milan and London Recordings 8.110270

Gigli Edition, Vol. 10: Milan and London Recordings 8.110271

Gigli Edition, Vol. 11: Milan, Berlin and Rome Recordings 8.110272

Heifetz – Brahms / Glazunov: Violin Concertos 8.110940

Heifetz – Elgar / Walton: Violin Concertos 8.110939

Heifetz – Mozart / Mendelssohn: Violin Concertos 8.110941

Heifetz – Prokofiev / Gruenberg: Violin Concertos 8.110942

Heifetz – Tchaikovsky / Wieniawski / Sibelius: Violin Concertos 8.110938

Heifetz – Vieuxtemps: Violin Concertos Nos. 4 & 5 8.110943

Kapell – Prokofiev: Piano Concerto No. 3 / Khachaturian: Piano Concerto 8.110673

Kapell – Rachmaninov: Piano Concerto No. 2 / Rhapsody on a Theme of Paganini 8.110692

Koussevitsky – Mussorgsky: Pictures at an Exhibition / Ravel: Boléro & Ma Mère l'oye 8.110154

Koussevitsky – Sibelius: Symphonies Nos. 2 & 5 8.110170

Kreisler/Rachmaninov – Beethoven / Schubert / Grieg: Violin Sonatas 8.110968

Levitzki – Complete Recordings, Vol. 1 8.110688

Levitzki – Complete Recordings, Vol. 2 8.110769

Mengelberg – Brahms: Symphonies Nos. 1 & 3 8.110164

Mengelberg – Strauss: Ein Heldenleben / Tod und Verklärung 8.110161

Menuhin – Beethoven / Franck / Lekeu: Violin Sonatas 8.110989

Menuhin – Beethoven: Violin Sonatas Nos. 7 & 9 8.110775

Menuhin – Brahms / Schumann: Violin Sonatas 8.110771

Milstein – Dvořák / Glazunov: Violin Concertos 8.110975

Milstein – Mendelssohn / Tchaikovsky / Bruch: Violin Concertos 8.110977

Moiseiwitsch – Chopin: 24 Preludes / Ballades / Fantaisie-Impromptu
8.111118

Moiseiwitsch – Chopin: Piano Works 8.111117

Moiseiwitsch – Schumann: Kinderszenen / Mussorgsky: Pictures at an
Exhibition 8.110668

Moiseiwitsch – Weber-Tausig: Rondo brillante / Liszt: La leggierezza /
Wagner-Liszt: Isoldes Liebestod etc. 8.110669

Petri – Brahms: Paganini and Handel Variations 8.110634

Ponselle – Rosa Ponselle Sings Verdi 8.110728

Sammons – Mozart: Sinfonia Concertante / Elgar: Violin Sonata
8.110957

Schnabel – Beethoven: Piano Sonatas Nos. 1–3 8.110693

Schnabel – Beethoven: Piano Sonatas Nos. 4–6 & 19–20 8.110694

Schnabel – Beethoven: Piano Sonatas Nos. 7–10 8.110695

Schnabel – Beethoven: Piano Sonatas Nos. 11–13 8.110756

Schnabel – Beethoven: Piano Sonatas Nos. 14–16 8.110759

Schnabel – Beethoven: Piano Sonatas Nos. 17, 18 & 21 8.110760

Schnabel – Beethoven: Piano Sonatas Nos. 22–26 8.110761

Schnabel – Beethoven: Piano Sonatas Nos. 27–29 8.110762

Schnabel – Beethoven: Piano Sonatas Nos. 30–32 8.110763

Szigeti – Brahms / Mendelssohn: Violin Concertos 8.110948

Szigeti – Prokofiev / Bloch: Violin Concertos 8.110973

Talich – Smetana: Ma Vlast 8.111237

Tauber – Lieder 8.110739

Tauber – Operetta Arias 8.110779

Thibaud/Casals/Cortot – Beethoven: Archduke Trio / Kreutzer Sonata
8.110195

Thibaud/Casals/Cortot – Haydn / Beethoven / Schubert: Piano Trios
8.110188

Thibaud/Casals/Cortot – Mendelssohn / Schumann: Piano Trios
8.110185

Walter – Mahler: Symphony No. 9 8.110852

Naxos Historical Opera and Musicals
Borodin: Prince Igor 8.111071–73
Delius: A Village Romeo and Juliet 8.110982–83
Giordano: Andrea Chénier 8.110275–76
Mussorgsky: Khovanshchina 8.111124–26
Ponchielli: La Gioconda 8.110112–14
Porter: Kiss Me, Kate / Let's Face It 8.120788

Rodgers & Hammerstein: Oklahoma! 8.120787
Rodgers & Hammerstein: South Pacific 8.120785
Sullivan: The Mikado 8.110176–77
Tchaikovsky: Eugene Onegin 8.110216–17
Verdi: Otello 8.111018–19
Wagner: Die Meistersinger von Nürnberg 8.110872–75
Wagner: Die Walküre, Acts I & II 8.110250–51
Wagner: Parsifal 8.110221–24
Wagner: Tristan und Isolde 8.110068–70
Wagner: Tristan und Isolde 8.110321–24

Acknowledgements

Many people helped with this book and my fulsome thanks go out to them all. First and foremost is Klaus Heymann who was, inevitably, the primary source for so much detailed information. His reputation for an unbelievably rapid response to email queries was more than validated through this process of researching, writing and checking. His accurate recall of facts and figures was almost equally unbelievable; fortunately I think he also enjoyed the opportunity to reflect on the past twenty-five years, since he is, by nature, the kind of man who rarely looks in the rear-view mirror.

Secondly, thanks to my editor Genevieve Helsby, who had the challenging task of working through my sometimes artistic (sketchy) grasp of grammar and occasionally wayward accuracy. There were thousands of tiny points to confirm, to question, to change, which she did not only with unfailing patience and diligence, but also while simultaneously running her busy Naxos editorial department.

The book had its beginnings in many discussions with David Patmore, the record historian and Naxos writer, who helped considerably in its emerging shape, particularly with regard to the history of the classical record industry which he knows so well. I am also grateful for interest expressed by David Shelley – deputy publisher of Little, Brown UK – in the history of Naxos, and his offer to publish this book.

All the Naxos contributors mentioned in these pages also

responded generously with their time and knowledge. Performers, administrators, salesmen, editors, publicists, producers, engineers from Hong Kong to Sweden, from Korea to the US, from Australia to Hungary – they all rose to the challenge of answering many and sometimes odd questions, having little idea what would happen to the answers. Of course, having been part of Naxos for nearly two decades myself, I knew many of these people already, and had visited a lot of them in their offices or seen quite a few in concert! But contact over the book showed again what a remarkable group of highly capable people they are – passionate about their work and committed to the label. In the end, it is the contribution of individuals, starting with Klaus Heymann, that has made Naxos. After twenty-five years, it is very far from being a corporate entity!

Index

Aagaard, Thorvald 343
Abbado, Claudio 14
Abeille Musique 405–9
Abendroth, Hermann 206
Adam, Antoine 33
Adams, John 186, 214, 231–2
Ailey, Alvin 347
Alain, Jehan 269
Albanese, Licia 276
Albinoni, Tomaso 279, 385
Alcántara, Theo 265
Alfvén, Hugo 392
Alkan, Charles-Valentin 59, 289
Allegri, Gregorio 259
Allen, Sir Thomas 229, 378
Alsop, Marin 91, 119, 181–6, 232, 234,
    251, 256, 298, 321, 366, 375, 417,
    420
Alwyn, William 160, 174, 363
Amadis 269–71
Anderson, Anthony 82, 90, 157, 248,
    331, 362–4, 366–7
Anderson, Keith 71, 82, 300, 327–31,
    362
Anderson, Leroy 215
Anderson, Marian 277
Andry, Peter 12
Angel, David 156–9
Angus, David 299
Anthony, Adele 232
Antill, John 221
Appenheimer, Günther 313, 314, 321
Arensky, Anton 194
Armstrong, Louis 278
Arnold, Malcolm 236, 363
Arnold, Samuel 306
Artaria Editions 101, 176, 256, 304–6,
    309
Arthaus Musik 104, 350, 366, 374, 387,
    402
Ashkenazy, Vladimir 4
Asturias Symphony Orchestra 265
Atterberg, Kurt 328
Auden, W.H. 219

Babbitt, Milton 380
Bach, C.P.E. 94, 162, 163, 177, 319,
    413
Bach, Johann Sebastian 6, 39, 73, 75, 76,
    99, 138–9, 142, 148, 155, 203, 204,
    207, 208, 223, 242, 250, 259, 260,
    268, 275, 279, 289, 343, 345
Bach, Wilhelm Friedemann 163
Badley, Allan 100, 101, 176, 304–5
Balakirev, Mily 194, 285
Balanchine, George 219
Baltimore Symphony Orchestra 182
Barbagallo, James 290
Barber, Samuel 91, 182, 183, 184, 226,
    380
Barrett, Sean 299, 323
Bartholdy Quartet 170
Bartók, Béla 125, 137, 138, 141, 142,
    153, 183, 185, 188, 261, 289, 302,
    319, 320, 355
Basie, Count 278
Bax, Arnold 90, 172, 221, 236, 358, 363,
    364
BBC 3, 119, 150, 183, 201, 202, 296,
    297, 366
  orchestras 209, 214, 215, 357
  Proms 173, 181, 201, 215
Beach, Amy 378
Beale, Simon Russell 295
Beaver, Steve 46, 83–4
Bechet, Sidney 278
Beck, Franz Ignaz 304
Beecham, Sir Thomas 2, 276
Beethoven, Ludwig van 4, 7, 9, 15, 30,
    73, 74, 75, 78, 79, 109, 124, 132,
    133, 138–40, 141, 142, 145, 148,
    152–3, 173, 176, 179, 180, 198,
    200–1, 207, 208, 223, 247, 251,
    259, 261, 269, 275, 276, 305, 357,
    378, 385, 387, 410, 420
Beiderbecke, Bix 278
Beijing Symphony Orchestra (BSO)
    245–6
Belcea Quartet 159

Belgian Radio and Television
    Philharmonic Orchestra (BRT) 85,
    251
Berg, Alban 261, 347
Berio, Luciano 225
Berkeley, Lennox 160
Berlin Philharmonic 10, 14, 179, 201,
    366
Berlioz, Hector, 31, 215, 280
Berman, Boris 320
Bernold, Philippe 162
Bernstein, Leonard 3, 4, 91, 182, 183,
    220, 226, 347, 366, 375, 378, 379
Bilbao Symphony Orchestra 265, 317
Biret, Idil 142–6, 174, 188, 191, 225,
    241, 254, 408
BIS 3, 10, 112, 360, 393, 402, 418
Bizet, Georges 179, 261
Björk 237
Björling, Jussi 99, 273, 275–6
Blake, David 355–6
Bliss, Arthur 236, 358
Bloom, Leopold 297
Blumenthal, Daniel 289
BMG 11–12, 45, 46, 77–8, 83, 84, 349
Boccherini, Luigi 168, 242, 268
Böhm, Karl 347
Bohus, János 318
Bohuslav Martinů Philharmonic
    Orchestra 325
Bolcom, William 181, 212, 213, 216,
    226, 227–8, 233, 321, 375
Bose, Dr Amar G. 38
Boulez, Pierre 143–5, 233, 241, 249,
    254, 363, 408
Bournemouth Symphony Orchestra 96,
    183, 221, 234, 357
Brahms, Johannes 15, 75, 85, 119, 131,
    138, 143, 144, 145, 148, 154, 174,
    177, 181, 184, 185, 188, 191, 198,
    201, 220, 223, 251, 252, 269, 275,
    281, 289, 326, 420
Bramall, Anthony 75, 179
Breiner, Peter 75, 135, 181, 187, 242–6
Brendel, Alfred 138
Brian, Havergal 58–9, 180, 285
Bridge, Frank 156, 172, 173, 236
British Piano Concerto Foundation 364
Britten, Benjamin, 157, 158, 209, 237,
    261, 327, 365
Brodsky Quartet 237
Bromley, Peter 60, 241, 266, 309, 331–4
Bronsart, Hans 39
Brouwer, Leo 168
Brown, Timothy 241, 364
Bruch, Max 75, 76, 131, 147, 153, 193,
    252, 275
Bruckner, Anton 39, 50, 95, 96, 252

Budapest Radio Symphony Orchestra 53
Buffalo Philharmonic Orchestra 229,
    381
Buffalo Symphony Orchestra 379
Burton, Anthony 302
Busoni, Ferruccio 145, 289
Butcher, Sarah 323
Butterworth, George 364
Buxtehude, Dietrich 260, 268
Bylsma, Anner 170
Byrd, William 202, 253, 249
Byrén, Mats 82, 388, 389

C Major 402
Cage, John 224, 320, 362–3
Callas, Maria 99, 276
Camden, Anthony 95
Candide 39, 44
Cannabich, Christian 305
Capella Istropolitana 68, 72, 73, 75, 85,
    179, 180, 251, 313, 314
Caplet, André 407
Cardoso, Manuel 205
Carreras, José 14–15
Carter, Elliott 226
Casadesus, Jean-Claude 408
Casals, Pablo 99, 275
Casella, Alfredo 61, 266, 267
Cassuto, Álvaro 317
Castelnuovo-Tedesco, Mario 165, 266,
    267, 268
Castile and León Symphony Orchestra
    265
CBS/Columbia 2–4, 12, 91, 228, 317,
    374
CD Journal 397
CD(s):
    analogue recordings on 14
    birth of 8–12
    decline of 104, 413
    deletions 280
    downloads/streaming v. 413–14
    DVDs and 374
    first Naxos 11
    improved formats of 102
    LPs v. 8, 11, 14, 57, 65–6, 67, 76–9,
        356
    pirated 65, 104, 115–16, 242, 336,
        394, 401–2, 416
    proliferation of 11, 13–14
Celibidache, Sergiu 347
Chadwick, George Whitefield 375, 378
Challenge Classics 402
Chandos 10, 90, 113, 215, 366, 376,
    394, 405, 418
Chapí, Ruperto 265
Charpentier, Marc-Antoine 96, 408
Chen Gang 47, 48, 49, 130

China Central Broadcasting 63, 64
China National Publications Import and
    Export Corporation 402
China Records 64
Choir of Clare College, Cambridge 240,
    364
Choir of St John's College, Cambridge
    237, 317, 364
Chopin, Frédéric 123, 137, 142–6, 148,
    174, 175, 190, 259, 269, 303, 385
Christopher Nupen Films 367
Chrysalis 46
Cimarosa, Domenico 164, 305
City of London Sinfonia 357
Čiurlionis, M.K. 59, 282, 289
Clarinet Classics xiv, 88
Classical Recording Company 323
ClassicsOnline (COL) 114, 116, 342,
    346, 367, 377, 409, 413, 416
Clements, Mike 204
Cliburn, Van 415
Coates, Eric 180
Coates, Gloria 226
Collegium Records 240, 364, 366
Collins Classics 236, 239, 309, 365
Collins, Wilkie 294
Cologne Chamber Orchestra (CCO)
    206, 207, 251, 386
Colorado Symphony Orchestra 182, 234
Concentus Hungaricus 140
Constable, John 258
Copland, Aaron, 184, 220, 380, 382
copyright 71, 87–90, 115–18, 223, 224,
    245–6, 274, 278, 333, 345, 394
Corelli, Arcangelo 40, 279
Corghi, Azio 328
Corigliano, John 226, 228–30, 378, 380,
    381
Cornelius, Peter 276
Corp, Ronald 156, 160
Cortot, Alfred 142, 143, 273
Costa, Sequeira 289
Coste, Napoléon 168, 268
Coutaz, Bernard 357
CPO 93, 360, 370
Craft, Robert 102, 216–19, 224, 303
Craker, Chris 357
Cresswell, Lyell 221
Creston, Paul 380
Cribbins, Bernard 365
Crumb, George 226
Cuckston, Alan 290
Cui, César 282
Cullingford, Martin 414–21
Curtin, Joseph 134
Curzon, Frederic 180
Czecho-Slovak Radio Symphony
    Orchestra 324

Czepiczka, Kai 403, 405
Czerwenka, Oskar 276

Dacapo 370
Daniel, Paul 318
Dante, ii, xiv, 88, 297, 347
DAT (Digital Audio Tape) 75, 124, 134,
    139, 308, 314, 316
Daudet, Alphonse 300, 348
Daugherty, Michael 227, 232–4, 376,
    379
David, Félicien 59, 407
Davis, Carl 366
Davis, Colin 16
Davis, Miles 278
de Almeida, Antonio 267
de Brito, White 201
de Falla, Manuel 265–6
de los Ángeles, Victoria 276
de Saint-Georges, Chevalier, 101, 128,
    131, 135, 208
de Sarasate, Pablo 170–1
de Victoria, Tomás Luis 202, 253
Debussy, Claude 85, 153, 164, 407, 408
Decca 1–4, 6, 7, 14, 175, 215, 317, 361
Degas, Rupert 299
Delaware Symphony Orchestra 73, 180
Delos 309, 380
Denève, Stéphane 321
Denon 11, 66, 69, 80, 350, 351–2
Denton, David 82, 90, 93, 96, 156, 201,
    203, 248, 314, 354–9, 361, 364
Denton, Rona 355–6, 361
Desprez, Josquin 363
Detroit Symphony Orchestra (DSO) 213,
    215, 234
Deutsche Grammophon (DG) 1–5, 7, 10,
    14, 39, 149, 161, 162, 204, 361,
    398, 419
Deutsche Grammophon Gesellschaft
    (DGG) 2
Deutsche Harmonia Mundi 3, 355, 394
Devich, János 150
Devienne, François 163
Devoyon, Pascal 407
Diaghilev, Sergei 194
Diamond, David 379, 380
Diapason d'Or 157, 187, 250, 407,
    430–4
Die Musik in Geschichte und Gegenwart
    ('MGG') 51, 197, 328
Diekamp, Ludger 384, 385, 387
digital rights management (DRM) 115,
    337, 346
Ding, Shande 47
Dmitri Ensemble 240
Dohnányi, Ernő 137, 142, 153, 380, 382
Domingo, Placido 4, 14

Donau 269–71
Donizetti, Gaetano 261, 280, 347
Donohoe, Peter 157, 364
Doppler, Franz 162
Doppler, Karl 162
Dorchester Abbey 202
Dostoevsky, Fyodor 294
D'Oyly Carte Opera Company 277
Drahos, Béla 179, 251, 319
Druckman, Jacob 380
Du Mingxin 49, 78
Dupré, Marcel 269
Dvořák, Antonín 138, 147, 154, 182,
     185, 188, 192, 198, 253, 382
Dylan, Bob 229, 381

ECM 10, 394
Éder, György 149–53
Éder Quartet 319
Edison, Noel 234
Edlinger, Richard 78
Egues, Richard 270
Eicher, Manfred 10
Eisenlohr, Ulrich 168–70, 252
Ejiofor, Chiwetel 297
El Vallès Symphony Orchestra 266
El Wakil, Mohamed 352
Elektra Nonesuch 3, 7, 12, 253
Elgar, Edward 147, 157, 174, 180, 198,
     220, 275, 358
Elora Festival Singers 234
EMI 1–3, 7, 12, 14, 39, 99, 117–18, 182,
     191, 204, 215, 344, 384, 419
Emmanuel, Maurice 407
eMusic 114, 115, 346, 416, 418
English Chamber Orchestra 93, 156
English Northern Philharmonia 318,
     357, 358
Ensemble of the Chinese University 327
Erato 3, 12, 376
Erkel, Ferenc 59, 289
Erle, Broadus 129
Escudero, Francisco 265
Espoir Classique 406
Essex Trading 38
Esterházy, House of 151
EuroArts 367, 374, 388, 402
EuroBeat 83–4
Eurodisc 45

Faber Music 201
Failoni Orchestra 199
Falletta, JoAnn 175, 229, 379, 381, 382
Falvay, Attila 149–53
Falvay, Mária 153
Fargo 11, 69, 405
Farley, Carole 226, 227, 258
Fauré, Gabrielle 203, 204, 205

Fawkes, Richard 298, 323, 419
Fejérvári, János 149–53
Ferrara, Franco 209
Ferrie, Edward 294
Ferrier, Kathleen 276
FG Naxos 389, 395
Fias, Gábor 150
Filipec, Goran 195
First Impression Music 402
Fischer, Edwin 275
Fitelberg, Grzegorz 190
Fitz-Gerald, Mark 241
Flagstad, Kirsten 276
Florida Philharmonic Orchestra 220
Flynn, Benedict 297
Fnac 409
Fokine, Michel 194
Fono 383–4, 386
Ford Motor Company Fund 230, 378
Franck, César 130, 162, 171, 269, 363
Franova, Tatjana 290
Franz Liszt Academy of Music 137, 140,
     318
Fred Sherry String Quartet 217
Friedman, Ignaz 275
Fuchs, Joseph 42, 127
Fuchs, Kenneth 380
Fuchs, Robert 289
Furtwängler, Wilhelm 276, 286, 328,
     329, 396

Gallagher, Jack 382
Gallois, Patrick 161–4, 320
Garofalo, Carlo 282
Gävle Symphony Orchestra 176
Gedda, Nicolai 276
Geest, Teije van 93
George, Stefan 330
Gerhard, Roberto 289
German, Edward 290
Gershwin, George 161, 220, 277
Ghedini, Giorgio Federico 266, 267
Gianneo, Luis 289
Gieseking, Walter 99
Gigli, Beniamino 276
Gillinson, Clive 16
Gimell 60, 366
Giulini, Mauro 6, 9
Glass, Philip 184, 208, 210, 231–2
Glazunov, Alexander 59, 154, 193, 194,
     254, 290
Glemser, Bernd 188
Glennie, Evelyn 234
Gluck, Christoph 289, 301
Godard, Benjamin 407
Godowsky, Leopold 290
Goethe, 25, 297, 299, 348
Goldmark, 198 *Penthesilea* 197

Gombert, Nicolas 204
Goodman, Benny 278
Górecki, Henryk 191, 235, 236, 253
Görner, Lutz 300
Gortázar, Isabel 100
Gossec, François-Joseph 101, 306
Göteborgs Domkyrkas Gosskör 392
Gould, Glen 139, 275
GRAMMYs 98, 105, 181, 214, 215,
   225, 227, 228, 231, 232, 233, 234,
   241, 250, 269, 310, 370, 375, 376,
   378, 381, 425–6
Gramola 57
Gramophone xiii, 58, 86, 105, 199, 250,
   356, 411, 414–21
   awards 105, 158, 182, 355, 427
   Klaus interviewed by 414–21
Granados, Enrique 243, 268
Grandage, Michael 297
Grappelli, Stephane 278
Greenfield, Edward 86, 356–7
Grieg, Edvard 130, 138, 253, 269
Griffith, Hugh 299, 302
Grodd, Uwe 176
Grohovski, Valeri 195
Grzegorz Fitelberg Concert Hall 190
Guarneri del Gesù, Giuseppe 133–4,
   137
Guerrero, Giancarlo 233, 376
Gulda, Rico 177
Gunzenhauser, Stephen 73, 132, 154,
   179, 180, 313
Gutman, Natalia 146

Hagen, Daron 382
Haitink, Bernard 3, 4
Halász, Michael 131, 147, 196–201
Hand, Gregory 228
Handel, George Frideric 73, 205, 242,
   253, 261, 320
Handley, Tim 186, 214, 222, 228, 321,
   357, 381
Haneke, Michael 177
Hansa 45
Hansen, Birger 394
Hanslip, Chloë 214
Hanson, Howard 375, 377, 379, 380
Hänssler Classic 384, 402
Harbison, John 226
Harden, Wolf 75, 133
Harmonia Mundi UK 3, 80–1, 355–6,
   357, 402, 415, 419
Harris, Roy 91, 184, 226
Harty, Sir Hamilton 210
Hashimoto, Qunihico 212
Haydn, Joseph 76, 94, 100, 101, 137,
   138, 141, 142, 149–53, 157, 159,
   161, 163, 164, 179, 180, 207, 208,

239, 242, 251, 255, 256, 304–6,
   319
Haysom, Graham xiv, 81, 90, 92, 355,
   358–1
He Zhanhao 47, 48, 130, 255
Heifetz, Jascha 99, 255, 275
Helsby, Genevieve 102, 303, 435
Helsingborg Symphony Orchestra 392
Henley, Darren 298
Henze, Hans Werner 168, 255, 268
Hersch, Michael 184, 256
Hesse Radio Orchestra 30
Hessischer Rundfunk 30
Heymann, Barbara (Klaus's sister) 29
Heymann, Brigitte (Klaus's sister) 29
Heymann, Ferdinand (Klaus's father) 29,
   31
Heymann, Henryk ('Rick') (Klaus's son)
   20, 44, 132, 402, 403
   birth of 43
Heymann, Klaus xiii, xvi, 10–11, 19–28
   agencies run by 40, 46, 62, 63, 64
   A&R method of 307
   Artaria Editions launched by 101
   arts and humanities background of 20
   birth of 10, 29
   business acumen of 20–1, 31, 51–2,
      60, 62, 103
   childhood of 29
   competitive nature of 22
   complete cycles and 59–60
   'cultured' home life of 29–30
   Deutsche Schubert-Lied-Edition and
      168
   diverse businesses of 62
   early employment of 22, 34–5, 62
   education of 31–3
   fast decision-making of 89
   foresight of 367
   Gramophone interviews 414–21
   grandmother of 29, 30
   K&A Productions and 93, 314
   loyalty and 23, 27, 125
   Marco Polo founded by 10, 50
   meets Takako 129
   music-education projects supported by
      23, 102, 116–17, 309, 338, 345,
      367, 417, 420–1
   musical passion of 22, 25, 30–1, 52
   Naxos created by 13
   Owner-Operator Award won by 24
   personal fortune of 97
   PolyGram prosecutes 44
   pre-Marco Polo 242
   reading passion of 31
   recognition achieved by 105–6
   record shop opened by 44
   retirement and 28, 414

Heymann, Klaus – *continued*
  risk-taking nature of 25, 28, 62
  secret of success of 423
  sobriquets of 20, 24, 136
  sporting passion of 22, 31–2, 33,
    365–6
  Takako marries 43, 128
  technological advances embraced by
    21, 22, 83, 102, 107–22, 304,
    317, 367, 413, 415–16
  turning 'failure' to 'learning' 103
  wine appreciated by 27–8
  worldwide distribution and 349–409
Heymann, Paula (Klaus's mother) 29, 30
Heymann, Takako (Klaus's wife) *see*
    Takako Nishizaki
Hildegard of Bingen 204, 256, 259
Hindemith, Paul 256, 290
Hinterhuber, Christopher 126, 176–7,
    319
Hirsch, Rebecca 209, 237
historical recordings 98, 100, 117
Hitchcock, Wiley 91
HK label 48, 50, 130, 328
HK Marco Polo 50, 281; *see also* Marco
    Polo Records
HMV 2, 356, 359, 396
hnh.com 108, 109, 112, 336
Ho, John 65
Hodge, Les 399
Hofmann, Leopold 101, 256, 305
Hogwood, Christopher 6
Holst, Gustav 400
Homer ii, xiv, 88, 294, 298
Hommel, Christian 207
Homs, Joaquim 289
Honegger, Arthur 211, 290, 291
Hong Kong Academy for Performing
    Arts 95, 327
Hong Kong Business Awards 24
Hong Kong Coliseum 49
Hong Kong Philharmonic Orchestra 41,
    42, 47–8, 50, 51, 53, 74–5, 209,
    281, 308, 369–70
Hong Kong Records 44
Horenstein, Jascha 39, 95
Horovitch, David 322
Horowitz, Joseph 91
Horowitz, Vladimir 275
Hosokawa, Toshio 225
Houston, Whitney 46
Hugh, Tim 210, 237
Hugo, Victor 197, 294, 347
Hummel, Johann Nepomuk ('Jan') 140,
    177, 305
Humphries, Barry 283, 365, 400
Hungarian Radio Competition 73
Hungaricus, Concentus 319

Hungaroton 3, 38, 45, 52, 73, 75, 76,
    124, 139, 318, 319
Hurford, Peter 6
Hurst, George 358
Huxley, Aldous 219
Hyperion 10, 90, 360, 393, 419

Ibert, Jacques 59
Ibsen, Henrik 297
Idil Biret Archive (IBA) 145
Ifukube, Akira 194, 397
Imai, Nobuko 127
Ink Spots 274
Inkinen, Pietari 321
Intégral Distribution 409
Ippolitov-Ivanov, Mikhail 282, 286
IRCAM 233
Italian Institute (Budapest) 74, 138, 139,
    150
Ito, Yuji 397
iTunes 112–13, 114, 115, 346, 373, 416,
    418, 421
Ivanovs, Jānis 193, 195, 286
Ives, Charles 225, 375, 377
Ivy 396, 398

Jackson, Garfield 157–8
Jackson, Laurence 156, 160
Jacobs, Paul 241, 269, 376
Jahn, Jörg-Wolfgang 170
Janáček, Leoš 191, 242, 243, 347
Jandó, Jenő ('JJ') 73–4, 125, 133,
    137–42, 153, 174, 191, 251,
    318–20, 357
Japan Philharmonic Orchestra 129
Järvi, Neeme 234
Jason, Neville 295–6
Jean, Kenneth 58, 132
Jenkins, Arthur Ka Wai 297
Jive Records 46
Joachim, Joseph 51, 131, 196, 328
Johansson, Lars 393
Johnson, Stephen 302, 303
Jolly, James 366
Jones, Aled 298
Jones, Toby 297
José, Antonio 265
Joseph Meyerhoff Symphony Hall 182
Joyce, James 89, 294, 295, 297
Judd, James 173, 179, 219–22
Juilliard School 42, 46, 127, 128, 129,
    133, 192
Junkin, Jerry 229

K&A Productions 93–4, 309–19, 362
Kabalevsky, Dmitry 194
Kaczyński, Lech 143
Kaiser-Lindemann, Wilhelm 148

Kaler, Ilya 154–5, 251, 320
Kalinnikov, Vasily 59, 282
Kalkbrenner, Friedrich 177
Kang, Dong-Suk 407
Karayev, Kara 194
Karłowicz, Mieczysław 155, 191
Kassai, István 289
Katayama, Morihide 211, 397
Kavafian, Ida 234
Kaznowski, Michal 156
Keenlyside, Perry 298
Kektjiang, Lim 47
Kempff, Wilhelm 142, 145
Kennedy, Nigel 14
Ketèlbey, Albert 290
Khachaturian, Aram 161, 192, 193
Kissin, Evgeny 138
Kitt, Eartha 277
Kleiber, Carlos 4–5, 6
Kleiber, Erich 276
Klemperer, Otto 3, 6, 9, 39
Kliegel, Maria 125, 146–9, 192, 237, 251
Kobow, Jan 170
Koch International Classics 217
Kocsis, Zoltán 140, 318
Kodály Quartet 76, 86, 149–53, 251, 319, 406
Kodály, Zoltán 137
Koechlin, Charles 407
Koehne, Graeme 210
Kopernicky, Karol 321
Korean Broadcasting System (KBS) 404
Korngold, Erich Wolfgang 261, 290, 363
Koukl, Giorgio 325
Kraft, Bonnie 165–8, 320, 321
Kraft, Norbert 164–8, 243, 265, 267, 320, 321
Kraus, Joseph Martin 164, 305, 393
Kraus, Sylvie 131, 135
Kreisler, Fritz 42, 46, 99, 128, 130, 133, 134, 136
Kun Woo Paik 187
Kwon, Hellen 199

Lachner, Franz 59, 282
Lagerqvist, Håkan 82, 248, 388–95
Lamberti, Giorgio 86
Lancaster Symphony Orchestra 180
Langlais, Jean 269
Larsson, Lars-Erik 392
Lassus, 201, 206 Masses for Five Voices 205
Latvian National Symphony Orchestra 193
Lau, David 214, 228
Laura Turner Concert Hall 215, 231, 378
Lauro, Antonio 268
Laux, Stefan 169

Lawlor, Fergus 81, 90, 358, 360, 361
Le Concert Spirituel 96, 408
Leaper, Adrian 179, 188
Lebrecht, Norman 121
Lebrun, Eric 269
Ledin, Marina 91, 193, 249, 371
Ledin, Victor 91, 193, 249, 371
Lee, Mr 68
Lei, Edith 249, 308, 325
Leinsdorf, Erich 276
Leipzig Chamber Orchestra 386–7
Lenárd, Ondrej 59, 179
Lennick, David 274
Lenni-Kalle Taipale Trio 270
Leoncavallo, Ruggero 261
Lesser, Anton 293, 294, 296, 299, 323
Leventritt Competition 42, 127
Levine, James 3
Levy, David 38
Lewis, Edward 7
Liadov, Anatol 290, 328
Liang Shan Bo 48
Ligeti, András 319, 376
Ligeti, György 145, 225
Lihua, Tan 246
Lilburn, Douglas 221
Lin, Cho-Liang 252
Linz 269–71
Lippert, Herbert 199
Liszt, Franz 137, 139, 142, 145, 173, 174, 175, 177, 193, 249, 253, 254
Liu, Hsin-Ni 195
Lloyd-Jones, David 172, 358
Lobo, Duarte 205
Locatelli, Pietro 306
London Philharmonic Orchestra (LPO) 16, 119, 184, 199, 251, 366
London Symphony Orchestra (LSO) 16, 95
Lopes-Graça, Fernando 174
Loughran, James 144
LPs 133, 349
    cassettes v. 7
    CDs v. 8, 11, 14, 57, 65–6, 67, 76–9, 356
    durability of 7
    'Music for Pleasure' 12
    zenith of 1
Ludwig, Michael 229, 381
Lully, Jean-Baptiste 96, 261
Lutosławski, Witold 188–9, 215, 231, 235, 236
Lyapunov, Sergei 194, 290
Lydian 269–71
Lyrita 3

McCarthy, Cormac 299
McCawley, Leon 173

McCleery, 302
McCormack, John 277
McCowen, Alec 297
MacDowell, Edward 290
McGraw Hill 372
McGregor, Ewan 297
Machaut, Guillaume de 204, 205
McKay, George Frederick 227
McKeich, Andrew 399–401
McKellen, Ian 297
MacMillan, James 209, 240
McMillan, Roy 322
Madrid Community Orchestra 265
Maggini Quartet 105, 155–61, 237, 239,
      314, 317, 358, 363, 366
Mahler, Gustav 4, 39, 50, 188, 198, 200,
      253, 303, 420
Mailer, Prof. Franz 60
Malipiero, Gian Francesco 267
Mallon, Kevin 320
Maloney, Michael 297
Malory, Sir Thomas 293
Mandela, Nelson 148
Mangoré, Agustín Barrios 168
Marco Polo Catalogue 67, 248, 254,
      283–92, 353, 373
   alphabetical listing 289
   'Chamber Music' 287–9
   'Chinese Classics' 283–4, 348
   'Light Music and the Strauss' 286–7
   'Marco Polo Classics' 284–5
   'Marco Polo Film Music' 290–1, 332,
      348
   'Opera' 285
   'Orchestral Music' 285–6
   'Piano Music' 289–90
Marco Polo France 405, 407, 408,
      409
Marco Polo Records ix, 13, 50–3, 73,
      100, 146, 180, 187, 193, 224, 243,
      280, 281–92, 325–9, 336, 370, 383,
      393, 403, 411
   artist contracts and 55–6
   complete cycles 59–60
   digital format embraced by 65–6
   diversity of 62
   'dream label' status of 58
   first recordings of 51, 52, 65–6, 67,
      131, 134 234, 248, 257, 266–7
   founding of 10, 50, 52, 60, 61, 65,
      132, 281, 328
   'Gothic' Symphony and 59
   Hong Kong HQ of 10, 13
   Kreisler Edition reissued by 133
   'Label of Discovery' 124, 281, 292
   Mandela and 148
   musical standards maintained by 135
   national anthems and 243–6

Naxos overshadows 360
Novecento works of 60
pre- 242
rapid expansion of 314, 331–2
recording, producing and editing
      procedures 313, 318
sales 283
Takako and 128, 131, 134
Western nature of 57
worldwide distribution 349–409
Mark, Jon, 98, 99
Mark-Almond 98
Markevitch, Igor 209
Märkl, Jun 321
Markson, Gerhard 146
Marsh, Roger, 297
Marston, Ward 99, 273, 316
Martin, Laurent 289
Martinů, Bohuslav 325
Marton, Ivan 68, 323–5
Martucci, Giuseppe 61, 266
Mascagni, Pietro 61, 261, 347
Masó, Jordi 289
Massenet, Jules 261
Maupassant, Guy 300
Maxwell Davies, Sir Peter 156, 159, 160,
      238–9, 240, 302, 317, 363
May, Karl 31
Mayuzumi, Toshiro 211
MCI 63, 64
Media 7 405, 408, 409
Melchior, Lauritz 276
Melodiya 3, 68
Mena, Juan José 265
Mendelssohn, Felix 30, 40, 75, 76, 126,
      131, 132, 148, 153, 161, 162, 211,
      220, 268, 269, 320
Mendelssohn-Bartholdy, George 40,
      44–5
Menotti, Gian Carlo 225
Menuhin, Yehudi 4, 275
Mercadante, Saverio 163
Meridian 3
Messiaen, Olivier 188–90, 241, 269,
      321, 376
Metropolitan Opera ('Met') 117
Meyerbeer, Giacomo 261, 285
Meyer-Eller, Sören 299
Michelangeli, Arturo 9
Middle Kingdom 291–2
MIDEM xiii, xiv, 10, 46, 57, 82, 88, 110,
      188, 195, 208, 311
MIDEM Classique xiv, 10, 188, 383,
      393
Milken Archive of Jewish Music 379
Miller, Glenn 278
Milnes, Sherrill 4
Milstein, Nathan 347

Milton, John 88, 293, 380
Minolta 40
Miricioiu, Nelly 86
Moeran, E.J. 156, 157, 288
Moiseiwitsch, Benno 99, 117, 275
Montemezzi, Italo 61
Monteverdi Choir and Orchestra 366
Monteverdi, Claudio 301
Moorani, Riyaz 114
Moroi, Saburo 211
Morris, Joan 227
Morris, Johnny xv, 365
Moscheles, Ignaz 39
Moscow Symphony Orchestra 193
Motown 46
Mozart, Wolfgang Amadeus 1–6, 25,
    75–6, 79, 100, 101, 123, 125,
    127–8, 133, 134, 136, 137, 138,
    140, 141, 162, 164, 171, 174–5,
    180, 198–200, 208, 220, 247, 251,
    252, 259, 261, 269, 281, 301, 303,
    304, 314, 319, 321, 326, 365, 386,
    393, 420
Müller, Othmar 177
Müller-Brühl, Helmut 206–8, 251
Munich Philharmonic Orchestra 30
Municipal Opera (Augsburg) 179
Murakami, Haruki ii, 299
Music City USA 379
Music Masters 217
music piracy 65, 104, 115–16, 242, 336,
    394, 401–2, 416
Music and Video Distribution (MVD)
    351
Music Week xiii, 13
musicology x, 91, 100, 101, 114, 211,
    262, 304, 323, 336, 340–1, 371,
    387, 418
Musikverein (Vienna) 131, 176
Mussorgsky, Modest 73, 138
Mute 46
MVC 367
Myaskovsky, Nikolay 59, 194, 198, 282,
    290, 328
Myers, Paul 317

Nachéz, Tivadar 134
Nagoya Philharmonic Orchestra 47
Nagy, Péter 75
Naïve 374, 394, 409
Nancarrow, Conlon 24
Napster 416
Nashville Symphony 214–15, 229, 231,
    233, 321, 369, 375–9
Naxos:
    artist contracts and 55–6
    audiobooks, see Naxos AudioBooks
    awards won by 158, 182, 187–8, 391,
        393, 407, 425–34; see also
    GRAMMYs
    becomes digital service provider
        113–14
    board 27
    catalogue, see Naxos Catalogue
    CD sales of 87–8, 91, 99, 100,
        113–14, 117, 144, 145, 147
    character of 411–12
    court cases involving 44, 117–18, 121
    creation of 13, 123
    customer loyalty to 419
    dedicated production facility of 314
    digital distribution 367
    distribution companies 18, 27, 44, 46,
        61, 65, 74, 77, 79–83, 90, 92–3,
        104, 110, 121–2
    diversification of 62, 94
    early days of 74, 132
    enters mainstream stores 356
    equal-fee basis of 120, 124, 140
    expansion of 100
    'fathers of' 71
    fifteenth anniversary of 91
    financial turnover 360
    first CDs of 11, 69, 70
    first decade of 385
    'Gothic' Symphony and 59
    husband-and-wife team of 25–6
    Internet and 107–22
    Klaus offers to CEOs 412
    Ltd 70
    market share 360, 363
    music education and 23, 102, 116–17,
        309, 338, 345, 367, 417, 420–1
    musical standards maintained by 135
    naming of 70
    national anthems and 243–6
    'national' recording programmes of
        397
    one-conductor cycle of 179
    parent company of 108
    precursor to 45–6
    prejudice experienced by 153
    public-domain repertoire and 224
    public perception of 95, 105
    rapid expansion of 314
    recognition achieved by 105–6
    recording, producing and editing
        procedures 311–22
    recordings statistics of 249–50
    recording/release schedule 307–11,
        318
    rivals of 387
    SADiE software and 311, 316
    'specialist' nature of 76
    Takako and 26, 134, 138
    'white-wall' status of 396

Naxos – *continued*
  Woolworths and, *see main entry*
  worldwide distribution 349–409
Naxos of America 27, 341, 350, 351,
  369–88
Naxos AudioBooks ii, xiv–xv, 88–9, 97,
  101, 116, 183–4, 249, 293–306,
  309, 322–3, 347, 360, 362, 370
  'Classic Fiction' series 294
  'Classic Non-Fiction' series 295
  German, *see* Naxos Hörbücher
  Grimms' *Fairy Tales* 294
  'Histories' series 298
  'In a Nutshell' series 299
Naxos Australia, *see* SAVD
Naxos Books 101, 102, 219, 302–4, 309,
  330, 385, 419
  biographies from 101–2, 303
  children's books from 102
  'Discover' series 302, 303, 304
  e-texts and apps 102, 344, 348
  'Life and Music' series 304
  'Portrait' series 304
  websites to accompany 303
Naxos Catalogue 248–80, 353, 373,
  408, 410
  'American Classics' 90–1, 184, 225, 229,
    249, 262–4, 310, 332, 348, 371,
    375–8
  anthologies 258
  'Best of' series 259, 365, 390
  best-selling recordings from 126, 128,
    144, 145, 147, 148, 158, 165,
    179, 187, 188, 237, 242, 253,
    259, 260, 265, 274, 385, 388,
    391, 392–3, 395, 414, 415
  'British' music series 357
  'British Piano Concerto' series 210,
    364
  'Budget Classics' 45, 300, 328, 363
  'Central Classics' 250–61
  children's choral music 260
  'Chill with' series 259
  Christmas-themed series 259
  'Cinema Classics' 259
  'Clarinet Classics' 360
  'Classics at the Movies, The' 259
  'Collections' listing 258
  'Complete Piano Music of Liszt' 332
  deletions 280
  'Deutsche Schubert Lied Edition' 252
  'Early Music Collection' 260, 348
  'Easy Listening Piano Classics' 260
  'English Piano Concerto' series 420
  'English Song Series' 365, 420
  'exploitation' 258
  'Great Conductors' 276
  'Greek Classics' 260

'Guitar Collection' 164–8, 267–8,
  332, 348
'H' listing 254, 255–6
'Immortal Performances' series 117
'Italian Classics' 260, 266–7
'Japanese Classics' 211, 212, 397–9
'Jubilee' series 385
'Laureate Series' 167, 168, 249, 260
lieder recordings 252
'Listen, Learn and Grow' series 259
'Liszt Complete Piano Music' 173
'Melodies of Love' 348
monthly Top Ten 365
Naxos Web Radio streams 348
'19th Century Violinist Composers'
  260
NML and 339–42, 416
'Opera Classics' 261–2
'Organ Encyclopedia' 268–9
'Piano' 348
pre-releases 334
rapid expansion of 331–2
'Recordings in the Pipeline' 308–9
'Robert Craft Collection, The' 217
'Romantic Piano Favourites' 260
'S' and 'T' listings 257–8, 260
'salon' favourites 260
'Sets/Series' section 260–1
'Spanish Classics' 260, 264–6, 332
'Tintner Memorial Edition' 252
'Trio' series 385
'Trumpet' recordings 260
'Very Best of' series 259, 332
'Vocal and Choral' 260
wedding music 260
'Wind Band Classics' 332
'Z' listing and beyond 258
Naxos Denmark 389, 395
Naxos Deutschland 352, 382–8
Naxos Digital Japan 398
Naxos DVD 104–4, 116, 278–80
  'Jazz Icons' series 280, 376
  'Musical Journeys' 278–9
Naxos Educational 255, 300–2, 309,
  372, 374
  'Art and Music' series 302
  'Classics Explained' 301
  'Discover' series 302
  'Life and Works' series 301
  'Opera Explained' 301
  'Portrait' series 302
Naxos Far East 20, 351, 401–3
Naxos Finland, *see* FG Naxos
Naxos in France, *see* Abeille Musique
Naxos Germany 104
Naxos Global Distribution 403
Naxos Global Logistics (NGL) 350–4,
  388, 409

Naxos Group 352
Naxos Historical 117, 272–8, 363
   'Great' series 274–5
   websites to accompany 275
Naxos Hong Kong 339
Naxos Hörbücher 299–300, 348
Naxos Japan 396–9
Naxos Jazz 270–1, 274, 277, 278
Naxos Korea 403–5, 414
Naxos Music Library (NML) 21, 109,
   111–22, 186, 338–42, 344–6, 367,
   374, 377, 395, 398, 401, 404–5,
   409, 413, 420–1
   apps 399, 417
   Jazz 346
   subscriptions 399, 415–16, 419, 421
Naxos Musicals 274, 277
Naxos Norway 389
Naxos Nostalgia 274, 277, 332
Naxos online music encyclopaedia
   418–19
Naxos Patrimoine 407
Naxos Promotions 355
Naxos Quartets 156, 159, 160, 238,
   317, 363
Naxos Spoken Word Library (NSWL)
   298, 341, 347–8, 404
Naxos Sweden 27, 248, 350, 351,
   388–95
Naxos Video Library (NVL) 342, 346–7,
   416
   'Global Treasures' series 347
Naxos Web Radio 348
Naxos website 102, 107–22, 247, 298,
   335–48, 403, 415–17
   apps 304
   books with 303
   BWV 51 345
   'Composers' section 343
   dial-up era of 336
   DRM and 115, 337, 346
   e-texts and apps 102, 304, 344, 348
   FTP site of 334
   global membership of 343
   metadata and 113, 337, 340, 373, 418
   newsletter 344
   NML and 21, 109, 111–22, 186,
   338–42, 344–6
   online platforms utilized by 112, 336,
   337
   'Sets/Series' section 343
Naxos White Wall 16, 81, 180, 334, 359,
   367, 396
Naxos World 98, 271–2, 332, 375
NaxosDirect 375
Nebolsin, Eldar 174–7, 190
Nelsova, Zara 193
New Zealand Chamber Orchestra 101

New Zealand String Quartet 320
New Zealand Symphony Orchestra
   (NZSO) 176, 211, 219–20, 221,
   243, 252, 321
Newman, Anthony 252
Nexus 387
NHK 10
Nicholas, Jeremy 303
Nicolaus Esterházy Sinfonia 179, 200,
   251, 319
Nielsen, Carl 180
Nietzsche, Friedrich 298
Nimbus 3, 10
Nin-Culmell, Joaquín 329
Niquet, Hervé 96, 408
Nishizaki, Atsushi (Takako's brother)
   396, 398
Nishizaki, Masako (Takako's mother)
   129
Nishizaki, Shinji (Takako's father) 43,
   129, 130, 136
Nishizaki, Takako Nishizaki (Klaus's
   wife) xi, 20, 24, 42–3, 46–9, 51–5,
   72–6, 124–5, 127–37, 138, 141,
   154, 197, 208, 224, 308, 315,
   320–1, 396, 397
   annual concerts performed by 135–6
   birth of 129
   Butterfly Lovers recorded by 47, 49,
   77, 128, 130, 135, 255, 403
   Chinese music recorded by 47–8
   concertos recorded by 101, 128, 131
   education of 129
   first review of 58
   Four Seasons recorded by 72, 75, 126,
   128, 132, 180, 252, 313
   Fritz Kreisler Scholarship won by 42,
   46, 128
   Guarneris chosen by 133–4, 137
   Juilliard attended by 127, 128, 129,
   133
   Juilliard Concerto Competition won
   by 127
   Klaus marries 43, 128
   Klaus meets 129
   Kreisler Edition and 133
   Leventritt Competition and 42, 127
   'Mrs Heymann' sobriquet of 136
   Naxos and 25–6
   Takako Nishizaki Violin Studio
   formed by 136
   violin competitions adjudicated by
   136
   violin lessons given by 136
   violin pop songs of 242
Nock, Mike 97, 270
Nopp, Otto 321
Norberg-Schulz, Elizabeth 199

Norddeutsche Rundfunk 119
North, Nigel 168
Northern Chamber Orchestra 165, 204
Northern Sinfonia 357
Norton, Jim 294, 297
Nyman, Michael 210, 253, 366

Obert-Thorn, Mark 98, 272–3, 316
OehmsClassics 402
Ohguri, Hiroshi 397
Ohki, Masao 211
Ohzawa, Hisato 194
Olga Musik 394
Olympic Games 243–6
Onczay, Csaba 138, 251
Ondine 164, 395
Opus 3, 38, 52
Opus Arte 104, 367, 374, 402
Orbón, Julián 266
Orchestra of St. Luke's 217, 219, 230
Orchestra Sinfonica di Roma 267
Orchestre National de Lille 408
Orchestre National de Lyon 215, 241, 321
Orff, Carl 39, 40, 224
Orgonášová, Luba 86
Osaka Philharmonic Orchestra 397–8
Ottensamer, Ernst 177
Otterloo, Willem van 31
Our Price 356, 359, 367
Outram, Martin 156
Overseas Weekly 33–4, 35
Oxford Camerata 47, 90, 96, 133, 201, 202, 204, 256, 359, 364

Pacific Audio Supplies Ltd 64
Pacific Mail Order System 37
Pacific Music Co. Ltd 64, 77, 78, 83, 84, 242
Pacifica Quartet 226
Pacini, Giovanni 261
Paganini, Nicolò 131, 154, 155, 170, 268
Paik, Kun Woo 407
Paleczny, Piotr 188
Palestrina, Giovanni Pierluigi da 134, 201, 202, 259
Paley, William 2
Parker Quartet 225
Pärt, Arvo 208, 210, 241, 253, 302, 382
Patmore, David 435
Paton, Laura 294
Pauk, György 188
Pavarotti, Luciano 4, 14, 15
Pears, Peter 327
Penderecki, Krzysztof 189–91, 236
Penguin 121, 86, 250, 356
Penny, Andrew 267

Pentatone Classics 374
Perlman, Itzhak 42, 127, 347
Perry, Ted 92, 360
Persichetti, Vincent 380
Peter Breiner and His Chamber Orchestra 242
Petermandl, Hans 290
Peterson-Berger, Wilhelm 392
Petitgirard, Laurent 241
Petrenko, Vasily 175, 178, 254, 311–12, 366
Pfitzner, Hans 420
Philharmonia Orchestra 144, 217, 218
Philips 1–3, 7, 15, 16, 215, 361
Phoenix Studio 141, 153, 200, 319
Piazzolla, Ástor 168, 170, 268
Pierné, Gabriel, 215, 216
Pierre, Fabrice 162
Pinza, Ezio 277
Pirate Bay 394
Piston, Walter 379, 380
Pittsburgh Symphony Orchestra 230
Pizzetti, Ildebrando 61, 266–7, 288
Plato 298, 347
Pleyel, Ignaz Joseph 101, 145, 164, 305
Plitmann, Hila 229
Polish National Radio Symphony Orchestra (PNRSO) 187, 188, 189, 191, 235, 236, 241, 253, 407
Polish State Philharmonic Orchestra 234
Pollack, Christian 322
Pollini, Maurizio 4
Polskie Nagrania 3, 189
PolyGram 7, 14, 15, 44, 76, 77, 78
Ponder, Michael 321, 357
Ponti, Michael 39, 40, 44, 56, 133
Popper, David, 148, 192
Porter, Cole 274
Poulenc, Francis 363, 407, 408
Powell, Robert 323
Prandelli, Giacinto 276
Preiser Records 384
Prentice Hall 372
Primrose, William 275
Prokofiev, Sergei 48, 187, 195, 283, 302, 400, 407
Prophone 395
Proprius 395
Proust, Marcel 295
Prunyi, Ilona 289
Puccini, Giacomo 261, 301
Purcell, Henry 204
Pushkin, Alexander 300

Qabala Music Festival 195

Raat, Ralph van 232, 382
Rachmaninov, Sergey 98, 99, 138, 144,

145, 174, 177, 188, 193, 194, 195, 215, 253, 272, 275
Radio France 144, 408
Raff, Joachim 59, 282, 329
Rahbari, Alexander 85, 251
Rameau, Jean-Philippe 261, 269, 363
Rautavaara, Einojuhani 163, 363
Ravel, Maurice 153, 164, 215, 407, 408
Rawsthorne, Alan 160, 210, 363
RCA 2–4, 11–12, 46, 130, 215
Record Geijutsu 396, 398
Record Review 150, 201
recording formats 65, 116, 339
  audiobooks xiv, xv, 88–9, 183, 293–306
  audio cassettes 7, 89
  audiophile 284
  BD-Audio 229, 317
  Blu-ray/Blu-ray Audio 102, 229, 309, 317, 411, 421
  CD 1, 8–13, 102, 104, 284, 298, 303, 352, 411, 417
  CD-R 316
  CD-ROM 297, 303
  download/streaming 77, 104–5, 108–10, 114–16, 127, 187, 217, 223, 242, 280, 298, 325, 334, 336, 374, 394–5, 413–14, 415–17, 421
  DVD/DVD-Audio 102–4, 116, 278–80, 317, 342, 347, 352, 361, 366–7, 387–8, 401, 417
  e-readers 404
  Laserdisc 103, 278
  LP 1, 7–8, 11–14, 39, 57, 65–6, 67, 76–9, 133, 327, 349
  MP3 115–16, 298, 341, 420
  SACD 102, 317
  smartphone 304
  78s 7, 316
  tablet 304
  U-matic 66
  VHS 278–9, 284, 366–7
  videodisc 8
RED 418
Reference Recordings 402
Reger, Max 254, 269
Reinecke, Carl 162, 163
Reiner, Fritz 276
Reinhardt, Django 278
Residentie Orkest 31
Respighi, Ottorino 51, 54, 58, 131, 266, 282, 382
Revox (HK) Ltd 38, 40, 62, 64
Rhapsody 416
Rheinberger, Joseph 268
Rhenish Philharmonic Orchestra 197
Richter, Sviatoslav 194
Ries, Ferdinand 101, 126, 176, 305

Riesel, Yves 144, 405–9
Rihm, Wolfgang 126, 170
Rimsky-Korsakov, Nikolai 194, 279, 282, 381
Ringeissen, Bernard 289
Riordan, Marcella 294, 297
Rippon, Angela 365
Robinson, Christopher 237, 317
Rochberg, George 226
Rodrigo, Cecilia 265
Rodrigo, Joaquín 161, 165, 168, 254, 265–6, 268, 302
Rorem, Ned 226
Rosbaud, Hans 30
Rose Consort of Viols 359
Ross, Graham 240
Ross, Tony 365
Rossini, Gioachino 261, 269, 280, 290
Rostropovich, Mstislav 146–7, 258
Rowlands, Phil 311–12
Royal Academy of Music 201, 205
Royal Liverpool Philharmonic Orchestra (RLPO) 119, 173, 176, 178, 221, 254, 311, 366
Royal Opera House 5, 33
Royal Philharmonic Orchestra 147, 214
Royal Scottish National Orchestra 91, 96, 182, 252, 321, 357, 358
RTÉ National Symphony Orchestra 96, 252
RTVE Symphony Orchestra and Chorus 180
Rubackyté, Múza 289
Rubbra, Edmund 160, 208, 210, 363
Rubinstein, Anton 59, 128, 131, 197, 282, 285, 286, 290
Rubinstein, Arthur 99
Rübsam, Wolfgang 268
Russian Philharmonic Orchestra 193, 194, 196
Rutter, John 240–1, 364, 366
Rydl, Kurt 199
Rzewski, Frederic 177, 226

Saarbrucken Radio Symphony Orchestra 146
St. Louis Symphony 230
Saint-Saëns, Camille 144, 147, 148, 365, 407, 408
Saito, Hideo 129
Sallinen, Aulis 347
San Carlos Opera 33
Santander International Piano Competition 174
Santos, Joly Braga 317
Sarnoff, David 2
Sasaki, Ryuichi 398
Sauer, Martin 313

Sauguet, Henri 407
SAVD 399–401
Scarlatti, Domenico 249, 254
Schäuble, Niko 270
Scheidemann, Heinrich 268
Scherbakov, Konstantin 290
Scherer, Barrymore Laurence 302, 303
Schermerhorn, Kenneth 74, 214, 369,
    375, 377
Schiff, András 73–4, 140, 318
Schirmer, G. 230
Schmid, Rosl 30
Schnabel, Artur 275
Schnittke, Alfred 146–7
Schoenberg, Arnold 177, 208, 216–19,
    224, 261
Schola Cantorum 201, 202, 364
Schreker, Franz 261, 329
Schreker, Heymann 198
Schröder pianos 145
Schubert, Franz 30, 130, 134, 138, 141,
    152–3, 157, 168–9, 174, 177, 192,
    196–7, 200, 251, 252, 253, 301,
    381
Schuman, William 91, 226, 379, 380
Schumann, Robert 25, 154, 188, 201,
    252, 253, 269, 288, 326, 420
Schütz, Heinrich 205
Schwarz, Gerard 263, 379, 380, 381
Schwarzkopf, Elisabeth 276
Scofield, Paul 296–7
Scriabin, 44, 143
Sculthorpe, Peter 221
Seattle Symphony Orchestra 379, 380,
    381
Selby, Jim 83, 369–70, 372–4
Select Music, UK/Select Music and Video
    Distribution Ltd xiv, 27, 81, 82, 90,
    92, 157, 248, 331, 351, 354–69,
    420
Seo, Kazunori 162
Serebrier, José 226, 276
Serra, Joaquim 266
Shakespeare, William 171, 266, 295,
    296, 299, 347
Sherab Ling Monastery 98, 375
Sherry, Fred 217
Shield, William 306
Shima, Mamoru 397
Shimono, Tatsuya 397
Shirley, Wayne 91
Shostakovich, Dmitri 88, 94, 147, 154,
    158, 178, 192, 194, 224, 241–2,
    254, 302, 387, 420
Shostakovich, Irina 241
Sibelius, Jean 75, 88, 154, 180, 210
Siepmann, Jeremy 255, 301, 302, 303
Simon, Klaus 232

Sinfonia Finlandia Jyväskylä 162, 163,
    164
Singapore Symphony Orchestra 51, 53,
    54, 131, 281
Sinigaglia, Leone 61
Sivelöv, Niklas 317
Slatkin, Leonard 181, 212–16, 227, 229,
    231, 312, 321, 375, 378, 420
Slovak Chamber Orchestra 72
Slovák, Ladislav 94, 254
Slovak National Opera Orchestra 72
Slovak Philharmonic Chorus 85
Slovak Philharmonic Orchestra 53, 54,
    58, 68, 72, 131, 132, 179, 197, 313,
    324
Slovak Radio Symphony Orchestra
    58–9, 72, 75, 94, 179, 199, 243,
    244, 246, 254, 377
Slovak Sinfonietta Žilina 322
Slovart 52, 324
Smetana, Bedřich 188
Smillie, Thomson 301
Smith, Bessie 274
Soames, Benjamin 294
Soames, Nicolas 88, 293
Soames, Victoria xiii
Sobotka, Wolfgang 314
Söderman, August 392
Soler, Antonio 254
Solti, Georg 3, 9, 33, 396
Sonart 399, 400
Sonic Solutions 316
Sony 8, 12, 78
Sousa, John Philip 91
Spohr, Louis (Ludwig) 51, 131, 134,
    289
Spotify 416
SRB Records 68
SRI 165
Staatskapelle Weimar 190
Stamitz, Johann 101, 363
Stanzeleit, Susanne 160
Starker, János 146, 147
Stenhammar, Wilhelm 317, 392
Stereo Sound 397
Stern, Isaac 4, 9
Stevenson, Juliet 297, 322
Stevenson, Robert Louis 300
Straub, Dr Stefan 387
Strauss, Johann Jr 59, 60, 261, 276
Strauss, Johann Sr 59, 321–2
Strauss, Josef 59
Strauss, Richard 24, 31, 190, 197, 198,
    211, 252, 276, 380
Stravinsky, Igor 31, 88, 102, 145,
    216–19, 224, 301, 302, 303
Studer-Revox (HK) Ltd 40, 46, 63, 64
Sturgeon, Jim 83, 369

Süddeutsche Rundfunk 119
Suk, Josef 382
Summerly, Jeremy 90, 96, 201–6, 364
Supraphon 3, 38, 45, 52, 68
Surif, Valentin 289
Suzuki Method 20, 43, 127, 129, 136
Suzuki, Shinichi 42, 43, 127, 129, 136
Swarowsky, Hans 209, 210
Swedish Chamber Orchestra 162, 393
Sydney Symphony Orchestra 210
Szabó, Tamás 150
Székely, István 75, 318
Szymanowski, Karol 59, 134, 155, 187,
    190, 191, 235, 257, 261

Tabakov, Emil 162, 257
Takagi, Kazuhiro 397
Takako Nishizaki Violin Studio 136
Takemitsu, Tōru 167, 184, 211, 225,
    241, 257
Tallis, Thomas 201, 204, 205, 253, 257,
    365
Taneyev, Sergey 155, 257, 286
Tartini, Giuseppe 40, 257
Tatum, Art 278
Tauber, Richard 277
Tavener, Sir John 148, 204–5, 209,
    237–8, 253–4, 257, 302
Taylor, John 357
Tchaikovsky, Piotr ('Peter') 48, 75, 123,
    128, 131, 132, 147, 154, 178, 180,
    188, 193–4, 198, 243, 253, 258,
    259, 347, 366, 400, 410, 420
Tebaldi, Renata 276
TEC, SL 100
Telarc 3, 215, 394
Teldec 12, 376
Telefunken 45, 47, 133
Telemann, 208
Thalberg, Sigismond 39, 290
Thessaloniki Symphony Orchestra 267
Thiollier, François-Joël 408
Tichy, Georg 199
Time Warner 12
Timson, David 295–7, 298, 299, 301
Tintner, Georg 95–6, 252
Tintner, Tanya 95
Tippett Quartet 173, 358
Tishchenko, Boris Ivanovich 194
Toho School of Music 129
Tokyo University of Fine Arts and Music
    212, 399
Tolstoy, Leo 295
Toscanini, Arturo 2, 396
Tóth, Erika 149–53
Tóth, Ibolya 138, 140–1, 148, 153,
    318–20
Tournemire, Charles 329

Tower, Joan 215, 226, 230–1, 376, 378
Tower Records 356, 371, 372, 374, 396
Toyama, Yuzo 397
Trekel, Roman 168
Trenet, Charles 277
Tsujii, Nobuyuki 415
Tuck, Rosemary 290
Turner, Laura 215, 231
Twentieth Century Classics Ensemble
    217
Tyberg, Marcel 382
Tydeman, John 296–7

Ugetsu 270
Ulster Orchestra 209, 211, 232, 237,
    240
Unicorn-Kanchana 3
Universal 361, 376
University of Texas Wind Ensemble 229

Valdés, Maximiano 265
Valentine, Alan 231, 377, 378, 379
Vallé, Orlando ('Maraca') 270
Vanguard 349
Vanhal, Johann Baptist 101, 131, 135,
    208, 304, 305
Varady, Júlia 347
Varèse Sarabande 3
Varèse, Edgard 224
Vaughan, Sarah 278
Vaughan Williams, Ralph 105, 157, 158,
    173, 220–1, 236, 364, 366
VEB Deutsche Schallplatten 3
Ventapane, Lorenzo 133
Verdi, Giuseppe 261, 280, 301
Vermeer Quartet 153, 320
Verne, Jules 294
Victor 2, 48
Vienna Philharmonic Orchestra 161
Vienna State Opera 85, 196, 198, 199
Vienna State Orchestra 198
Vierne, Louis 269
Villa-Lobos, Heitor 165, 268, 288, 376
Virgin 46, 406
Vītols, Jāzeps 193
Viva 389
Vivaldi, Antonio 14, 40, 72, 75, 126,
    128, 132, 164, 170, 179–80, 203,
    207, 252, 279, 313, 385, 391
Vladar, Stefan 251, 407
Voll, Chris 83, 104, 383–8
von Bahr, Robert 10, 112
von Bülow, Hans 289
von Karajan, Herbert 3, 4, 6, 9, 10, 14,
    76, 276, 396
von Matačić, Lovro 209
von Suppé, Franz 134
von Zemlinsky, Alexander 177, 220

Vox-Turnabout 39, 44, 95, 144, 215, 349, 383

W.W. Norton 372
Wagner, Richard 261, 284, 289, 301–2, 329, 345, 400
Wagner, Siegfried 61, 285, 329
Walls, Peter 221
Walter, Alfred 60
Walter, Bruno 276
Walton, Andrew 93, 156–8, 204, 222, 311–18, 357, 358, 362, 398
Walton, William 236
Ward, Nicholas 165
Warner 7, 12, 344, 376
Warsaw Philharmonic Orchestra 155, 190
Wass, Ashley 171–4, 221, 363, 364
Wearn, Jonathan 117, 272
Webern, Anton 208, 211, 217, 276
Weill, Kurt 413
Weir, Simon 323
Whitacre, Eric 234
White Cloud 98
Whiteman Paul 277
Whitfield, June 365
Whitfield, Peter 298
Wieck, Clara 134
Wieniawski, Henryk 43, 242
Wildner, Johannes 85
Williams, Alberto 289
Williams, Heathcote 294, 297
Wilson, Terrence 233

Winter, Richard 57, 80, 272
Wit, Antoni 155, 175, 179, 187–91, 198, 235, 236, 241, 253, 407
Witt, Friedrich 162
Wong, S.K. 107, 112, 335
Wood, Henry 147
Woolf, Virginia 294, 295
Woolworths xiii, 13, 14, 16, 80, 350, 354–5, 356–7
Wordsworth, Barry 75, 179, 180, 251
Wulfson, Eduard 195
Wuorinen, Charles 226

Xhosa lullabies 148

Yablonsky, Dmitry 179, 191–4
Yablonsky, Oxana 192
Yamada, Kôsçak 209, 211, 398
Yang, Tianwa 126, 170–1
Yashiro, Akio 209, 211
'Yellow Label' 1, 161
Yellow River 291–2
YouTube 168
Ysaÿe, Eugène 155, 170
Yuasa, Takuo 208–12, 237, 240
Yüksel, Şefik 145

Zagreb Philharmonic 78
Zander, Benjamin 327
Zenker, Martin 270
Zhu Ying Tai 48
Zyman, Samuel 343

338.76178 S676

Soames, Nicolas, 1950-
The story of Naxos : the
extraordinary story of the
independent record label
Central Nonfiction CIRC -
2nd & 3rd fls
12/12